T0306096

Liberalism and Chinese Economic Development

Liberalism and Chinese Economic Development brings international contributors together in order to consider economic, political, social and legislative aspects of China's modernization. This volume explores how liberalism is received and perceived, and whether it is adapted or adopted upon the basis of centuries of Chinese civilization and decades of capitalism.

China's role in the global economy is an undeniable force. This book examines both historical and contemporary dimensions surrounding the question of Chinese liberalism, exploring China's economic development in a comparative context. In particular, this text explores differences from the Western model, and more specifically, the relationship between Chinese economic thought and European traditions. This text assesses China's economic development at both a macro and a micro level, and also considers its relationship with its neighbours.

Campagnolo answers whether free-trade and capitalistic economic developments are long sustainable without other types of liberal developments. Or is the idea that political liberties and economic freedom go together merely a Western ideology? This is a uniquely wide-ranging book, suitable for scholars of the Chinese economy, the history of economic thought, economic philosophy and international political economy.

Gilles Campagnolo is Research Professor at the National Center for Scientific Research and at Aix-Marseilles School of Economics, France. He is also the Global Coordinator for the European Union program "Liberalism in between Europe and China".

Routledge Studies in the Modern World Economy

For a complete list of titles in this series, please visit www.routledge.com

Recently published titles:

Liberalism and Chinese Economic Development

Perspectives from Europe and Asia

Edited by Gilles Campagnolo

LONDON AND NEW YORK

First published 2016
by Routledge
2 Park Square, Milton Park, Abingdon, Oxon OX14 4RN

and by Routledge
711 Third Avenue, New York, NY 10017

Routledge is an imprint of the Taylor & Francis Group, an informa business

The work leading to this invention has received funding from the European Union Seventh Framework Programme (*FP7/2007–2013*) under *grant agreement* n°PIRSES–GA–2012–317767.

British Library Cataloguing in Publication Data
A catalogue record for this book is available from the British Library

Library of Congress Cataloging in Publication Data
Names: Campagnolo, Gilles, editor.
Title: Liberalism and Chinese economic development : perspectives from Europe and Asia / edited by Gilles Campagnolo.
Description: New York : Routledge, 2016.
Identifiers: LCCN 2015044506| ISBN 9781138909199 (hardback) | ISBN 9781315694115 (ebook)
Subjects: LCSH: Economic development--China. | China--Economic policy--21st century. | China--Foreign economic relations. | Economics--History. | Liberalism.
Classification: LCC HC427.95 .L5734 2016 | DDC 338.951--dc23
LC record available at https://lccn.loc.gov/2015044506

ISBN: 978-1-138-90919-9 (hbk)
ISBN: 978-1-315-69411-5 (ebk)

Typeset in Times New Roman
by Saxon Graphics Ltd, Derby

Contents

Figures

Tables

Contributors

Andrea Altobrando is currently a Visiting Professor at the Hokkaido University, Japan. He got his PhD in co-tutorship from the Bergische University of Wuppertal (Germany) and from the Turin University (Italy), and a second PhD from the Padua University (Italy). His main research topics are: Phenomenology of Subjectivity and Philosophy of Mind; Intercultural Philosophy and Phenomenology of Intersubjectivity; Phenomenology of Knowledge and Epistemology. He is Executive Editor of *Metodo. International Studies in Phenomenology and Philosophy*.

Guimei Bai is a Professor of public international law and human rights law at Peking University Law School, Beijing, China. Her fields of interest are theories of international law, mechanisms of human rights protection and human rights education. She has a special interest in issues related to the right to self-determination of peoples, minority rights and rights of women and children. She is an active member of the LIBEAC Network.

Olga Borokh is a Leading Researcher at the Russian Academy of Sciences, Institute of Far Eastern Studies, Moscow. Her fields of interest are: the history of Chinese economic thought since the early twentieth century, with a focus on Western impact on Chinese economics and contemporary economic debates in the People's Republic of China.

Igor Botoev is an Associate Professor at the Buryat State University, Eastern Siberia, Russia. In addition to his PhD in Japanese studies, his fields of interest are in Japanese language and Japanese culture and he has a special interest in issues related to Japanese business in Russia. He has sojourned for long periods in Japan, especially in the northernmost large island of Hokkaido.

Gilles Campagnolo is a Full Research Professor at the National Center for Scientific Research (CNRS) France, in the research-unit in Economics, GREQAM, UMR7316, the co-Editor of the *Review of Economic Philosophy* and the Editor of this volume. He is a Senior Member at Aix-Marseilles School of Economics (Aix-Marseilles University). His former publication with Routledge was *Criticisms of Classical Political Economy: Menger, Austrian Economics and the German Historical School* (2010, paperback reprint 2013).

His fields of interest are liberal theories of economic development, Austrian (Mengerian) economics, economic liberalization, modernization in global context. His studies on modernization brought him to economics and economic policy making in China and Japan, where he is regularly invited. Campagnolo is the global Network Coordinator for the European Union Marie Curie IRSES program LIBEAC ("Liberalism In Between Europe and China"), whose main deliverable is this collective volume.

Jean-Sébastien Gharbi is an Assistant Professor at the research-unit REGARDS (University of Reims Champagne-Ardenne, France). His work deals with economic theories of justice and economic philosophy, in particular with methodological, epistemological and ontological underpinnings of economic theories. He is also one of the founders and the co-manager of the Philosophy-Economics Network. He is an active member of the LIBEAC Network.

Sang-Jin Han is a Professor of sociology at Seoul National University, Korea and an invited Professor under contract at Peking University in Beijing. His fields of interest are the sociology of urban life, risk governance and participatory action of the citizens. His works have been edited and translated from Korean in other languages. He has been a correspondent and a close acquaintance with late Professor Ulrich Beck, the author of *Risiko-Gesellschaft* (1986). He is an active member of the LIBEAC Network.

Qunyi Liu is an Associate Professor of economics at Peking University in Beijing, China. Her fields of interest are: East Asian economies, economic integration, and the history of economic thought.

Masataka Muramatsu is an Associate Professor of philosophy and ethics at the University of Hokkaido in Sapporo, Hokkaido, Japan. His fields of interest are: ethics, French philosophy, especially nineteenth-century and contemporary French philosophy. He has also a special interest in the reception of Western philosophy and social sciences in Japan. He is an active member of the LIBEAC Network and the research team coordinator for the Japanese partner within LIBEAC.

Santiago Pinault is a PhD candidate in philosophy and economic philosophy at Aix-Marseilles University. His fields of interest are the influence of the Austrian school of economics in adjacent social sciences, with a focus on Friedrich Hayek and Karl Polanyi, and the governance of economic transition towards liberal markets in the context of authoritative regimes (Chile and China in particular). He is an active member of the LIBEAC Network.

Yoshihide Sakurai is a Professor of sociology and social studies at the University of Hokkaido in Sapporo, Hokkaido, Japan. His fields of interest are in sociology of religions, especially in contemporary religions in Japan and comparative study of religious culture in East and Southeast Asia, and he has a special interest in issues related to engaged religions and cult problems, that is function/dysfunction of religion in society. He is active in the LIBEAC Network.

Young-Hee Shim is a Professor of sociology at Hanyang University, Korea and an invited Professor under contract at Peking University in Beijing. Her fields of interest are related to family relationships, social analysis of urban life and comparative aspects of East Asian societies. She is an active member of the LIBEAC Network.

Olga Tugulova is an Associate Professor at the Buryat State University, Eastern Siberia, Russia. In addition to her PhD in Asian (Chinese) studies, her fields of interest are Russian–Chinese relations and the evolution of bilateral partnerships, together with Chinese language, culture and social anthropology.

Bo Xu is an Assistant Professor at Southwestern University of Finance and Economics in Chengdu, China. He got his PhD from Peking University, Beijing. His fields of interest are: political philosophy, history of political thought, and Western political thought and China's modern transition. He is an active member of the LIBEAC Network.

Lizhi Zhao is a PhD candidate in public international law, International Law Institute of Peking University. His fields of interest are: theories of international law, mechanisms of human rights protection and human rights. He is an active member of the LIBEAC Network.

Acronyms

AIIB	Asian Infrastructure Investment Bank
APEC	Asia-Pacific Economic Cooperation
CAT	Convention Against Torture and Cruel, Inhuman, Degrading Treatment or Punishment
CCB	China Construction Bank
CCP	Chinese Communist Party
CDB	China Development Bank
CEDAW	Convention on Elimination of All Forms of Discrimination against Women
CERD	Committee on the Elimination of Racial Discrimation
CRC	Convention of the Rights of the Child
CRPD	Convention on the Rights of Persons with Disabilities
EC	European Community
ESHET	European Society for the History of Economic Thought
EU	European Union
EU-PIRSES	European Union Programme for International Research Staff Exchange Scheme
FBO	Faith-Based Organization
FP7	European Union Seventh Framework Programme
FRA	European Union Agency for Fundamental Rights
FRP	Fundamental Rights Platform
GAROP	Global Alliance for the Rights of Older People
GDP	Gross Domestic Product
ICCPR	International Covenant of Civil and Political Rights
ICESCR	International Covenant on Economic, Social and Cultural Rights
LIBEAC	Liberalism In Between Europe and China
MT	Modernization Theory
NATO	North-Atlantic Treaty Organization
NGO	Non-Government Organization
NPO	Non-Profit Organization
OEWG	Open-Ended Working Group (on the Convention for the Rights of Older Persons)
OP CEDAW	Optional Protocol to CEDAW
PRC	People's Republic of China
R2P or RtoP	Responsibility to Protection
RCIF	Russia–China Investment Fund

RDIF	Russian Direct Investment Fund
RFP	Russian forest products group
RWI	Raoul Wallenberg Institute for Human Rights and Humanitarian Law
SEZ	Special Economic Zone
UN	United Nations
UPR	Universal Periodic Report of the UN Human Rights Council
US or USA	United States (of America)
USSR	(Former) Union of Soviet Socialist Republics

1   Introduction

In search of the meaning of
liberalism in a China
confronting crisis

Gilles Campagnolo

Has the tremendous rise of the Chinese economy already met (some) limits? In other words, has mainland China encountered forces that may hinder its apparently inevitable development into the first world power? And what forces may decelerate China's growth, a phenomenon already visible? Conversely, what forces may help China overcome obstacles on the path explicitly taken by Chinese leaders towards realizing the "Chinese dream"? This is the main topic of this volume.[1]

These questions accompany a scholarly puzzle: whether some of the forces at play are internal, whether they stem from the very sources of the Chinese development path and are furthermore embedded in its culture and civilization, much rather, for instance, than from resistance on the part of East Asian neighbors, which share with China the rich heritage of many common values.

This reflection agrees with the facts too: as of 2015, China has in fact met some difficulties, more than the usual worries already raised by specialists, in its most extraordinary experience, the most baffling success story of modernization in the contemporary era. Both at first sight and in retrospect, the present times are the period of China's economic development since 1978, together with the 1992 turn, two major steps which have been much discussed. In 1978 Deng Xiaoping oriented the country anew towards prospects of wealth and more economic freedom. In 1992 the CCP Plenary Session marked a second turn towards some full-fledged economic capitalist economy including "liberal"/pro-free trade measures. Deng made his famous "Southern tour" to illustrate swiftly this shift in the discourse. Now, would the year 2015 stand at the other end of the trajectory, with the result of unprecedented growth and accumulation of wealth (in absolute terms) being halted, or at least slowing down? No one slammed on the brakes, that is certain. On the contrary, the authorities are sustaining economic activity more than ever when a multifaceted crisis threatens. What about China?

China has arguably experienced, in proportion to its size and with respect to its demography, the most important change for its effective and, even more, potential impact on the history of mankind since Great Britain first trod the path of the industrial revolution. It took China roughly one third of a century to develop economically so as to stand at the forefront of international economic powerhouses. In the first decade and a half of the twenty-first century, China got from that event more respect, even fear (for instance, regarding the threat to levels of employment in the West), and attention concerning its economic situation than for centuries before. After Japan already at the end of the nineteenth century and Taiwan and (South) Korea after World War II, China has been diagnosed as the single player that is insuring that the center of gravity of the world economy shifts to the Asia–Pacific region. Let us not forget that both the United States and Russia have a Pacific coastline.[2]

For all other major powers, China now offers both immensely new opportunities and worries. China itself, put in this new "global" role, has opportunities and duties on the scene of world economics like never before – with the tasks and perils that go with it. In particular, each and every power-player in the world, to begin with its neighbors, has had not only to take into account this power–state–party entity, but also to contend (and perhaps to contain) this new high-stake international player that, once "awakened" (according to the famous saying attributed to Napoleon), is now acting at global scale not only strategically, but also, and most importantly because this is the new aspect, in terms of the economy.

This being said, China's role was given a further push since the other powers suffered greatly from the global major crisis that originated in 2008 in the United States with the so-called *subprime* and Lehmann Brothers default crisis. Sequels followed that shook the West arguably much more than China or other regions of the world. Sovereign-debt crisis in Western European countries displayed the relative weakness of the West – even in front of Russia, that had recovered since the collapse of the Soviet model, a trauma that China spared itself, for better or worse with respect to consequences in socio-economic or political terms. From 2008 on, the crisis reached such dimensions that it was named a *Great Recession*, like that of the 1890s, and recalling the *Great Depression* of the 1930s. In a so-called "globalized" world with most Western nation-states proving relatively penniless and weak, and to some extent leaderless (as on the issues of global climate-change, the United States' reluctance made it a laggard on the issue while, for once, French diplomacy met a much-needed success in ending the December 2015 world-meeting COP21 with the unanimous signature of the binding so-called "Paris Protocol" to succeed the "Kyoto-Protocol"), then may it be the case that China could ever be a leader for the twenty-first century? Or are there some obstacles in the nature of its development and/or its civilizational traits that would hinder that geopolitical role?

This book aims to point out some internal socio-cultural and even philosophical traits that impact the economy, at the micro scale of the agents' behavior. Methodologically, the assumption is that these are causally related to macroeconomic effects which are generally widely felt and registered in various types of national and international statistics, that strangely enough do not always coincide. Talks about the "Beijing consensus" (opposed, or at least independent from so-called "Washington consensus") may lead to think China may be contemplating such a role of leader. The question is not whether this is possible, but which inner forces contribute or hinder such a "central" role *in the minds*. As China is traditionally the "Middle Kingdom" (or rather *Central* Kingdom, 中国 *Zhongguo*, since 1949 under the guidance of a *Central* Standing Committee of the Chinese Communist Party – CCP henceforth), this means that all others countries are but peripheral. Now, on the regional and global scale, is this sustainable?

If power depends on economic development and the latter In turn on free/liberal economic practises, then are both sustainable in the long run *without* the other traits that liberalism is/was said to bring to the fore in the West (especially democratic politics in the sense understood, notably in the West, as multiparty elections, among other features)? Or is liberalism but one Western ideology? Would China reject parts of it while digesting others, as the CCP did for Marxism, in a sense, leading to an interpretation by the CCP that differs quite a lot from the Western views on Marxist ideology (needless to say itself originally a Western product)?

Add, however that China gives evidence that the role of major player is set as a goal: in 2014 and 2015, China managed to set up a major tool (the Asian Infrastructure Investment Bank, known as AIIB), to orientate financial investments in countries that are close to the new center of gravity of the world economy. Notice though, that rulings and procedures for the AIIB are clearly not the same as those of the World Bank with its headquarters in Washington, or as those practised by the International Monetary Fund and commonly recognized in the West. Governance and the understanding of finance may differ from the Western liberal stands – and yet, the UK, Germany, France and Italy take part in the scheme, while Japan and the US do not. Besides geo-strategy (the subject of a different book from this one), a kind of world-view underlying economic and socio-political development is at stake. The AIIB is just a (major-scale) example. The meaning of *liberalism per se* is at stake: what has become of early British political thought of the seventeenth century (John Locke to name only one thinker) and French philosophy of the eighteenth century Enlightenment? The very notions of universality vs. plurality, what "individual" means are at play since, in any given society, such traits display the original models of life, mindsets and frameworks that run the whole system of behaviors, and the cogs and wheels of the economic machine in the end.

Such notions provide the frame for economic exchange and any socio-economic order, while, as a matter of fact, they are diverse, even if they have been partly imported and adapted/adopted. The nature of these notions in China is of utmost significance if, or rather since, the whole world has entered a mutation where China plays a, if not *the*, major role. Does it mean, since the whole world has entered a crisis, that the change is such that these notions will be decisive? One should recall this warning by a French sinologist: "Conceptions that we have about the state, about what is 'political', how 'public service' contrasts with 'private activities', etc. either have no existence in China, or do have a totally different meaning" (Billeter 2000: 107).

Facts about China in 2015 put in global perspective and the "Chinese dream"

Understanding fundamental notions in the background will provide keys to grasp how a country that is already a geographic and demographic giant, already known for social and environmental evils, namely mainland China, is now facing both success and the elements of crisis that go with it, while the political turmoil that lasted for most of the twentieth century is over since the end of the Cultural Revolution. Facts and some historical perspective are needed here to form the background upon which the contributions in this volume will make most sense for the reader.

Economic facts, then: China is still in 2015 (yet may well not be, according to demographic forecasts, by 2030) the most populated country in the world. China comes globally second in terms of GDP (second to the USA since China overcame Japan on that criterion around 2010). China is also newly a large foreign direct investor in many countries around the world, both developed (first owner of US Bonds and present in all sectors in the European Union, buyer of all kinds of minerals from Australia) and under-developed (Africa and Asia). China's ever larger growing investing power gets no better illustration than the AIIB: through investing heavily in the development of many other economies, China (with allied partners) will rival the International Monetary Fund and already compelled the World Bank to insert the *renminbi* into the basket of five most-in-use currencies.

In historical perspective, China displays traits more significant than just now being wealthy. The issue is whether it is an over-powerful nation – and how it may confront crisis. It has become more powerful than neighboring Japan in the 2010s for the first time in the Modern era. In undertaking to reshape the Asian–Pacific region around its mainland territory, China has begun an expansionary policy with neighboring areas, especially those among still sparsely populated regions (like Siberian Russia) and is facing opposition in the so-called "pearl necklace" of the South China Sea. But the issue is whether the economy can sustain China in regaining its ancestral central role. And this is where the history of imported liberalism matters. Is China dependent on Western notions or can China bring forth a model (and which one?) without reaching the peak of a trajectory that has effectively left unprecedented traces in the historical records of national accounting since these have been in existence and – given that these are both recent in history and contemporary with industrialization where growth is highest – thus probably in the whole history of mankind?

Once again, some impressive figures: in 2015, China has overcome the United States in terms of exports of merchandize for two decades or so. And the pace of growth during the past three decades, with two-digit figures, has had the consequence of tremendously reducing the level of poverty, pushing the front line of developed China from the sea coastal regions always further inland and well into traditionally poorer inner countryside of its Western provinces. Pockets of poverty, and even misery, do however remain sometimes in areas that would be large enough to include whole countries in other regions of the world. But this is in a country where, at a moment when China is quitting the one-child policy (officially cancelled from October 2015), the mere margin of error relative to the exact figure of the population is higher than the whole count of the population of countries like France, Germany, or Japan.

Now, the point is that the Chinese government in this situation regards it to be the duty of CCP governance, by either Communist or newly popular again (neo-) Confucian standards, to serve well a population busy getting rich. It is true that in remote provinces, this still means providing enough help for development so that all have enough to eat. In Shanghai and along the coastal areas, it means, though, a lifestyle on a par with that of the large metropolitan cities of the world. Not every Chinese lives in the main "global cities" of Beijing, Shanghai or Tianjin, but for those who do, they live "*almost* like" the people in any other "global city" of the world – and with time many more cities of that kind will arise in China. Obviously, there are also social evils that come with such wealth.[3]

Actually and quite naturally, much remains implicit and adding the qualification "*almost* like" implies both a divergence, for instance in political activities, and similarities. So, despite the fact that post-modern life has standardized some attitudes which give the appearance of commonalities to all, the need exists for the study of civilizational features and traits of socio-economic "embeddedness" within a cultural analysis that shall help to explain social and economic behaviors.[4]

In this regard, one of the most paradoxical aspects is probably the following: on the one hand, China is still suffering from diseases typical of a "young" capitalist country in an environment that has grown at a fast-pace. The experience of catastrophic events shows that point well: the mega-explosion which destroyed part of the city of Tianjin in the summer of 2015 illustrates what happens in the complex situations of mega-cities that have grown out of multi-industry and potentially defective (and destructive) development.[5] There are numerous examples of such major accidents, due to mis-construction on sites as significant as industrial complexes, chemical plants, railways; many are also due to cases of corruption. They cast a spell on countries and cities that usually carry or have just left, thanks to fast-paced development, the status of being labeled as "Third-World". Difficulties of this kind are still felt in China – like pants leaving bare skin where teenagers grew too quickly to adjust the hems.

On the other hand, evoking the image of "youth" about a country that rightfully boasts one of the longest (if not the longest) tradition of civilization in human history sounds strange. China is *both* a post-modern capitalist society and the most traditional culture, at the forefront of modernity and still with traits pertaining to the most traditional. Such is the case of many so-called "Third World countries", some of which are also now on the rise, like also Brazil, Russia, India, South Africa (under the new denomination of "BRICs"). If Brazil is something of a newcomer in world history, India may boast a history as old at least as China's. But in China the paradox reaches its peak. When was the time that just sneezing in the US could give a cold to the rest of the world? The position newly taken by China at the international level implies a continuous assessment of *this* country's demeanor as well henceforth.

China now boasts world-level scientific achievements, with its first Nobel Prize in science (medical sciences, in 2015), and manufactures the computers of tomorrow (harvesting "game-playing farms" for instance) while using characters/ ideograms dating back to the first traces that human hands left on pebbles or turtle-shells. Chinese dynamism makes it all the more striking that China's growth will continue to rise along a model of modern capitalism that, after all, dates back *only* to the Western industrial revolution. By bridging the times before and after modernity in the contemporary world, and doing so in not much more than a third of a century, China mixes syndromes of societies with long development and new abundance. Has therefore China reached the peak of such a development path, and does China have the means to put together pieces of a new economic and socio-intellectual model?

Now, for all the excitement that such a perspective may bring, and which motivated this volume, let it be known that the Party has an answer: the apogee will come when the country feels self-assured, dominant (and possibly less sympathetically, arrogant), stable and prosperous. Goals are set under the guidance of the CCP for a zenith already planned and scheduled: it has got a name, given by the Standing Committee and conveyed in Party literature. It is called the "Chinese Dream". And it is set to be realized in 2049 – for the centenary of the People's Republic of China.

Notice, then, that whether this "dream" becomes a reality or not, it will still be three-quarters of a century, *less* than one hundred years, since China took the first steps into modern capitalism, since the moment when the CCP, under the leadership of Deng Xiaoping, decidedly turned away from the remnants of Mao Zedong's teachings and prioritized the accumulation of capital rather than socialist distribution. That policy of the initial stage of reforms applied in the People's Republic of China after 1978 and 1992 has led insofar to changes unpredicted at the time. Why not share in the "Chinese Dream" then?

How China faces crisis and some key notions that may shed light on China facing crisis

In 2015, not much more than a third of a century after 1978 and less than a quarter of a century after 1992, does the type of full-fledged economic capitalism that has been implemented and prevails go along with some form of socio-economic, or even socio-political liberalism? If precisely the issue is whether the one is sustainable without the other, then how long is economic liberal development sustainable without political liberalism being granted? But the kind of economy implemented is also at stake, and the agents' behavior that goes with it. Are there signs that the impressive results aimed at, and largely achieved, are shaken in the midst of the waking dream in which the country would be soon (at historical scale) living?

Specialists of China have, all the time that development was taking place, pointed to failures and gaps in various facets of this incremental development, to begin with the disparity between regions and the difficulties of social and environmental nature overall.[6] Yet, the signs that, in 2015, surface are of a different nature: they confirm less the fact that there would be 'gaps in accumulation' (which remains true however), than they prove the fact that evils accompany the whole process of accumulation and are part of its very outcome.

In any case, if there is a crisis in China, much of it looks nowadays like the ones experienced in industrialized countries.

Providing some more facts about the crisis that struck China in 2015 this time may come as a starting point and the stimulus to realize the need for deeper views on economic circumstances and their socio-cultural embedding. China faces shocks of the two kinds mentioned above, suffering some shocks that plagued only countries with a well grown capitalism. In 2015 in Shanghai, the stock exchange crisis recalls in many ways each and every major bubble and crash crisis. Surely, another blow came thereafter from distrust (or even slanders) of the economic picture drawn by parties adverse to China. Anyhow, from the end of August 2015 to the Fall of the same year, and thereafter, investors and economists all over the world followed the fluctuations of the Chinese stock market, and moreover Chinese production lines, with concern in the face of huge losses that had affected investors and could endanger construction and manufacturing. Were the shocks big enough to shake the fundamentals of the Chinese economy?

It does not pertain to this book to examine this difficult and delicate question. Moreover, only the future holds the keys to a correct answer. But facts can be recalled and key notions that run deep below the waters of the tempest may be summoned up. A crisis strikes after preliminary warnings, simply most observers realize retrospectively. Headline news may be enough to raise eyebrows, and worries throughout the world. But they surface only because of deeper moves. The contributors in this volume examine concepts that have brought long-run evolution and long trends in the history of China and/or East Asia. They do even more since they deal with the mindsets that frame these trends, like for instance Ma and van Zanden (2011). These trends are also economic indicators that appear at various levels of analysis. From instantaneous to long-time analysis, together they thus provide a multi-layered economic analysis, like the studies by French historian and thinker Fernand Braudel. We are thus reminded that there are strata in the analysis of economic structures and that they are based upon concepts and can be approached through conceptual qualitative analysis as much, if not better than, through mere modeling. This Introduction starts from elements of the 2015 crisis to open a volume that draws on deeper longer-term analysis.

The instantaneous: between June 1, 2015 and September 10, 2015, the Chinese Stock Exchange, beginning with the Shanghai Index, crumbled down violently by 37 percent, a phenomenon wherein instant trading played a large part. Not only did trillions of Yuan, an instant before regarded as solid by many investors, melt in the air. First of all, this new crowd was only the Chinese branch of a cohort we know from old in the liberal West and that was hit at every step of capitalist modernization, the "small speculators" who come in flocks to stock markets just to be fleeced, at least most of them. But not only did these small investors lose their savings, also cross-participations in all industries actually created a much heavier blow from the impact of the stock crunch, one that went far beyond stock-companies directly trading on the market. Companies that did trade on the market and companies that were not listed were mostly just as badly affected since participations are huge and intricate in the Chinese economy. The networks of interpersonal relations (*guanxi*, 关系), historically known as a basis for business, for instance of regional chambers of commerce pushing sociopolitical change (Chen 2011), are very resilient as a scheme, but whether the CCP supports their own networks or not, they also very easily transfer risk and collateral damages. What is a guarantee of resilience, on the one hand, is a system that transfers huge shocks to the whole structure, on the other hand.

The latter structure, *guanxi*, is community-based in essence, like the family or religious groups, and it is antagonistic by definition to individualism as some Western version of liberalism may conceive it. Individualism acts exactly the other way round. Now, what helps investment more and what hampers progress? Anyhow, the starting point of second thoughts about the Chinese situation comes, in the second decade of the twenty-first century, quite obviously with the issue of its rate of growth. The two-digit rate of growth maintained for decades has been lost. It was already blown with the Great Recession that started in 2008 since the world crisis struck China as well, for the simple reason that China exported more to the world than any other of the country that bought Chinese products. One may just recall how the catching up of products "made in Germany" against British exports around 1900 (while this was thoroughly realized and assessed in the UK only *after* World War I)[7] made Germany both dependent in turn and powerful, but thus vulnerable to external shocks. The same was true of Japan in the 1930s, in addition to the difficulty to access indispensable raw materials. China faces this situation at an even larger scale.

Despite major endeavors and quite appropriate measures taken by the CCP Standing Committee, official statistical bureaus have been compelled to reduce the figure of the Chinese growth-rate. By 2015, they had sworn to see a 7 percent growth-rate – sworn to the Party. This figure, rehashed *ad nauseam*, had become quasi-sacred. The figure finally released was 6.9 percent. This is a typical situation where doubt begins to creep in – as in the years of the art of interpreting Soviet official data. Chinese statistics are plentiful, but all remain subject to various kinds of review overall (reviewed everywhere except, by definition, in the official literature of the original provider – but who believes official figures only?). Practically speaking, economists and specialists know well that, from the winter of 2014–15, Chinese growth slowed down. The press may not say it, and it may still take time (how long?) for public opinion to become aware, but the fact is that a rate of growth that would more than please any other developed country comes as a disappointment to the Party. And this has unpleasant consequences for the country they rule. Precise indicators such as imports (in terms of volume at least), production of electricity, industrial manufacturing, etc. all tend to show the same inversion of their curves. The trend is clear, the "sacred" figure merely wishful.[8]

At the same time (before the summer of 2015), warning signs after decades of higher growth had been ignored. After the shock, with the whole economy suffering, the government attempted to calm down players, even threatening some (mostly domestic investors) with penal sanctions. Is then such interventionism precisely not an issue *per se*? Financial markets may be subdivided and a differentiated treatment applied to *national* and *international* investors, or to *private* and *institutional* financiers, and funding bodies may be regulated by the CCP at will, but what is then left of free trade in finance, of voluntary investment in mere stocks (funding the economic activity), and not only in derivative products? One must confess that the question can be asked in other places around the world (in 2008 the US government was not the last to raise a finger and to implement relief-packages), but what is then liberalization when there is systematic resort to "big government"? It may well be that liberalization is not what is happening. Then the question is whether liberalism is key to economic development – but is not this in turn what the CCP bet upon to develop China, with such success for so long? The issue is not only whether an economic liberal path may be trodden without a political liberal path: it is also whether, confronting crisis, China will trust enough liberal views to go on. And also whether developmental needs do not bring with them a process of individualization that runs underground, little noticed, yet deep in the minds of the people who are getting both more and more education and a better acquaintance with the laws of trade and of the market. A modern economy requires talent, and education/training, abroad and/or at home, pushes the idea of individual investment into one's labor-power.

Now, these aspects of economic development – how individualization comes into play, which universal creeds are assumed, which are denied, and so on – make the common thread that relates the contributions in this volume in various areas of inquiry towards a common goal. Each contributor takes the reader to a field that displays reality *beyond* mere actual economic facts. Each delivers knowledge on principles and information far deeper embedded in the history, philosophy and sociology of the Chinese and Eastern Asian background. This deliberate approach is quite obviously a gamble in thinking that cultural economics and comparative history and philosophy of economic thought are the necessary background to sustaining core pure economics. In the book at hand, we all sustain the idea that the role of social sciences is comprehensive and explanatory. Obviously, this goal is far from exhaustive in any respect. All contributors aim simply at providing some keys for the understanding of Chinese economic development by highlighting facts that they analyze with their own tools. Now and thereafter, down the line, they make the reader able to grasp more of the background upon which to observe China confronting elements of crisis and pursuing its growth with greater or lesser chances of reaching the "Chinese dream" scheduled for its future.

Perspectives from Europe and Asia

To fulfill the goals mentioned in the previous pages, this volume provides the reader with perspectives from Europe and Asia. Conceptual tools are used to make sense of economic facts, which are indeed not always easy to understand, but may appear quite mechanical with respect to the underlying layers of civilizational material in which they are embedded.

Economics is more than mechanics since mechanics (economics in a reductive view) always requires interpretation; one can grasp its meaning only when provided with concepts to do so: among our contributors, some make sense of economic analysis of modern capitalism and trade in discussing the import of the notion of "liberty" as understood by Chinese and Japanese scholars, some in examining its application on the concrete level to business and some approach the economic agent through the "individual". What these notions consist in makes the mind hesitate and consider alternative paths, concepts of universality, plurality and singularity, implemented within the framework of rules, customs and codes of a particular civilization.

Concerning the contemporary crisis-like historical development, actors and observers wonder: what "liberalism" may it be when, as shown by the 2015 crisis, the CCP interferes in markets with effects surfacing that are clearly undesirable, such as capital leaving markets, fleeing China like a hemorrhage? Is it that the idea of liberalism is absent, weakened, or will it be fostered when this result is openly assessed by Chinese economists in turn? Outside of China, will investors judge that, after all, stock markets there are still the playground of Party officials? If one recalls that China was still in 2015 asking to be recognized by the World Trade Organization as a full-fledged market-economy, then one hesitates to tread on unsafe ground with plain intervention. Now, since some Western governments display the same tendency, is it "Western liberalism" as such, or liberalism as an ideal that is at stake? One more paradoxical element is that when governmental measures are taken on the advice of opponents of economic liberalism, these are quickly taken over by hardline conservatives, opponents of civic and individual liberties in China. Indeed, the situation is complex enough to require some more clarification at technical level[9] and at conceptual level as well: what to infer from this interference? If the position newly taken by China in Eastern Asia and at international level implies to assess a renewed understanding of "liberalism" in historical, social and even philosophical dimensions, then liberalism is not only far from being effective, but its contents as well come under scrutiny.

This is precisely what the group of scholars gathered here aims to scrutinize: both the benefits and the risks associated with diverse views on liberalism and some of its most commonly associated forms, namely individualism, rationalism, universalism, and the respect of liberties in social and economic dimensions. Is liberalism present, in what sense, and is it perceived as a "model", a threat or a guise of Western ideology? Is it, after all, merely inconsistent when one puts together the pieces of this puzzle? Politics adds one more layer, whether it is not clear that this may hold all pieces together in a profuse reality or add uncertainty.

This book is a qualified selection of contributions on liberalism and Chinese development from a multidisciplinary and comparative Eurasian perspective. It examines the issue of liberalism in China, bearing on some elements from Japan and including a study on Siberia bordering China. It contributes to the debate on how long economic development is sustainable with social evils from both early and later stages of capitalist development, while wondering whether some form of liberalism (and which form, a Western version of it?) is being implemented.

Papers in this volume were presented and discussed in various settings, that contributors indicate, their collection originating with a seminal meeting of the session dedicated to the European program "Liberalism In Between Europe and China" (LIBEAC) at the conference of the European Society for the History of Economic Thought (ESHET) hosted at the University of Lausanne, Switzerland in May 2013, around the theme "Liberalism in the History of Economic Thought".

The methodologies adopted throughout the twelve chapters following this Introduction are as diverse as the backgrounds of the specialists that contribute to that undertaking in comparative development thought of the history of economics and economic thought, economic philosophy and socio-economics. Yet all aim at resorting to a variety of disciplines to question today's economic reality. Yesterday's traces formed the mindset and framework that has shaped China and East Asia, since the time when capitalist and industrial modernization began. All contributors bear in mind cultural imports from the West being accepted, rejected or modified. In adapting/adopting so-called "liberal" values, most often related to the market, East Asian societies have had to meet notions and realities such as the individual agent, legal freedom and the "rule of law", freedom of expression, and so on. This has shaken and changed older ways as well as the agents' behavior. Contributors come from European and Asian academic backgrounds and their perspectives, including Korean and Russian, provide us with keys for understanding, deter clichés, and instead present the reader with a renewed understanding of trans-cultural grounds.

In this perspective, this book is transnational, transdisciplinary and of "trans-value". This is quite natural when one recalls that, since the nineteenth century, the core of the Chinese reception of Western ideas has run along, or against, the Chinese motto *"zhongxue wei ti, xixue wei yong"* (中學為體 西學為用 "Chinese learning as the substance, Western learning as an instrument"). When upheld, it was never sufficient to support modernization. The instrumentalist view it displays seemed detrimental in the end, failing to grasp what produces techniques, that is what lies behind the instrument yet without which one can use the instrument neither effectively nor for long. Once Chinese elites realized they were compelled to try to integrate more Western *Weltanschauung* than mere technical tricks, they split between those who enthusiastically endorsed Western values (or what they understood these to be) and those who brutally rejected them. Naturally, things are never that simple.

Even rejection may mean a need for much deeper endeavor into reception. Maoism, officially meaning a sequel of the Marx–Engels–Lenin–Stalin tradition, thus derived from one part of Western philosophy, and with Marxism stemming from Georg Wilhelm Friedrich Hegel's rationalist and "Prussian" approach to the world, the model of the nineteenth-century Western heritage was well anchored. "Chinese Marxism" does still surprise more than one Western specialist of Marx, but no part of the world (except North Korea) has a proportionally higher number of scholars claiming to be Marxists in the twenty-first century than China. Lip service is paid to official ideology, but Marxism is not proclaimed as the only true scientific and most advanced doctrine. It has ceased to be for Chinese intellectuals the ultimate criterion to judge other historical or contemporary doctrines. Since China turned to capitalist entrepreneurship, liberal values, always much criticized, have pervaded the discourse even of officials. Is this a sign of parallel liberal democratization? Or an ideological tool the West tends to impose on the rest of the world? What does individualization of behavior mean, if anything at all in the East Asian civilizational context? Are so-called "liberal" values present, and under which form or guise?

Contributions

The volume is divided into three parts. The first part deals with the history of economic thought, examples dating back from early liberal Western thought to the reception of Western liberal values in China till the end of the twentieth century. Theories of modernization related to liberal values are anchored in this latter period. The second part is about the adaption/adoption of the concept of *individual*, and related notions of individualism, individualization and their indeterminacy in civil society. Whether the adaption/adoption of the latter is necessary (or not), inevitable (or not), at the domestic level but also in relation to international bodies and legislation, the debate over this conceptual background related to the development of a market-enhanced economy makes up a third part.

Philosophical and legal, statistical and sociological inputs are needed to study such principles of socio-economic life. Even though some thinkers commented on in this volume were philosophers rather than economists, their widely differing ideas influenced the formation of economic thinking. Socio-economic analysis, in turn, proves well enough the effect of beliefs, religious and philosophical, in concrete life. Applied elements of legal issues also frame liberalization and the terms of exchange: is liberalism synonymous with universalism, pluralism, or some other notion, either from the European traditional conceptual heritage or from new forms of multiculturalism? Law and long-term economic change (Ma and van Zanden 2011) are linked, all the way down to circumstances where states have to take into account new bodies of international law, bodies that illustrate new economic partners (NGOs for instance). This is all against a background of politics, with both outer and inner influences on the forms of "capitalism" and "surveillance" adopted: discipline matters, and it is as strict under the rules of the market as under those made by the Party. Conversely, Western individualism may give hope for freedom and/or liberties.

Western liberalism therefore makes sense first in relation to rationalism, which means both the rationality of the economic agent (and decision theory makes it its object of study among major fields in economics) and the rational process that leads to collective decisions ("democracy", with all sorts of limits regarding collective-choice, as so-called "Arrow theorem" demonstrates). This twofold display of reason in history, with freedom of labor and trade, on the one hand, and the "rule of law", on the other hand, is historically anchored in the French Enlightenment and subsequent philosophy best conveyed in German rational criticism: Immanuel Kant's three *Critiques* in the 1780s were as much of a starting point for Western liberalism as Adam Smith's 1776 *Wealth of Nations*.[10] This is where this book starts. The four chapters constituting Part I follow the chronological order of topics dealt by contributors in the history of economic thought, beginning with the question how one most fundamental matrix of Western modernity, Kantian philosophy, made it to China.

In Chapter 2, Bo Xu traces the diffusion of knowledge about Immanuel Kant in China as embodying the transfer of the liberal spirit of Enlightenment from Europe to China, since Kant was said to embody the outcome of the French philosophers (Montesquieu, Rousseau and Condorcet, among others) and to build a critical theory that led to German Idealism. In turn, the main philosophy representative thereof, G. W. F. Hegel's, is reckoned as a source of Marxism (Marx putting Hegelianism "on its feet" or, according to a different standpoint, rather "upside-down"). Xu examines Chinese translations and interpretations of Kant, putting them in the changing historical context of modern China.

European systematic thinking on liberty, like Kant's, bore fruits with theories of rationality and knowledge (*Erkenntnistheorie*) in practical applied fields. Many genealogies can be traced to philosophers and economists. Under spotlight in Chapter 3 is the introduction of elements of applied Western precepts by the translator of Smith's classical work in Chinese (1902): Yan Fu. In Chapter 3, Qunyi Liu introduces a less known facet of the achievements by Yan Fu, though. Yan had translated not only Smith's classical book but eight other such Western books in total, including John Stuart Mill's *On Liberty* and his *Logic* (both in 1903), *A History of Politics* (by E. Jenks) and *The Spirit of Laws* (from the English translation of the French treatise by Montesquieu). These translations won him a reputation as an educationalist and a thinker.[11] Yan was then appointed president of Fudan University and Peking University, but he had also, earlier on, been active as the manager of a mining business, the so-called Kaiping Mines (Hebei province) where he happened to meet Herbert Hoover, later to become US president, then employed by the British board of directors as chief engineer and general manager.

In Chapter 4, Olga Borokh shows further how principles of freedom and rationalism were advocated in the economy, and borne by great characters among other newly Western-oriented Chinese elites in republican-era China. Some elites were more reluctant towards so-called "Westernization". Indeed, along the precept 中學為體 西學為用 ("Chinese learning as the substance, Western learning as an instrument") and under the pretense of the influence of more traditional concepts and historical circumstances specific to China, liberal values were more commonly rejected than accepted. Yet some thinkers, economists, statesmen and/or entrepreneurs put liberal thought forth. Borokh introduces the characters of Gu Yiqun (1900–92), later appointed to the International Monetary Fund, who pushed for Western economic liberalism, and Tang Qingzeng (1902–72), who represented somehow the former's scholarly counterpart in seeking to elaborate some form of economic liberalism with Chinese roots.

Promotors of liberal values and ideas have indeed always had to try to "educate" their fellow men in ideas that strengthened liberties, whether brought from the West or genuinely anchored in China's own traditions: this meant that the Chinese could, and ultimately would, reckon the benefits of liberal practice in economic and social life. The meaning of economic liberalism in republican-era China was not limited to intellectual exercise but would combine further scholarship and practicalities of business life. Some of these thinkers attempted to test ideas in reality, as best they could amidst hustle and bustle, all sorts of adventure and entrepreneurship. Pillage by "Lords of War", failures of the Guomindang Party of Jiang Jieshi would not stop them but in October 1949, a much more stable power was established on the mainland by the Chinese Communist Party (CCP) with rigorous control of the economic, political, social and ideological aspects of life: liberal values were over for a while.

Periods of calm and tempest would follow under Mao Zedong, for instance the "Great Leap Forward" and the "Cultural Revolution". In any case, a first era of opening-up to liberal/Western thoughts had ended. They would re-emerge thirty years later, in a second era of opening-up. Chapter 5, by Jean-Sébastien Gharbi, discusses precisely the meaning of modernization and what kind of modernization theory (or MT) can be provided as tools to analyze (and accompany) this surge. Indeed, since W. W. Rostow's *Stages of Economic Growth*, his "Non-communist Manifesto" (Rostow 1959), the idea that economic growth, liberalization, modernization and individualization of societies happen more or less together as societies live through economic stages, much was written – and statements had to be qualified. Predictive goals were over-ambitious, as the picture all along arguably remains puzzling, yet brings forth very interesting by-products.

Part II aims at conceptually sorting out types of individualization in East Asia and their salient characteristics. Western liberalism makes sense with individualism. The methodology here brings together philosophical investigation and socio-economic research. The former is based on major texts and the latter on survey data, quantitative and qualitative. Four chapters deal with the adaption/adoption of this central concept of a liberal *civil* society. Between family and state, the fact that the individual is alone to find his/her own place in the network of economic and social relationships characterizes a "civil society" since Adam Ferguson coined the term during the Scottish Enlightenment, simultaneously with Smith grounding classical economics on "self-love". Whether these two notions, that were simultaneously born, have much in common is precisely what needs to be determined; or it is sometimes left undetermined, as Andrea Altobrando (Chapter 6) notices: when reaching East Asian shores, these notions were both met, first in Japan, with skepticism and wonder due precisely to this indeterminacy. How could these terms serve as ideals? If a modern civil, or *bourgeois* society, is based on them, is it not *weak* by definition? Studies on individualization in East Asia stemmed from there, often arguing that the individual in East Asia is supposedly "different" from that of the West. This alleged divergence (but what is it?), though, is one more puzzle to deal with, which all four contributions in Part II tackle each in its way.

In Chapter 6, Andrea Altobrando thus starts by assessing the simple fact that when East met West, so to speak, clearly Japan led the way since, from the Meiji era, in the last third of the nineteenth century, onwards, Japan confronted the adaption/adoption of these notions of individualism and self-love while coining terms for philosophy and economics as a science.[12] Forced to open up to the rest of the world, and specifically to Western powers, in the middle of the nineteenth century, Asia, and in particular China and Japan, saw Western individualism either as barbarian and threatening or as palatable and attractive, sometimes both. Anyhow, the Western attitude deeply impressed their people, in the sense of admiration or repulsion. They adopted the sciences and wondered whether to adopt and/or adapt individualism as well. Altobrando discusses how thinker Nishida Kitarô, arguably the most famous Japanese philosopher of the twentieth century, dealt with the issue of the individual, starting from studies of Hegel[13] and Martin Heidegger.

How individualism may impact genuine local attitudes, including the socio-economic agent, is further developed in Chapter 7 by Masataka Muramatsu, who wonders at what makes the Japanese people attached to their own version of "self-love" (自愛 *jiai*) which bears on narcissism. Is it appropriate to build any positive attitude in the economy, however despicable in other regards? One must recall that the very basis of Smith's assessment of the nature of the economic agent, in his *Wealth of Nations*, is "self-love". But is Japanese self-love of the same kind? Another major Japanese thinker of the twentieth century, Masao Maruyama, described it as perilous while seeking its origins in traits common with Chinese Confucian community spirit. Would, paradoxically, a genuinely East Asian understanding of "self-love" enhance a type of market economy that would be conformist and definitely alien to "liberal" values?

While philosophers deal in principles, sociologists display what to observe as their counterparts from observed facts: Sang-Jin Han and Young-Hee Shim debate, in Chapter 8, the dual process of individualization that took place in families and societies in East Asian countries. Family, long considered one of the most important institutions to form strong networks, is at the basis of the cliché of the Asian collective-oriented mind: ties among family members are very much based on Confucian traditions, which are strong in China and Korea especially. Individualization may change all that quickly, they argue, and from this perspective of social change, does individualization in society beat individualization in the family context? Answering this query, they find it is questionable in East Asia to define individualization exclusively in terms of self-interest. So, while philosophers focus on fundamental traits of the essence of the individual, sociologists recall that in the main three countries of East Asia considered in this volume remarkable change is going on, putting the family at risk as individualization spreads over a new urbanity.

In Chapter 9, Yoshihide Sakurai stresses further that very point. There are characteristics of individualization in East Asia, particularly in Japan, a mostly Buddhist country, but also in Korea, more influenced by Christianity, not to speak of China, officially atheist under the CCP guidance. All three societies are deeply Confucian in some way, but individualize alongside an objective decline in subjective happiness and deteriorating "self-felt" well-being. Japan is a striking example (illustrated in surveys by the Cabinet Office) of the visible symptoms that crisis brings in the face of post-modernity. Is the liberalization of society pushing toward *this* type of society for all East Asia, and in a not-too-distant future, thus suffering from diseases of the "post-modern" environment? China may indeed suffer simultaneously from being a country still young in terms of capitalism and yet already elderly, that is sharing traits identical with Japan in terms of individual lifestyle, solitude and ageing phenomena. Because there are "many Chinas" in that sense, the concept of "individual" leads one to wonder what type of society liberal economic development may establish: will it be a Western-looking one or one of an altogether new type?

The four chapters that make up Part III question this very issue and test various hypotheses, related both to external/international relationships and domestic issues that mix economics and politics. Indeed, one major element of what any liberal society is about is the "rule of law" and its universalistic basis. This offers an unprecedented challenge to China, first to be considered from a legalistic point of view and then impacting the course of the economy and the society with heavy consequences on how to face times of crisis.

To incorporate liberal values into society requires knowing what it is to implement them in legal terms. Confronting the contemporary mesh of notions put forth by Western liberal thinkers topical in this incipient twenty-first century, Lizhi Zhao considers in Chapter 10 "what liberalism is it?" Drawing on the essay by Gerry Simpson entitled "Two Liberalisms" (Simpson 2001), Zhao assesses that a considerable part of international legal scholarship, with a very effective impact on international bodies, such as the World Trade Organization, regards so-called 'liberalism' (whose sense Zhao tries to define) as the basis of contemporary law. Now, when and how is this received in China and what then should one think if Western positions somehow lack consistency? Within the institutional framework indispensable for a most ancient country to be a new home for capitalist entrepreneurship, what Western main source to rely on, if Western forms of liberalism seem too intricate or complex? May a genuine Chinese understanding seem more appropriate?

This thread is further spun by Guimei Bai in Chapter 11, speaking up for the under-privileged and under-considered. Yes, there are different liberalisms in international law, but some are gentler to the weak than others. Her chapter, inspired by her experience as a witness of periods when China was not open and as a member of the Human Rights Institute at Beijing University, discusses the virtue and limits of Anne-Marie Slaughter's liberal theory of international law from the works initiated by Slaughter in the 1990s on law among "liberal states". Liberal internationalism develops not only in the context of international human rights law, at the heart of Slaughter's theory, but has an impact on international economic matters as well. The role of states and civil society, of NGOs particularly, is at stake under compliance with international conventions, extending liberal theory to trade issues as well and comparing the potentialities of China with

European experiences and United Nations bodies. Since Western liberalism is also about values and fundamental rights, will a new body of global laws be universalistic or pluralistic? Business reality creeps in, but it may work towards new situations where lawyers promote *individualistic* needs in common with liberal economists.

Because China has to cope with the realities that emerge from the very development of its kind of "capitalism under surveillance" then when crisis strikes, this creates new terms of economic exchange. Social change as a consequence may also affect *international* transfers (in fortune, in knowledge, in values) in the long-run, as a shift in the gravity center of the world economy to the East takes place.

Like Bai, I have memories, so let the reader allow me to recall one here. I was in Beijing, in September 2012, when China launched its first aircraft-carrier in the midst of the crisis about the so-called Diayoyu/Senkaku islands disputed with Japan. The whole world talked about the quite tense circumstances (I would then avoid speaking Japanese with Japanese-speaking friends in the open). At the same time a Conference of Asian–Pacific countries was being held. This made headlines in China while it was barely given attention by public media in the West: the event was organized by President Vladimir Putin in Vladivostok, the Russian Far-East capital which faces the coast of Japan. The shift to the Asian–Pacific region was blatant, and clear to Moscow, Beijing, Seoul and Tokyo … and Washington! The "Eastern vector" of Russian development, as it is called, deepens economic cooperation with the entire region, and China comes first – also, naturally, Japan, Korea and Mongolia tend to follow suit. To the Chinese economy, this is a major addendum, while Japanese investors are overcome by an ever growing Chinese presence in Siberia. Igor Botoev and Olga Tugulova discuss this new opening towards Siberian regions in Chapter 12.

Grounding principles and international agreements are decisive to the outcome of a China facing crisis. Back home, internal political order will be ensured, as Santiago Pinault warns in Chapter 13. Domestic politics may well mean internal trouble. The media are under surveillance: for how long, though? Is it sustainable to develop an "information economy" while locking up information? However, all political lines get blurred with liberalization, and liberal-minded Westerners may be actually a little less liberal than they pretend, while some liberties do exist in China in the economy and beyond. What the new mindsets will permit remains unclear as long as the authorization for anything must come from the Standing Committee. Is the combination of a more and more elitist recruitment and self-assured elites referring to Chinese Marxism and Neo-Confucianism simultaneously bringing a solution? While Western democracies are crippled by the global economic crisis, with social unease and political unrest at home in the West as well, does China seem to converge towards their "model(s)" or tread a new path – and does the latter mean building a model anyway? Older traditions survive better, but, in that respect, the liberal West is not necessarily favored with regard to China. Conversely, do both, after decades of capitalist trade, share more traits than they may think or do they advocate models that diverge?

All in all, while socio-economics relationships are getting individualized for better (and worse), economics as a science displays its need for historical, philosophical, sociological and legal inquiry. The three parts in this volume are spotlights on each ground, with a deep conviction that economics without resort to these other pieces of knowledge remains somewhat dull and enigmatic indeed. The reductive view in economics may well go on for a while, as long as all goes well, but times of crisis are times when the marginal value added by adjacent sciences to economics rises dramatically. Only the individualization of socio-economic relationships renders individual behavior understandable within a given civilizational context. Exchange should be totally free; this is what liberalism says. What such freedom means needs exploring, be it only to counter the attacks of all those who, for various reasons, not always inspired by sympathy for the weak, would pick on liberal values and their implementation. What is sustainable development as long as full freedom, starting with freedom of expression, is not granted? And this would in turn allow the following question to be raised, perhaps not to please self-claimed liberal Westerners: what if the nature of the difference in systems was not an issue of nature, but of degree? What if China had reached a point where Chinese citizens may consider a different trend to a post-modernized world than that which the Western powers have followed?

Beyond the sketches provided in this book, the next issue would therefore be geo-strategy. But it does not pertain here. This volume deals with liberalism in various modes and forms and facts past and present: other interpretations are for prospective, not science. Liberalization, industrialization and individualization go together to an extent that permits economists, philosophers, sociologists and law and political sciences scholars, from Europe and from Asia, to work together. What the outcome is, this is for the twenty-first century to show. In this volume, we delineate the elements of a China now confronting potential crisis on its development trajectory.

The book at hand thus provides plenty of food for thought about liberalism in the course of Chinese development at a time when this development is facing crisis and obstacles that require to clarify its very essence.

Guidelines for the reader

In this volume, "East Asia" means *North*-Eastern Asia, specifically territories where Chinese characters are/were used and/or commonly understood. Besides China, that includes Japan, Korea and some parts of Siberian Russia/Manchuria/ Mongolia where local peoples and Han Chinese have long interacted, peacefully or not, back and forth the Great Wall (a movement restarted with Siberian trade). To be precise, neither Taiwan, nor Hong-Kong or Singapore or communities of Chinese in neighboring *South*-East Asia or overseas are dealt with. Focus is on mainland China, with hints at Japan regarded as the *locus for detour* of Western ideas entering China especially in the early twentieth century.

This use of ideograms to designate an area obviously bears on culture: the Chinese script carries notions anchored in Chinese thought. Yet English transliteration is needed: for Chinese, it follows the *pin yin* system (with occasional older transcriptions, when still in use for names of persons or localities). Transcription of Japanese follows the 'modified Hepburn' standard. For instance and as a result, 'economics' is *jingjixue* in Chinese, *keizaiguku* in Japanese, and this word is, like more than a few, written identically in both languages: 経済学. One must know that pronunciation may vary considerably among the many Chinese "dialects" (Mandarin being the official and common language, *putonghua*) but characters are read everywhere. Also, where characters differ (between ancient and "modernized"), simplified Chinese is adopted for Chinese, except for names dating back to before the 1949 simplification or names used in other Chinese-speaking parts. Also Chinese and Japanese names usually follow a reverse order compared with the West – confusion is avoided according to need by contributors (whose names all follow the Western standard). In most chapters, characters are also shown for key notions and for names, with a twofold advantage: it corresponds to real use (since the region of study is selected following that criterion) and it is useful for readers mastering these languages besides English. Concerning translations of excerpts and various passages from other languages to English, these are the contributors' own except where indicated.

Last, the reader will become aware of a trend that I, the Editor, wish to stress here, to end this Introduction: there was a time when studies on Asian cultures were mostly the fruit of (sometimes adventurous) missionaries, diplomats or scholars, almost all "specialists" of some Asian language or art (to begin with martial arts). This forged Asian studies *per se*. One felt moved either by a sense of attraction and admiration, or fear and even repulsion, and at times both feelings mixed in awe. Quite strange behaviors would result, like Westerners adopting habits or outfits already absolutely outdated for locals, who were keen on the contrary to "Westernize" their lifestyle. This could also lead to rigorous scholarship in the end, but tainted with either paternalism (sympathetic in the best case) or downright racism (in the worst). Anyhow such attitudes cannot be upheld any longer. Notice that they were due not only to naïve newcomers to these regions, but to scholars of two categories: favorably biased admirers or arrogant paternalists, patronizing their own science. In the twenty-first century, these species will vanish. We connect with all colleagues on an equal level; this is one outcome that rising economic power has been and is quickly achieving. Self-confidence is more commonly shared, and even some Westerners seem to have their reliance on Western values shaken by the shift of the center of gravity of the world economy to the Asia–Pacific region. Being heir to older patterns of behavior is the one mistake that would hinder some more mutual understanding. What comes and what must come is a new type of scholars who fit the global need for education and knowledge: on both sides, they are "masters of their trade" and teach their disciplines, as specialists of philosophy, law, sociology or economics rather than some under-determined "Asian studies". They debate with their counterparts on even ground in a world of global knowledge.

Notes

1   Support from the European Union International Research Staff Exchange Scheme program (EU–PIRSES) is acknowledged for the work leading to this volume. Funding was received for the project as a whole from the European Union Seventh Framework Programme (*FP7/2007–2013*) under *grant agreement* n°PIRSES–GA–2012–317767. I wish to thank contributors to the programme, to this volume in particular, as well as the professional staff at Routledge. This volume is the deliverable collective volume dedicated to this program.

2   Note that both President Obama from the United States as well as President Putin from Russia look first at their Pacific Coast (the former intently making his first presidential 2008 trip not to Europe but in the opposite direction, and the latter paying renewed attention to the *economic* Siberian scene along the Chinese border; see Chapter 12 in this volume).

3   These cities compete for the highest standards in various fields. Concerns are common between them, like safety, risk governance or participatory involvement of citizens. Family life in a context of individualization (see Chapter 8 in this volume) is at stake, while anonymity may be a suffering (see Chapter 9 in this volume). Indexes, such as the "Safe Cities Index", publish the results of such competition on global criteria. Beijing is recorded together with Shanghai, and Tokyo or Seoul, and Western capitals. Generally speaking, this Index and others of the kind demonstrate that, in the twenty-first century, lifestyle in the cities of the West is *no longer* the only benchmark of advanced (material) civilization.

4   The common knowledge of standard clichés about "the East", starting from Asian ethnic food and "China-towns" around the world, was once compared by a Chinese colleague to what "American pizza" is to the original taste of the dish from Naples: an *ersatz* that hides more than it reveals. One finds it palatable as long as one does not know what the real stuff is.

5   Moreover, one should take into account that the higher the expectations about government action on the part of the population, the higher the risk that citizens get deluded. Some reports show that many inhabitants from the Tianjin area (probably representative of a bigger part of the Chinese population) had such expectations and were quite disappointed. In Chapter 8 of this volume, the contributors provide some background with a survey where the question of "If a disaster occurred, how much help do you think the following people or groups could give you?" shows that while family turned out to be the most reliable social group in degree of expected help in case of a disaster, showing also strong solidarity besides family (more than 90 points in Beijing), between friends and neighbors, reliance on government help was exceptionally high (67 points). Conversely, insurance companies and civic groups (NGOs) performed poorly in Beijing, in comparison with Tokyo or Seoul. Now, when confronted with reality, it also means that the risk of disappointment with government is higher and the crisis felt even more deeply in China, with the feeling of being abandoned if authorities fail to be up to the task.

6   One example suffices to show the immensity of the environmental issue: the Shandong province would use more coal each year than Germany and Japan put together. Far from being an argument to spare China the burden of heavy anti-pollution environmental efforts, according to Piketty and Chancel (2015), does not a carbon-equivalent consumption figure of six tons/year/person in China (whereas it is even roughly twice that amount in Western Europe) speak enough for the efforts to be demanded of the Chinese population (which is much more than twice as numerous than the whole European Union population, thus impacting much more globally)? The atmosphere in Beijing (and many other Chinese cities) is sufficiently "smoggy" to convince not only each and every visitor, but all common-sense observers, including the CCP Standing

Committee members: no "dream" can be achieved in conditions where any rosy picture of life is painted deep grey by a highly polluted environment.

7   Concerning the exports of manufactured goods, the German territories, though starting (after the Napoleonic wars) from mere craftsmanship crippled by lack of infrastructure, especially in transportation means, reached first place and ranked as soon as 1900 *ahead of* Great Britain in terms of exports. "Made in Germany" products became famous worldwide and surpassed the economic pioneer leading-nation, Britain, hegemonic in trade since the eighteenth century. From 1900 on Germany was first – as a report of the British House of Commons demonstrated … only in 1918! The most reliable source is the collective *Final Report of the Committee on Commercial and Industrial Policy after the War*, House of Commons, London, 1918.

8   With the release of the Chinese data set CGSS 2015 (new release of the Chinese general social survey which is only available in Chinese at the time of writing this Introduction) one may try to apply some specific models to answer questions more efficaciously than from quasi-fictitious propaganda goals. The more precise the questions, the better: for example, what are the determinants of one's investments (in business, in development projects, but also in education, etc.) in such a context?

9   Technically speaking, efforts were made to reassure market investors (especially foreign ones, since domestic ones can easily be threatened). This comes with monetary adjustment – twice in the same month of August 2015 – leading to more comforting prospects.

10 Smith's reception in China is dealt with by Qunyi Liu (Liu 2013), in the book edited by Ying Ma and Hans-Michael Trautwein, in the same series (Ma and Trautwein 2013). Qunyi Liu contributes to the present volume as well, with another topic. Regarding Smith in East Asia, Masataka Muramatsu, another contributor to this volume, presented elements of the reception of Smith in Japan at the seminar chaired by the Editor of this volume (Aix-Marseilles Economic Philosophy Department, May 2010).

11 About the works of Yan Fu as a translator, the reader may refer to Cui and Forget (2013). More generally, the collective volume edited by colleagues Ma and Trautwein in 2013, with some same contributors as in this volume (including the Editor), is much recommended and may be regarded as a "complementary good" (to use economic parlance) for readers regarding parts bearing on the history of economic thought.

12 Japan early cultivated a tradition of Western studies, yet for a long time almost exclusively *Dutch* studies (蘭学*rangaku*), in pre-modern, pre-*Meiji* times, during the Edo-Shogunate that spanned from 1603 to 1868. Some Japanese scholars coined the terms for imported knowledge and new sciences: Nishi Amane did so for "philosophy" (哲学 *tetsu-gaku*) in 1862 while "economics", as the name for the discipline as it is utilized since then, is *keizaigaku* in Japanese, *jingjixue* in Chinese, in both cases, the characters being written 経済学. The term is made up of the characters 経 and 済 (while 学 means "study" in academic disciplines, like "-logy" or "-nomy" in Western language) short-hand for a four-character saying: 経世済民 (Japanese *keiseizaimin*) that combines two expressions: "govern the country" (Japanese 国を治める, *kuni wo osameru*) and "protect the people" (Japanese 人民を済, *jinmin wo sukuu*).

13 It is this sense of an "individualized society" that Hegel used when speaking of "*bürgerliche oder 'Bourgeois' Gesellschaft*" in his 1821 *Principles of the Philosophy of Right (Grundlinien der Philosophie des Rechts)*, which in turn conveys the essence of views by classical economists Smith, David Ricardo and Jean-Baptiste Say. We must still ask today: what does "liberal" mean in the relationship between the individual and socio-economic institutions in a "system of needs" (*ein System der Bedürfnisse*)?

References

Billeter, François (2000) *Chine trois fois muette* [*China: Three Times Mute*], Paris: Odile Jacob.

Chen, Zhongpin (2011). *Modern China's Network Revolution: Chambers of Commerce and Sociopolitical Change in the Early Twentieth Century*, Stanford, CA: Stanford University Press.

Cui, Yang and Evelyn Forget (2013) 'Yan Fu, individualism and social order', in Ying Ma and Hans-Michael Trautwein (eds.), London and New York: Routledge, 56–87.

Liu, Qunyi (2013) "The reception of Adam Smith in East Asia" in Ying Ma and Hans-Michael Trautwein (eds.), *Thoughts on Economic Development in China*, London and New York: Routledge, 35–55.

Ma, Debin and Jan Luiten van Zanden (eds.) (2011) *Law and Long-Term Economic Change: A Eurasian Perspective*, Stanford, CA: Stanford Economics and Finance, an Imprint of Stanford University Press.

Ma, Ying and Hans-Michael Trautwein (eds.) (2013) *Thoughts on Economic Development in China*, London and New York: Routledge.

Piketty, Thomas and Lucas Chancel, *Carbon and Inequality: From Kyoto to Paris*, report addressed at Iddri-PSE conference on November 3, 2015.

Rostow, W. W. (1959) *The Stages of Economic Growth: A Non-Communist Manifesto* (subtitle added: 1960 edn.), Cambridge: Cambridge University Press.

Simpson, Gerry (2001) 'Two Liberalisms', *European Journal of International Law* 12(3): 537–71.

Part I

History of thought

Contributions to the reception and
adoption/adaption of Western thought

2 The reception of Kant in China

Bo Xu

Introduction

The reception of the German philosopher Immanuel Kant, like the reception of many other Western thinkers, was initiated in China by those enlightened Chinese intellectuals who saw the necessity of importing Western ideas, as well as Western technology and institutions, so as to transform the Old China into a new and modernized country – since the Old China had exposed its weakness and backwardness in its unexpected and disastrous confrontation with the West since the mid-nineteenth century. Learning and exploring Western ideas, including economic, political, social and even philosophical ideas, therefore transcended mere academic interest, and came to be tantamount to very serious social efforts by the Chinese intellectuals aiming at China's revival through modernization (Wang, J.C.F. 1999: 9).

In this massive and dynamic process, however, Chinese intellectuals were not merely passive or docile learners: they had not only to adapt to and interpret in their mother language, namely Chinese, those newly imported Western ideas and theories which were almost alien to their own tradition, but also to reconcile these, consciously or unconsciously, with Chinese traditional thought and culture. In other words, Chinese intellectuals both absorbed and modified Western ideas and theories which were generally acknowledged as recipes for China's modernization. It was this dualistic work, rather than a more genuine devotion to Westernization, that laid the intellectual foundation of China's modernity.

Although the above historical context is supposed to be a general guide for the inquiries of the Chinese reception of Western thinkers and their thoughts, a few explanatory remarks still need to be made in the case of the reception of Kant. After all, it is not clear, at least on the surface, how Kant's three *Critiques*, which deal with the theory of knowledge, ethics, aesthetics and teleology respectively, have anything to do with the urgent concern of Chinese intellectuals about transforming China into a strong and modernized country. Partly for this reason, Kant actually received his due attention in China much later than those Western thinkers, such as Adam Smith and Jean-Jacques Rousseau, from whom one could expect to draw direct economic or political suggestions. Nevertheless, the Königsberg latecomer gradually gained his fame and popularity among Chinese intellectuals as they deepened their inquiries into the Western civilization and therefore turned to those Western philosophers *par excellence* who had laid the fundamental concepts, categories and values that shaped the intellectual framework of that civilization.

In the West, Kant is expressly renowned for his assertion of the limits of human knowledge and his defense of human freedom. These two points, however, are not separate. Together they constitute a blueprint for human rights and dignity in a secular and modern age, which actually makes Kant one of the fountainheads of the liberal tradition and in particular a major reference point of contemporary liberalism. For example, it is well known that John Rawls (1971, 1980), perhaps the most influential liberal thinker in the West since the 1970s, bases his moral and political theory on a Kantian foundation. How then has Kant, as an acknowledged exponent of liberal ideas and values in the West, been received and interpreted in China in the course of China's striving for modernity?

This chapter examines the Chinese translations and interpretations of Kant by situating them in the changing historical context of modern China. Special attention will be paid to the modifications that Chinese intellectuals have made on Kant's philosophy so as to adapt it both to Chinese intellectual traditions and political and socio-economic circumstances.

Moreover, we expect that this historical examination will shed some light on the comparative issue of liberalism in between the West and China that particularly concerns this collective volume. In the last few decades, China's turn to a market economy and high rates of economic growth, but along with its maintenance of the authoritarian regime, have made it particularly necessary to reconsider the assumed correlation between free market and liberal democracy that is largely based on the Western experience. Inquiring into how some basic notions of liberalism, such as freedom, rights and individualism, have been introduced to China, but also been reconciled with traditional Chinese emphasis on community, tradition and authority, as in the present case of the reception of Kant, will permit us to go further to ponder over China's somewhat distinctive developmental model as well as the meaning of liberalism.

Early reception

Kant's name was mentioned in Chinese intellectual circles for the first time no later than 1886, when Kang Youwei (康有為, 1858–1927), a forerunner of the Chinese Enlightenment and a future leader of the abortive Hundred Days Reform of 1898, referred to Kant's nebular theory (usually known as the Kant–Laplace hypothesis) and epistemology in his *Zhutian Jiang* (諸天講 *On the Heavens*), written in that year, but published almost forty years later. Living in a country in which scientific knowledge had been traditionally regarded as inferior to moral practice and therefore to a considerable degree neglected,[1] Kang and many of his contemporaries developed a complicated attitude towards modern Western scientific and technological achievements. The failure of China in the two Opium wars that happened in the mid-nineteenth century gravely damaged the Middle

Kingdom's age-old pride in the face of modern Western techniques and stimulated the so-called "Self-Strengthening Movement" (洋務運動) in the second half of the nineteenth century, focusing on military and industrial reforms through massive importation of Western science and technology. The Movement also prompted a great number of Chinese intellectuals to learn from the West. Kang's *Zhutian Jiang* resulted from that intellectual endeavor, in which a lot of Western astronomical theories, from Thales' to Albert Einstein's, were introduced to the reading public in China.

Kant's nebular theory was also touched upon in that work for the purpose of introducing Western scientific achievements, but it should be noticed that his epistemology was explored by Kang for two different purposes: on the one hand, it was used as a philosophical justification for modern materialistic cosmology (He and Hong 2009: 4); on the other hand, it was explored to reveal the limits of Western science. When Kang in his *Zhutian Jiang* jumped from the physical level to the metaphysical level and discussed the problem of the existence of God, he referred to Kant's agnostic stance. However, he quietly transferred this Kantian stress on the limits of human cognition to the limits of Western science. For Kang, the existence of God was unknown only if we limit our inquiry to the material-corporeal world as modern Western science actually did, but that God does exist was so evident a truth that no justification was even needed. Kang therefore did not embrace Kant's agnostic stance wholeheartedly, but adopted it merely in the sense that it demarcated a boundary for Western science, within which only material-corporeal things were to be studied. This, for Kang, ultimately determined that Western science was at best but second-class learning. Kang wrote harshly that:

> It is true that Newton, Laplace, and Darwin could reveal [the laws of] those material-corporeal things. But could they foreknow those incorporeal things? Chuang-Tzu says that human life is limited but its knowledge is limitless. Newton, Laplace and Darwin would therefore be overconfident if they attempted to start from their very limited knowledge to a complete apprehension of the Heavens, and a total rejection of God.
>
> (Kang 1990: 171)

Other early introducers, such as Yan Fu (嚴複, 1854–1921), Zhang Taiyan (章太炎, 1869–1936) and Wang Guowei (王國維, 1877–1927), treated Kant's philosophy in a similar way. Yan, a key figure in transmitting Western thought to China by his great activity of translation, praised Kant, along with other agnostics like David Hume, as an insightful sage whose teaching could combat an overwhelming scientism coming from the West (He and Hong 2009: 6).

By contrast, a much more optimistic attitude towards modern Western science was expressed about half a century later by a Chinese logical positivist Hong Qian (洪謙, 1909–92), who once studied philosophy in Germany under the supervision of Moritz Schlick, the founding father of the Vienna Circle, and served as an assistant to him. For Hong, Kant's theory of knowledge was neither a kindly reminder of the limits of modern science, nor a philosophical foundation for it. In a word, Kant's theory of knowledge was outdated for modern science, especially in that it endorsed a kind of transcendentalism, that is, it argued for the existence of certain *a priori* cognitive principles. Though, for Kant, these *a priori* principles could serve merely as forms of the human mind in organizing the materials of knowledge provided by experience and therefore were necessarily presupposed by all empirical knowledge, Hong still criticized Kant from a radically empirical perspective:

> Kant's transcendentalism is completely incompatible with modern science, both in its theoretical principles and methods of thought. Modern science, in view of its development, could be fairly said to prove the adequacy of the philosophical conceptions of empiricism in applying it to science as well as the rejection of all kinds of theoretical principles of metaphysics which are based on non-empirical intuitions. The spirits and meanings of modern science thus differ fundamentally from those of classical science. This is the reason why Kant's transcendentalism has lost the influence that it used to enjoy, and it also accounts for the same fate of all unscientific schools of philosophy as well as Kant's critical philosophy.
>
> (He and Hong 2009: 21)

Although Kant had been brought into the view of Chinese intellectuals firstly with his nebular theory and epistemology, which catered to their great concern about modern Western science, a more comprehensive introduction of Kant also appeared around the turn of the twentieth century. The introducer was Liang Qichao (梁啟超, 1873–1929), a student of Kang Youwei and an activist during the Hundred Days Reform. After the failure of the Reform, Liang fled to Japan and stayed there until 1912, where he exerted an increasingly influence over Chinese reading public through his writings. From 1901 to 1904, Liang published in the Journals *Qingyi Bao* (清議報 *Discussion*) and *Xinmin Congbao* (新民叢報 *New People*) a series of introductory articles about some important Western thinkers, including Aristotle, Francis Bacon, Thomas Hobbes, René Descartes, Spinoza, Montesquieu, Rousseau, Adam Smith, Kant, Jeremy Bentham, Johann Caspar Bluntschli, Charles Darwin and Benjamin Kidd. The article about Kant (published in several parts in different issues) was entitled "The teaching of the greatest philosopher of modern times: Kant", and has been regarded as the first Chinese treatise on Kant (He and Hong 2009: 11; Yang 2001: 49; Ding 2009: 33). It probably, in Chinese intellectual circles, offered the first treatment of Kant's theory of knowledge and ethics in combination.

Liang did not read Kant directly, however. His knowledge of Kant, as has been shown by Huang Kewu (1998), was through a Japanese channel. It was mainly through the Japanese thinker, dubbed "Japan's Rousseau", Nakae Chomin's (中江兆民, 1847–1901) translation of a work by French scholar Alfred Fouillée, his historical account of philosophy, *Histoire de la philosophie*, that Liang got acquainted with Kant's thought. In understanding and interpreting Kant's thought, Liang reconciled it with Yogacara Buddhism and Neo-Confucianism. For example, Liang used the Buddhist expression "*wuru*" (物如 reality of thing) to translate the Kantian conception "thing-in-itself" ("*Ding an sich*"), which was adopted later by some Chinese intellectuals in their writings, and he also attempted to make use of his knowledge of cognitive theories of Yogacara Buddhism and Neo-Confucianism to give explanations of Kant's epistemology.

However, by doing so, Liang actually differentiated himself from Kant's "pessimistic" attitude towards human cognition. According to Kant, what could indeed be known by human beings was appearance, but not the thing-in-itself. Yet, those Eastern intellectual traditions to which Liang resorted actually held much more "optimistic" attitudes towards human cognition and knowledge, and finally led Liang to concede the possibility of knowing the thing-in-itself and acquiring the cognition of the totality of all objects (Huang 1998: 134), even though he admitted that this kind of knowledge was inferior in certainty if compared with physics, which dealt with appearance or corporeal things (Liang 1988: 56).

Liang also explored the moral meaning of the Kantian distinction between the thing-in-itself and appearance. This distinction, as Liang rightly asserted, led to a dualistic concept of a human being: in the phenomenal sense, a human being was a corporeal being, filled with desires and submitted to the law of necessity, but in the noumenal sense, a human being was a free being. Being free was not being licentious or lawless; on the contrary, it meant to submit oneself to the dictation of the higher part, or the "true" part of the Self. This Kantian teaching of personal autonomy, as Liang highly praised, revealed the essence of morality, repelled the vicious teaching of utilitarianism, and was similar to traditional Chinese moral doctrines. Furthermore, Liang saw a parallel between personal autonomy and civic obedience to sovereignty. It should be noticed that when Liang read and wrote on Kant, he, as a reformist, was taking issue with revolutionaries in China. He thus extended Kant's moral teaching to political aspects, laying stress on the necessity of performing one's civic duty:

> Freedom must be presupposed by obedience. If citizens do not obey the sovereign, they will lose their freedom which is endowed by sovereignty. If a human being does not obey his/her conscience, then he/she loses his/her freedom since his/her inner categorical imperative fails in applying to him/her. Therefore, one who respects freedom must pay homage to the freedom of conscience. If a xiaoren (小人 a base person) does not possess freedom with awe, if his/her conscience is overwhelmed by his/her desires, and his/her true self is overwhelmed by his/her corporeal self, then he/she is a prisoner of the Heaven. This is exactly opposite to Kant's conception of freedom.
>
> (Liang 1988: 62–63)

Despite contributing to spreading Kant's thought in China, Liang's introduction was charged by his contemporary critic Wang Guowei as a distortion of Kant's thought due to its *amateurism* and concealed political purpose. Even Liang himself was not quite satisfied with his introduction (Huang 1998: 108–9). More thorough and professional Chinese reception of Kant would then wait for the younger generation.

Reading Kant from the 1920s to the 1940s

Although Kant's thought had been introduced in China around the turn of the twentieth century, no Chinese translation of his major works had appeared during that first period. This fact may suggest that Kant did not belong to the best received Western thinkers in the early stage of the transmission of Western thought to China, whereas the Chinese translations of some other great Western thinkers' works had already appeared.

The classics of political economy and liberalism, especially Adam Smith's *The Wealth of Nations*, John Stuart Mill's *On Liberty* and *System of Logic*, and Montesquieu's *The Spirit of Laws* were translated single-handedly by Yan Fu in the first decade of the twentieth century. And Rousseau's *On the Social Contract* was available to Chinese intellectuals even a little earlier, firstly through the Japanese translation by Nakae Chomin, whom we already mentioned, in the late nineteenth century and then, in 1900, the Chinese translation by Yang Tingdong who at that time was a student in Japan. In comparison, the first Chinese translation of Kant's major work, the *Critique of Pure Reason*, came in 1935. Before that, only a letter of Kant about mind-cure and his lectures on education had been published in Chinese in 1914 and 1926 (Ding 2009: 33).

Nevertheless, the enthusiasm for Kant was growing as time went by. Several articles on Kant's transcendental idealism, theory of space and time, and educational thought appeared during 1919–22. His epistemology was even discussed in comparison with Karl Marx's in a 1922 article by Wang Zhongjun, indicating the diverse intellectual interests at that time. The first Chinese version of Kant's biography also came in 1922. It was translated from Karl Vorlander's *A Biography of Kant* by Luo Zhanglong and Shang Zhangsun.

With the coming of the bicentenary of Kant's birthday, the Chinese reception of Kant reached its first peak. In 1924, the Journal *Xueyi* (學藝 *Arts*) dedicated a memorial issue to Kant with twenty special articles. Another memorial issue with fifteen special articles was published by the Journal *Minduo* (民鐸 *People's Bell*) in the next year. These articles touched upon almost all aspects of Kant's philosophy. Considering the journal *Xueyi*, for example, apart from three introductory articles about Kant's theory of knowledge, ethics and aesthetics, there were several articles focusing on other specific themes, including his theory of space and time, teleology, astronomy, logic, religion, pedagogy, philosophy of history, philosophy of laws and theory of perpetual peace. Moreover, four other kinds of articles were also included in these two commemorative issues: (1) biography and chronicle of Kant; (2) Kant's influence; (3) Kant in relation to some specific issues, such as "Kant and natural science" and "Kant and socialism"; (4) Comparison between Kant and other thinkers, such as "Kant and Dewey".

For some commentators like He Lin and Hong Handing, the rising enthusiasm for Kant since the 1920s was no coincidence. It was the great concerns about science and democracy, as were evoked in the May Fourth Movement of the late 1910s and early 1920s, which impelled Chinese intellectuals to turn to Kant. For Kant's philosophy seemed to respond to those two concerns properly. He and Hong write as follows:

> Although Kant's thought had been introduced to China as early as in the period of the Hundred Days Reform, the climax of the reception of Kant appeared in 1924 and 1925. This is probably due to the spirits of democracy and science that burst forth in the May Fourth Movement. For Kant's theory of knowledge is connected with science, and any discussion on epistemology must refer to Kant's theory of knowledge; besides, Kant talks about free will and practical reason, which are necessarily related to democracy and freedom.
>
> (He and Hong 2009: 23)

In the modern history of China, the May Fourth Movement marked a watershed moment, not only for its strong demand for democracy and science, but also for its radical embrace of Western ideas and bitter criticism of the Confucian heritage. The principle of "*zhongxue wei ti, xixue wei yong*" (中學為體　西學為用 "Chinese learning as the substance, Western learning as an instrument"), which had been widely accepted as the guiding principle in the early stage of the transmission of Western thought to China, was largely defied by the radical intellectuals of the younger generation, who were extremely indignant at the incompetence of their government in the face of the imperialistic aggression of the West and Japan, especially when the Treaty of Versailles in 1919 let China cede its territories in Shandong to Japan, and held high expectations for radical political and social changes based on various Western doctrines ending in "-ism" – and known as "-isms", for example liberalism or Marxism – instead of the Confucian tradition (Mitter 2005: 18). In a word, *openness* to Western ideas was prompted to a new and much higher level in the spiritual atmosphere of the May Fourth Movement.

Two new channels were extremely important in shortening the intellectual distance between the West and China. The first was that some renowned Western thinkers were eager to spread their doctrines to China. John Dewey was invited to China and gave lectures there during 1919–20, and the same invitation was offered to Bertrand Russell during 1920–21, which have been recorded as crucial moments in the modern development of Chinese thought. The second channel was that more and more young Chinese students were studying in Europe and America. Thus, unlike the older generation who largely relied on the Japanese intermediaries, the younger generation, then, could much more easily get direct access to Western thought and were expected to bring back more genuine and valuable teachings. For example, Hu Shi (胡適, 1891–1962), a representative of Chinese liberalism, was a student of John Dewey. And Zhang Junmai (張君勱, 1887–1969), a key figure in spreading German thought to China, once studied in

Germany under the supervision of Rudolf Eucken, a German philosopher famous for his *Lebensphilosophie* and the 1908 Nobel Prize laureate for literature, whose philosophy was particularly welcomed and explored by modern Chinese conservatives to resist scientist-materialist ideas and foster *jingshen wenhua* (精神文化 spiritual culture) (Campagnolo 2013: 110–12).

The Chinese reception of Kant also benefited from the above channels. During 1922–23 a German biologist and philosopher Hans Driesch, as the replacement of Eucken, was invited to China for lectures. Though Driesch was lecturing in China mainly for his neo-vitalism, he gave a speech on Kant's philosophy during his stay in Beijing, which is said to have some influence in spreading Kant's thought in China (He and Hong 2009: 18). Yet a more remarkable contribution was made by Chinese students studying in the West. For example, Zhang Yi (張頤, 1887–1969), who had studied classical German philosophy in Germany and England and received his doctorate from Oxford University, taught the philosophy of Kant and Hegel at several Chinese universities after his return in 1924. And Qu Junong (瞿菊農, 1901–76), once studying philosophy in Harvard University, translated Kant's lectures on education in 1926 and contributed an article on Kant's critical philosophy in an influential Chinese journal named *Zhexue Pinglun* (哲學評論 *Philosophical Review*) in 1928.

Another Chinese student named Zheng Xin (鄭昕, 1905–74) also returned from Germany in the 1930s, where he had studied the philosophy of Kant under the supervision of the Neo-Kantian scholar Bruno Bauch. When he returned, Zheng brought back to his far-away land the most professional treatment of Kant. He taught at Peking University thereafter and published his work on Kant with the title *Kangde Xueshu* (康德學述 *On Kant's Theory*) in 1946. Strictly speaking, this work was an interpretation of Kant's *Critique of Pure Reason*. However, what should be noticed is that unlike the first *Critique*, which makes denial of speculative metaphysics only after its illustration of the possibility and *a priori* prerequisites of empirical knowledge, Zheng began his book directly with the criticism of *xuanxue* (玄學 metaphysics). Once a student affected by the spirit of the May Fourth Movement, Zheng took the criticism of *xuanxue* as a criticism of traditional Chinese philosophy, arguing that the method of Chinese philosophers was intuitive, pursuing the apprehension of the whole and totality, and contrary to the scientific method that required analytical and concrete reasoning (Zheng 2011: 65–66). However, *xuanxue* was impossible only in terms of knowledge, but not morality. The Kantian distinction between knowledge and morality was well received and emphasized by Zheng:

> Human behavior is the product of one's own self, grows out of one's motivation, and is the first cause of it. Being one's own master is called free will. If nature is explained by the concepts of freedom (for example the divine will), it is the end of natural science. If morality is explained by causality, tracing your behavior to genes (like character and intelligence) or the environment (such as the political, economic and social environment), and claiming that your behavior is determined by these genes or this environment,

then [it is claiming that] you do not possess free will and are determined by external mechanics (causality) … The dignity of a human being lies in self-constraint, namely in obeying the universally binding laws that one has proscribed to oneself.

(Zheng 2011: 7–8)

Kant's concepts of morality and freedom also helped increase his popularity in China, as they were generally thought to have affinities with traditional Chinese moral doctrines. And not surprisingly, his popularity went beyond the limited academic groups. It is said that Mao Zedong (毛澤東, 1893–1976) in his youth had been influenced by Kantian ethics (He and Hong 2009: 22–23), though he probably extended the Kantian teaching of autonomy to a more positive sense, namely to self-striving or realization (Li Zehou 2008: 135–37).

Translations of Kant's major works finally came in the 1930s, which can be seen as fruits of the rising enthusiasm for Kant largely stimulated by the spirit of the May Fourth Movement. The first Chinese translation of the *Critique of Pure Reason* appeared in 1935. The translator was Hu Renyuan (胡仁源, 1883–1942), who once served as the president of Peking University and the Minister of Education. Since this translation was reported to be so difficult for understanding that students would rather turn to English translations (Wang, T. 1999: 74), it might have had very limited circulation. Almost at the same time, another Chinese translation of the first *Critique* was done by Lan Gongwu (藍公武, 1887–1957), a left-wing intellectual, but it did not get published until 1957. For these reasons, Chinese translations of Kant's moral philosophy probably had a higher popularity at least until the late 1950s, as Kant's *Critique of Practical Reason* and *Groundwork for the Metaphysics of Morals* were translated into Chinese by Zhang Mingding and Tang Yue (唐鉞, 1891–1987) respectively in 1936 and 1939. Besides, Kant's *Observations on the Feeling of the Beautiful and Sublime* was translated into Chinese by Guan Wenyun (關文運, 1904–73) in 1940. It is the first Chinese translation about Kant's aesthetics.

Kant and Neo-Confucianism

Up to now, we have examined the Chinese reception of Kant in the first half of the twentieth century. We can learn from this story that attention on Kant rested particularly in his theory of knowledge and ethics, as they met Chinese intellectuals' great concerns about modern science and morality. What we did not mention yet is the possible conflict between these two concerns. A mechanical and therefore deterministic view of the order of the world endowed by modern science might be opposite to, and destroy all sorts of moral ideals that are based on the conception of free will. How to reconcile them is a particularly Kantian theme. But in the modern history of China, conflict emerged and was thereafter closely linked to another dilemma between a new and high-level openness to Western ideas and a strong nationalistic attitude, which had both been evoked in the May Fourth Movement. Then there existed an intellectual possibility to associate the endeavor of saving morality from an overwhelming scientism with resistance to "Westernization".

On February 14, 1923, Zhang Junmai delivered a speech at Tsinghua University, arguing for the difference between science and *Lebensanschauung* and the inaptitude of applying the former to the latter. Zhang's speech was harshly criticized about two months later by Ding Wenjiang (丁文江, 1887–1936), who held a firm belief in the omnipotence of science, and was followed thereafter by a series of debates with more and more participants joining in, including Hu Shi and Liang Qichao. The debates are usually referred to as *"kexue yu xuanxue de lunzhan"* (科學與玄學的論戰 "debates over science and metaphysics"), since Zhang's argument for *Lebensanschauung* was refuted by Ding as *xuanxue* (玄學 metaphysics). Although the debates only lasted for about two years, they had so great an impact upon the subsequent development of modern Chinese thought that even when Zheng Xin published his work on Kant more than twenty years later, as we have seen in the previous section, he began his work with a discussion of the theme of *xuanxue*.

During the debates, proponents of *kexue* (科學 science) and *xuanxue* overlapped to a considerable degree with proponents of "Westernization" and traditional culture. Zhang himself was a nationalist and a defender of Confucianism. Besides, it was not difficult for the proponents of *xuanxue* at that time to find strong support in an intellectual atmosphere favoring traditional Chinese culture, as a movement that reacted to the radical defiance of the Confucian heritage emerged almost at the same time. In January 1922, a journal named *Xueheng* (學衡) was initiated in Nanjing. It also named itself in English *The Critical Review* and indeed held highly critical views of the May Fourth Movement's attraction to "Westernization" and attempted to revive traditional Chinese culture. It can be seen as the formal beginning of a strong and continuous cultural trend, among various trends contending with one another, calling for a return to the Confucian past in the face of the Western challenge. Needless to say, it is far from a total rejection or ignorance of Western ideas, but an absorption of them into the substance of the Confucian tradition, reminding us of the earlier principle of *"zhongxue wei ti, xixue wei yong"* (中學為體　西學為用 "Chinese learning as the substance, Western learning as an instrument").

In this trend, Kant, among all great Western thinkers, is particularly favored and explored by the so-called Neo-Confucian scholars in their efforts to renew Confucianism so as to make it accommodating for the context of modernity and in synthesis with Western rationalism as well as "humanitarianism". Indeed, Many Neo-Confucian scholars, such as Xiong Shili (熊十力, 1885–1968), Liang Shuming (梁漱溟, 1893–1988), Zhang Junmai, Feng Youlan (馮友蘭, 1895–1990), and Tang Junyi (唐君毅, 1909–78), referred to Kant and his theories in their writings.

But the most remarkable thinker is Mou Zongsan (牟宗三, 1909–95), who, along with many other Chinese intellectuals, moved to Taiwan and once to Hong Kong and carried on his academic activities in these two places after the founding of the New Republic in the Mainland in 1949. Not only was Mou the first Chinese scholar to translate single-handedly Kant's three *Critiques* and *Groundwork* (though from English versions instead of the German original) in the 1980s and early 1990s, when he had already reached a very old age, but he also developed his Neo-Confucian philosophy with originality from a transformation of Kant's philosophy (Chan 2006: 125). His affinity to Kant can even be easily learned from the titles of some of his works, which bear obvious Kantian themes, like *Renshixin zhi Pipan* (認識心之批判 *Critique of the Cognitive Mind*), *Zhi de Zhijue yu Zhongguo zhexue* (智的直覺與中國哲學 *Intellectual Intuition and Chinese Philosophy*), and his *magnum opus, Xianxiang yu Wuzishen* (現象與物自身 *Phenomenon and Thing-in-itself*). In a word, "Mou's monumental oeuvre represents the attempt to back up Confucian ethics with Kant's philosophy, while also taking Daoism and Buddhism into consideration" (Müller 2006: 148).

Two reasons might account for this interest in Kant on the part of Neo-Confucian scholars, and in particular Mou. The first is that Kant, in the history of Western philosophical thought, represents a revolution against, or a reversal of, two orthodox opinions: (1) the Platonic preference for the 'other-world' over this world, and (2) the Aristotelian assertion of the superiority of philosophical contemplation over moral practice. Kant's critical philosophy, however, has two opposite consequences. That is to say, the speculative use of reason is inferior to the practical use of reason, on the one hand, and the experience of this world becomes the appropriate material of knowledge, on the other hand. These two consequences make Kant, more than any other Western thinker, particularly palatable to traditional Chinese learning, for the latter is well known for focusing on practical philosophy, in sharp contrast to its neglect of contemplative philosophy, and it is also famous for its secularism as well.

The second reason is that the key concept of Kant's moral philosophy is "autonomy", which means the self-imposition of the universal moral law that is derived from practical reason rather than emotion or desires, and which is so often thought to be coincident with the Confucian moral teaching.[2] For example, a typical Kantian definition of morality could be easily found in one of the leading Neo-Confucian scholars Tang Junyi's writing:

> Moral life is always an internal life, and moral imperative is always an imperative that one imposes on oneself: one strives to dominate, change and transform oneself … When we identify moral life with the life that one dominates oneself, we are in line with other moral philosophers who argue that moral life is the life that one overrules oneself, one regulates for oneself, and moral life is the life of autonomy rather than heteronomy.
>
> (Tang 1946: 2, 4)

Despite these affinities, for many Neo-Confucian scholars, including Mou Zongsan, limitations are also revealed in Kant's philosophy, which, fortunately enough, can be overcome by traditional Chinese wisdom. Thus, the Neo-Confucian adoption of Kant is not only good for Confucianism itself, but benefits Kant and Western philosophy even more. As the representative of

Neo-Confucian scholars in bridging Kant and Chinese philosophical traditions, Mou actually modified Kant's philosophy in several aspects (Chan 2006). Here, we are just going to make a brief examination of the most remarkable one, that is, the problem of intellectual intuition and its relation to the thing-in-itself, so as to illustrate in what sense Chinese philosophy is interpreted as transcending Kant's philosophy.

The term "intellectual intuition" (*intellektuelle Anschauung*) is adopted by Kant *negatively* to show the limits of human cognition. One of the most well-known conclusions from Kant's critical philosophy is that human cognition is limited to appearance, while things-in-themselves, though being real in their own right and serving as the existential basis of appearance, are unknowable to us. "Intellectual intuition" is simply impossible for human beings, since what we know, in terms of the content, originates from what we intuit, and what we intuit are only what things appear to be for us through our sensory organs. In a word, our intuition is by nature sensuous, which cuts us off entirely from things-in-themselves. By contrast, intellectual intuition, when conceived as corresponding to things-in-themselves, is the sort of intuition that we do not possess and might only be ascribed to the superhuman being, like God. In the *Critique of Pure Reason*, Kant makes it very clear that both the concepts of intellectual intuition and thing-in-itself, or *noumenon*, are used negatively to denote the cognitive limitations of a human being:

> If, therefore, we wish to apply the categories to objects which cannot be regarded as phenomena, we must have an intuition different from the sensuous, and in this case the objects would be noumena in the positive sense of the word. Now, as such an intuition, that is, an intellectual intuition, is no part of our faculty of cognition, it is absolutely impossible for the categories to possess any application beyond the limits of experience. It may be true that there are intelligible existences to which our faculty of sensuous intuition has no relation, and cannot be applied, but our conceptions of the understanding, as mere forms of thought for our sensuous intuition, do not extend to these. What, therefore, we call noumenon, must be understood by us as such in a negative sense.
>
> (Kant 1946: 187)

Kant's denial of intellectual intuition to human beings, however, dissatisfies Mou, who considers it a weak point in Kant's philosophy that eventually makes Kant's endeavor to establish a moral metaphysics impossible, but only a moral theology instead, and finds in traditional Chinese philosophy more brilliant and convincing teachings on this issue. Mou explores the Chinese treatment of intellectual intuition and its relationship to the thing-in-itself firstly in his 1971 work *Zhi de Zhijue yu Zhongguo zhexue* (智的直覺與中國哲學 *Intellectual Intuition and Chinese Philosophy*), and then much more systematically in his *magnum opus, Xianxiang yu Wuzishen* (現象與物自身 *Phenomenon and Thing-in-itself*), about four years later. In Mou's view:

For Kant, all human knowledge must depend on sensible intuition; only God has intellectual intuition, hence it is impossible for Kant to establish a moral metaphysics. He can only appeal to the demands of practical reason to formulate a moral theology. But for the major Chinese traditions, even though humans are admittedly finite beings, they are still endowed with the ability to grasp the Way, as both transcendent and immanent, regardless of whether the Way is understood in Taoist, Buddhist, or Confucian terms. The Chinese simply believe they are capable of penetrating into the ineffable mystery of ultimate reality and that there is no longer a wide gap of phenomenon and noumenon, of subject and object. It is in this sense that intellectual intuition, understood in the sense of personal realization of the Way beyond the conceptualization of the intellect and language expressions, must not be excluded from humans.

(Müller 2006: 149)

Mou's modification of Kant in regard to the problem of intellectual intuition is doubtless original, but it might also be easily blamed for its retreat from Kant's critical position and return to the pre-Kantian dogmatism (Deng 2006), as one of Kant's greatest contributions to Western philosophy lies precisely in his assertion of the limits of human cognition. Nevertheless, how to evaluate Mou's modification in itself is not our primary concern; instead, what should interest us here is the implication of Mou's conscious departure from Kant.

The crucial point behind Mou's attempt to go beyond Kant is a reassessment of the problem of human finitude and creativity. It has been shown by some commentators like Wing-Cheuk Chan (2006) and Stephan Schmidt (2011) that Mou's understanding of Kant's critical philosophy is heavily influenced by his reading of Martin Heidegger's interpretive book *Kant and the Problem of Metaphysics*, in which Kant's *Critique of Pure Reason* is not interpreted as a work of epistemology, as is usually thought, but as a work of ontology. The difference lies in the following: while the epistemological interpretation focuses on *a priori* conditions of our cognition, the ontological interpretation focuses on *a priori* conditions of the world, namely the objects of our cognition (Chan 2006: 126). Thus, following Heidegger, who has already regarded intellectual intuition as creative, when it is distinguished from sensuous intuition that is characterized by its finitude and perceptiveness, Mou claims that intellectual intuition creates its own objects and is, in this sense, infinite. Although such a creative intuition is also denied by Heidegger himself to human beings, Mou finds in traditional Chinese philosophy, including Confucianism, Daoism and Buddhism, the affirmation of it as such. In Confucian terms, for Mou, *liangzhi* (良知 good knowledge) is an intellectual intuition that a human being possesses, which is not only the transcendental ground of moral action, but also the "ontological (creative) principle of realization", producing all things in existence (Mou 2008: 160, 166). Daoism and Buddhism have similar ideas, though expressed in different ways.

Two conclusions can be drawn from Mou's affirmation of intellectual intuition to the human being within Chinese philosophical traditions: First, the gulf between nature and freedom which is embedded in Kant's philosophical system and continues to trouble Western philosophy no longer exists, as nature and freedom are synthesized into a much more comprehensive and creative notion of morality. For Mou, "in moral metaphysics, *benxin renti* (本心仁體 original mind and the nature of benevolence) that brings about moral creation is always integrated into the One with the creation of the cosmos" (Mou 2008: 166). Second, by ascribing intellectual intuition to human being, Mou is actually asserting human infinitude which, of course, should not be understood as immortality, but rather as unlimited potentiality of mortal sagehood to create, change and transform oneself as well as the world. John Berthrong comments rightfully:

> Human nature can change and, in fact, is human nature because it is not structurally constrained as other animals seem to be bound by their natures. The soul of the Confucian is what the person seeking sagehood decides to become – you are what you will to be, and you become more fully human as you create your own world as moral community.
>
> (Berthrong 1994: 117)

Reading Kant from the 1950s to the late 1970s

In October 1949, a much more stable power was established in Mainland China by the Communist Party with rigorous control on economic, political, social and ideological aspects of life in the country. As the official ideology, Marxism, actually understood as a theoretical development from Marx and Friedrich Engels to Lenin, Stalin and Mao Zedong, was not only proclaimed as the only true scientific and the most advanced doctrine, but also became the ultimate criterion by which to judge other historical as well as contemporary doctrines. It has been argued that the reception of Western philosophy in Mainland China after 1949 might be influenced by the guidelines proposed by the Soviet official Andrei Zhdanov, in which "the central aim of philosophical work" was defined as "the development of Marxism-Leninism" and "all reactionary philosophical systems still in discussion" were required to "be mercilessly criticized" (Müller 2006: 144–45).

This tight ideological control did not remove Chinese attention from Kant since Kant was in turn recognized as the founder of classical German philosophy, which had been regarded by Lenin, along with English political economy and French utopian socialism, as one of the three theoretical sources of Marx's doctrine. Nevertheless, attention given to Kant was far surpassed by attention given to his successor, Georg Wilhelm Friedrich Hegel, simply because the latter had a closer intellectual linkage with Marx.

Furthermore, the image of Kant became much simplified until the end of the 1970s: he was regarded as a gutless member of the *bourgeoisie* who attempted, though in vain, to work out a compromise scheme between scientific materialism and reactionary idealism. When Tang Yue's translation of the *Groundwork* was reprinted in 1957, a preface was added, in which Kant's bourgeois identity was mentioned:

> There are two schools among Western bourgeois ethical theorists: one focuses on the purity of the motivation of action, claiming that the rightness or wrongness of action could be judged before its empirical consequences; the other puts emphasis on the consequences of action, claiming that the rightness or wrongness of action must depend on whether its consequences are good or bad. While the former school is represented by the present work of Kant, the latter school is represented by John Mill's Utilitarianism.
>
> (Tang 1957: Preface)

Here, Tang just contrasted Kant's ethical theory with Mill's utilitarianism within the same bourgeois camp. But in the preface to his 1960 translation of *Kant's Critique of Practical Reason*, Guan Wenyun described the nature and influence of Kant's philosophy from the viewpoint of the dichotomy between materialism and idealism as follows:

> In general, materialism and idealism are inextricably mixed together in Kant's philosophy. In this sense, Kant is a dualist. But Kant eventually moves through his dualism towards agnosticism and subjective idealism ... Classical German idealist philosophy, which had been founded by Kant, was later developed by Fichte and Schelling in their philosophy and reached its climax in Hegel's philosophy.
>
> (Guan 1960: Preface)

Interestingly, when Kant was primarily criticized for his "bourgeois" doctrine, his discussions about property rights, contract and money, which were mainly developed in *The Metaphysical Elements of the Doctrine of Right* (the first part of the *Metaphysics of Morals* and usually referred to as *The Doctrine of Right*) and should have become a major target of this criticism, were almost neglected. Overshadowed by his three *Critiques* and the *Groundwork*, Kant's *Doctrine of Right* had actually been ignored in Chinese intellectual circles and was not translated into Chinese until 1991.

Nevertheless, for a span of thirty years, the most remarkable academic achievement was the translation work that was done. In 1956, an official translation program that targeted more than 1,500 foreign classical works was launched, though due to political reasons only a very small part of them were accomplished by the Commercial Press (Ding 2009: 37). Several translations about Kant appeared: Lan Gongwu's translation of the *Critique of Pure Reason*, which had already been finished about twenty years before, now got printed in 1957 by the SDX Joint Publishing Company and was reprinted in 1960 by the Commercial Press. It was the second publication of the Chinese version of the first *Critique*, but considering the quality of the previous publication of Hu Renyuan's version, it might arguably be the first readable one. In regard to Kant's moral philosophy, as we have already mentioned above, Tang Yue's translation of the *Groundwork* was reprinted in 1957, and a new Chinese version of the *Critique of Practical Reason* by Guan Wenyun was offered to the Chinese reading public in 1960.

Compared with his theory of knowledge and ethics, Kant's aesthetics so far had received much less attention from Chinese intellectuals. Indeed, there were some discussions on that topic before 1949. And Cai Yuanpei (蔡元培, 1868–1940), the most honored president of Peking University and modern Chinese educator, even made use of Kant's aesthetic thought in support of his proposal for aesthetic education, which was regarded by him as a substitute for religion (He and Hong 2009: 15). However, the interest aroused in Kant's aesthetics could only be satisfied by the translation of the original works. We might recall that the Chinese version of Kant's *Observations on the Feeling of the Beautiful and Sublime* had already been published in 1940. But it was not enough.

With the publication of the translation of Kant's *Critique of Judgment* in 1964, all of Kant's three *Critiques* were now available in Chinese. The first part of the third *Critique*, namely the part on aesthetics, was translated by a famous Chinese aesthetician Zong Baihua (宗白華, 1897–1986). In his short postscript, Zong pointed out the significance of the third *Critique*, that is, it marked the completion of Kant's philosophical system and had a great impact on the later development of Western aesthetics. However, in order to make it politically acceptable, Zong also had to emphasize that the present work was translated for criticism due to its bourgeois characteristics (Zong 1964: Postscript).

The second part, namely the part of teleology, was translated by Wei Zhuomin (韋卓民, 1888–1976). As an expert on the philosophy of Kant and Hegel, Wei put most of his effort into translation. After all, in those years of high political pressure, translation bore relatively low risks. Despite his involvement in the translation of the third *Critique*, Wei is probably the third Chinese translator of the first *Critique*, though his translation was published very late, in 1991, fifteen years after his death. He also offered translations of some important Western studies on Kant to the Chinese reading public in the 1960s, such as John Watson's *The Philosophy of Kant as Contained in Extracts from His Own Writing* and *The Philosophy of Kant Explained* and Norman Kemp Smith's *A Commentary to Kant's 'Critique of Pure Reason'*. These translations must be a great boon for Kant's Chinese readers, as interpretations of Western thinkers and thought were in general dominated by the Soviet paradigm of Marxism.

Reading Kant from the late 1970s until the 2010s

The publication of Li Zehou's *Pipan Zhexue de Pipan: Kangde Shuping* (批判哲學的批判: 康德述評 *Critique of Critical Philosophy: A Commentary on Kant*) in 1979 marked a new phase of the Chinese reception of Kant. As one of the earliest fruits of the cessation of ideological control in the post-Mao period, Li's commentary on Kant actually had a great impact on the intellectual atmosphere of the 1980s. And it is in this way that Kant entered into China's post-Mao enlightenment.

Li's commentary was a reflection both on the political and social crises of Mao's period and on the new situation of post-Mao China. For Li, it was Mao's voluntarism, which overstated the capability of human agency in transforming both the external and inner worlds and neglected the constraint of objective laws, that could be largely responsible for China's crises such as the Great Leap Forward (大躍進) and the Cultural Revolution (文化大革命). Furthermore, Mao's voluntarism was in no way a divergence with respect to Chinese intellectual continuity. It borrowed much from the traditional Chinese belief in the infinitude of moral will, and, more surprisingly, was even inherited in new fashions of thought in the post-Mao period, though in different forms and probably without being aware of the fact. Socialist humanism, which was particularly welcomed by many post-Mao intellectuals as an alternative to Marxism-Leninism, in a certain sense had the same problem with Mao's voluntarism in Li's analysis, as it just concentrated on the ethical or subjective aspect of human being, without paying due attention to the scientific or objective aspect.

Meanwhile, the reality of human agency should not be overridden by the opposite extreme of scientific determinism with its political result, totalitarianism. In this sense, Li found himself confronting a typically Kantian problem, that is, how to reconcile human freedom with scientific necessity. Furthermore, Kant's dualistic view of human being was regarded by Li as particularly valuable for contemporary philosophers to address the philosophical problem of human subjectivity based on a synthesis of natural character and sociability, and humanism and scientism as well (Li 1987). However, what eventually lay under Li's synthesis was not the Kantian transcendental idealism, but rather the Marxist conception of human practice in history. Chong Woei Lien comments:

> The drawback of Kant's doctrine of the a priori, Li stated, is that it ignores history. The forms and categories of the understanding are only a priori from the point of view of the individual; from the point of view of the collective, they are a posteriori, that is, derived from experience. Humankind, while engaging in the technical transformation of external nature, also transforms its inner nature. The process of the "humanization of nature" ("ziran de renhua" 自然的人化) works in two ways: humankind humanizes external nature in the sense of making it a place fit for human beings to live in, and at the same time, by this very activity, it humanizes its own physical and mental constitution by becoming increasingly de-animalized and adapted to life in organized society. This is how the forms and categories of the human understanding evolved over time: the need to coordinate labor gave rise to an increasingly sophisticated language and a standardized conception of space, time and logic. In this way, the human species moved progressively away from its animal beginnings.

> (Chong 1999: 129)

Although Li's modification of Kant's doctrine of the 'a priori' was heavily influenced by Marx and his practical and historical philosophy, it was doubtless a break with the dogmatic Marxism which was promulgated by the Party. Furthermore, Li's philosophy of human subjectivity, to some extent, deviated from the orthodoxy of Marxism, as it attached great importance to the cultural and psychological structure of human being. This was actually what Li owned to Kant:

> While Marx focused on the crucial aspect of the capacity of the collective human subject to engage in economic production by means of 'tools', Kant provided Li with the philosophical framework to reflect on the mental and ideal aspects of human nature.
>
> (Chong 1999: 121)

Li's commentary on Kant was not the only indicator of the paradigm shift in Western philosophical studies in the post-Mao period. In 1978, a nationwide conference on the history of Western philosophy was held in Wuhu, at which sentiments in favor of academic freedom were strongly expressed, and it was requested that Zhdanov's guidelines be abandoned, and that idealist philosophy be treated with fairness and objectivity (Ding 2009: 39). Three years later, to commemorate the bicentenary of the publication of Kant's *Critique of Pure Reason* and the 150th anniversary of Hegel's death, another conference on classical German philosophy was held in Beijing, and some renowned Western experts on the philosophy of Kant and Hegel were invited to deliver speeches, which marked the re-embracing of Western academic achievements.

At the turn of the twenty-first century and from then on, more translations of a higher quality have been offered to the Chinese reading public. Deng Xiaomang's translations of Kant's three *Critiques* appeared in the first decade of the twenty-first century, and have rapidly become widely read. Another popular translation of the *Critique of Practical Reason* was offered a little earlier by Han Shuifa in 1999. Despite these major works, Kant's minor works have also attracted Chinese intellectuals' attention. For example, Kant's essays on history were collected and translated into a volume by He Zhaowu in 1990, with an eye-catching title "Critique of Historical Reason". Whether this title was used in an appropriate way, it called attention to Kant's philosophy of history, which had long been ignored and overshadowed by Hegel's and Marx's historicism.

And when Deng Xiaomang published his translation of Kant's *Anthropology from a Pragmatic Point of View* in 1986, he apparently thought that Kant's empirical anthropology developed in this work should deserve much more attention and even, surprisingly enough, concluded that it was the destination for Kant's critical philosophy (Deng 1986). Needless to say, the publication of translations of Kant's minor works indicated an extensive interest in Kant as well as a tendency to treat Kant's writings as a whole. From 2003 to 2010, Li Qiuling, as the chief translator and editor, put out the first Chinese version of the collected works of Kant, based on the famous *Akademie-Textausgabe*, in nine volumes.

This progress in translation just reveals one aspect of Kant's popularity in contemporary China. Martin Müller's analysis of the database of articles published in Chinese academic journals from 1994 to 2004 shows that there were

798 articles on the topic of Kant during that ten-year period, ranking him actually the fourth in discussion among a number of selected Western philosophers, that is, after Marx, Lenin and Engels, but before other non-Marxist philosophers including Aristotle, Hume, Hegel, Nietzsche, and Heidegger (Müller 2006: 141–42). A considerable number of works about Kant that have been published after 2004 also suggests that Kant remains one of the most-discussed Western philosophers in China during the last decade.

In general, Chinese works about Kant over the last decades of the twentieth century and the first decade and a half of the twenty-first century have touched upon almost all aspects of Kant's philosophy, from his theory of knowledge, ethics and aesthetics to his theories of religion, laws, politics, history and astronomy. Several Chinese versions of Kant's biography have also been offered (Han 1997; Cheng 1999; Hou 2008). Furthermore, analytical, historical and comparative methods are adopted either to examine some specific elements of Kant's philosophy or to reconstruct it as a whole. In particular, the meaning of Kant's philosophy for China catches many Chinese intellectuals' attention. Whether Kant's philosophy could be interpreted as similar to Confucianism as well as other Chinese philosophical traditions remains one of the favorite topics and inspires many comparative studies. In his *Rujia yu Kangde* (儒家與康德 *Confucianism and Kant*), Li Minghui (1990) at Academia Sinica of Taiwan compared Kant's ethical theory with Confucian moral teaching, especially the teaching of Mencius, reasserted their similarity, and therefore defended his master Mou Zongsan's treatment of Kant.

Arguing against Li, Feng Yaoming (1989) analyzed each pair of basic concepts of Plato, Aristotle, Kant, Confucianism and Buddhism and concluded that it was Plato rather than Kant that stood closest to Confucian thinking, though his analysis concentrated on metaphysics rather than ethics. Comparison is also adopted to emphasize the incompatibility between Kant's philosophy and Confucianism. For example, Deng Xiaomang, as one of the leading Kant scholars in the Mainland, is also a famous critic of the Neo-Confucian scholars' effort to reconcile traditional Chinese philosophy with modern Western thinkers such as Kant. For him, traditional Chinese philosophy lacks the conception of free will, which is crucial to Western ethics (Deng 2001).

Kant's own image of China is also explored (Zhao 2010), though his Sinophobia might be a disadvantage for the intellectual effort to associate Kant's philosophy with traditional Chinese culture.

With China's huge transition over the past few decades, an increasing awareness of individual freedom and rights has been witnessed among contemporary Chinese people. Kant, as an acknowledged exponent of liberal ideas and values, has also been touched upon by Chinese scholars in this regard. His theory of right is highlighted in the recent attention on his political thought (Li 2007; Zhao 2009; Wu 2010; Zhao and Huang 2011), and his idea of the Enlightenment, especially his appeal for "man's emergence from his self-incurred immaturity" (Kant 1991: 52), is explored in relation to its possible meaning for contemporary Chinese society (Deng 2010; Li 2010).

Concluding remarks

In 2015, it has been about one and a quarter centuries since the first Chinese reference to Kant. Tremendous progress has been achieved in translation and interpretation, which makes Kant nowadays one of the best-known as well as the most-discussed Western thinkers in China. This evolution accompanied the major changes that made China what it is at present.

Kant was introduced to the Chinese reading public in the context of China's encounter with Western civilization and its attempt to learn from that civilization so as to make its own modernization, and has played a significant role in the evolution of modern Chinese ideas. His philosophy, especially his epistemology and ethics, is arguably one of the most important resources for Chinese intellectuals who wish to approach modern Western science and morality and seems to correspond properly to the nation's vehement and long-lasting aspiration for science and democracy, the spiritual fruit of the May Fourth Movement.

Indeed, the diversity of understandings and interpretations of Kant can be easily noticed among Chinese intellectuals, which renders the implication of Kant's philosophy for contemporary China rather complicated. Some regard Kant as an incarnation of the Enlightenment, whose ideas could help enlighten the road to liberalization and/or modernization, be they synonymous or not. But there are other interpretations that tend to depreciate the value of Kant's philosophy: for example, we might easily recall that Kant's philosophy was criticized for its idealism and was claimed to have been superseded by the scientific materialism of Marx when Marxism was predominant in Chinese intellectual circles.

Nevertheless, during the Chinese reception of Kant, the most influential and remarkable approach has been to associate Kant's philosophy with traditional Chinese culture and therefore to develop a renewed understanding of the relationship between China and modernity. Kant's defense of freedom and morality in the face of the rising modern science with its mechanical and hence deterministic worldview has enabled those "conservative" intellectuals in China even to gain a foothold within Western civilization to preserve China's age-old humanism and its traditional emphasis on moral practice in the course of China's striving for modernity. Moreover, Kant's conception of autonomy is utilized, in a direction especially represented by Mou Zongsan, to clarify the essence of traditional Chinese ethics, so as to make the latter accommodating for the context of modernity.

However, a fundamental difference can also be noticed here. For Kant, the defense of freedom and morality is intertwined with the revelation of the limits of human knowledge. In the preface to the second edition of the *Critique of Pure Reason*, Kant makes a very famous statement that in defense of morality he must "abolish knowledge, to make room for belief" (Kant 1946: 18). But for many Chinese intellectuals, the very notion of the cognitive limitations of human beings is hard to accept. From very early on, Kant's epistemology has been explored by many of his Chinese readers to denote the limits of Western science rather than the limits of human being. Modification is then made to Kantian ethics, as in the case of Mou's affirmation of intellectual intuition to the human being, which links morality with human infinitude rather finitude.

Therefore, if we wish to go further in asking whether the dissemination of Kant's thought in China has inspired a liberal spirit or tendency, we see why the answer might be quite complicated. Indeed, by introducing and translating Kant, new concepts and ideas focus on individual freedom, dignity and rights have been imported to Chinese intellectual circles; moreover, they might even reform Chinese intellectuals' self-understanding of their own tradition when they are interpreted to be parallel with traditional Chinese thought and, in particular, utilized to clarify the essence of traditional Chinese ethics. However, these new concepts and ideas have also been reconciled with traditional Chinese thought and values and adapted to the special historical circumstances of modern China, which gives new meanings to the original Western notion of individualism.

Here, and to conclude, some brief contrast between Mou and Rawls might be illuminating. Both of these scholars formulated their theories on an acknowledged Kantian background. However, in constructing the fundamental principles for modern democratic society, Rawls chose to hypothesize human beings placed in the original position, behind the so-called "veil of ignorance" and displaying reciprocal dis-interest about one another, like isolated or detached beings (Rawls 1971). In comparison, Mou went to the other extreme, envisioning the humankind as related with all things, both natural and social, and integrated with them into "the One", or "the Whole". Mou therefore seems to suggest a different image of the individual, not characterized by one's solitude and self-centered tendencies, as they may be revealed in some popular interpretation of the hypothesis of the *homo economicus*, but rather by one's relationship with others, communities and by altruistic aspiration, a point which may be reinserted into economic thinking only by putting new grounding foundations under its superstructure.

Acknowledgements

This chapter is an outcome of my academic visit to Aix–Marseilles University in the fall of 2013 within the LIBEAC ("Liberalism in between Europe and China") project. I wish to express my gratitude both to the project and to the university, for the generous financial help as well as the comfortable working conditions. I am also deeply grateful to Professor Li Qiang, who recommended me to the project and suggested the initial topic to me, and Professor Gilles Campagnolo, the coordinator of the project, who warmly received me in France and provided me with kind and valuable advice. An earlier version of this chapter was presented in a workshop held at GREQAM, Aix–Marseilles University (Aix-en-Provence, September 2013). Comments from and discussions with attendees benefited me a lot.

Notes

1   The fact that traditional Chinese learning is strong in moral philosophy but weak in contemplative science has been recognized both by Chinese and European scholarship. Feng Youlan (1973: 3), one of the leading Chinese philosophers of the twentieth century, commented that traditional Chinese learning was not "primarily for the seeking of knowledge, but rather of self-cultivation, it was not for the search of truth, but for the search of good". Feng's comment seems to coincide with the earlier judgment made by some European observers in the early period of the Enlightenment, when the so-called "sinophilia" was at its highest. For example, Gottfried Wilhelm Leibniz once contended in his *Novissima Sinica* that Chinese surpassed Europeans in practical philosophy, though they were equal in the industrial arts and fell behind in contemplative sciences (Jones 2001: 20–21).
2   Not all Confucian philosophers are interpreted in the sense of endorsing "autonomy" as the essence of morality. One of Mon Zongsan's boldest, but also most controversial, arguments is that Chu Hsi, an acknowledged exponent of Neo-Confucianism, expounds morality in a heteronomous rather than autonomous way.

References

Berthrong, John (1994) *All Under Heaven*, Albany: State University of New York Press.
Campagnolo, Gilles (2013) 'Three Influential Western Thinkers during the "Break-Up" Period in China: Eucken, Bergson and Dewey', in Ying Ma and Hans-Michael Trautwein (eds.), *Thoughts on Economic Development in China*, London and New York: Routledge: 101–35.
Chan, Wing-Cheuk (2006) 'Mou Zongsan's Transformation of Kant's Philosophy', *Journal of Chinese Philosophy*, 33 (1): 125–39.
Cheng, Zhimin (1999) *Kangde [Kant]*, Changsha: Hunan Education Publishing House.
Chong, Woei Lien (1999) 'Combining Marx with Kant: The Philosophical Anthropology of Li Zehou', *Philosophy East & West*, 49: 120–47.
Deng, Xiaomang (1986) 'Pipan Zhexue de Guisu' ['The Destination for Critical Philosophy'], in the Institute of Philosophical Studies of Hubei University (ed.), *Deguo Zhexue* (vol. 2) [*German Philosophy* (vol. 2)] Beijing: Peking University Press.
——(2001) *Xin Pipan Zhuyi [New Criticism]*, Wuhan: Hubei Educational Press.
——(2006) 'Mou Zongsan Dui Kangde Zhi Wudu Juyao: Guanyu Zhixing Zhiguan' ['Examples of Mou Zongsan's Misinterpretation of Kant: On Intellectual Intuition'], *Journal of Jiangsu Administration Institute*, 25: 14–20; 26: 12–15.
——(2010) 'Kangde Zhexue Dui Zhongguo Qimeng De Yiyi' ['The Meaning of Kant's Philosophy for the Chinese Enlightenment'], *Zhongguo Tushu Pinglun [China Book Review]*, 7: 102–07.
Ding, Donghong (2009) 'Bainian Kangde Zhexue Yanjiu Zai Zhongguo' ['Kant Studies in a Century in China'], *Shijie Zhexue [World Philosophy]*, 4: 32–42.
Feng, Yaoming (1989) *Zhongguo Zhexue de Fangfalun Wenti [The Problem of Methods of Chinese Philosophy]*, Taipei: Yunchen Cultural Company.
Feng (Fung), Youlan (1973) *A History of Chinese Philosophy*, 7th edn (vol. 1), Princeton: Princeton University Press.
Guan, Wenyun (translation) (1960) *Shijian Lixing Pipan [Critique of Practical Reason]*, Beijing: The Commercial Press.
Han, Shuifa (1997) *Kangde Zhuan [A Biography of Kant]*, Shijiazhuang: the People's Press of Hebei.

He, Lin, and Hong, Handing (2009) 'Kangde Heigeer Zhexue Dongjian Ji' ['The Dissemination of Kant's and Hegel's Philosophy from the West to the East'], in xixue dongjian wenxian yanjiu guan of Sun Yat-Sen University (ed.), *Xixue Dongjian Yanjiu* (vol. 2) [*Study on the Dissemination of the Western Learning to the East* (vol. 2)], Beijing: The Commercial Press.

Hou, Hongxun (2008) *Kangde* [*Kant*], Hong Kong: Zhonghua Book Company.

Huang, Kewu (1998) 'Liang Qichao yu Kangde' ['Liang Qichao and Kant'], *Bulletin of the Institute of Modern History, Academia Sinica*, 30: 101–48.

Jones, D.M. (2001) *The Image of China in Western Social and Political Thought*, New York: Palgrave Macmillan.

Kang, Youwei (1990) *Zhutian Jiang* [*On Heavens*], Beijing: Zhonghua Book Company.

Kant, Immanuel (1946) *Critique of Pure Reason*, trans. J.M.D. Meiklejohn, London: J.M. Dent & Sons Ltd.

——(1991) *Political Writings*, ed. Hans Reiss, Cambridge: Cambridge University Press.

Li, Mei (2007) *Quanli yu Zhengyi: Kangde Zhengzhi Zhexue Yanjiu* [*Right and Justice: A Study on the Political Philosophy of Kant*], Beijing: Social Sciences Academic Press.

Li, Minghui (1990) *Rujia yu Kangde* [*Confucianism and Kant*], Taipei: Linking Publishing Company.

Li, Qiuling (2010) 'Kangde yu Qimeng Yundong' ['Kant and Enlightenment'], *Journal of Renmin University of China*, 6: 65–70.

Li, Zehou (1987) *Pipan Zhexue de Pipan: Kangde Shuping* [*Critique of Critical Philosophy: A Commentary on Kant*], Beijing: the People's Press.

——(2008) *Zhongguo Xiandai Sixiangshi Lun* [*History of Contemporary Chinese Thought*], Beijing: SDX Joint Publishing Company.

Liang, Qichao (1988) 'Jinshi Diyi Dazhe Kangde Zhi Xueshuo' ['The Teaching of the Greatest Philosopher of Modern Times: Kant'], in *The Collected Works of the Ice-drinking Room* (vol. 13), Beijing: Zhonghua Book Company.

Mitter, Rana (2005) *A Bitter Revolution: China's Struggle with the Modern World*, Oxford: Oxford University Press.

Mou, Zongsan (2008) *Zhi de Zhijue yu Zhongguo Zhexue* [*Intellectual Intuition and Chinese Philosophy*], Beijing: China Social Sciences Press.

Müller, Martin (2006) "Aspects of the Chinese Reception of Kant", *Journal of Chinese Philosophy*, 33 (1): 141–57.

Rawls, John (1971) *A Theory of Justice*, Cambridge: The Belknap Press of Harvard University Press.

——(1980) 'Kantian Constructivism in Moral Theory', *Journal of Philosophy*, 77: 515–72.

Schmidt, Stephan (2011) 'Mou Zongsan, Hegel and Kant: The Request for Confucian Modernity', *Philosophy East & West*, 61: 260–302.

Tang, Junyi. (1946) *Daode Ziwo Zhi Jianli* [*The Construction of the Moral Self*], Shanghai: The Commercial Press.

Tang, Yue (1957) *Daode Xingershangxue Tanben* [*Groundwork for the Metaphysics of Morals*], Beijing: The Commercial Press.

Wang, J.C.F. (1999) *Contemporary Chinese Politics: An Introduction 6ᵗʰ edn*, Upper Saddle River: Prentice Hall.

Wang, Taiqing (1999) 'Du Dong Kangde' ['Understanding Kant'], *Dushu* [*Reading*], 10: 72–76.

Wu, Yan (translation) (2010) *Kangde: Quanli Zhexue* [*Kant: The Philosophy of Right*] (by Jeffrie G. Murphy), Beijing: China Legal Publishing House.

Yang, He (2001) 'Ershi Shiji Kangde Heigeer Zhexue Zai Zhongguo De Chuanbo He Yanjiu' ['Kant and Hegel in China during the Twentieth Century: Dissemination and Studies'], *Journal of Xiamen University (Arts & Social Science)*, 145: 49–56.

Zhao, Dunhua (2010) 'Lun Zuowei Zhongguo zhi di de Kangde' [*Kant as a Sinophobe*], *Journal of Renmin University of China*, 6: 144–46.

Zhao, Ming (2009) *Shijian Lixing de Zhengzhi Lifa* [*Political Legislation of Practical Reason*], Beijing: China Legal Publishing House.

Zhao, Ming and Huang, Tao (translation) (2011) *Kangde de Quanli Tixi* [*Kant's System of Rights*] (by Leslie Arthur Mulholland), Beijing: The Commercial Press.

Zheng, Xin (2011) *Kangde Xueshu* [*On Kant's Theory*], Beijing: The Commercial Press.

Zong, Baihua (translation) (1964) *Panduanli Pipan: Shangjuan* [*Critique of Judgment: The First Part*], Beijing: The Commercial Press.

3 Yan Fu and Kaiping Mines

The meaning of economic liberalism in early modern China

Qunyi Liu

Introduction

The assertion of modern liberalism in China took place no earlier than the nineteenth century. Like other early modern doctrines, liberalism had been treated as a central value to secure wealth and power that enabled Western nations to surpass China. Demonstrating a different perspective from its Western origin, liberalism had more economic implications than philosophical and political ones in pre-industrial but yearning-for-development China. Yan Fu (1854–1921), a Chinese thinker and translator, labeled it *guoqunziyou* (国群自繇 State Liberalism). He had introduced through translation a few Western masterworks of liberalism and promoted economic liberalism in Chinese society at the turn of the twentieth century. Thanks to his contributions, Yan is dubbed "the Father of Liberalism" in China.

Concerning Yan's liberal thoughts, almost all of the previous studies have focused on their inward meaning domestically, that is, how liberalism is coordinated with the genuine local traditions and why liberal thoughts are referred to frequently in China's reformation and revolutions. Schwartz's work (1964) is one of the leading foreign studies. The author holds that Yan regarded the dilemma between the West and China and thought of Western liberalism as a path to enrich the state and strengthen the army. The extreme side of individual liberalism nevertheless is neglected by Yan.

Li's "On Yan Fu" (1977) is one example of the typical literature in China. Li referred to Schwartz's work for the first time in China, and consequently enriched the former's arguments with a detailed explanation of the context of Yan's activity. Li emphasizes the blow that resulted from the defeat in the Sino–Japanese War (1894–95), which hit Yan and other Chinese elites seriously. Therefore, the transmission of Western thoughts and the subsequent reforms were not at all gradual and accommodating. Like Schwartz's work, Li's also takes the position that Yan paid more attention to the state than to the individual. Li nevertheless disagrees with Schwartz on the point that Yan embraced Western liberalism enthusiastically and recognized completely the essence of individual freedom and autonomy. What confuses Li is the conflict between the state and the individual.

A quarter-century later, Huang (2000; 2008) intends to mediate the conflict and does what Metzger points out in his preface to Huang's book, that is, "to identify the significant issues left unresolved by this voluminous, confusingly complex literature" (Metzger 2008: xv). Adopting Metzger's epistemological optimism in Yan's thoughts, Huang is also in agreement with Li that Yan could understand Mill's work and liberalism without distortion. Furthermore, he explains the causes of the failure of Chinese liberalism, that is, its failure to give the government the central role to mold a positive and optimistic liberalism. These pieces of literature, however, have not supplied scholarship with solutions to two dilemmas: at a microscopic level, concerning Yan and at a macroscopic level, China.

The last two decades of Yan's life are labeled as conservatism. Yan returned to the traditional Chinese world and indulged in Chinese traditional thoughts, especially Taoism. He was one of the active founders of the *kongjiaohui* (孔教会 Confucius Society) and even received the title of *jinshi* (进士 imperial scholar) from the last emperor in 1909. He was a proponent of a constitutional monarchy and the restoration of Qing's emperor even after the 1911 "bourgeois" revolution. His reverse of fortune symbolizes the failure of Chinese liberalism. Therefore, in China, there is a mystery about the opening policy adopted by the central-planning government since 1978: what has pushed the authorities to turn to economic liberalism?

Let us restate Yan's thought within the framework of State Liberalism. Yan had translated the well-known declaration of Mill, according to whom "Over himself, over his own body and mind, the individual is sovereign" (Mill 2001: 13), but along with an extension. His translation went as follows: "Over himself, over his own body and mind, the individual is sovereign, like a state" (Yan 1981a: 11).

Yan had thus put forward a different subject of liberalism – the state. In his perspective, the state is a sovereign individual with full rights of freedom and autonomy, like an individual. With this divergence from Mill and the extension added to the Western original sentence, Yan had actually completed his own systematic view on liberalism in the developing and at that time crisis-ridden country. His own later reversal just disclosed his strong belief in the state. He was conscious that it was anarchism in the 1911 Revolution that had ruined the order of early modern society and led to possible chaos. Now, so-called State Liberalism has actually been the mainstream until today, so that the government in modern China succeeds in setting up a free market economy with both a liberal heritage and the separation of economic from political liberty.

In the following discussion, I attempt to analyze the meaning of Yan's liberalism along the pathway of liberty – that is, state liberty – and State Liberalism through his translations as well as the only economic practical experience he had, at Kaiping Mines. The first section introduces Yan's brief biography in relation to Kaiping Mines. The next section focuses on his translation of *On Liberty* by Mill (*qunji quanjie lun*, 群己权界论 Yan 1981a) and *The Spirit of the Laws* (*L'Esprit des Lois*, by French Enlightenment philosopher Montesquieu,

Fayi 法意Yan 1981b) to discuss his understanding of liberty and state liberty. Then another section explains his economic practice with State Liberalism in Kaiping Mines. The last section provides a few concluding remarks and attempts to solve both dilemmas.

Yan Fu's life and Kaiping Mines

Yan was born into a traditional family. His father was a famous doctor of Chinese medicine and had Yan taught classics such as *sishuwujing* (四书五经 *The Four Books and The Five Classics*) and philosophy books of the Song and Yuan Dynasties. Unfortunately, Yan had to give up his regular study when his family was bankrupted by the death of his father. He continued his study at a "new-style" school of Fuzhou in 1866 and trained to be a ship's captain. With his educational and social background, Yan took the Imperial Examination in order to be a bureaucrat, but he failed as many as three times before he was sent by the Qing government to Britain in 1877. It was in the UK that Yan began to read English books of different disciplines including politics and economics, and there he became a believer in the new ideas of Darwinism.

After two years of study at Portsmouth University and Greenwich College, he came back to China and taught at the Foochow Naval Academy and Peiyang Naval Academy for about twenty years. Yan began to delve into the translation of Western books after the Sino–Japanese War. The first work he translated was Huxley's *Evolution and Ethics* (published in 1896), which inspired the reformists' camp and influenced finally even the government. Yan had translated eight books in total, including *The Wealth of Nations* (translated in 1902, Yan 1981c), *On Liberty* (1903), *Logic* (by Mill, 1903, Yan 1981d), *A History of Politics* (by E. Jenks, 1903, Yan 1981e), and *The Spirit of the Laws* (from the English translation by Montesquieu, 1904–09, Yan 1981b). His translations won him a reputation as an educationalist and a thinker in China, and then he took up the positions of the president of Fudan University and of Peking University in 1906 and 1912 successively. Before and during the time Yan was doing the translations, he had also written several comment essays in newspapers, such as *Lun shibianzhiji* (论世变之亟 *On the Speed of World Change*, 1895) and *Yuan qiang* (原强 *On the Origin of Strength*, 1895).

But Yan's one and only contact with actual economic practice was during his working experience in Kaiping Mines.

Kaiping Mines are located in what is nowadays Tangshan, a city of Hebei Province, which is near both Beijing and Tianjin. After being united with another plot of mines, these mines became, and remain so even today, one of the most important coal companies in northern China. The Mines had been discovered in the 1870s at the time of the so-called "Self-Strengthening Movement" (1861–95) of the Qing Dynasty. Until the 1890s it produced every day as many as 2,000 tons of coal. The Mines contributed so much to the industrial development of the weakening Qing government that it became one of the two successful industrial models of the Movement.[1] The Mines also introduced the first foreign managers into Chinese companies: Herbert Hoover (1874–1964), later to become a US president, was at a time employed by the British board of directors as chief engineer and general manager. Foreign managers also brought foreign loans from Britain to the Mines. Yet, as a negative result of this financing, Hoover and his British employer maneuvered the Mines into being sold to the British at the turn of the twentieth century. The Qing government, however, was quite annoyed by the unexpected sale, because the Mines, like other natural resource enterprises, had been regarded as state-owned in China down the ages. Facing what was regarded as an infringement and an unfair deal on the part of foreigners, the former managing official, Zhang Yi (1846–1913), invited Yan, as the general manager, to deal with the business of this joint venture and to fight the deal in order to keep ownership. Yan held the position in 1901, and later in 1905. He went to Britain with Zhang to sue the British board of directors, because the Chinese government believed that the deal was a total fraud. Yan and his colleague did not succeed in their legal suit, even though they obtained a positive judgment at some point. In 1908, Yan was nominated as a consultant again in a new deal on the Mines between the late Qing government and the British government. His efforts proved more theoretical than practical.

Yan's successive nominations to the Mines' top position were due to several reasons. The first and the most apparent one was to make use of his language ability and his early experience in Britain. The Qing government was so badly in need of such kinds of elites to make contact with foreigners in the process of reformation that most of the intellectuals with more or less foreign experience had been promoted to appropriate, or inappropriate, positions. Yan was one of many typical examples. His major in education was ship's captaincy, but he was nominated to manage an important state-owned company, coping with mines and land extraction, about which he had limited knowledge. In one of his letters to his best friend, Yan had written:

> I am not confident that I can go well with the foreign and Chinese colleagues. Probably I can know more about it after a period of time. I accepted the position just for the salary of 500 Yuan, but the job is not what I am interested in.
>
> (Wang 1986: 540)

Yan's letter also demonstrated his needy economic condition after the Boxer Rebellion (1898–1900) and the following Eight-Nation Alliance War (1900). Yan's house in Tianjin had been destroyed in the war and he had to flee to Shanghai. He even lost the translational script of *On Liberty* in the accident. Therefore, he had no choice but to accept the nomination in order to scrape a living.

Yan's life and his practice in Kaiping Mines also display the context of his unique understanding of Liberalism, that is, *state liberalism* instead of *individualistic liberalism*.

The meaning of liberalism in Yan Fu's translations: from liberty to state liberty

Yan Fu referred to liberty and liberalism in several of his commentary essays and in translated books, among which *Lun shibianzhiji* (论世变之亟 *On the Speed of World Change*, 1895), *Yuan qiang* (原强 *On the Origin of Strength*, 1895), *On Liberty* (1903) and *The Spirit of the Laws* (1904–9) were most referable. It is certain that Yan had demonstrated some variation in his understanding, yet his strong proposition on *guoqun ziyou* (国群自繇/由, State Liberalism) never changed.

Also, Yan was not the first translator of freedom/liberty in China. It was as early as the beginning of the nineteenth century that some translations appeared in English–Chinese dictionaries edited by missionaries who came to China to teach Western ideas and to preach religious beliefs. In one of Yan's essays, *Lun shibianzhiji* (论世变之亟 *On the Speed of World Change*, 1895), he commented on the word "liberty" as such in a very spontaneous manner, as if his readers had already been familiar with the necessary knowledge. He wrote as follows:

> 'Freedom' or 'liberty' is a word with which Chinese sages have been deeply cautious for a long time and hence never tried to set up a rule for it. On the contrary, it is stated by Westerners that man is born with heavenly endowments, among which freedom is the most important. Everyone has freedom, and every nation also has freedom, so that laws should be enacted to avoid infringement to man and nations... Two of the Chinese concepts, *shu* (恕 forgiveness) and *xieju* (絜矩 measurement) are most similar to the Western rule of freedom. But they can be identified as similar concepts at most, not as the same in essence. Why? *shu* and *xieju* concern social communication among people, while freedom in the Western countries signifies the individual person through the relationship between man and the physical world. The concept of freedom is different from the above ones and then the social system in China is also different from the Western nations as a natural consequence.
>
> (Wang 1986: 2–3)

Yan pointed to the different concepts of freedom in the Western countries and China. The word had a quite substantially negative meaning in China so that it had been neglected deliberately among Chinese elites. In order to explain the Western concept, Yan first removed the negative content of the concept through the argument formulated by the French thinker Jean-Jacques Rousseau. His words remind the readers of the famous sentence that "Man is born free; and everywhere he is in chains. One thinks himself the master of others, and still remains a greater slave than they" (Rousseau 1762, trans. Cole 1782: Book 1.1). To Yan, freedom arose from restriction on individual behavior, so he selected two traditional Chinese counterparts related to the notions of *limit* and *boundary* to explain this difficult concept. Yan nevertheless admitted that there is actually no totally identical Chinese word for freedom, as freedom is extremely individualistic in the Western world. It is interesting to note that Yan put "state" with "individual" together, which is even a common dichotomy in nowadays China.

In this other later essay already mentioned, *Yuan qiang* (原强 *On the Origin of Strength*, 1895), Yan clearly stated a comparison of freedom between individual and state, that is to say: "It is the most important for people to have freedom, while for a state independence" (Wang 1986: 17).

Yan's understanding of freedom in the above two essays is still relatively incipient and obscure, but through the translations of two master works of philosophy that he would later produce, Yan improved his knowledge substantially, and just in the introductions and commentaries of his translational work, he put "state" and "liberty" first meaningfully, and then literally together so as to distinguish himself from his Western mentors.

Yan began his translation of Mill's work in his somewhat dark period, after the so-called Hundred Days (百日) Reform of 1898. He coined and adopted throughout his translation a special Chinese word *ziyou* (自繇), instead of *ziyou* (自由). As he explained again in the "Translator's Directions to the Reader" (Wang 1986: 132), he noticed that the latter traditionally contained some negative meaning. Moreover, he wrote that 'liberty' was a notional term from philosophy, which was also different from the functional Chinese *you* (由). Conversely, *you* (繇) means "pass through" or "by way of", which is actually a variant to *you* (由) with the same meaning. The reason that Yan changed the Chinese character was presumably attributed to the shock he received at the time of the *coup d'état* of August 1898.

Yan sensitively noticed the difference of concepts in Mill's work, such as "freedom" and "liberty". He compared "freedom" and "justice" with "liberty" and concluded that the former was synonymous with "liberty", while the latter was related to "liberty", but not exchangeable with it. He added the legal factor to it and completed the concept of "Liberty" in the preface of the same book.

As was already analyzed by Schwartz in his book (1964), Mill's arguments were not very relevant to Yan's concerns. Yan aimed at wealth and power for the state, but Mill's book was apparently insufficient to contribute to that aim. In order to stress the state instead of the individual, Yan twisted some original words in the book. Almost all of the words related to "government" were translated into "state", and furthermore, Yan asserted that the beneficiaries of "individuality" were the individual, the national society and the state as well. While Mill meant that "it is through the cultivation of these personal impulses, vivid and powerful, that society both does its duty and protects its interests", Yan changed the sentence into

> Statesmen must realize that it is only by fostering superior people of this type that they can be said to have fulfilled their heaven-imposed duty. The honor of their race and the strength of the state can only be achieved thus.
>
> (Schwartz 1964: 140)

All of the above efforts tended quite obviously to focus on the state.

Yet the pathway from individual liberalism to state liberalism was comparatively long to go. Yan spent at least three years, as he disclosed in the title of the book. He translated simply at first *Ziyou lun* (自由论 *On Liberty*) and shifted to the published title of *Qunji quanjie lun* (群己权界论 *On the Boundaries of the rights of the Society and of the Individual*) in 1903.

In the subsequent translation, *Fayi* (法意 *The Spirit of the Laws*, 1904–9), Yan did not only put the two words together, but also made the frankly suggestion that state liberty should override individual liberty.

To translate the concept of liberty in the following paragraph of Montesquieu's book, Yan used for the first time *guoqun ziyou* (国群自繇 state liberty), in spite of the fact that the original text was "political liberty". For another word, "independence", Yan's choice *wuzhi* (无制 no bondage) demonstrated to some degree his negative attitude towards individual liberty. Except for the above two words, he followed the author's analysis and translated every word into Chinese and then spared no compliment after the paragraph, asserting that the concept put forth was the "essence of liberty" (Wang 1986: 969).

> It is true that in democracies the people seem to do what they want, but political liberty in no way consists in doing what one wants. In a state, that is, in a society where there are laws, liberty can consist only in having the power to do what one should want to do and in no way being constrained to do what one should not want to do.
>
> One must put oneself in mind of what independence is and what liberty is. Liberty is the right to do everything the laws permit; and if one citizen could do what they forbid, he would no longer have liberty because the others would likewise have this same power.
>
> (Montesquieu 1748: 155)

Yan agreed with Montesquieu that the state is "a society where there are laws". To build such a state, he said in the latter translation that laws should be the essential institution to set up in the first place (Wang 1986: 971). Yan hence expounded in his own political view a conservative attitude towards reformation and revolution. During the Hundred Days Reform, Yan never became a member of the inner circle with Kang Youwei (1858–1927) and Liang Qichao (1873–1929), although Yan was definitely an intimate friend to the reformists, especially to Liang and consistent with their reform assertions to a certain extent (Campagnolo 2013: 109–10).

Yet partly because of the shock from Sino–Japanese (1894–95) before the reform, and the death of the famous "Six Martyrs" after the reform, the gentleman Yan Fu also showed his other face of being radical in *Fayi*. Contrary to the obscure opinion expressed in the translation of Mill's work, he followed the logic of Montesquieu's philosophy of history to minimize the role of individual liberty and asserted in the commentaries on Montesquieu that China at that time was in the crisis of being conquered, and that state liberty should take precedence over individual liberty.

Individual liberty is paramount for Western countries to pursue the well-being of their citizens. It is true because without pursuing liberty the Europeans could not survive from the oppression and exploitation of monarchies and lords in history. However, the truth is not applicable for today's China, where individual liberty is not as stringent as state liberty. Concerning the foreign invaders at the door, it is indeed urgent for us to build a state in the world through state liberty instead of individual liberty.

(Wang 1986: 981)

According to his own translations, Yan's logic of state liberty was to conform to Montesquieu's meteorological climate theory, taken in a broad sense. By placing an emphasis on environmental influences as a material condition of state, Yan went so far as to assert that certain states such as Britain, France and the US were superior to Russia, owing not only to individual liberty but to geographic conditions first and the liberty of the state second. Yan thought that China was geographically quite similar to the US, which was a positive condition for development, but unfortunately China was not as strong as the US. The reason was just attributable to the lack of a modern state (Wang 1986: 984).

Yan, like other intellectuals such as Liang Qichao (Campagnolo 2013: 109) and Sun Yat Sen (1866–1925) in the late Qing Empire, was convinced that there were no states at all in Chinese history. He referred to the argument of Chinese thinkers such as Liu Zongyuan (773–819) in the Tang dynasty and Gu Yanwu (1613–82) in the Ming dynasty to explain the "non-state circumstances" within Chinese traditional political theories (Wang 1986: 948). In fact, Yan admitted in his translating work that *tianxia* (天下under heaven) was always the only concept to support political sovereignty in China. Chinese emperors had held the view that they were divinely appointed to their land by universal order, which was to some degree absurd in the modern world system, especially when faced with the challenge from the Western world. Therefore, there was no choice but to follow the Western powers to retrieve national independence as the initial condition to develop state liberty.

However, Yan was not a complete nationalist, in spite of his radical opinion about the state. In his times, the minority Manchu controlled the government and the concept of race impacted not at all on state liberty, whereas the foreign threat was on the top of the agenda. Yan's seemingly conservativism after the 1911 Revolution disclosed his basic standpoint that was faithful to the state, not to the nation, that is, favorable to a stable political system and an integrated society including both the majority and the minority.

In a word, once he had been enlightened by his work on *On Liberty* and *The Spirit of the Laws*, Yan gradually worked out a new system of state liberty based on his former learning of Chinese philosophy and his understanding of the Western world. Nevertheless, the liberty he meant was still substantially abstract and remained a philosophical concept until this liberty evolved into liberalism considered as a methodology. In his translations, Yan attempted to design the political and economic system for a country according to his ideal. However, both of the above-cited books basically belong to philosophical work with little analysis of efficient policies. Yan's opinion about state-building was scattered in the translations in the introductions and commentaries. No more work was then completed until Yan's economic practice in Kaiping Mines.

From state liberty to state liberalism: the case of Kaiping Mines

It was by coincidence that Yan got involved in the business affair of Kaiping Mines (1901–8), just as he was working on his translation work of *On Liberty* (1898–1903) and *The Spirit of the Laws* (1904–9). This experience of economic practice enriched his understanding of liberalism, especially in the economic perspective.

Yan noted well that his opinion about state liberty diverged from the traditional individual liberty in the West and xenophobic trends within the China of his times. He pointed it out in one of the footnotes of *On Liberty*: "The following part is discussing free trade and its principle is different from individual liberty" (Wang 1986: 101) and in his commentary on *The Spirit of the Laws*: "some of the Chinese students who studied abroad opposed radically the foreign capitals in the Chinese railroading and mining industries to prevent the foreigners from getting profit in China" (Wang 1986: 1005).

Yan explained reasonably in several commentaries what state liberty meant. Such state liberty should be implemented with at least two dimensions, that is to say, domestic and international. Based on a complete legal system, the state enjoys the full rights of liberty domestically. Let us take the case of economic policy for example: there should be no limit to trade and investment, as long as the traders and the investors abide by the laws. Contrary to other conservative and reformative elites of the time, Yan promoted foreign direct investment and foreign loans enthusiastically, which was the best evidence of his understanding of economic liberalism. However, he stressed the independence of the state in its international dimension. The sovereign of the state is as important as the right to which the individual as such is entitled and it would bring a catastrophe if the state has no full right in the world system, which is similar to Kang Youwei's argument about China's future in *Datong shu* (大同书, Grand Unity) (Campagnolo 2013: 109).

From the standpoint of liberalism Yan started his career in Kaiping Mines as a novice, but he threw himself actively into the work in order to adapt to the new position as soon as possible. In the second letter to the same friend mentioned above, he described his trip to the Mines in Tangshan and even gave a comment on joint-venture management and ownership:

I went to the Mines in Tangshan on the second of May and came back on the sixth . . . [I think], if we Chinese still retain the right and ownership, we can strive to reform and succeed in the economic development. But if we lose the ownership or are cheated by foreigners so that we lose it, the foreigners can drive us Chinese out in the name of clearance, and then we have got nothing

no matter how profitable it is. At that time we will become the landowner who
has lost his landownership.

(Wang 1986: 541)

Yan could deal with management in a somewhat professional manner one month
later. In the July of his first year in Kaiping, he made an announcement to
stockholders stating both in Chinese and in English that he could declare that the
joint venture was finally set up. He explained in detail why a foreign partnership
should be undertaken and stressed the importance of the latter even with the
circumstances of crisis then existing in the whole country. This liberal type of
attitude was conveyed in the comments he wrote for the mass media. In 1902, he
gathered all of the possible information in his management and drew the sketch
of a blueprint for railways and mining in China (Yan 1902).

The commentary essay *Lukuang yi* (路矿议 *On Railroading and Mining*, 1902)
was divided into three parts. At first, Yan pointed out the priority of railroad and
mining in economic development through a comparison between Western
countries and China. The building of railroads should be given even more
precedence as the transportation system can increase both supply and demand at
the same time. In the second part, Yan was not content with a mere theoretical
description and he put forth several feasible policy suggestions to foster the two
leading industries. His open policy to foreigners, including technicians, investors
and bankers was unprecedented in the plan; and finally, Yan even drafted an
organizational plan and operational charter for the Railways and Mining Bureau
(see Figure 3.1).

The management system that Yan designed was multi-layered. At the head of
the Bureau was the Chancellor of Railways and Mining, in charge of both industries
together. Yan indicated that railways and mining were interactive and had
continuous spill-over effects through cooperation. Contrary to the state-owned

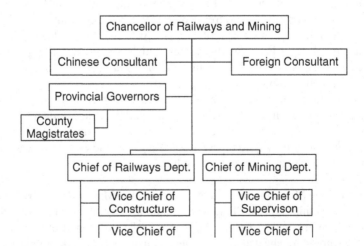

Figure 3.1 The organizational structure of the Railways and Mining Bureau by Yan Fu

pattern traditional in Chinese history, in Yan's system the Bureau enjoyed autonomy from the central government, which Yan thought of as a symbol of economic liberty and a source of economic vitality. Furthermore, companies in both industries could retain ownership for up to fifty years, so as to effectively attract both private and foreign capital, but the basic condition was that the controlling shareholders should be from China and that companies should be owners for at most fifty years. Yan's open policy was geared toward not only investors, but also foreign managers. He suggested employing foreign consultants to assist the Chancellor. The reason behind it was apparently the motto *xixueweiyong* (西学为用 Western learning for practical application). Hence, through the whole structure of centrally owned property rights in railways and mines, these rights were shared by both the private sector and foreign investors, while State Liberalism could be achieved domestically.

Now, the reality was not as rosy as expected. Yan dreamed of an ideal state with liberal ideas, but China at that time was not strong enough to resist economic invasion from the Western powers. According to the *Memorandum Relating to the Reorganization of the Chinese Engineering and Mining Company* (Brad 2014), Kaiping Mines had been transferred to a British company and renamed "Chinese Engineering and Mining Company" by Hoover as early as February 1901, just before Yan took his position. Yan got knowledge of the fact in the same year and complained in his letter to his friend. Upon the order of the Qing government, Yan went to Britain with Zhang Yi to attempt to regain ownership of the Mines. Before taking on the trip, Yan had submitted a testimony to the government for Zhang (Wang 1986: 137–42). He verified in that document that Zhang was prone to increase the foreign working capital used to manage the company. On such a special occasion that could cause war, there was no other choice than to transfer the ownership temporarily to the foreigners as an effective measure to protect the assets and stockholders' interest. However, Yan learned more concerning Zhang at the High Court of London and he hesitated to insist on state liberalism in the international perspective later on.

Yan's involvement in the Mines lasted in all for more than seven years, and his attitude at the end had indeed changed substantially. In 1908, Yan was nominated by another Qing official to deal with the merger between Kaiping Mines and Ruanzhou Mines, aiming to regain ownership from British managers (Ma 2005). In the documents he prepared, Yan (1998) insisted repeatedly on the sovereignty of the Qing dynasty, although that was virtually uncompromised by his principle of the free market in his former design and his proposition of an international perspective for State Liberalism. He proposed five conditions for negotiating with foreign managers:

First, the [Chinese] government does not acknowledge the ownership by British managers, and thus there is no possibility to repurchase the Mines with private or public capital.

Second, the ownership of British managers is completely illegal.

Third, Zhang Yi, the former General Manager of the Mines, was nominated as an agent of the government, and thus he had no right to sell the Mines to anyone.

Fourth, all of the natural resources including coal are owned by the Chinese government, and thus note that the Mines have been acquired by the foreigners illegally.

Fifth, therefore, the British managers should withdraw from the company and stop their infringement on the rights of the Chinese government.

(Yan 1998)

Yan's suggestion would quite certainly be refused by the British side. Also, we should note that, after the 1911 Revolution, the British colonist acquired the ownership of Ruanzhou Mines through another agreement with official agents and merged the two Mines into one, namely Kairuan Mines. Yan's practice in the case of Kaiping was left aside but it has left more to be understood than it actually achieved.

Concluding remarks

An attempt can be made to analyze the evolution of Chinese liberalism through Yan Fu's efforts. Assuming an "Impact-Response Model" (Fairbank 1942), let us consider that Chinese liberalism originated from the European classical works. To the extent that Yan created the special Chinese word *ziyou* (自繇) to break away from the traditional meaning in China, and to the extent that Yan designed an ideal system to realize liberty through anti-governmental measures, Yan was a "liberal". However, we cannot discern in Yan's translations the substantial persistence of traditional values, in spite of the elegant form of his beautifully crafted traditional Chinese sentences, because the target of liberalism regarded as a methodology was to build a modern state that had never actually existed in earlier Chinese history. The motivation derived from the impact of foreign invaders, who were evidently also newcomers to the Empire in a history of thousands of years, led Yan to adopt a practical attitude in separating economic business affairs from political systems with diversified domestic and international dimensions. He is thus identified as being both pro-*laissez-faire* in economic affairs while a nationalist in political and especially in international perspective (see Table 3.1).

In contrast with some commentators, we cannot discern a reverse course in Yan's trajectory and his return to the tradition in his late years, since not only the conditions and circumstance of his times but also his response to these were changing during his whole life. The so-called "Chinese tradition" we learn about has itself already been processed by intellectuals like Yan and diffused through their widely transmitted works. Yan's attitude, however, offers a hint to help us understand the "open policy" of the Chinese government after the Third Plenary Session of the Eleventh Central Committee in 1978, that is, the point that economic liberty can be definitely isolated from the political. Meanwhile there

Table 3.1 Yan Fu's state liberalism

State liberalism	inward	outward
economic	√	√
political	?	×

remains an obscure standpoint with respect to internal political affairs that appears as important as the tough outward response to foreign rivals.

To conclude, Yan's arguments on liberalism may remind us of a verse written by Edmund Clerihew Bentley – and cited in Amartya Sen's work *On Ethics and Economics* (Sen 2004: 1) – that goes like this:

John Stuart Mill
By a mighty effort of will
Overcame his natural bonhomie
And wrote *Principles of Political Economy*.

While J. S. Mill had overcome his bonhomie to argue for the natural rights of human beings against the government, which he thought as opposite to the liberty of individuals, Yan Fu had put the government (or the state) on an equal status with the individual and tried to resolve efficiently the direct conflict between them.[2]

Acknowledgements

This chapter is a revised version of a paper with the same title which I read at the ESHET meeting in 2014 (session "Liberalism In Between Europe and China – LIBEAC project", organized and chaired by Gilles Campagnolo) and I am grateful for the valuable criticism contributed by Olga Borokh on that occasion.

Notes

1 The other one was Jiangnan Shipyard in Shanghai.
2 Due to research time limitation, we do not compare either the *Patriarcha* embodied in the debate between Robert Filmer (1588–1653) and later John Locke (1632–1704), or Liberal Paternalism (Dworkin 2014) with the State Liberalism of Yan Fu. But we consider those as a further and indispensable topic.

References

Brad, D. (2014) 'Memorandum Relating to the Reorganization of the Chinese Engineering and Mining Company', <http://delong.typepad.com/sdj/2007/07/kaiping-mines-m.html> (accessed May 1, 2014).
Campagnolo, G. (2013) 'Three Influent Western Thinkers during the "Breakup" Period in China: Eucken, Bergson and Dewey', in Y. Ma and H. Trautwein (eds.), *Thoughts on Economic Development in China*, Abingdon: Routledge, 101–35.

Dworkin, G. (2014) 'Paternalism', in Edward N. Zalta (ed.), *The Stanford Encyclopedia of Philosophy* (Summer 2014 Edition), <http://plato.stanford.edu/archives/sum2014/entries/paternalism/> (accessed May 1, 2015).

Fairbank, J. (1942) 'Tributary Trade and China's Relations with the West', *Far Eastern Quarterly*, 2: 129–49.

Huang, K. (2000) *Ziyou de suoyi ran: Yan Fu dui Yuehan Mier ziyou zhuyi sixiang de renshi yu pipan* (*The Raison d'être of Freedom: Yan Fu's Understanding and Critique of John Stuart Mill's Liberalism*), Shanghai: Shanghai Bookstore Publishing House.

——(2008) *The Meaning of Freedom: Yan Fu and the Origins of Chinese Liberalism*, Hong Kong: The Chinese University Press.

Li, Z. (1977) '*Lun Yan Fu*' (On Yan Fu), *Historical Research*, 2: 67–80.

Metzger, T. (2008) 'Foreword', in K. Huang, *The Meaning of Freedom: Yan Fu and the Origins of Chinese Liberalism*, Hong Kong: The Chinese University Press, xi–xxii.

Ma. Y. (2005) '*Zhongying kaiping meiguang quanli jiufen de zai renshi: yi Yan Fu wei zhongxin*' (Rethinking the Dispute of the Ownership of Kaiping Mines between Britain and China: Based on the Analysis of Yan Fu), in Institute of Modern History, Chinese Academy of Social Sciences (ed.) *Jindai zhongguo yu shijie- dierjie jindai zhongguo yu shijie xueshu taolunhui lunwenji* (*Modern China and the World: An Anthology of the Second Conference of Modern China and the World*), Beijing: Social Sciences Academic Press, 2:186–209.

Mill, J. (2001) *On Liberty*, Kitchener: Batoche Books. (First published 1859.).

Montesquieu, C. (1748) *De l'esprit des lois*; ed. and trans. A. Cohler, B. Miller and H. Stone, *The Spirit of the Laws* (Cambridge Texts in the History of Political Thought), Cambridge: Cambridge University Press.

Rousseau, J. (1762) *Du contrat social ou principes du droit politique*; trans. G. Cole (1782) *The Social Contract or Principles of Political Right*, <http://www.constitution.org/jjr/socon.htm> (accessed May 1, 2015).

Schwartz, B. (1964) *In Search of Wealth and Power: Yen Fu and the West*, Cambridge, MA: The Belknap Press of Harvard University Press

Sen, A. (2004) *On Ethics and Economics*, Malden: Wiley-Blackwell.

Yan, F. (1902) '*Lukuangyi*' (On Railway and Mining), *Waijiaobao* (Foreign Affairs Journal), 1902: 12–13.

——(1981a) *Qunji Quanjie Lun* (trans. *On Liberty*), Beijing: The Commercial Press.

——(1981b) *Fayi* (trans. *The Spirit of the Laws*), Beijing: The Commercial Press.

——(1981c) *Yuanfu* (trans. *The Wealth of Nations*), Beijing: The Commercial Press.

——(1981d) *Mule mingxue* (trans. *Logic*), Beijing: The Commercial Press.

——(1981e) *Shehui tongquan* (trans. *A History of Politics*), Beijing: The Commercial Press.

——(1998) '*Guanyu Kaiping kuangquan jiufen de shuotie*' (A Comment on the Kaiping Mines' Suit), ed. G. Li, *jindaishi ziliao* (Materials for the Modern History), 93: 225–34.

Wang, S. (ed.) (1986) *Yan Fu ji* (Collected Works of Yan Fu), Beijing: Zhonghua Book Company.

4 Liberal economic thought in Republican China

Olga Borokh

Introduction

In the 1930s economic debates in China were focused on the problems of the role of the state in the economy. The ideas of control and planning gained huge influence among the professional economists, and in those years, scholars who supported a controlled economy (*tongzhi jingji* 統制經濟) and criticized the path of free-market economy could be called "mainstream".

Most influential Chinese economists of the Republican era graduated from leading American universities in the 1920s. During their studies in the US they got acquainted primarily with the ideas of liberalism and free competition that assumed no direct intervention of the state in the economy. However, among the Chinese scholars, the Great Depression caused a huge disappointment with this Anglo-American model of a free economy. Growing pressure on China from Imperial Japan also led scholars and politicians to seek a strategy of rapid modernization for the sake of preparing military confrontation.

The introduction of Western economic thought began in China in 1902 with the publication of the classical work of Adam Smith in Chinese translation by well-known thinker Yan Fu. The *Wealth of Nations* advocated the principles of free economy that were not easily accepted by the educated Chinese due to "influences of traditional concepts and specific historical circumstances" (Zhong 2007: 230).

Recognition of a high role for the state in economic life and cultural stereotypes of neglect of commerce were inherited from China's past. For hundreds of years, Confucianism had praised the moral norm of "duty" (*yi* 義) and despised the pursuit of individual "profit" (*li* 利). Since the middle of the nineteenth century, after defeats in the Opium wars, China suffered from the dictates and intervention of foreign powers. Early efforts at modernization failed due to the weakness and conservatism of the Qing dynasty. Chinese reformers wanted their nation to become rich and strong again through centralization of power, implementation of state control over the economy and protectionism in international trade. Anti-imperialist slogans of Chinese revolutionaries looked more convincing than liberal pro-free trade suggestions to open domestic markets to inflows of foreign goods and capital.

The idea of economic freedom was deeply unpopular among the Chinese intellectuals because it provided no recipes for accelerated industrialization and the protection of the national economy from external pressure. Conversely, scholarly voices that resounded in favor of economic freedom in the atmosphere of predominant ideas favoring a controlled economy therefore deserve special attention and careful study. Gu Yiqun and Tang Qingzeng were the most prominent Chinese liberal economists of the 1930s. Both were exposed to Western economic ideas. However, they developed different approaches towards the adaptation of liberalism in China.

Gu Yiqun and Western economic liberalism

In the 1920s Gu Yiqun (Gu Jigao) (顧翊群, 顧季高, 1900–92) studied economics in the United States. In 1924 he returned to China. In 1936 he held a post as the advisor to Executive Yuan. He worked in the banking sphere and participated in the Bretton Woods Conference, and in 1946 he was appointed to the International Monetary Fund.

The liberal views of Gu Yiqun were influenced by his trip to Europe and the United States in 1934–35. In Switzerland he communicated with economic experts from the League of Nations and the Bank for International Settlements. In Geneva he had conversations with economists of the International Chamber of Commerce Theodore Gregory and Bertil Ohlin (Gu 1935a: 5). He met with bankers and government officials in France, the United Kingdom, Germany and the United States. His stay in London at the end of 1934 was notable for numerous contacts with scholars. In his report about his trip overseas, Gu Yiqun wrote that he had "many discussions on monetary theory and China's monetary policy" with Ralph Hawtrey. He also mentioned meeting Arthur Salter, John Maynard Keynes, Theodore Gregory, Hartley Withers, Lionel Robbins, Friedrich Hayek and Hugh Dalton (Gu [1935d] 1994: 311). The principal goal of Gu Yiqun's trip was "the investigation of monetary systems and financial problems" of major Western powers, and after his return to China his main efforts were concentrated on the preparation of currency reform. However his scholarly interests expanded beyond the issues of stable currency and trade tariffs: he criticized the planned economy from the standpoint of the ideas of leading Western economists.

Gu Yiqun underlined that only the market was capable of allocating resources effectively. In his article 'Economic Thought and Social Transformations' (1935) he proposed three criteria of evaluation of an economic system: (1) Is this system capable of ensuring rational and balanced increase of capital accumulation? (2) Can this system regulate changes of the economic cycle without causing big damage to the spiritual and material life of the people? (3) Can it guarantee fair distribution of income so that everyone possesses purchasing power that allows living a decent life? (Gu 1935a: 10).

Gu Yiqun applied these criteria to evaluate three different types of economy. The planned economy of the Soviet type is made distinctive by its system of state ownership of the means of production and "absolute dictatorial government", which suppresses the role of private initiative from the people. The controlled economy is based on private property and is aimed at carrying out industrialization by the methods of state intervention in the economy to counterbalance external influences. Gu Yiqun declared that these two types of economic control did not fit China's needs. The third type, described by liberal economists and supported by Gu Yiqun, is a private economy where the state control is intended only for encouragement of free competition, prevention of monopolies and the goal of maintaining rational distribution of wealth (Gu 1935a: 9–10).

Criticism of the Soviet planned economy

Gu Yiqun used rich factual material that illustrated actual problems of the Soviet economy like shortage of goods, low level of consumption, bad quality of industrial products. The scholar had got these facts from Western publications, primarily from the book of the Soviet émigré economist Boris Brutzkus, *Economic Planning in Soviet Russia* (Brutzkus 1935).

This peculiar feature makes articles of Gu Yiqun look different from most Chinese economic publications of the 1930s. Chinese Marxists used positive information about the USSR to illustrate the advantages of socialism and to prove the necessity to copy this path in China. Supporters of the capitalist controlled economy were also somewhat attracted by Soviet achievements in rapid industrialization and implementation of Five-Year Plans. Gu Yiqun disapproved of the Soviet experience and focused on its failures.

He admitted that the Soviet economy had facilitated accumulation of capital for accelerated growth in the means of production. However, this kind of accumulation of capital sacrificed human consumption; as a result, the losses surpassed the achievements. Without free market criteria the elaboration of plans of production was not based on consumers' demands, but on ideal notions of the authors of the plan. Gu Yiqun observed that the Soviet planned economy had no ability to react flexibly to changes in the economic cycle, and because of that it did not fit the second criterion in evaluating the economic system. Under capitalism, fluctuations restore the equilibrium between production and consumption, so that the economy and society can progress continuously (Gu 1935a: 13). Gu Yiqun argued that Soviet Russia paid no attention to the balance of supply and demand; therefore produced goods were simply not necessarily needed by society. He cited the impressions of an American journalist who had visited Soviet shops: the more essential an article is, the harder it is to get, and conversely, the more non-essential it is, the greater its output – "sporting goods, pictures and busts of leaders, books even flowers and balalaikas and lipsticks are to be had on almost every block of the main streets" (Lyons 1935: 306).

Gu Yiqun declared that the planned economy of the USSR could be considered a "wartime economy" focused on the problems of defense instead of the well-being of the people. His remark was that "now Soviet Russia is not at war" (Gu 1935a: 14), which shows that he rejected the use of planning and control for the accelerated build-up of military potential in the pre-war period. As an economist, he declared that the principle "today's wealth is more important than future wealth" can be considered as an economic law. In other countries people cut their consumption and turn to savings voluntarily, their savings contribute to creation of capital, then future wealth and today's wealth are in mutual balance. In Soviet Russia the government forcibly limited consumption, and accumulated funds, often in order to direct them towards production which would bring no guaranteed success.

Thinking from a liberal standpoint, Gu Yiqun praised highly the freedom of choice of consumers. He doubted that economic planners acting "like engineers in a drawing room" were capable of defining constantly changing patterns of human consumption. The idea of maintaining the mutual balance of production and consumption on the basis of the plan looked senseless to Gu Yiqun. He asked the following hypothetical question: if all the 160 million inhabitants of Soviet Russia were to want to have a car, can the government produce these cars and distribute them? In a market economy this question can get a solution through the competition of the automotive industry with other branches of industry for initial factors of production, such as capital and labor force. And what will happen if under the instructions of the Soviet government 160 million cars are produced but 10 million people will prefer to receive an apartment instead? If the government permits it, then the plan will fail and should be rejected. If the government does not permit it, then that will become "forcibly adjusted" consumption, actually very well described by the Chinese saying: "to cut the feet to fit the shoes" (Gu 1935b: 28).

Gu Yiqun underlined that free markets play an indispensable role not only within the national economy, but also in world economic development:

> Now the planned economy is implemented only in Soviet Russia; though this country has no free market it still can use the markets of countries of the capitalist system as an evaluation criterion of national production. Let us assume that the ideal of the supporters of the planned economy will be realized and the whole world will implement this system, then the evaluation criteria will be completely lost. How will the Americans know that they should not encourage the cultivation of tung trees, and how will the Chinese know that they should not produce cars? Let me ask, whether such production is not a blind production.
>
> (Gu 1935b: 28–29)

Many Chinese intellectuals favored the Soviet model, which had neither unemployment nor crises. Gu Yiqun commented that there was also no unemployment under the slavery system, and that, with such a low level of real wages as in Soviet Russia, unemployment could be eliminated in the capitalist countries as well. He supposed that the United States and Britain could easily stop the economic crisis by copying Russian methods of controlled consumption and lowering the real income of peasants and workers. But in that case these countries should abandon liberal democratic policy and let the standards of living of the population fall, which was unacceptable to them (Gu 1935b: 28).

"I do not deny the successes of Russia in defense and in the realization of big projects at all, but I profoundly believe that this system should not be envied", wrote Gu Yiqun (Gu 1935b: 30). He compared Soviet achievements with the construction of Egyptian pyramids, the building of the Great Wall under Emperor Qin Shihuang (259–210 BC) and the digging of the Grand Canal by Emperor Yang Di (569–618) of the Sui dynasty. Economists recognize that these were projects of huge scale, but they do not consider them to be economic projects, because the rewards obtained by the people did not correspond to their sacrifices. History proved this point, because the Qin and Sui dynasties were overthrown by revolutions.

> The economic system and policies which are needed today in China should help us reach rapidly the level of modern states with the least sacrifice and at the same time cultivate the habits of a democratic policy. Realizing a planned economy, I am afraid, does not fit this purpose!
>
> (Gu 1935b: 30)

In the interest of preventing a currency crisis in China and to foster the creation of economic foundations for future development, Gu Yiqun recommended focussing on currency reform and the means of attracting foreign capital. He noted that failure in these undertakings would cause only minor damage, while attempts to copy the experience of Soviet Russia would lead to unpredictable consequences (Gu 1935b: 30–31).

Gu Yiqun criticized Chinese Marxists for treading the "heretical way" in economic science by announcing the inevitable collapse of capitalism and proclaiming that the planned economy was the object of study of economics. He believed that acquaintance with foreign economic ideas could help reveal the erroneous nature of the planned system. He asserted that many "pure economists" like Nicolaas Gerard Pierson, Ludwig von Mises, George Halm, Boris Brutzkus, Friedrich A. von Hayek and Lionel Robbins had since long unambiguously stated that the Soviet economic policy failed to correspond to economic principles. Gu Yiqun underlined that these economists were not "lackeys of imperialism" and they had no motives to demonstrate hostility to Soviet Russia. However, all of them did "love truth" and could not force themselves to say that the system with great sacrifices and small efficiency was better than the existing system. These economists do not deny the numerous shortcomings of the economies of big capitalist countries; at the same time and with the support of theory they have shown that the economic system of Soviet Russia has even more defects. Gu Yiqun especially recommended reading *Economic Planning in Soviet Russia* by Brutzkus (1935) and *Collectivist Economic Planning: Critical Studies on the Possibilities of Socialism* edited by Hayek (1935) (Gu 1935b: 26).

Shortcomings of a controlled economy

By the mid-1930s Chinese economists learned to distinguish the Soviet planned economy based on state ownership from the controlled economy with private property. According to Gu Yiqun, the latter is focused on the development of productive forces and support of industrialization. To achieve these goals the state uses protective duties, control and other methods to shield the national economy from unfavorable foreign impacts. As a result this system nourishes monopolies in the economy and fosters the class of big capitalists (Gu 1935a: 9–10).

Gu Yiqun turned to the analysis of the views of Friedrich List, which were frequently used in China for substantiating a protectionist policy that encourages the development of national economy. Since the 1920s there were supporters of List's state protectionism among the Chinese economists. For example, one of the leading economists of the Republican period, Ma Yinchu (馬寅初, 1882–1982), favored the studies of the ideas of List in China instead of the theory of Marx (Ma 1924).

Gu Yiqun sought to demonstrate that List's ideas do not contradict economic liberalism. First of all, List did not advocate introducing duties on imports of agricultural products. On the contrary, List asserted that tariff protection should not cover agriculture. This thesis looked especially well-timed against the backdrop of problems discussed in China in the 1930s when an inflow of cheap foreign products was seen as a threat to domestic agriculture. To prove his position Gu Yiqun quoted List's words that "the imports of natural products must everywhere be subject to revenue duties only, and never to duties intended to protect native agricultural production" (List [1841] 1909: 247; Gu 1935a: 15).

List had also specified that free trade with advanced economies was capable of stimulating the development of backward nations. Gu Yiqun cited his words according to which protectionism should not "exclude foreign competition at once and altogether, and thus isolate from other nations the nation which is thus protected" (List [1841] 1909: 143).

List had advised the governments of the less advanced nations to encourage the national manufacturing industries in the first period of their development. Commercial restrictions are "justifiable only until that manufacturing power is strong enough no longer to have any reason to fear foreign competition, and thenceforth only so far as may be necessary for protecting the inland manufacturing power in its very roots" (List [1841] 1909: 144). Gu Yiqun observed that "orthodox" economic theory claimed that, if a branch of industry did not correspond to local conditions, then there was no need to support it artificially in the early period of development. List's recommendations were more proactive, but he had also laid down an important additional condition: when the given industry becomes developed, it should be no more under protection, and otherwise there will be a danger of monopolies emerging from this situation (Gu 1935a: 16).

According to Gu Yiqun, the history of the development of industry in foreign countries showed that in Germany, in the United States and in Japan recommendations by List had only been half-implemented. After the industries of these countries became developed, protectionist measures were not relaxed, leading to numerous economic imbalances and strengthening of economic etatism. Gu Yiqun noticed that protective duties had led to the formation of monopolies in many branches of industry in the United States. Though the productive forces in the United States had reached a high level of development, constant increase in duties made trade with the United States unprofitable in turn for other countries. According to him, this was one of the causes of the world economic crisis in the 1930s.

Using his criteria of evaluation of economic systems, Gu Yiqun demonstrated the negative side of such a state-protected monopolistic economy. Despite all their successes in accumulating capital, monopolies are incompatible with balanced economic development. At the initial stage of development and under the pretext of the preservation of "stable market conditions", monopolistic capitalists prevent changes in the economic cycle. Later, they cannot constrain these changes anymore and then the fluctuations become sharp, bringing the problems of unemployment and bankruptcies. The world economic crisis was triggered by excessive development of monopolistic enterprises; subsequently the regulation of the consequences of the crisis became difficult and took too much time. Monopolies hamper the fair distribution of surplus and make the losses of the consumers in society exceed the benefits of monopolistic producers. According to Gu Yiqun, this tendency leads to visible inequality of income in society and creates conditions for spreading extremist ideas, as could be seen in Germany and Japan (Gu 1935a: 17).

The liberal model of limited state control

Gu Yiqun expressed his readiness to support a controlled economy in China. However, this control was to be limited to government actions to prevent monopolies from emerging and to supervise relationships between capitalists and workers in the interests of the well-being of the masses. He expressed confidence that the Chinese government could make a maximum effort in future economic construction. The authorities have more trained staff than private enterprises; many important branches like railways, telegraph, finances and shipping are in the hands of the government. "Government's economic policy actions render a great influence on the national economy, therefore the policy of non-action (*wuwei* 無爲) is not appropriate at all" (Gu 1935b: 26).

Such a "liberal" understanding of control as elaborated by a then "orthodox" school in economics was the cornerstone of the views of Gu Yiqun. He considered government intervention necessary to prevent certain individuals and groups from obtaining special rights that could be used to infringe upon the freedom of the others. The Chinese scholar found the sources of this policy in Adam Smith, specifically in the dispute with the Mercantilists, where the British father of economics put stress on social justice, since, in Gu Yiqun's view, Smith supported *laissez-faire* in every way to ensure elimination of privileged classes and to create possibilities for free development of the majority of the people (Gu 1935a: 17).

Gu Yiqun attempted to address his mainstream colleagues in China by assessing that the liberals did not oppose the state *per se* and did not exclude its notion from their economic concepts. He called erroneous judgments of List those passages where the German economist criticized the "orthodox" school for recognizing only the individual and the world, but for ignoring the state. Gu Yiqun underlined that Smith did not reject the necessity of selective "super-economic sacrifices", assuming a possibility of actions in the interests of the state without consideration of the economic interests of the people. According to Smith, there are some cases "in which it will generally be advantageous to lay some burden upon foreign for the encouragement of domestic industry" (Smith [1776] 1904, *Wealth of Nations*, IV.ii.23). Gu Yiqun also mentioned Smith's recommendations to use duties to regulate the import of saltpetre to Great Britain to enable the nation to produce gunpowder, as well as Smith's support in favor of The Navigation Acts in the interests of developing British shipping.

Gu Yiqun claimed that, for what he called the "orthodox" school, the state was a starting point for discussion about any economic theory. At the same time, this school proposes to harmonize the interests of the individuals and the state, and also the economic interests of various states in the world economy; it supports neither class struggle within the nation nor economic wars on a global scale. If the government is able to use laws to prevent the emergence of monopolies, to ensure social peace and to eliminate excessive risks for the enterprises, then the interests of various classes will be coordinated and conflicts will not arise. Therefore economic control supported by the "orthodox" school consists in numerous steps of social transformation which are carried out in due time and piecemeal instead of thought of and enacted by some unitary plan. According to Gu Yiqun, it is so because liberals do not trust the doctrine of the "supremacy of state" (*guojia zhishangzhuyi* 國家至上主義) (Gu 1935a: 17).

The "orthodox" school believes in the possibility of harmonizing gains and losses in the relations between national economies and the world economy. Following the principles of the division of labor, each country should develop its production in the areas in which it holds the strongest positions and carry out mutual exchange of products with other countries. Gu Yiqun presented an ideal image of a world economy in which free trade stimulates the development of backward economies:

> All countries, for the purpose of maximum exchange of goods, and the advanced countries, for the purpose of helping backward countries towards industrial development, should have a common monetary unit in the form of an international gold standard, and they should allow maximum free circulation of goods by reducing duties and concluding commercial treaties following the most-favored-nation treatment; the advanced countries should invest in backward countries to develop their productive forces and to let the whole world enjoy common prosperity.
>
> (Gu 1935a: 18)

Facing the harsh realities of the post-crisis world economy of the mid-1930s, Gu Yiqun admitted that there was an evident gap between the "cold judgments" of theories and actual "emotional actions of humans" who favored policies of self-sufficiency in economic development. He observed the rapid progress in the world economy since the second half of the nineteenth century, when the gold standard had been established. On the contrary, in the years close to the time he wrote, when many countries adopted the ideas of state economy, the standards of living of population in these countries had sharply declined. "As a result the confidence in international cooperation among the academic supporters of liberalism became stronger" (Gu 1935a: 18).

The link between economic liberalism and political democracy remained unbreakable for Gu Yiqun. He concluded that phenomena of low efficiency in democracies and the transitional phase to dictatorships that happened in those years all over the world were of a temporary nature. He expressed confidence in the future revival of democracy, when economic liberalism would inevitably replace all other systems of state control over the economy. State functions will be restricted to support fair competition and the division of labor, in the interests of maintaining maximal social and economic effectiveness of production and distribution of goods and labor services. To substantiate these ideas, Gu Yiqun referred to *Economic Planning and the Tariff: An Essay on Social Philosophy* (1934) by American scholar James Gerald Smith and *The Great Depression* (1934) by British economist Lionel Robbins (Gu 1935a: 18).

Gu Yiqun believed in the practical viability of the liberal socio-economic system that allows people to develop freely without facing monopolistic abuse and other restrictions on production. Though this system cannot avoid completely the changes in the economic cycle, the flexibility of its economic organization will make its regulation relatively and comparatively easy. There will be a possibility to prevent economic wars which cause damage to other countries and bring no benefits to the nation. Certainly, according to the distribution of national income, the capitalists who take risks receive more money than workers. However, against the background of decreasing risks in the economy and the increase in social stability, the government will cease to give covert support to capitalists, and this gives grounds to some hope that the share of the interests and profits within national income will decrease every year, while the share of wages will increase (Gu 1935a: 18).

Gu Yiqun has underlined that, in his liberal views, there was no room for some extraordinary or bizarre judgments which had gained popularity around the globe. Widespread criticism of the "old social order" is accompanied by an almost religious admiration of the utopian system of the state economy that was yet not tested in practice. Real successes of new social systems that emerged in Europe after World War I were not as big as depicted by propaganda (Gu 1935a: 21). And the implementation of these radical ideas led to dangerous self-isolation from the world economy:

> Soviet Russia used a planned economy; as a result, the system of prices and costs became torn away from the world system, and as a result the people there endure huge difficulties. Now China should seek to accommodate itself

to [world] influence instead of avoiding it. China suffered for a hundred years because it did not recognize earlier the necessity to correspond to world tendencies. Do we really still not realize it today?

(Gu 1935a: 22)

The comparison of Soviet planned economy, state-controlled economy and liberal economic control was expected to compel the majority of non-biased scholars to admit that the third type of economic system "has comparatively few defects and is easy to implement" (Gu 1935a: 18–19). The liberal economy will help China to put into practice the teaching of Sun Yat-sen (孫中山, 1866–1925) that was the foundation of the official ideology of the ruling Kuomintang. The goals of "equalization of land rights" and "regulation of capital" proposed by the founder of the Republic could be achieved if the emergence of monopolies and big capitalists was prevented.

The openness of the Chinese economy

Gu Yiqun called himself a supporter of "the school of international economic equilibrium" (*guoji jingji junheng pai* 國際經濟均衡派) based on three simple liberal principles: division of labor, private property, free exchange. The realization of these principles on a global scale promotes overall development of the economy when all participants receive benefits. If backward countries (including China) really want to develop their economies, they should participate in global economic processes (Gu 1935c: 9).

The scholar consistently defended the thesis that all benefit from international trade. Gu Yiqun illustrated the ideas of the international division of labor and comparative costs by the metaphor of the relationship between a professor and a rickshaw driver. It would be better for the society if a university professor concentrates on research and hires a rickshaw to pull the cart instead of doing both.

If the rickshaw driver has no ability to do research, then after the professor will have spent all his strength in research, it will be easy for the rickshaw driver to provide him with labor service: it will not be exploitation. If the rickshaw driver wants to do research, but has no abilities, [this attempt] will be useless. He can continue to pull his cart actively and spend his remaining energy on research to achieve a position in life. If he cannot do research and does not want to pull a cart, only cursing the professor as exploiter, then it means that that rickshaw driver consciously reconciled himself with his backwardness and it is impossible to find a medicine for his rescue.

(Gu 1935b: 16)

In those years, China's patriotic intellectuals worried that the Western "professor" will ride the Chinese "rickshaw" without any prospect of improvement for the latter under the existing framework of the division of labor between the advanced

West and backward China. Politician Zhang Naiqi (章乃器, 1897–1977) criticized the supporters of openness to international trade on this basis. He claimed that pro-free trade scholars believed that backward China should buy cheap foreign goods to increase the well-being of the people; they hoped that an unfavorable balance in foreign trade could turn into foreign investment. "They completely deny unequal exchange; they say that when the rickshaw driver carries a professor, it can not be considered as unequal exchange". Using Gu Yiqun's figurative example, Zhang Naiqi declared that the rickshaw driver was already exhausted and the professor gave him little money: "Ah! Why should we become rickshaw drivers? Is it defined by destiny? Why cannot we preserve our human status and learn some technology? Why can other countries import foreign capital and machinery during the large-scale construction of their national economy?" He declared that the position of Gu Yiqun represented "classical slavish philosophy" (Zhang [1935] 1997: 244–45).

Now, according to Gu Yiqun, the Chinese paid a high price to take part in international trade. The scholar felt compassion for Chinese enterprises of the old type, which were defeated in natural selection, but he opposed government measures to protect them. Self-isolation from the world would deprive China of the motivation for technical changes and of the benefits from international trade. Gu Yiqun stressed that qualitative changes in the Chinese economy became possible only due to the expansion of communication with the world economy. Before opening to navigation, China was a closed economy with an insignificant volume of foreign trade. In *The Distribution of Wealth* (1899), American economist John Bates Clark had identified such a society as being "static" (Clark [1899] 1908: 60). Gu Yiqun concluded that by means of military force, unequal treaties and cheap production, foreigners quickly transformed Chinese society from a "static" into a "dynamic" one. This influence was manifest in the fast growth of the population and the increase of desires on the part of consumers. These changes caused improvements in the methods of manufacturing and they led to capital increase and to the progress of China (Gu 1935c: 10).

International trade became a source of financial and industrial capital for China; it also helped to feed the growing population and to maintain living standards in Chinese cities. Breaking links with the external world was equal to disaster: "There will be bankruptcy of manufacturers of export goods, transport will stop, cities will blossom no more, and there will be chaos in society" (Gu 1935b: 21). At the same time, China should make every effort to get rid of unequal treaties imposed by foreigners, precisely in order to develop international trade even more actively and to strive for revival of the Chinese economy.

Thus Gu Yiqun highly praised economic theory and urged young Chinese intellectuals to study it diligently in order to get rid of their fascination with empty slogans. Nevertheless his primary concern was the application of theory to urgent practical problems of China; he was not engaged in purely academic reasoning. A different version of economic liberalism came from the academic circles of the Republican era.

Tang Qingzeng and economic liberalism with Chinese roots

A well-known historian of Chinese economic thought, Tang Qingzeng (唐慶增, 1902–72) was another prominent defender of liberalism. In the 1920s he studied economics in the United States at Harvard University and the University of Michigan, and received his Master's degree from Harvard. Tang Qingzeng's liberal views were greatly influenced by his teacher from Harvard University, the professor of economics Frank William Taussig. After returning to China in 1925, Tang Qingzeng taught economics and the history of economic thought; he was a professor of Fudan University and the chair of the economics department of Daxia University in Shanghai.

In 1933 he took part in the discussion on the modernization of China organized by *Shenbao yuekan* (申報月刊 – *Shenbao Monthly*) magazine. In its special issue on modernization, among twenty-six articles dealing with this theme altogether, only his contribution titled "Modernization of production in China should use individualism" urged following the direction of a free capitalist economy (Tang 1933b).

Individualism versus socialism in China's modernization strategy

Having addressed the question of choice between individualism and socialism, Tang Qingzeng underlined that "no teaching or institution in the world is absolutely right or absolutely wrong – if it suits the state A, it does not necessarily suit the state B" (Tang 1933b: 60). He did not reject socialism as such, believing that socialism responded to the needs of countries where the main problem was inequality of the rich and the poor.

In Tang Qingzeng's textbook, *An Introduction to Economics*, we can find a reference to the opinion of Taussig (Tang 1933a: 33). In his *Principles of Economics*, Taussig wrote: "The essential end which socialism tries to attain is a change in distribution" (Taussig [1911] 2013: 467). Tang Qingzeng supported this idea and claimed that socialism was focused on distribution, but in China the top priority belonged to the problem of developing production. He warned that it was very important not to mix the sequence of solving these problems. In backward countries, like China, it is necessary to begin with the search for methods of increasing wealth. Later, when sufficient wealth is generated and inequality in distribution gradually surfaces, the state should start searching for ways of regulating this inequality, including the use of socialist methods.

For thousands of years, China had focused on the equal distribution of wealth and did not pay attention to production. Premature transition to socialism brings dangers of sticking to material backwardness, and in Chinese conditions the historical experience of isolation predisposes the people to self-sufficiency. Individualism is the only way of increasing wealth. To let the Chinese get enough food and clothing (*wenbao* 溫飽), it is necessary to develop production, to master new methods and to create new enterprises. Of the three factors of production, China does not lack labor and land, therefore the only yet most important problem is capital increase. Gain-seeking behavior is rooted in human nature. Removing obstacles to modernization will stimulate people to do business: the bigger the gains they receive, the more enthusiastically they will invest in production. If China embraces socialism and leaves people little hope to receive gains, or even totally deprives them of this hope, then there will be insufficient sources of capital. In this case the so-called new methods of production and new enterprises will turn into delusion. People will remain stuck in desperate conditions forever and will not be able to escape this trap (Tang 1933b: 61).

Tang Qingzeng rejected the arguments according to which, if overproduction generates crises in the United States and Europe, then the development of private enterprises in China will bring a similar outcome. According to Tang Qingzeng, the supporters of this point of view do not realize that the main part of the Chinese population lives in dire poverty without any possibility of satisfying their basic needs for clothing, food and shelter. After an increase in production, the purchasing power of the Chinese will grow, and the country with its big population and big territory will be able to consume different goods. Then the standard of living in China will rise, and the hopes for a good material life will be easy to satisfy.

Tang Qingzeng underlined that China should not try "to reach what is beyond China's grasp by copying Soviet Russia" (Tang 1933b: 61). Those who advocate socialist methods praise the example of the USSR, which calls itself a socialist state, where the production grows every year and the wealth increases. Tang Qingzeng noticed that Soviet Russia provided foreigners with unreliable statistics; its stress on propaganda made it impossible to judge the real economic situation only on the basis of Soviet official data. Some foreign scholars conducted their own surveys and cited opposite data. And if a hugely overpopulated China was to repeat the Soviet experience and started to establish big state trusts, operating them would be extremely difficult to manage.

Tang Qingzeng admitted that the idea of 'individualism' had taken a bad reputation in China: having heard this word, the people "plug [their] ears and quicken [their] pace", they condemn this "-ism" as the source of evil and the cause of poverty of the nation (Tang 1933b: 61). The scholar quoted from the *Yin Wenzi* (尹文子) – the book of ancient Chinese philosophical "school of names" (*ming jia* 名家):

> The venerable elder from Kangqu named his servant Shan Bo (善搏 Good Fighter) and named his dog Shan Shi (善噬 Good Biter). For three years visitors did not appear on the threshold of his house; the venerable elder was surprised and asked about it. He was told the truth. He changed [the names], and visitors began to come again.
>
> (*Yin Wenzi* quanyi 1996: 151, my translation[1])

The Chinese are unhappy with individualism because they are misled by its bad reputation related to its name. In reality they naturally act in their own self-interest and benefit, at the expense of others (*zi si zi li, sun ren li ji* 自私自利, 损

人利己). According to Tang Qingzeng, there is no capitalist class in China, so there is no individualism to talk about. But the founder of liberal economic theory, Adam Smith, in *The Theory of Moral Sentiments* (1759), had explained that individualists pay attention to sympathy among the people and do not dream of defeating others. However the Chinese make no distinction between black and white: in time of political disturbance and economic failure, they groundlessly blame individualism for all troubles (Tang 1933b: 61).

Tang Qingzeng recommended utilizing both internal and external sources of capital for the needs of modernization: "If there is only national capital, it will not suffice, if we lean only on foreign loans, it will not be a wise policy" (Tang 1933b: 62). To support the building of national capital, he suggested the restriction of consumption and the reduction of squandering of capital. He admitted that in practice it would not be possible to limit human desires, but it was necessary to find a way to persuade the people to cut expenditure so that the standard of living would not exceed existing productive forces. The Western concept that the growth of wants leads to an increase in production is applicable to countries where the most basic needs are already satisfied, hence it does not suit modern China. Besides that, the largest component of spending of the Chinese does not go into production, and "from the standpoint of society, it is a big defect" (Tang 1933b: 62).

The scholar pointed to the problem of "anti-economic" behavior by the Chinese, who are inclined to gambling and doing illegal business. Their love of a comfortable life and their unwillingness to work has generated among the Chinese a desire to receive unearned goods and has become a means to make speculative activity blossom. Tang Qingzeng warned that personal vanity had created in China the phenomenon of the coexistence of the backward manufacturing of the eighteenth century with the consumption of the twentieth century (Tang 1933b: 60).

Liberal economic policy in the context of the history of Chinese economic thought

In 1936, in his article entitled "Observing from the point of view of history which economic policy should be carried out in our country", Tang Qingzeng provided historical arguments about the necessity of a liberal economy. He cited an old Chinese saying according to which an orange tree growing in the south of Huaihe River can bear sweet fruits, but turns sour if planted in the north. Local conditions are important, and foreign economic experience must be accommodated to national specifics, to the social and cultural environment, to local human habits. Attempts to copy Western economic policies in China will fail if implemented without consideration of traditional Chinese economic policy.

> Old institutions continue to exist; they are certainly valuable because they are firmly established. Besides, the history of China is long, and traditions and habits could not be destroyed at once. Therefore it is necessary to take gradual

measures to do away with the old and set up the new, so that, on the one hand, it would be possible to adapt to the new environment, and on the other hand, to avoid contradiction with old habits. Then the life of the national economy will gradually take the right track.

(Tang 1936a: 174)

This accent on history and traditional institutions was different from the general mood of Chinese intellectuals of that time who aspired to break away from the past and to find abroad new spiritual sources for the progress of China. Tang Qingzeng declared that looking back into history in order to solve contemporary problems was not any kind of "restoration of antiquity" or "return to feudalism". The key watershed is between true and false, not between the old and the new.

Tang Qingzeng was an influential historian of Chinese economic thought and the author of one of the earliest comprehensive studies on this theme published in China (Tang 1936b).[2] The depth of his historical expertise increased the value of his interpretations of traditional economic policy. If Ma Yinchu and other supporters of a controlled economy asserted that China had always implemented some kind of rigid state regulation of economic life (Ma 1935: 52), Tang Qingzeng focused his attention on the historical roots of a free economy in China.

The scholar developed his own interpretation of the idea of *laissez-faire* (*fangren* 放任) in the context of Chinese history and culture. Tang Qingzeng declared that, historically, economic policy in China tended towards non-interference of the state in the economy: the people competed with each other in their struggle for profit, but the state was not their contender. In the past, the successes of government-run state enterprises were always small, and even in the midst of unfavorable conditions private enterprises were able to survive. The scholar recognized the historical importance of the ancient Chinese reformers, but he also stressed that politicians like Shang Yang (390–338 BC), Wang Mang (45 BC–AD 23) and Wang Anshi (1021–86) failed when they attempted to pursue interventionist policies. On the contrary, the Duke of Zhou (Zhou Gong), who dates back to the eleventh century BC, and the Tang dynasty officials Liu Yan (716–80) and Lu Zhi (754–805), succeeded thanks to their policies of non-interference (Tang 1936a: 176).

Tang Qingzeng considered the idea of economic *laissez-faire* to be fundamental for two major ancient Chinese schools of thought – Daoism and Confucianism. He believed that the economic ideas of the Daoists were based on the philosophy of non-action (*wuwei*), as this school propagandized the principle of *laissez-faire* (*fangrenzhuyi* 放任主義). Confucius also supported *laissez-faire* and opposed the policy of intervention.

To make a clear distinction, Tang Qingzeng outlined the difference between "absolute *laissez-faire*" of Daoists and "relative *laissez-faire*" of Confucians. Daoists Lao Zi and Zhuang Zi called to a return to nature and proposed an absolute principle of *laissez-faire*. Founders of the early Confucian school Confucius and Mencius supported the principle of "benefiting people by things that are beneficial to them" (*yin min zhi so li er li zhi* 因民之所利而利之) (*Analects*

論語, XX. 2). All their suggestions in the economic sphere implied no government interference. Confucian ideas included the equal distribution of wealth (*jun fu* 均富), the system of "well-fields" (*jing tian* 井田) in the distribution of products between the peasants and the authorities,[3] attention being given to agriculture and the promotion of commerce. In Tang Qingzeng's view, Confucians propagated a relatively mild or limited principle of *laissez-faire*. It was different from the absolute or unlimited non-action of the Daoists (Tang 1936b: 168), which was formulated with the following words by Lao Zi: "the people will be equitable, though no one so decrees" (*min mo zhi ling er zi jun* 民莫之令而自均) (*Daodejing* 道德經, 32, translation by Lau 1989: 49).

Tang Qingzeng noticed that, in traditional China, *laissez-faire* policy had been connected with the satisfaction of needs of the people (*zu min* 足民). The primary task was to supply the people with food to solve the problem of the sources of subsistence (*shengji* 生计). The scholar cited the words of Confucius according to which when it is not enough for people, how can it be enough for the ruler (*Analects*, XII. 9). It meant that if the economic problems of the people are solved, then the state revenues are guaranteed, so the people are the most important factor in the economy. The quest for sources of taxes was for a long time considered as the main way of solving financial problems, and Tang Qingzeng recommended accepting this principle in the contemporary situation as well (Tang 1936a: 176).

The broad popularity of the ideas of planning and economic control in Republican China relied upon the attractiveness of foreign successes brought by government interference. Tang Qingzeng observed that, in the past, Europe had followed the principle of *laissez-faire* and that it was only after World War I that there was some marked preference for state intervention. He warned that attempts to copy this policy in China would obstruct business activity and hamper the accumulation of capital.

> The wants of the contemporary people are more complex than in the past, therefore today it is impossible to take completely the position of non-interference. In my humble opinion, the policy that we should accept today should inherit the former spirit of laissez-faire. It should also find the way to avoid the shortcomings of intervention.
>
> (Tang 1936a: 176–77)

Tang Qingzeng outlined the main principles of economic policy in China. First of all, in the field of production, the main principle is private business. However, if private entrepreneurs do not want or have no possibility to be engaged in certain kinds of production, for example in heavy industry, their functions should be taken over by the state. Second, the state may support private enterprises directly or provide incentives (for example, tax exemptions). Third, so as to receive good results from the economic activity of the people, the state guarantees special business rights (for example, by the registration of trade-marks) and protects the people's livelihood (for example, by means of introducing labor laws, food-quality control, etc.). Fourth, the state safeguards the people's interests, maintains social stability and protects individual freedom, private entrepreneurship and contractual rights (Tang 1936a: 177).

Tang Qingzeng gave particular attention to those concepts of traditional Chinese economic thought which he considered to be inapplicable in the contemporary world. First of all, it is the idea of equal distribution of wealth, which was at the center of Chinese economic policy for a long time. Confucius said that rulers worry not about scarcity of goods, but about their uneven distribution (*bu huan gua er huan bu jun* 不患寡而患不均) (*Analects*, XVI.1). It was supposed that, after equal distribution of wealth, the people can live peacefully. According to Tang Qingzeng, due to such ideas, in old China

> desires were scarce, the aspiration to frugality was propagandized, material needs were very low, therefore, while carrying out some economic policy, the rulers needed only to maintain equality in the distribution of property, and then it was possible to live in peace.
>
> (Tang 1936a: 175)

He noticed that in the past such policy had had certain value, but now when "the people are poor and the wealth is exhausted", and there was no sense in adhering to it. He underlined again that one must follow some sequence of actions in realizing an economic policy. The new economic course in China should support production by the means of creating the conditions for capital accumulation: first, the nation should get rich, and only after that is achieved may the state take care of redistributing wealth by means of taxation.

The traditional policy of economic self-sufficiency (*zi zu* 自足) does not correspond to modern conditions either and has become an obstacle to China's progress. From the point of view of Tang Qingzeng, in international economic situation of his day, it was impossible to use the methods of self-sufficiency and to remain isolated from world markets. China needed to work together with the foreign powers by establishing communications and finding common interests: it is absolutely necessary to benefit from the international division of labor (Tang 1936a: 176).

Tang Qingzeng on modern civilization

In the 1920s and 1930s Chinese intellectuals held intense debates on the relationships between Chinese and Western civilizations. The supporters of the idea of borrowing foreign achievements debated with the traditionalists, who attempted to protect Chinese national culture from the destructive impact of external influence and focused on the negative sides of Western civilization.

Tang Qingzeng observed that many people complained about the unequal distribution of the benefits of modernity and voiced their support for socialism (Tang 1932: 251). However, in Tang Qingzeng's view, they did not take into consideration the fact that, around the world, the number of wealthy people was increasing and there was a tendency towards a gradual alleviation of poverty. There is no reason to argue that a bad economic system allows capitalists to exploit the working class. He claimed that, in the mid-1930s, the life of workers was better than the life of the upper class in the previous century. At the same time, Tang Qingzeng acknowledged that inequality was an inevitable phenomenon (Tang 1932: 252).

The moralizing attacks on market economics were also put in doubt. The scholar rejected the reasonings according to which the modern economy was the "economy of money" and "people became slaves of money". Money is the instrument of transactions and a tool to achieve goals; higher goals can also be reached by means of money (Tang 1932: 252). There is no need to limit profit-seeking behavior, and this question deserves more careful consideration. According to Tang Qingzeng, the greatest flaw of socialism is that, after its realization, the enterprising spirit of the people and their sense of responsibility decrease: therefore it will be better to allow people to pursue their economic self-interest (Tang 1932: 253).

A contemporary researcher of the history of Chinese economic thought of the Republican period, Sun Daquan, noted that, in the article "Economic science and modern civilization", Tang Qingzeng used the notion of "capitalist system" (*ziben zhidu* 資本制度) only once (Sun 2010: 147; see Tang 1932: 253). However Tang Qingzeng's numerous statements about "modern civilization" based on private property and freedom of entrepreneurship unmistakably signified the modern capitalist system. Sun Daquan concluded that Tang Qingzeng "accurately and consistently glorified and protected modern capitalist material civilization; it was extremely rare in Chinese intellectual circles where the influence of state capitalism and socialism was widespread" (Sun 2010: 148).

Tang Qingzeng insisted that healthy economic ideas were a tool of the development of civilization, and such ideas were generated in the process of a successful development of economic science. He noticed that the popularity of Marx's *Das Kapital* in Europe and the United States peaked in the 1880s and 1890s, when academic circles worshipped this book as the "Bible of Socialism". Later on, new intellectual trends appeared in world economic thought, and there were also changes in industry and commerce. In this new context, the doctrine of Marx lost its former influence and could be compared with an arrow at the end of its flight. Foreign economists did not support this teaching anymore: for example, Taussig wrote that the facts had forced socialist scholars and their leaders to acknowledge that Marx's predictions concerning the economic evolution were erroneous (Tang 1931: 14).

The scholar believed that the problems of China's workers were caused not by capitalist robbers, but by the sharp increase of prices in the years when he was writing, the influence of the civil war, the aggression of imperialist powers and the chaos in the currency system (Tang 1931: 19–21). He added that that situation could be improved by the accumulation of capital, some active action to protect the interests of workers, eliminate the consequences of armed confrontation, abolish unequal treaties and implement currency reforms (Tang 1931: 21–22).

Tang Qingzeng concluded that Marxism would not help to solve China's problems; that, on the contrary, it would pit workers against capitalists and lead to the interruption of production. He underlined that he was not calling for abandoning the study of Marx's economic ideas. He suggested that more attention be paid to the real problems of China and to remember that it is impracticable to follow foreign theories blindly (Tang 1931: 22).

Conclusion

Gu Yiqun's and Tang Qingzeng's criticism of state interventionism in the economy was consistent and based on Western liberal theory. Both scholars were skeptical about Marxism. Their clear and unambiguous liberal economic ideas were expressed in the mid-1930s at the height of the so-called "golden decade" of relative prosperity of Chinese capitalism between the national unification of 1927 and the Japanese aggression of 1937. It was a period of growing confidence in private entrepreneurship in China, which also encouraged scholarly interest in free markets.

In the 1940s though, the leading representatives of the Chinese economic mainstream had abandoned the idea of a controlled economy because of their disappointment with the policy of state control and the loss of any hope in the Kuomintang government's ability to take the guiding role in economic development. For example, in the mid-1930s, Ma Yinchu fought against economic individualism, but in the later half of the 1940s he concluded that the epoch of free capitalism in China belonged to the future and not to the past (Ma [1947] 1999: 208).

Nevertheless this deep intellectual transformation did not contribute to the popularity of *laissez-faire* economics. Chinese political liberalism of the second half of the 1940s embraced the ideas of the so-called "third way" and borrowed heavily from Western socialists. Though Chinese liberals "studied ideas from England and America", they were inspired "not by the classical liberalism of Locke, Adam Smith and Hayek, but by the New Liberalism and social democracy of Bentham, Mill, Laski, Russell and Dewey" (Xu 2014: 768). Contemporary researcher Liu Junning observed that the Chinese liberals of the 1940s promoted the ideas of "equal wealth" and the "mixed economy", while in the West similar approaches were disapproved by Hayek as "the road to serfdom" (Liu 1998: 9).

After the revolution of 1949, economic liberalism disappeared from the Chinese intellectual scene for more than three decades. Liberal economic ideas regained importance at the end of the twentieth century, when the Chinese reformers proclaimed such goals as "openness" and a "socialist market economy". A contemporary researcher of Chinese economic thought, Zhong Xiangcai from the Shanghai Academy of Social Sciences, commented that the critical rethinking of the controlled economy by China's economic liberals of the 1930s "became an important intellectual resource for the subsequent transformation of the Chinese economy" (Zhong 2007: 231). In the late 1970s the authorities abandoned the idea of egalitarian distribution of wealth and motivated the most active members of society to seek individual profit, "to get rich first", in order to facilitate economic growth. Tang Qingzeng's recommendations to prioritize the accumulation of capital instead of focusing on socialist distribution were similar to this policy of the initial stage of reforms applied in the People's Republic of China after 1978. His arguments in favor of economic cooperation with the external world as well as Gu Yiqun's criticism of trade protectionism and self-isolation also correspond to the policy of "openness" in contemporary China.

Sun Daquan noticed that, in the Republican period, Gu Yiqun was more influential than Tang Qingzeng (Sun 2006: 273). This could be partly attributed to their difference in social status: Gu Yiqun served as a high-ranking economic official, while Tang Qingzeng was employed as a university professor whose primary concern was the history of ancient Chinese economic thought and basic economic theory for the needs of higher education. In a longer historical perspective, it seems less significant to try to evaluate the personal influence of each thinker than to compare the intellectual traditions represented in Chinese economic science by both Gu Yiqun and Tang Qingzeng.

The way they sought to apply Western liberalism to Chinese realities and their methods were different. Gu Yiqun relied upon Western economics to find answers to the practical problems of China's economy, and he focused primarily on currency reform and the international trade balance. He transplanted foreign ideas into China, but did not attempt to contextualize them in the local cultural setting. Tang Qingzeng made a significant effort to find the roots of liberal economic ideas and *laissez-faire* policy in the Chinese tradition proper; he was concerned by the cultural and psychological obstacles to the reception of liberalism in modern China.

Both lines of thought exist in contemporary Chinese economic science. Proponents of Western economic ideas have formed a prominent group that has significantly influenced the search for new reformist ideas in China since the 1980s. They apply universal principles of mainstream economics to the Chinese economy. Another group of scholars tends to focus on the development of "Chinese economics", which takes into consideration the factors of culture and institutions. The roots of the debates in the PRC at the turn of the twenty-first century, about the mutual compatibility of Western individualism and traditional Chinese moral ideas, could be traced back to Tang Qingzeng's publications of the 1930s. Seen from this angle, his intellectual legacy is no less significant than the ideas of Gu Yiqun. Issues of how to adapt mainstream economics in China that were debated in the 1930s will keep their importance in the future.

Acknowledgements

This chapter is a significantly revised version of a paper presented at the annual conference of the European Society for the History of Economic Thought (ESHET, Lausanne, May 2014, session "Liberalism Between East and West", co-sponsored by the LIBEAC project and chaired by Professor Gilles Campagnolo) and later at the conference of the Society for the History of Chinese Economic

Thought (中國經濟思想史學會) in Chengdu in October 2014. Valuable comments and thought-inspiring questions from the participants of these scholarly gatherings are highly appreciated. I am grateful to Gilles Campagnolo, the Editor of this volume, for helping me to improve the quality of this chapter.

Notes

1 A good French translation of *Yin Wenzi* published in the early twentieth century is the following: "*Un notable de K'ang-kiu (康衢) donna pour nom à son petit domestique: Chan-po (善搏 Bon pour donner des coups de cornes), et à son chien: Chan-cheu (善嚙 Bon pour mordre). Ses amis ne passèrent jamais devant sa porte pendant trois ans. Le notable, s'en étant étonné, demanda pourquoi. On lui dit ce qu'il en était réellement; les noms furent changés et les amis revinrent.*" (Masson-Oursel and Kia-Kien Tchou 1914: 593).
2 About Tang Qingzeng's views on history of Chinese economic thought, see Borokh (2013).
3 "Well-fields" or nine-square land distribution system was described by ancient Confucian thinker Mencius (372–289 BC). The Chinese character "jing" (井well) represents the scheme of borders between the fields in communities of eight peasant families. The field in the center was cultivated collectively on behalf of the ruler; the eight surrounding fields were cultivated by individual families.

References

Borokh, Olga (2013) 'Chinese Tradition Meets Western Economics: Tang Qingzeng and his Legacy', in Ying Ma and Hans-Michael Trautwein (eds.), *Thoughts on Economic Development in China*, London and New York: Routledge: 136–57.
Brutzkus, Boris (1935) *Economic Planning in Soviet Russia*, with a foreword by F. A. Hayek, London: Routledge & Sons.
Clark, John Bates ([1899] 1908) *The Distribution of Wealth: A Theory of Wages, Interest and Profits*, New York: Macmillan.
Gu, Jigao (1935a) 'Jingji sixiang yu shehui gaizao' ['Economic Thought and Social Transformations'], *Minzu* [*The Nation*], 3.8: 1–22 (1313–34).
——(1935b) 'Ru chao guo yu Zhongguo you da hai fou' ['Is There Real Great Harm from Unfavorable Balance of Trade for China'], *Shehui jingji yuebao* [*The Social and Economic Monthly*], 2.5: 15–31.
——(1935c) 'Zhongguo xin huobi zhengce yu guoji jingji junheng. Shang' ['China's New Monetary Policy and International Economic Equilibrium, Part 1'], *Dongfang zazhi* [*The Eastern Miscellany*], 32.23: 5–16.
Gu, Yiqun ([1935d] 1994) 'Gu Yiqun chengbao pu Ou kaocha geguo bizhi jinrong wenti de jingguo' ['Gu Yiqun's Report of the Tour to Europe for Investigation of the Monetary Systems and Finance Problems in Various Countries'], in *Zhonghua Minguoshi dang'an ziliao huibian. Di wu ji di yi bian. Caizheng jingji (Wu)* [*Collection of Archival materials on the History of the Republic of China, vol. 5, collection 1, Finance and economy (5)*], Nanjing: Jiangsu guji chubanshe [Jiangsu Ancient Books Publishing House]: 310–12.
Hayek, Friedrich A. (ed.) (1935) *Collectivist Economic Planning: Critical Studies on the Possibilities of Socialism*, London: Routledge & Kegan Paul.
Lau, D.C. (translator) (1989) *Tao Te Ching – Chinese Classics*, 2nd edn, Hong Kong: Chinese University Press.

84 *Olga Borokh*

List, Friedrich ([1841] 1909) *The National System of Political Economy*, trans. Sampson S. Lloyd, with an Introduction by J. Shield Nicholson, London: Longmans, Green and Co.

Liu, Junning (1998) 'Beida chuantong yu jindai Zhongguo de ziyouzhuyi' ['Traditions of Peking University and Liberalism in Modern China'], in Liu Junning (ed.), *Beida chuantong yu jindai Zhongguo – ziyouzhuyi de xian sheng* [*Traditions of Peking University and Modern China – Harbingers of liberalism*], Beijing: Zhongguo renshi chubanshe [China Personnel Publishing House].

Lyons, Eugene (1935) 'The Customer Is Always Wrong', *The American Mercury*, July: 301–9.

Masson-Oursel, Paul and Kia-Kien Tchou (1914) 'Yin Wen-tseu', *T'oung pao*. Second Series, Vol. XV, No. 5. Leiden: E.J. Brill: 557–622.

Ma, Yinchu (1924) 'Makesi xueshuo yu Lishite xueshuo erzhe shu yi yu Zhongguo' ['Which of Two Teachings – Marx's or List's – is Suitable for China?'], in *Ma Yinchu yanjiangji* [*Collection of lectures of Ma Yinchu*], Shanghai: Shangwu yinshuguan [The Commercial Press]: 220–29.

——(1935) *Zhongguo jingji gaizao* [*Transformation of the Chinese Economy*], Shanghai: Shangwu yinshuguan [The Commercial Press].

——([1947] 1999) 'Zhongguo jingji zhi lu' ['The Path of the Chinese Economy'], in *Ma Yinchu quanji. Di 12 juan* [*The Complete Works of Ma Yinchu*, vol. 12], Hangzhou: Zhejiang renmin chubanshe [Zhejiang People's Publishing House]: 455–62.

Robbins, Lionel ([1934] 2007) *The Great Depression*, Auburn, AL: Ludwig von Mises Institute.

Smith, Adam ([1776] 1904) *An Inquiry into the Nature and Causes of the Wealth of Nations*, 5th edition, London: Methuen & Co., Ltd.

Smith, James Gerald (1934) *Economic Planning and the Tariff: An Essay on Social Philosophy*, Princeton: Princeton University Press.

Sun, Daquan (2006) *Zhongguo jingjixue de chengzhang – Zhongguo jingji xueshe yanjiu (1923–1953)* [*Growth of Chinese Economics – Research of the Chinese Economic Society (1923–1953)*], Shanghai: Shanghai sanlian shudian [Shanghai Joint Publishing Company].

——(2010) 'Tang Qingzeng jingji sixiang yanjiu' ['A Study of Tang Qingzeng's Economic Ideas'], in *Di shisi jie Zhongguo jingji sixiangshi nianhui lunwenji* [*Collection of Papers of the 14th Annual Conference of Society for Chinese History of Economic Thought*], Wuhan: Zhongnan University of Economics and Law: 137–53.

Tang, Qingzeng (1931) 'Makesi jingji sixiang yu Zhongguo' ['Economic thought of Marx and China'], *Jingjixue jikan* [*Quarterly Journal of Economics*], 2.4: 14–23.

——(1932) 'Jingjixue yu xiandai wenming' ['Economic science and Modern Civilization'], *Jingjixue jikan* [*Quarterly Journal of Economics*], 3.3: 241–54.

——(1933a) *Jingjixue gailun* [*Introduction to Economics*], Shanghai: Shijie shuju [World Book Store].

——(1933b) 'Zhongguo shengchan zhi xiandaihua ying cai gerenzhuyi' ['Modernization of Production in China Should Use Individualism'], *Shenbao yuekan* [*Shenbao Monthly*], 2.7: 59–62.

——(1936a) 'Cong lishi shang yi guancha wo guo jinhou ying cai zhi jingji zhengce' ['Observing from the point of view of history which economic policy should be carried out in our country'], *Jingjixue jikan* [*Quarterly Journal of Economics*], 7.1: 173–78.

——(1936b) *Zhongguo jingji sixiang shi. Shang juan* [*History of Chinese Economic Thought*, vol. 1], Shanghai: Shangwu yinshuguan [The Commercial Press].

Taussig, Frank William ([1911] 2013) *Principles of Economics*, vol. 2, New York: Cosimo Classics.

Xu, Jilin (2014) 'Zai ziyou yu gongzheng zhijian: shehui minzhuzhuyi zai Zhongguo' ['Between Liberty and Justice: Social Democracy in China'], in Xu Jilin (ed.), *Xiandai Zhongguo sixiangshi lun. Di er juan* [*History of Modern Chinese Thought*, vol. 2], Shanghai: Shanghai renmin chubanshe [Shanghai People's Publishing House]: 753–75.

Yin Wenzi quanyi [Full translation (into vernacular Chinese) of *Yin Wenzi*] (1996), in *Shenzi, Yin Wenzi, Gongsun Lunzi quanyi* [*Full translation (into vernacular Chinese) of Shenzi, Yin Wenzi, Gongsun Lunzi*], Guiyang: Guizhou renmin chubanshe [Guizhou People's Publishing House]: 101–67.

Zhang, Naiqi ([1935] 1997) 'Jingji lunzheng zhong de liang tiao luxian' ['Two lines in economic debates'], in *Zhang Naiqi wenji. Shang juan* [*The Works of Zhang Naiqi*, vol. 1], Beijing: Huaxia chubanshe [Huaxia Publishing House]: 239–51.

Zhong, Xiangcai (2007) 'Lun Zhongguo lishi shang de jingji ziyou sixiang' ['On the Ideas of Economic Liberty in Chinese History'], in Gu Hailiang, Yan Pengfei (eds.), *Jingji sixiangshi pinglun. Di er ji* [*Review of History of Economic Thought*, vol. 2], Beijing: Jingji kexue chubanshe [Economic Science Press]: 221–36.

5 Modernization theory, Chinese modernization and social ethics

Jean-Sébastien Gharbi

Introduction

The expression "modernization theory" (MT) refers to the tradition of theoretical and empirical studies into how and why countries modernize. Since the modernization process is as complex as societies themselves are, this tradition of thought is not exclusively economic but deals also with history, and the social and political sciences. Nevertheless, economic aspects are crucial in MT insofar as it can be broadly summarized, at first glance, as advocating the idea that the economic development of a country leads it to adopt (Western) democracy, with the development of a market economy as a side-effect.

Since the first contributions to this field (Rostow 1959; Lipset 1959; Huntington 1968), MT gave rise to strong criticism targeting its neglect of different aspects as well as many of its ideological presumptions. Despite the merits of much of this criticism, the MT research program not only survived a temporary loss of influence, but it also enjoyed a strong revival in the 1990s, becoming the dominant theory of social evolution. This revival was linked to what Huntington called the "third wave of democratization" (Huntington 1991),[1] that is to say the remarkable progress towards democracy that took place between the 1970s and the 1990s all around the world. Indeed, between 1972 and 1994, "the number of democratic political system [had] more than doubled, from 44 to 107. Of the 187 countries in the world [in 1994], over half (58 percent) [had] adopted democratic government" (Shin 1994: 136).

MT is used not only in a descriptive way, that is, to explain *a posteriori* what happened. MT proponents also claim that "socioeconomic development brings roughly predictable cultural changes – and beyond a certain point, these changes make democracy increasingly likely to emerge where it does not yet exist and to become stronger and more direct where it already exists" (Inglehart and Welzel 2005: 15). In other words, MT also pretends to have a prospective use.

This pretension to be able to predict the evolution of countries is of particular interest for a study of liberalism in between Europe and China,[2] because it directly asks the question whether Chinese economic growth will automatically, within any foreseeable future, lead China to adopt (a Western version of) democracy. It is worth making clear that questioning such a claim as to whether it provides elements to anticipate China's evolution is not tantamount to extrapolating theoretical accounts, and Inglehart and Welzel say with confidence the following:

> If [Chinese] socioeconomic development continues at the current pace (as it shows every sign of doing) [...] we predict that China's socioeconomic liberalization process and its experimentation with local-level democracy will spill over to the national level so that China will make a transition to a liberal democracy within the next two decades.
>
> (Inglehart and Welzel 2005: 190–191)

Therefore, this chapter does not intend either to discuss China's evolution or to adjudicate whether it may become democratic in a Western way (or not), but to focus on the relevance of MT when used in order to predict the evolution of societies – and the evolution of Chinese society in particular, with regard to the Chinese economic development and the values underlying it above all. With some historical depth, reminders of the Chinese background and a retrospective outlook, we may learn much about the pretension of Inglehart and Welzel to be able to predict China's evolution. Therefore, this chapter consists in a (somewhat historical and) *methodological* debate on the possible uses of MT from a perspective of economic philosophy. The point made here is that MT proponents implicitly assume, sometimes contrary to their explicit claims, that *social ethics* that exists in a given society either does not strongly depend on past traditions of thought, or that any further link with such traditions is not of any importance. Consequently, MT implies that upholding "worldviews" commonly shared in a society can in some way rather quickly change. According to the present study, these two cases neglect the importance of social ethics in any possible foresight of economic and/or political change.

The remainder of this chapter is organized as follows. The first section presents in more detail the historical development of MT. The criticism addressed to the first generation of MT is made clear, as well as how it led to adjustments and revisions that form contemporary MT. The second section deals with Chinese societal philosophy, regarding economics and social ethics, with special attention being paid to Confucianism – along with specific reasons for such a choice of focus. The final section provides an assessment of the prospective use of MT in the Chinese case.

Modernization theory

In this section, after summarizing the first MT contributions, such as the seminal works of Rostow (1959), Lipset (1959), and Huntington (1968), it will be necessary to provide an overview of the criticisms that have been addressed to what is considered as the first generation of MT. It is worth noting that a large part of these criticisms were accepted and taken as contributions to MT. This section ends by discussing more recent MT claims, and by highlighting that its research program is similar to that of its founders.

The first contributions to modernization theory

The first contributions to modernization theory can be dated back to the 1950s. In 1959, for instance, Rostow advocated the idea that economic growth leads any country from a form of so-called "traditional society" to a modern one. In other words, according to Rostow, economic development literally "drive[s] [countries] to maturity" (Rostow 1959: 8). Thus, Rostow opposes modernity and tradition and considers that the goal of the modernization process is to break away from traditional dimensions of earlier societies, in order to reach the situation of a society of high mass consumption. One of Rostow's aims in his seminal paper was to contrast the American conception of what modernity is (and what it should be) with the Marxist one. Indeed, the latter pretended to be an alternative to the American worldview as Marxism pretended to provide a consistent, full-fledged theory of modernization.

Later on, in his two books (1960, 1971), Rostow extended the position of his important paper and the "stages of economic growth" got explicitly linked with the issue of political systems, particularly with democracy. It is worth mentioning that the term "democracy" does not appear whatsoever in his 1959 paper. It is only in his extended and more developed position presented in the two books that Rostow (1960, 1971) understands democracy as the final step of modernization for a country.

The position of another pioneer of MT, Huntington, as expressed first in 1968, is theoretically related with that of Rostow. For example, Huntington also considers that modernization leads countries from a traditional stage of society to a modern one (in which the weight and the importance of traditions are reduced almost completely to trifles). Huntington argues that social mobilization and economic development (two aspects that are, according to him, strongly interdependent) are the building blocks of modernization, thus also being its requirements. The modernization process is depicted by Huntington as progressive, inescapable, linear, homogenizing, and irreversible (Huntington 1968). As Rostow did a decade earlier, Huntington holds that democratization is an essential part of the modernization process, and, so to speak, its final product.

Without denying the importance of Rostow's and Huntington's contributions to the first generation of MT, it is the essay by Lipset "Some Social Requisites of Democracy" (Lipset 1959) that probably had been the most influential contribution to this field of research, and the first attempt to establish on an empirical basis a relationship between the level of a country's economic development and the probability of this country becoming democratic: "the more well to-do a nation, the greater the chances that it will sustain democracy" (Lipset 1959: 75).

While Lipset's contribution is often laid on the same shelf along with Rostow and Huntington, his essay was much more carefully crafted and brought qualifications in many crucial regards. First, according to Lipset, annual per capita income is taken as the main index for economic development, instead of being considered as its strict equivalent. As Wucherpfennig and Deutsch mention, Lipset does not intend to isolate wealth as the only variable for explaining democratization, but he rather identifies several social requisites of the democratic system, among which wealth stands along with education, industrialization and urbanization (a list that Lipset does not present as being exhaustive) (Wucherpfennig and Deutsch 2009: 2). Second, by calling these four aspects "requisites" and not "*pre*-requisites", Lipset refuses to advocate that there is a well-established causal relationship between these requisites and democracy, and he only talks about a *correlation* between them.

Although this text by Lipset in 1959 is mostly remembered for its first part, dedicated to democratic transition, namely to the question of testing the hypothesis that "democracy is related to the state of economic development" (Lipset 1959: 75), the second part is equally important. It deals with the question of democratic stability, arguing that "the stability of a given democratic system depends not only on the system's efficiency in modernization, but also upon the effectiveness and legitimacy of the political system" (Lipset 1959: 86). In a nutshell, Lipset was not only interested with the link between *social* requisites and the shift to democracy, but also with the issue of how these requisites play a role in political *stability*. Lipset strongly insists on the fact that the historical characteristics of Western development are of a unique type, and that societal factors are extremely important in developing democracy. He also emphasizes that the creation of cross-cutting cleavages in a society is much more important for democratization than economic development itself, and that there are different versions of democracy and varying developmental routes to reach them.

In other words, economics is a key issue, but it cannot be regarded as the only determinant. Modernization is not only an economic process, it is a social and economic process that involves far more than the study of per capita income. This conclusion that could be regarded as strictly common sense in fact stems from the analysis of empirical data about democratization. So, although Lipset comes to an agreement with common sense, his position cannot be reduced to it. Lipset ended his seminal paper with the following words:

> This conclusion does not justify the optimistic liberal's hope that an increase in wealth, in the size of the middle class, in education, and other related factors will necessarily mean the spread of democracy or the stabilizing of democracy.
>
> (Lipset 1959: 103)

Such a statement is quite far from some caricatural accounts of MT grounding works. Indeed, one can see that, contrary to Rostow in 1960 or Huntington in 1968, already in 1959, Lipset did not advocate the idea of some linear, universal, and necessary process that would inevitably link economic development with democratization.

Before delving into the criticisms made against the first generation of MT, one point needs to be stressed: according to the proponents of the first generation of MT, modernization cannot go on *without* some correlative shift in the market economy. In other words, although MT focuses on the link between economic development and democratization, "marketization" is considered as necessarily embedded in the process of modernization, an aspect sometimes made straightforwardly explicit. Interestingly, Rostow's 1971 book subtitle (*A Non-Communist Manifesto*) suggested that it should be read also as advocating *economic liberalism*, not just political liberalism and democratization.

Criticism of the first generation of modernization theory

To provide here a full and detailed presentation of all criticisms made against the first generation of MT works is a task that falls well beyond the scope of this chapter. For the purposes of the argument developed here, I shall limit myself to a general account of the main counterarguments to MT.

First, the "traditional *vs.* modern" dichotomy is biased, since the former is defined from the outset in negative terms with regard to modernity. This leads to the inability to take any serious account of differences existing between societies that are of this residual category, namely the "traditional" type (Bernstein 1971: 146). Moreover, this analytical hypothesis does not come from the empirical works on which MT is supposed to be based. Second, by considering that the experience of Western countries provides the model of what a modern society is (and since this is assumed to be unique and unified), then MT proponents indisputably make the ethnocentric assumption that amounts to assuming that modernization is nothing else but Westernization (Bernstein 1971: 147). The third point of criticism, which is also a consequence of the previous one, is the teleological aspect of MT. Indeed, the final step of any modernization process is considered as given, and as being completely exogenous to the process itself. Last, but not least, MT fails to address crucial aspects of the evolution of societies, such as uneven income distribution or public health.

All these criticisms stem from a theoretical point of view, but MT was also discussed on empirical grounds. For example, a study by O'Donnell looked into the consequences of development, mainly in Latin America countries, dealing with the question of the breakdown of democracies (O'Donnell 1973). O'Donnell set forth the thesis that, in the 1960s, in this area of the world, industrialization and subsequent economic development did not only fail to generate democracy, but also gave rise to a new form of authoritarianism, which he called "bureaucratic authoritarianism".

Many of these criticisms target mainly a less subtle version of MT and Lipset would probably have agreed with all of them as echoing his own precautions and reservations. But even Lipset's own account of MT is not immune to criticism. For example, Rustow points out that, in his 1959 essay, Lipset often "slips from the language of correlation into causality" (Rustow 1970: 342), which seems to imply that correlations ensure the chance of some causal connection, here leading from modernization to democratization.

Przeworski, with Limongi in 1997 and with others in 2000, followed the idea that Lipset's seminal study fails to establish *more* than a correlation between economic development and democratization, and that it is necessary to ask whether development leads to democracy, what can be called "endogenous democratization" (Przeworski et al. 2000), or if development only *helps* to maintain democracy (in other words, if this is some kind of "exogenous democratization"). After having analyzed a large dataset of time-series from 1950 to 1990, Przeworski and Limongi (1997) and Przeworski et al. (2000) claimed that modernization (that is to say, here, the increase of annual per capita income) has little influence on whether a government becomes democratic. Although they agree with Lipset that an increased annual income per capita results in an increased likelihood of sustaining democracy (independently of the educational level or of the existence of democratic history), this conclusion challenges one of the grounding hypotheses of MT:

> This is therefore no longer a modernization theory, since the emergence of democracy is not brought about by development. Rather, democracy appears exogenously as a deus ex machina. It survives if a country is "modern," but it is not a product of "modernization."
>
> (Przeworski and Limongi 1997: 159)

Recent modernization theory

Recent modernization theory brings forth debates and criticisms different from those of the first generation of MT, which led to its revisions and adjustments which, in turn, incidentally, deeply resemble Lipset's research program from 1959 on (along with his reservations and precautions). MT scholars focused their efforts on clarifying how and why each aspect of economic development is linked with the evolution of a political system. Far from contributing to the abandonment of MT, the works by Przeworski and Limongi in 1997 and again in 2000 (Przeworski et al. 2000) can finally be interpreted as a *confirmation* of MT in a sense: "Przeworski and Limongi interpret their findings as a challenge to modernization theory, though it seems to me a revisionist confirmation – in fact, the strongest empirical confirmation ever" (Geddes 1999: 117; Acemoglu and Robinson 2005; Wucherpfennig and Deutsch 2009).

Boix and Stokes (2003) challenge the refutation of endogenous democratization by Przeworski and Limongi (1997) and Przeworski et al. (2000) on both theoretical and empirical grounds. On theoretical grounds, they argue that the conceptual distinction between endogenous and exogenous democratization is not convincing without a theory that links development with democracy only in a context of preexisting democracy. Such a theory is lacking, even in Przeworski et al. (2000). On empirical grounds, they argue that the conclusions by Przeworski and his affiliates rely, to a great extent, on the fact that the probability of a non-democratic system turning democratic does not monotonically increase with the rise of income. Boix and Stokes did indeed reanalyze the dataset by Przeworski et al. (time series from 1950 to 1990) and they even extended the series (going then from 1850 to 1950). They concluded that economic development has a strong endogenous effect on democratization.

In 2005, Inglehart and Welzel used data from Przeworski and Limongi (1997) and Przeworski et al. (2000) and calculated the ratio of shifts from an authoritarian regime to democracy, and the ratio of shifts from democracy to an authoritarian regime. They argued that the distinction between endogenous and exogenous democratization, which was so crucial to Przeworski and his colleagues, did not take into account the possible stability of regimes (depending on the annual income per capita). Inglehart and Welzel showed that the ratio of regimes shifting to democracy increases exponentially as the annual income per capita increases, which led them to conclude that modernization increases the probability of transitions to democracy, that is to say that MT's central hypothesis is getting confirmed by data gathered from Przeworski and his affiliates.

Epstein et al. (2006) provided another reappraisal of the central counter-argument by Przeworski and Limongi (1997) and Przeworski et al. (in 2000) against MT, while using once again their data: Epstein and his colleagues claimed that Przeworski and his co-authors failed to correctly estimate the standard of error in the model and that this is what led them to underestimate the impact of per capita GDP on democratization. In other words, Epstein concluded that the model and data of Przeworski in fact *do* confirm the central insight of MT (Epstein et al. 2006).

All recent contributions to MT thus also take account of the theoretical criticism of the first generation of MT. For instance, Inglehart and Welzel proffered a revised theory of modernization (Inglehart and Welzel 2005: ch. 1), which asserts, contrary to earlier versions of MT, the following points:

> The process [of modernization] is not deterministic [...]
> Religion and other aspects of a society's traditional cultural heritage are not
>   dying out and will not disappear with modernization [...]
> Cultural modernization is not irreversible [...]
> The process of cultural change is not linear [...]
> Modernization is not Westernization.
>
> (Inglehart and Welzel 2005: 46–47)

Nevertheless, according to this revised version of MT, effective "socioeconomic development is conducive to self-expression values" (Inglehart and Welzel 2005: 45). In other words, the rise of individual autonomy and values is integrally part and parcel of the modernization process. This is important insofar as it stresses that the most recent versions of MT do not abandon the idea that, as a matter of fact and as a side-effect, modernization also leads to the adoption of individualistic values and, consequently, to full market economy.

China and social ethics: the example of Confucianism

When speaking about social choice and the evolution of societies, it is important to address the question of social ethics as the background upon which agents thrive and upon which economic activities of all sorts are managed. That is why this second section is dedicated to social ethics. As the aim of this chapter is to assess the ambition of MT, and especially of the version proposed by Inglehart and Welzel, to predict China's evolution, we now pay attention to Chinese social ethics in particular.

First, when displaying what social ethics is, one has to stress the importance of history and traditions of thought in this field, to highlight that social ethics usually changes slowly and that it is submitted to a kind of path dependency. This is why it then seems unavoidable to focus especially on Confucianism among a wealth of Chinese traditions of thought, numerous and rich. In this perspective, one must also explain what to refer to when using the term "Confucianism". Finally a brief account of some Confucian claims relevant in terms of social ethics.

Social ethics and schools of thought

"Social ethics" can be defined as a set of values widely shared in a society. Of course, ethics may be said always to be "social" in some sense, since ethics is about *others*, about shared norms of behavior, and behaviors assessment. Nevertheless, it would be misleading to think that adding the word "social" to "ethics" is just a redundancy. Indeed, a contemporary society is never homogeneous in terms of an ethical system of judgment and evaluation. Rather, it is always made up of several groups with different representations of ethical norms. In other words, diverse ethical codes coexist and are not completely compatible with each other. In such a morally pluralistic society, the idea of social ethics does not refer to a complete system of ethics shared by everybody, as such a shared system does not exist, but rather to the set of values that is widely accepted or known as accepted in a given society. In a society that is "morally pluralistic", the set of widely shared values is incomplete: it is not a full system of morals. Each and every society has rules that everybody within it is expected to follow (even if not everyone thinks that such rules are constitutive of societal bonds, and even though some individuals personally do not adhere to values underlying these rules).[3]

Social ethics is made up of many factors, among which influential schools of thought are particularly significant. By "school of thought" is meant here a kind of intellectual tradition, which can be of philosophical or religious origin.[4] What makes a school of thought considered as significant in the history of a given society is precisely its influence on the way in which people in this society think and assess good or bad. Sometimes the influence of such a school of thought is reflected in some part of the law of the country. In other words, what makes a school of thought important is its impact on social ethics. Nevertheless, it is worth noting that the causality between schools of thought and social ethics does not go in one direction only. Indeed, schools of thought do not appear spontaneously: they stand in continuity with their time and culture – consequently, with social ethics.

Such a description could suggest that social ethics does not evolve at all – but this would be a wrong inference. Indeed, schools of thought are rather part of a dialectical relationship with the part of that country-specific culture which is a component of social ethics. This dialectical relationship implies that social ethics can change, but that it happens at a slow pace. On this point, it is noteworthy that when Inglehart and Welzel speak of changes in cultural values, they say that even when some changes may seem sudden and lumpy, they always reflect a long process of incremental value change (Inglehart and Welzel 2005: 39).

About Confucianism

Before going further, two questions need to be answered: (1) Why focus mostly on the sole issue of Confucianism while Chinese traditions of thought are both numerous and extremely rich? (2) What does one refer to when using the term "Confucianism"? In other words: *why Confucianism and which Confucianism?*

The first question is inescapable since Confucianism is only a part of the history of Chinese philosophy (Mou 2009; Lai 2008). Yet, the renewed interest in Confucianism in contemporary China at the beginning of the twenty-first century appears obvious and is indisputable. This movement, sometimes called a "Confucianist revival", aims to navigate between tradition and modernity in order to define China's cultural and political contemporary identity (Worsman 2012).

Therefore, it makes sense to pay special attention to Confucianism when discussing possible directions for the near past, present, and near future development of China. Furthermore, since the aim of this chapter is to discuss the pretension of Inglehart and Welzel to be able to predict China's evolution, and since the position advocated by Inglehart and Welzel is a specific version of MT, it is only natural to recall that the MT literature describes China as being generally "Confucian" (Huntington 1984: 208; Lipset 1994: 5). This Confucian characterization of China is also particularly blatant in the work by Inglehart and Welzel (Inglehart and Welzel 2005: ch. 3), although they naturally also mention the influence of Marxism/communism (Inglehart and Welzel 2005: 64). Consequently, focusing on Confucianism does not stem from any personal (and rather disputable) assumption that Confucianism exhausts Chinese cultural and political identity and social ethics.[5]

When used with no further specification, the term "Confucianism" refers to a very long tradition of thought that has been interpreted differently in different times and contexts. Different kinds of Confucianism, Neo-Confucianism, and, so to speak, "Neo-Neo-Confucianism" (that is to say contemporary Confucianism) have been developed over centuries and their consistency with each other is not complete (otherwise there would not be different versions of Confucianism anyhow).

Furthermore, since Confucianism rejects essentialism (Ames 2010: 67, 83 especially note 1), redefining Confucianism for each period seems to be constitutive of Confucianism of each period in time (Ames 2010). Daniel A. Bell, to whom I shall also refer here, is a contemporary proponent of Confucianism (Bell 2008a, 2008b; Bell 1995: 20).[6] Following in this regard the approach adopted by Bell in his paper dedicated to property rights in a Confucian perspective (Bell 2003: 220–221), the brief presentation that follows means only to focus on the two "founding fathers" of Confucianism, namely Confucius and Mencius. The former is "the first teacher of China" in his main text, reprinted over centuries, *The Analects* (Confucius 2003), where his teachings are gathered in the form of aphorisms compiled by his disciples, years after his death. The latter, Mencius, is known as the second most important figure in the Confucian tradition because he systematized the master's ideas, and reprints have stimulated comments for centuries as well (Mencius 1984). Naturally, Confucianism cannot (or should not) be reduced to references to Confucius and Mencius, but this has the twofold advantage of providing some easy identification basis acceptable to any Confucian.[7]

Important Confucian claims in Chinese social ethics

Now, as far as MT is concerned with some important Confucian claims, this is due to social ethics as a background, in particular as the background of economic behavior. That is precisely why it is of particular interest to pay attention to the three following Confucian claims in order to discuss the relevance of Inglehart and Welzel's prediction about China's future.[8]

The first one is about *material value*, that is to say, social welfare. In Confucianism, it falls to the government to provide good governance and, as a matter of moral duty, this includes a minimal level of welfare to everyone. The first function of the government is to ensure that everybody in need will receive help. This claim does not imply that people could, even less should, rely only on the government's charity and help. In order to explain how the assistance system is seen in Confucianism, Chan suggests we understand it as a "multilayer system" (Chan 2003: 236) in which family comes first, then the social network or community comes second (in case of family failure, for instance), and finally, the state comes third, as a kind of last-resort assistance. If someone is unable to help him/herself, has no family and no social network that can help (in other words, if someone is part of the "worst off" among the deprived people), then it is the moral duty of the government to provide him/her with a minimal level of welfare. The fact that the assistance provided by the government comes only as the solution of last resort does not reduce its imperative dimension.

This is where Confucian texts come in: according to Mencius, poverty is always the result of some political misrule (for instance, heavy taxation). If the government does correctly what governments have to do, then the people will be able to ensure their livelihood and to help their relatives in need and, next, their friends or neighbors in need. Consequently, the duty of the government to help people in need should not be a heavy burden, except if they fail to provide the largest part of the population with conditions in which people can ensure their own living as well as the living of their relatives (if necessary). In this latter case, the government would fail to fulfil their role.

Three remarks are in order here: (1) Saying that ensuring social welfare is the first task assigned to the government means that if it is necessary to choose between social welfare and anything else (education, individuals rights, etc.), social welfare will have primacy. (2) It does not mean that social welfare is a goal in itself (like, say, in an endless race for wealth): reaching a minimal level of welfare is necessary just as a means to be educated, and to develop the moral nature of the people. (3) The duty (of the family, the community and the government, taken in this order) to help the people in need should be understood as follows: that the people have a "right to food" (Bell 2003: 227, note 28). Children have a right to receive care from their parents, and parents have a right to be cared for by their children once they have become adults.

A second major point in Confucian social ethics has to do with property. In Confucian ethics, and in traditional China in general (Schurmann 1959), property is not private and individual, it is a family thing. This sheds light on the Confucian requirement according to which a son has the responsibility to pay for his father's misdeeds, and similarly, the father has to pay for his son's wrongdoings: "Fathers cover up for their sons, and sons cover up for their fathers. 'Uprightness' is to be found in this" (Confucius 2003: 13.18). Bell explains that Confucianism defends a system of values that sets constraints on private property rights and, consequently, sets limits on the extent of the *possible* outreach of any market economy realm (Bell 2003).

Confucianism is opposed to heavy-handed governmental control of the economic realm, namely to a high level of taxation (Confucius 2003: 12.9) and Confucian scholars assert that government should not fix the price of goods which are exchanged on the market (Mencius 1984: 3A.4). Starting from these two points, it could seemingly be tempting to conclude that Confucianism advocates for a very *liberal* position, and that it is strongly in favor of what could be called "a *full-fledged* market economy". Nevertheless, according to Bell, the Confucian representation of property has (at least) two significant limits which keep it far from the perspective of a full market economy (Bell 2003). First, the overriding value of *material* welfare (mentioned above) encompasses the fact that the state has to control the distribution of land and even its use (Mencius 1984: 3A.3). Second, another constraint falls on property rights. It originates from obligations that individuals have to each other within the family. This second point can be seen as a consequence of the family–property conception, yet it also comes from the very status that Confucianism gives to the family structure.[9]

The third aspect of Confucian social ethics in focus here pertains precisely to the importance of the family. In Confucianism, family is crucial insofar as it is the space in which one learns virtue: filial piety is at the core of all concepts of Confucian ethics. Filial piety is defined as gratitude toward parents for nurturing, instructing and loving. As already mentioned, within the family, productive adults have to take care of their family members in need. This duty is even stronger for elderly parents. Filial piety requires more than providing to elderly parents material comfort, it is about serving them, and serving them even if it means sacrificing one's own interest. In case of conflict, filial piety should have priority over any other duty, as for instance caring of wife and children (Bell 2003: 230), public duties or even the obligation to follow the law (Bell 1995: 23–24).[10]

Family is the first school of virtue in Confucianism (chronologically and in terms of importance), because filial piety is the utmost virtue and the source of all other virtues that can be applied in everyday life. Experiencing filial piety leads to learning responsibility and self-sacrificing love, and is "the essential way of learning to be human" (Tu 1989: 13, quoted in Bell 1995: 22). This understanding allows us to grasp another important point, which is that the proper behavior within the family is important not only in terms of ethics (that is within the moral sphere), but also in terms of politics. There is a continuity between what could be called the "private sector" and the "public sector", and there is no difference of nature between moral and politics: "In being a filial son and a good brother, one is already taking part in government" (Confucius 2003: 2.21 and Confucius 2003: 1.2 and 8.2).

Can modernization theory predict China's evolution?

In order to discuss Inglehart and Welzel's aspiration when they conceive of China's historical evolution for the coming years, one needs to clarify the scope of the conclusions they reach. Arguing against Inglehart and Welzel's pretension to be able to predict China's evolution does amount neither to rejecting the idea that China could soon become democratic, nor to advocating that very same idea. That is why it is important to stress that the goal of this last section is not to guess whether China will become democratic or not, but only to discuss the reasons that underlie the prediction of Inglehart and Welzel about China's evolution: the aim of the following pages is therefore to assess if this prediction is *theoretically* well- or ill-based.

Inglehart and Welzel share a position on the persistence of cultural traditions that deserves to be presented more in detail. On this occasion, emphasis must be put on the fact that their work results from their effort to take into account the impact of traditions and social ethics on the (possible) political change. Then, two different kinds of arguments must be displayed in this section, against Inglehart and Welzel and their contention about the predictability of China's future. On factual grounds, any possibility that China becomes democratic must be referred to Chinese social ethics and Confucian heritage. On methodological grounds, it can be argued that the theory of Inglehart and Welzel confuses what happened with what had to happen. This naturally does not disqualify all uses of MT, but limits the argument to its worth at the predictive level, while acknowledging that retrospective and factual uses are of interest as a basis for informed discussion, and lead to a better understanding of what has happened in the past, and why.

The revised modernization theory of Inglehart and Welzel

As MT has been challenged for taking no account (or at least, no sufficient account) of cultural and traditional aspects, it is worth mentioning that Inglehart and Welzel dedicate a full chapter to the question of the "value change and the persistence of cultural traditions" in their (Inglehart and Welzel 2005: ch. 2). To date, Inglehart and Welzel "provide what is perhaps the most comprehensive framework by linking socio-economic development and cultural prerequisites for democracy" (Wucherpfennig and Deutsch 2009: 5). Moreover, as mentioned at the end of the first section, their revised version of MT aspires to break with the weaknesses of classical versions of this theoretical tradition.

Inglehart and Welzel conduct an analysis of the evidence for which cultural change is displayed, based on Values Surveys, and this is arguably

> the largest investigation ever made of attitudes, values, and beliefs around the world. These surveys have carried out four waves of representative national surveys, in 1981–3, 1989–91, 1995–97, and 1999–2001. They cover 81 societies on all six inhabited continents, containing more than 85 percent of the world's population.
>
> (Inglehart and Welzel 2005: 48)

Their objective is to show not only that socioeconomic development causes changes in values, but also that these value-changes are oriented towards specifiable directions, and thus, they are predictable. In other words, they attempt to identify the dimensions of cross-national polarization in terms of political, social, and religious norms, values and beliefs on which people of economically rich countries differ from those of low-income countries. On the basis of their results of the econometric analysis of the World Values Surveys, Inglehart and Welzel identify two dimensions of values that are modified along with the modernization process: the "*traditional* versus *secular-rational* values" and the "*survival* versus *self-expression* values" (Inglehart and Welzel 2005: 49). Clearly, these two dimensions deserve more attention.

The first dimension polarizes the values of traditional societies (associated with low-income societies) and so-called secular-rational societies (which happen to be economically rich countries). Inglehart and Welzel explain that in low-income societies, family is considered as crucial, and divorce is usually rejected (as are abortion, euthanasia, and suicide). Likewise, in traditional societies one finds a high level of national pride, religion is important in people's life, and they respect authority, especially national authority. On the other side of the spectrum of this first dimension, there are exactly the opposite values. Namely, that family is not considered as crucial (divorce is accepted, as abortion, euthanasia and suicide are), the level of national pride is low, religion is usually not considered as important, respect for authority is low (notably regarding national authority). All these "secular-rational values" are characteristic of economically rich societies. Inglehart and Welzel deduce from these results that the traditional versus secular-rational dimension "is associated with the transition from an agrarian to industrial society" (Inglehart and Welzel 2005: 58).

The second dimension puts into contrast so-called "survival values", associated mostly with low-income countries, with "self-expression" values, associated particularly with modern societies. Inglehart and Welzel explain that in societies where there still exists material insecurity, that is to say, in low-income societies, people give importance to "economic and physical security above all; they feel threatened by foreigners, ethnic diversity, and cultural change – which leads to intolerance of gays and other outgroups" (Inglehart and Welzel 2005: 52). Moreover, on the "survival values" side, ordinary people usually do not speak of, or take part in, politics. On the other side of the second dimension, values are strictly opposed (the authors speak of "postmaterialist values") and focus on individual freedom above all, self-expression, subjective well-being, political activism, and tolerance of outgroups. Inglehart and Welzel interpret the survival versus self-expression values dimension as linked to the rise of a postindustrial society and a service economy (Inglehart and Welzel 2005: 58).

The above framework allows Inglehart and Welzel to represent the process of modernization for all the countries they study in a two dimensional-space (see Figure 5.1).

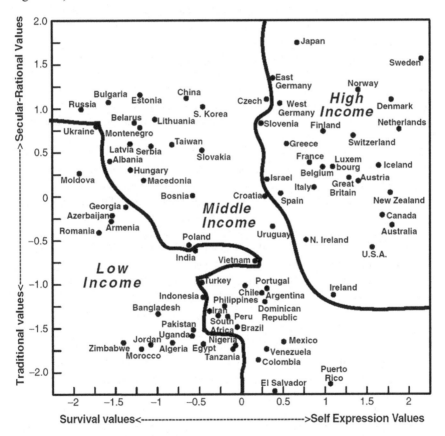

Figure 5.1 Economic levels and locations of eighty societies on a cultural map. Cultural locations reflect each society's factor scores on two major dimensions of cross-cultural variation.

Source: Inglehart and Welzel 2005: 57. Economic zones are from World Bank, *World Development Indicators, 2002.*

According to Inglehart and Welzel, their analytical framework aptly distinguishes two fundamental aspects of modernization and makes it possible to separate elements that were earlier on and until their analysis detrimentally confused with each other.

> Both modernization and a society's cultural tradition shape both secular-rational values and self-expression values, but historical factors have a greater relative impact on secular-rational values, whereas modernization factors have a greater relative impact on self-expression values.
>
> (Inglehart and Welzel 2005: 76)

Besides, distinguishing these two dimensions is supposed to ensure the immunization of the version of MT revised by Inglehart and Welzel against the classical theoretical criticism. For instance, in such a theoretical frame it is not very surprising to see an economically rich country in which social ethics gives an important role to religion. In Inglehart and Welzel's version of MT, the increase of per capita GDP does not necessarily cause the abandonment of traditional features (even if this move is highly probable). Similarly, Inglehart and Welzel hold that their version of MT does not equate modernization with Westernization, the argument being that they do not take the United States (where the importance given to religion and the level of national pride are high) as a model of modernity:

> The United States is not a prototype of cultural modernization for other societies to follow, as some postwar modernization writers assumed. [...] On the traditional/secular dimension, the United States ranks far below other rich societies, with levels of religiosity and national pride comparable with those found in some developing societies. The United States does rank among the most advanced societies on the survival/self-expression dimension, but even here, it does not lead the world. The Swedes, the Dutch, and the Australians are closer to the cutting edge of cultural change than the Americans. Clearly, modernization is not Americanization.
>
> (Inglehart and Welzel 2005: 65)

When Inglehart and Welzel assert that modernization leads to democracy, they are more demanding in that respect than a large part of MT literature ever was. Indeed, Lipset defined democracy very broadly, as follows:

> A political system which supplies regular constitutional opportunities for changing the governing officials. It is a social mechanism for the resolution of the problem of societal decision-making among conflicting interest groups which permits the largest possible part of the population to influence these decisions through their ability to choose among alternative contenders for political office.
>
> (Lipset 1959: 71)

Following Lipset, most MT proponents took "democracy" as meaning "elective democracy". Inglehart and Welzel go further and consider what they call "effective democracy", which is not only an institutional implementation of democracy: in other words, it is not "democratic in name only" as many "illiberal democracies",[11] "deficient democracies" and "low quality democracies" are. – Inglehart and Welzel's "effective democracy" is a political system that concretely protects and promotes the citizens' individual freedom, rights and autonomy (Inglehart and Welzel 2005: 9).

To sum up the version of MT given by Inglehart and Welzel, one should recall that their two-dimensional framework is not arbitrary, and that it does not stem from a pure theoretical analysis, but that it is based on their econometric analysis of four waves of long and detailed questionnaires of World Values Surveys. Second, one must recollect that they proposed a way of understanding socio-economic development that leaves room to social ethics as well as economics, which in turn makes it possible to account for modernization that does not completely break with all the traditional aspects of a society. Yet, despite all the attention paid to cultural aspects in each society, Inglehart and Welzel maintain in the end the following:

> The core of the human development sequence is the expansion of human choice and autonomy. As this aspect of modernization becomes more prominent, it brings cultural changes that make democracy the logical institutional outcome.
>
> (Inglehart and Welzel 2005: 2)

Modernization theory disputed: factual arguments

The way in which Inglehart and Welzel attempt to immunize their revised version of MT against some classical counterarguments formulated against MT remains disputable, and one may question whether their work allows them to predict China's evolution in the very next years.

First, their reply to the criticisms according to which in MT that modernization is only and necessarily Westernization, by saying that the United States is not the paradigmatic example and the one and only model of modernization, but a deviant case (see also Inglehart and Welzel 2005: 47) may seem insufficient. Indeed, knowing whether the United States has strong historical and cultural specificities is not the point here. On the one hand, individualistic values have been largely promoted and exported from the United States all around the world. On the other hand, the United States is obviously not the only representative of Western values. The strong historical link between the United States and Western Europe shows well enough that American individualism has its roots in a Western European tradition.

Also, if one takes into account differences between American social ethics and social ethics in Western Europe, despite the importance and influence of the United States in the contemporary world at the economic and ideological levels, it would be misleading to strictly identify "Westernization" and "Americanization" as Inglehart and Welzel tend to do in order to prevent criticisms of their position. Western European values are also very specific, especially when they are seen from outside the North American and European continents. From this perspective, "from outside", say, what is called "Western values" can be identified with social ethics that contains elements common to American and most European Union countries, with importance given to individual freedom and individual rights of the person as such being main reference values (regardless of whether these values are implemented or not).

This leads to a great challenge to the position presented by Inglehart and Welzel: in the case of Chinese social ethics, these social ethics seems not to be at all in accordance with Western values, especially with the individualistic dimension. For instance, Chinese social ethics, giving great importance to the family (in a different way than it could be given in the West), regards it necessary to make sure that productive people in a family can take care of their relatives in need and, if not, that the state can do that in their place, yet only in the last resort. That is why the Chinese could reject, in the name of such values, a political system if it does not support these points.

In other words, viewing the rise of individualistic values as typical markers of democracy and most likely to be adopted in a society in transition could be understood as a biased view when translated into the Chinese context, since it could be the very reason for China (possibly) *not* to adopt any Western-style democratic regime. Despite the attention given to societal values in their study, Inglehart and Welzel do not assign much weight to this element in the possible political change of a society.

Some Confucian countries (like South Korea and Taiwan) are strongholds of Confucian values and yet are generally said to have become democratic in the last third of the twentieth century. Therefore, the fact that a society is Confucian cannot suggest that it *cannot* become democratic. Taking this aspect into account leads to the question of the (in)dependency (of)/on the political trajectory of countries to their social ethics *vs.* socio-economic path. A fundamental question is whether a country's political trajectory should be considered as completely endogenous or as a partly exogenous variable. This question was already significant in the past, because political changes in Europe in the eighteenth and in the nineteenth centuries were not strictly independent from each other, and it is even more important today, in the age of so-called "globalization". The exogenous influence on the possible democratization process can be negative (as it was the case when the Soviet Union was maintaining Communist regimes in Eastern Europe by threatening to intervene militarily in case of trouble) or positive (which can be illustrated by the example of the United States supporting democratization in the Philippines or in South Korea). Inglehart and Welzel tackle explicitly these two kinds of *active* exogenous influences (Inglehart and Welzel 2005: ch. 9), but they do not address the effect of the impact of intercultural interactions on social ethics (which can be then called "passive influence").

It is difficult to measure the impact of intercultural interactions on social ethics, but it seems highly probable that a small country is more likely to be influenced from outside. The core question here is to determine whether countries strongly influenced by Confucianism that did become democratic are comparable with China. Inglehart and Welzel implicitly assume that the differences between China and other countries with the Confucian tradition are not relevant in such a context, the obvious difference being that China is a huge country with the world's largest population (at least until the 2010s), which may suggest a kind of resistance to outside impacts, along with the following argument: the bigger a country is, the less sensitive it is to external cultural and ideological influences.[12]

Since Inglehart and Welzel accept the idea that "prodemocratic social forces are still relatively weak [in China]" (Inglehart and Welzel 2005: 217), there are consequently only two ways to interpret their prediction about China's evolution. On the one hand, a first interpretation is grounded on the fact that they assume that Chinese social ethics will change endogenously very quickly. On the other hand, the second interpretation is based on the way that they think that Chinese social ethics will change because of influences from the rest of the world. These two possibilities are problematic because they do not fit with the fact that these authors claim that social ethics change is *always* a long process of incremental changes (Inglehart and Welzel 2005: 19).

Modernization theory disputed: methodological arguments

There is yet another argument that allows potential critics to dispute the possibility for Inglehart and Welzel to somehow predict China's evolution in the 2010s and 2020s. Indeed, these two authors assert that the modernization process is not deterministic (Inglehart and Welzel 2005: 46). Nevertheless, they also deduce from their data and from the correlations they find in them that "modernization theory implies that as societies develop economically, their cultures will tend to shift in a predictable direction" (Inglehart and Welzel 2005: 66). The only way to hold consistently these two claims at the same time is to assume that there is no strict determinism, but only a statistical and probabilistic one. In other words, it implies that, as the GDP per capita increases, the probability for a society to shift towards democracy tends toward 1. This interpretation fits their statement according to which "human development [...] makes democracy increasingly likely, where it does not yet exist, and increasingly responsive, where it already exists" (Inglehart and Welzel 2005: 76). As one can see, such a position is a kind of determinism, despite the claim otherwise made. Indeed, there is something paradoxical in the claim that the necessary rise of individual freedom and autonomy (even if this necessity is only statistical) will lead necessarily to the adoption of democracy, with no other possibility. Consequently, Inglehart and Welzel have to face a theoretical dilemma.

The first side of this dilemma consists in solving the tension between necessity and freedom by advocating that socioeconomic development makes it possible for members of a society to choose a political system which is different from, simply put, democracy. Embracing this alternative, however, means accepting the idea that the probability that a country adopts democracy when its GDP per capita increases tends, for instance, "only" to 0.90 or 0.95 (and not towards the full probability of 1). Yet, these figures (0.90 or 0.95) are chosen arbitrarily: let us only stress that if Inglehart and Welzel really think that human development strengthens individual freedom, they would have to abandon such (statistical) determinism, which in turn means that, on the basis of their theory, they cannot predict, but only bet on, the evolution of China.

The second side of this dilemma consists in advocating a position which is not explicitly endorsed by them, namely some "speculative philosophy of history", a position which claims that history has a "meaning" and a "direction". In this perspective, Inglehart and Welzel would need to embrace some strong philosophical assumptions. For instance, they should break with methodological individualism. They should also acknowledge that the work they did in analyzing the World Values Surveys is *not* the basis of their theory, but that their theory is based on some metaphysical understanding of causality and rationality. In other words, they would need to accept the idea that it is not their empirical work that leads them to, notably, predict that China will shift to democracy. Indeed, such a position cannot be deduced from empirical data: empirical inquiries can only highlight patterns but cannot establish that something is necessary. Until someone discovered a black swan, everybody thought that all swans were white...

The dilemma resulting from the tension between necessity and freedom is unavoidable when referring to data because of the already mentioned interdependency of the different countries' political trajectories. Because of this interdependency, even if each and every country in the world were to finally become democratic, it would not be sufficient to establish the case for the necessity of that claim. In other words, it is not because what happened has happened that it was necessary, or even very probable that it had to happen. As a reference to the French poet Mallarmé, one has to acknowledge that "a throw of the dice does not abolish chance". In other words, the fact that you roll a "2" on a six-sided dice does not alter the fact that you might have rolled any other side. Similarly, even if the process of world modernization finally leads to a total shift for democracy, it will not demonstrate that there was no other possible path.

Besides, Inglehart and Welzel work only on interpreting data. It means that there is room for many debates and alternative interpretations. Their narratives are not the one and only one correct. To illustrate this point, it suffices to point out that the answers given to World Values Surveys depend on what people meant when they say "God", with a capital, or "god(s)" without it, "religion", or even "family". On the question of meaning, translation cannot ensure that people around the world understand the same question. Typically, it is rather the contrary that is certain. Inglehart and Welzel interpret and aggregate their results in a short and caricatural story of a society that slowly abandons a large part of its traditional marks as its per capita GDP grows and that self-expression values get developed (Inglehart and Welzel, 2005: 52–54). Such a narrative could seem convincing and may be appealing, but it clearly goes further than what data and results strictly speaking may allow them to properly claim.

Conclusion

Modernization theory is a tradition of studies that addresses fundamental issues regarding the link between socioeconomic development and the nature of the political system adopted in a country. Such a topic is both very appealing and necessarily subject to much debate. Understanding how human societies work remains uneasy and complex. In other words, even when MT fruitfully highlights past events, it is already controversial by nature. It helps us to understand history though, and this is a fruit that is palatable when one does development economics. Where modernization studies are used to predict the evolution of countries, the story is different and MT clearly goes beyond what it can do while being scientific.

Inglehart and Welzel are arguably, as demonstrated in the previous pages, the proponents of the version MT that takes the best and fullest account of social ethics. They base their work on four waves of World Values Survey, which is also the largest investigation on people values and beliefs that has been made around the world. Nevertheless, they still do not give enough importance to social ethics when they aspire to predict the evolution of China towards democracy on the grounds of their work. While they intend to remain scientific, they extrapolate (Inglehart and Welzel 2005: 190–191). This remark leads back to what Lipset said in concluding his seminal paper in 1959, namely that MT studies *cannot* ensure that modernization will necessarily lead all countries to shift for democracy or to stabilize democracy where it already exists (Lipset 1959: 103).

Acknowledgements

This article benefited immensely from encounters and discussions made possible within the LIBEAC program during a research visit of the author at Peking University (Beijing, China), as well as from discussions with researchers who came to Aix-en-Provence. Special thanks are owed to Malgorzata Dereniowska for help in revising this chapter. The final product is the author's own responsibility.

Notes

1 The first wave of democratization identified by Huntington springs from the French and American revolutions and runs until 1926. The second wave is much shorter, running from the end of Second World War to 1962. According to Huntington's reading of the history of democracies, each wave of democratization caused a reverse wave (Huntington 1991: 16–21).
2 That is, within the LIBEAC program, the Marie Curie International Research Staff Exchange Scheme program funded by the European Research Council and coordinated by Gilles Campagnolo.
3 For instance, abortion is considered as ethically inacceptable and shocking in some societies, while it is allowed in some others. Usually, national laws reflect the widely pro- or contra-arguments to reach an agreement within each country. Besides, even if

abortion is considered as morally inacceptable in some specific society, some individuals may not personally share this disapproval. In other words, social ethics is a moral code that defines what is, and what is not, acknowledged as morally acceptable in a society.

4 In this context, determining whether a specific doctrine is philosophical or religious does not matter.
5 About the topic of what Chinese social ethics is and how it is changing, see He's book (He 2015).
6 Daniel A. Bell, the Professor of the Schwarzman Scholars Program at Tsinghua University (Beijing), must not be confused with Daniel Bell, the sociologist who is often presented as one of the proponents of MT (Wucherpfennig and Deutsch 2009: 6).
7 I also follow Bell (2003) in *not* referring to Xunzi, often considered as the third founding father of Confucianism due to the influence he had on the Legalist tradition, the main theoretical rival of Confucianism. On this issue which would take this chapter too far away from MT, see also Liu (1998).
8 This presentation of some Confucian claims is based on Bell (especially 1995 and 2003) and Chan (2003), and relies on their analysis and interpretations.
9 This is precisely where a full-fledged market economy finds strong opposition in the family system, or tends on the contrary to impinge on it, with more or less social disorder, as Chapter 8 in this volume shows.
10 This last aspect is an important point of disagreement between Confucianism and the Chinese Legalist philosophy.
11 Inglehart and Welzel (2005) do not refer here specifically to Daniel A. Bell's position about illiberal democracy, such as in Bell et al. (1995) – this author simply does not appear in their bibliography and when arguments meet, it is coincidentally.
12 Unlike India, the only similar country in terms of population, China has not been colonized by Western countries, which obviously contributed to modify national self-representation and, consequently, social ethics. The issue in China was with the Opium Wars of the nineteenth century and the subsequent Unequal Treaties, enhancing nationalism and the potential thirst for revenge.

References

Acemoglu, D. and J. A. Robinson (2005) *Economic Origins of Dictatorship and Democracy*, Cambridge: Cambridge University Press.
Ames R. T. (2010) 'What is Confucianism?', in W. Chang and L. Kalmanson (eds.), *Confucianism in Context: Classic Philosophy and Contemporary Issues, East Asia and Beyond*, Albany NY: State University of New York Press: 67–85.
Bell, D. A. (1995) 'Democracy in Confucian Societies: The Challenge of Justification', in D. A. Bell, D. Brown, K. Jayasuriya and D. Martin Jones (eds.), *Towards Illiberal Democracy in Pacific Asia*, London: Palgrave Macmillan: 17–40.
——(2003) 'Confucian Constraints on Property Rights', in D. A. Bell and H. Chaibong (eds.), *Confucianism for the Modern World*, Cambridge: Cambridge University Press: 218–35.
——(2008a) *China's New Confucianism: Politics and Everyday Life in a Changing Society*, Princeton: Princeton University Press.
——(ed.) (2008b) *Confucian Political Ethics*, Princeton: Princeton University Press.
Bell, D. A., D. Brown, K. Jayasuriya and D. Martin Jones (eds.) (1995) *Towards Illiberal Democracy in Pacific Asia*, London: Palgrave Macmillan.
Bernstein, H. (1971) 'Modernization Theory and the Sociological Study of Development', *Journal of Development Studies*, 7: 141–60.

Boix, C. and S. Stokes (2003) 'Endogenous Democratization', *World Politics*, 55: 517–49.

Chan, J. (2003) 'Giving Priority to the Worst Off: A Confucian Perspective on Social Welfare', In D. A. Bell and H. Chaibong (eds.), *Confucianism for the Modern World*, Cambridge: Cambridge University Press: 236–53.

Confucius (2003) *Confucius Analects: With Selections from Traditional Commentaries*, trans. E. Slingerland, Indianapolis, IN: Hackett Publishing.

Epstein, D., R. Bates, J. Goldstone, I. Kristensen and S. O'Halloran (2006) 'Democratic Transitions', *American Journal of Political Science*, 50: 551–69.

Geddes, B. (1999) 'What Do We Know About Democratization after Twenty Years?', *Annual Review of Political Science*, 2: 115–44.

He, H. (2015) *Social Ethics in a Changing China: Moral Decay or Ethical Awakening?* Washington DC: Brookings Institution Press.

Huntington, S. P. (1968) *Political Order in Changing Societies*, New Haven: Yale University Press.

——(1984). 'Will More Countries Become Democratic?', *Political Science Quarterly*, 99: 193–218.

——(1991) *The Third Wave: Democratization in the late Twentieth Century*, Norman, OK: University of Oklahoma Press.

Inglehart, R. and C. Welzel (2005) *Modernization, Cultural Change, and Democracy: The Human Development Sequence*, Cambridge: Cambridge University Press.

Lai, K. L. (2008) *An Introduction to Chinese Philosophy*, Cambridge: Cambridge University Press.

Lipset, S. M. (1959). 'Some Social Requisites of Democracy', *American Political Science Review*, 53: 69–105.

——(1994) 'The Social Requisites of Democracy Revisited', *American Sociological Review*, 59: 1–22.

Liu, S-.H. (1998) *Understanding Confucian Philosophy*, Westport, CT: Greenwood.

Mencius (1984) *The Works of Mencius* [Complete translation by D. C. Lau under the title *Mencius*], Hong Kong: Chinese University Press.

Mou, B. (2009) *History of Chinese Philosophy*, New York: Routledge.

O'Donnell, G. A. (1973) *Modernization and Bureaucratic-Authoritarianism*, Berkeley: University of California Press.

Przeworski, A. and F. Limongi (1997) 'Modernization. Theories and Facts', *World Politics*, 49: 155–183.

Przeworski, A., J. A. Cheibub, M. E. Alvarez and F. Limongi (2000) *Democracy and Development: Political Institutions and Material Well-being in the World, 1950–1990*, Cambridge: Cambridge University Press.

Rostow, W. W. (1959) 'The Stages of Economic Growth', *Economic History Review, New Series*, 12: 1–16.

——(1960) *The Stages of Economic Growth: A Non-Communist Manifesto*, Cambridge: Cambridge University Press.

——(1971) *Politics and the Stages of Economic Growth*, Cambridge: Cambridge University Press.

Rustow, D. A. (1970) 'Transitions to Democracy: Toward a Dynamic Model', *Comparative Politics*, 2: 337–63.

Schurmann, H. F. (1956). 'Traditional Property Concepts in China', *Far Eastern Quarterly*, 15: 507–16.

Shin, D. C. (1994) 'On the Third Wave of Democratization', *World Politics*, 47: 135–70.

Tu, W.-M. (1989) *Confucianism in an Historical Perspective*. Institute of East Asian Philosophies (Singapore) Occasional Paper and Monograph Series no. 15.

Worsman, R. (2012) 'Tradition, Modernity, and the Confucian Revival: An Introduction and Literature Review of New Confucian Activism', *History Honors Papers*. Paper 14 (cited 1 September 2015, <http://digitalcommons.conncoll.edu/histhp/14>).

Wucherpfennig J. and F. Deutsch (2009) 'Modernization and Democracy: Theories and Evidence Revisited', *Living Reviews in Democracy* (online journal, accessed September 1, 2015: <https://www.lrd.ethz.ch/index.php/lrd/article/viewArticle/lrd-2009-4>).

Part II

Liberalization and individualization

6 The essence of individuality in Kitarō Nishida's works

A contribution from Eastern Asia to a transcultural understanding of the meaning of individualism

Andrea Altobrando

Introduction

When East Asia, in particular China and Japan, were forced to open up to the rest of the world, and specifically to the Western powers, in the middle of the nineteenth century, individualism was something which deeply struck their people. They were moved both in the sense of attraction and admiration, as well as in the sense of fear and repulsion.

In this situation, on the one hand, the Japanese played a kind of *avant-garde* role in the confrontation with Western ideas. In particular, individualism constituted one of the main issues which troubled most Japanese intellectuals, novelists, writers, and philosophers (Walker 1979; Nolte 1984; Ikegami 1995). In China, on the other hand, which was at that time occupied by the foreign countries, the issue of individualism was not particularly hotly disputed, and one should probably consider some writings of Lu Xun (who incidentally studied in Japan at the very beginning of the twentieth century) in order to find a first thoroughgoing Chinese confrontation with both the existential and political situation of the individual in a post-traditional society.

One could perhaps object that some kind of individualism seems to be more deeply and traditionally rooted in China than in Japan, specifically in the Daoist tradition (Munro 1985; Brindley 2010). However, it is probably only after the encounter with Western thought that a "modern" political application of Daoist ideas concerning the individual became an issue (Lee 2013). This means that the Daoist translation of Western modern individualism, or, alternatively, the individualistic reappraisal of Daoism, has been realized only a few years after the tackling of the issue of "Western" individualism had already happened in Japan, and, quite likely, also on the basis of the related debates. Similarly, one should notice that the "father" of modern, Republican China, Sun Yat-Sen, received much of his modern education and, consequently, some of his ideas about social modernization, in Japan. It is thus quite likely he was influenced in his political thought by the very "father" of Japanese modern liberal thought, namely Yukichi Fukuzawa (諭吉福沢, 1835–1901) (Matthew 2015). In general, one has to acknowledge the influence of Japan as a medium through which Chinese intellectuals, between the end of the nineteenth century and the first decades of the twentieth century, especially the revolutionaries, found a gate to Western ideas and ideals.

In this scenario, one should not neglect that, until Commodore Perry knocked at the door of Edo Bay with his "black ships" in 1853, the Japanese culture, in terms of both lifestyle and of intellectual life, had heavily and almost exclusively been under the influence of the Chinese culture. For this reason, the Japanese full-scale confrontation with Western ideas and values is of great relevance to understanding how a traditional culture based to a great extent on both a Chinese social and scientific conception of reality can react as well as interact with the ideas and values coming from the West, more precisely from the United States and Europe. The intellectual as well as practical experience gained by the Japanese during the Meiji (1868–1912) and Taisho (1913–26) eras, and specifically the experience of the possibility of an individualistic worldview, can indeed be considered as the first substantial breakthrough of Western ideas and values in the so-called "Far East". It can be seen as a pathfinder for the learning and adaptability of such ideas and values against the background of traditional East Asian cultures, including first and foremost different languages and writing systems, as well as an example of how a traditional conception of the relationship between the individual and the society of Confucian lineage could either be overcome or transformed by a confrontation with Western models.

Considering all that has been mentioned up to this point, the reflections of the Japanese literates of the Meiji and Taisho eras can be considered instructive in order to understand and handle the transformations which are currently still happening both in Japan and in other East Asian countries. The very current socio-political situation in China can plausibly gain some useful insights from the conceptual endeavors regarding the individual, individualism and individuality which happened in Japan between the end of the nineteenth century and the first decades of the twentieth century. In this regard, the works of Kitarō Nishida, who is almost unanimously acknowledged as the father of modern Japanese philosophy, are among the most telling. Nishida himself, like almost all Japanese intellectuals until the Meiji era, was profoundly educated in the Chinese classics (Dalissier 2010; Yusa 2002). Moreover, he was quite familiar with, as well as fond of, some masterworks of the Western literature, e.g., Dante, Shakespeare, Goethe, Dostoevsky, Tolstoy, as well as the Bible (Yusa 2002). With this background, his conscientious investigations into "Western" philosophy and his restless attempts to systematically and logically assess the relationship between the individual and the universal also from an experiential point of view, clearly take on a paradigmatic relevance.

In what follows, after a brief sketch of the "philosophico-political" situation of individualism in the Meiji era, I will try to show how and why Nishida's "logical" assessment of the individual is still relevant not only for metaphysics and ontology, nor solely for the Japanese, the Chinese or in general the East Asian societies, but possibly for the entire contemporary world.

Some remarks concerning the situation of individualism in the Meiji era, with special regard to the "East Asian" collectivistic background

As already mentioned, at the end of the nineteenth century, the reaction of the Japanese towards Western culture, and more specifically towards the issue of individualism, was ambivalent. On the one hand, there was a fear of seeing their own, that is to say the (Sino)–Japanese tradition and culture, becoming more or less rapidly annihilated by the penetration of foreign ideas and habits. Individualism was both an ideal and a way of living which could deeply endanger the Japanese style of life. This would also mean that the order, at least the order established up to that point, would fall into ruin, and chaos – or foreign powers – would reign – as, indeed, it was in China and in most other Asian countries. On the other hand, it is exactly thanks to ideas and habits different from the ones to be found in China and Japan that, most likely, the foreigners had been so successful. Besides that, the absorption by means of learning of foreign ideas and habits could finally signify, instead of chaos, a better life for the Japanese people – as well as for all other Asian people.

Indeed, one could see not only the military power of the foreigners, but also their self-confidence which could likely be linked also to a more satisfactory life. Western civilization seemed to promise an economic rising, and, consequently, a better and more comfortable lifestyle as well as less hardship. There were, therefore, at least two different reasons to let the foreign, Western ideas and habits slightly enter Japan: to improve the Japanese power as a modern nation-state, and to improve the lifestyle of the Japanese people. The latter reason, moreover, could be interpreted in two ways, that is in the sense that, by learning the ideas of the Westerners, especially their scientific and technological knowledge, Japan could improve its ways of production and become richer in terms of both agricultural and industrial products – or in the sense that the Western lifestyle would be more satisfying, as well as healthier, for the people than the one followed up to that point. The introduction of foreign elements into the Japanese society could thus benefit the nation as a whole or the individuals living in the nation. It is quite clear that the two things do not necessarily go hand in hand.

It is, therefore, far from surprising that the issue of individualism was one of the main areas of dispute in the Meiji era, and that both intellectuals and politicians had to tackle it. In this regard, one should ask what specifically was, or could have been, meant by individualism for the Japanese of the Meiji era. Indeed, before the encounter with the West, in Japan, the idea of 'individuals' was certainly not unknown. Not only were the Japanese aware that there exist individual things, but they were also aware of the individual "inner" life of human individuals as such and of the difference between individual drives and interests and social order and goals.[1] The social rules that went together with the social policy were thought, indeed, exactly to control such elements and to avoid any danger they may pose to the social order. This is signally true of pre-Meiji Japan, which was in this regard strongly subjected to a Neo-Confucian ethics which segregated some individuals in specific spaces, like the pleasure districts (Walker 1979: 8ff.). Individual desires and drives, as well as specific emotions, were considered to be inopportune and even dangerous for the social, not to say *universal*, order. The latter corresponded to, and required, a quite strict hierarchy between classes and clans, as well as a rigid subordination of the individual to such a hierarchy and to a "division" that was not only that of labor, but also of all spheres of life into designated places. Consequently, the individual spontaneity and the individual desires had to be, if not annihilated, at least marginalized.

For this reason, for many Japanese people who appreciated the individualistic character of the Western culture, who tried to socially promote it and even fought for it, individualism was not simply the ideology of the winners. As such, it would perhaps have been not so interesting, and especially not so worth the struggle many Japanese undertook in order to see some "Western ideas" realized in Japan. Therefore, on the one hand, individualism was rather fascinating and desirable because it could finally give the possibility to express stifled emotions, feelings and desires. It was something to strive for because it would finally free the individuals from the yoke of servitude and strict hierarchy.

On the other hand, given the overwhelming strength of the Western nations, and acknowledging that this very strength was partially dependent on the individualistic consciousness of Westerners, individualism could become attractive, or at least interesting, even for those who were not in favor of an adoption of foreign lifestyles and social rules. The "conservatives", indeed, could anyway be interested in learning how to achieve the strength and power of the foreigners. To this aim, the capacity to understand and, at least partially, annex the so-called "Western spirit" or "Western mind" was required. Following this, also the conservatives were somehow forced to admit that, at least in part, individualism could be necessary in order to achieve certain desirable goals, such as building a stronger and more powerful nation. It is not only the history of Japan that one might have in mind here. In China, during the so-called "break-up period" (after the defeat at the hands of the Japanese in 1895), this was illustrated by the Chinese "modern-conservatives", or rather reformists, such as the thinker Kang Youwei (康有為, 1858–1927), who turned to Western philosophies, especially vitalism and the *Lebensphilosophie* of Rudolf Eucken (Campagnolo 2013: 110–15). In any case, as far as Japan is concerned, in the beginning of the Meiji era individualism was not plainly dismissed by the leading groups, but rather, even if not fostered, it was at least tolerated.

This being the case, the encounter with the West could have simply meant the discovery, or the necessity to acknowledge, that "individualistic societies", in which the individual initiative as well as individual desires were allowed, or even dominant, were more powerful than traditional societies – Japan and China included. As such, this would not have meant any discovery of new ideas, but simply that the Japanese choice for "collectivism", deeply anchored in the Neo-Confucianism inherited from China and Korea, and which was clearly dominant in matters of public ethics and law, was no longer able to guarantee the very same Japanese independence and stability.

However, this choice was not the case. When Japan collided with the West, something more than the "liberation" of the individuals was glimpsed. According to Janet Walker, during the Meiji Restoration, with the promotion of lower-ranking *samurai* to higher positions in society, the concept of the individual as such was introduced into Japan for the first time. The individual at stake here is "an independent social agent" and "a person with a private moral existence and inner life". If Walker is right, then the "individualism" glimpsed in the Western societies was not simply a new way to "govern", or more generally to (socially) deal with the individuals, but rather a new form of existence of the individuals *also*, and perhaps *primarily, with themselves* – as well as amidst their social embedding.[2]

Yukichi Fukuzawa was renowned for his efforts as the champion of this new model of humanity from the very beginning of the Meiji era (Craig 2009). In his writings of the 1860s and 1870s, Fukuzawa denounced the inequality among people and the obedience to hierarchy which had characterized Japan thus far. Fukuzawa identified the power, and in a certain sense the superior level of civilization, of the Western nations, indeed, with their ideals of freedom and equality. Such ideals would inspire people:

To be responsible for themselves;
To take initiative in all walks of life;
To be strong and vigorous citizens ready to defend their nation
(Fukuzawa 1960; see also Walker 1979: 17–20)

One can easily see that Fukuzawa, like other intellectuals in the Meiji era, promoted individualism not so much – or, at least, not solely – because the individual is considered as being a value in itself, but rather because a nation, and in general any community of individuals, is more valuable for the nation in that way. Fukuzawa did fight in favor of human rights, and maintained that 'it is a basic human right for a man to be able to attain his desires, as long as he does not obstruct others' (Fukuzawa 1960: 38). In this way, he spread one of the main principles of John Stuart Mill's liberalism in Japan (Mill 1991: especially 30, 72). Moreover, he claimed that all people, those of most humble condition as well, had to learn and study in order to avoid despotism, as it had happened so far. In order to achieve this, however, a specific kind of education was necessary in order to both implement and protect what could be regarded as some set of genuine human rights. Indeed, individuals cannot realize themselves as individuals by themselves from the beginning, but they rather need an imprinting, which cannot but come from the society.

Following this, the introduction of the concept of "human rights" *theoretically* makes the people free from hierarchical bonds. However, free human beings become possible only thanks to a certain type of state, which promotes and protects their rights, as well as it forms them to be autonomous and independent, fully responsible individuals. This being the case, a certain type of state is necessary for the realization of free human beings. Even if one assumed that human rights are not relative to a specific state or nation, still some kind of social organization would be necessary in order to realize them, that is to form citizens which are aware of human rights and to allow the citizens both to contribute to the realization of a just society and to see that human rights are respected by the institutions.

People like Fukuzawa risked their own life in order to promote the independence and autonomy of the individuals as well as equality among all human beings. Their struggle was exactly motivated by the fact that the mere *idea* of human equality, as well as of human dignity at all – is not sufficient in order to see human rights realized.

One may object here that, previously, the idea of equality among all human – as well as non-human – beings had already been affirmed in some of the Buddhist doctrines. However, from a Buddhist perspective, *this* world, that is to say the factual-material world we are embedded in, is totally without freedom, and a free existence is possible only through an awareness of one's own inner spiritual nature. Walker poignantly stresses that, for example, in most Buddhist traditions there is a somehow paradoxical idea of the individual as being both socially unfree *and* experientially free (Walker 1979: 6). Therefore, the Buddhist perspective seems to necessarily result in something which is politically irrelevant because it does not promote any actual reform, not even to speak of revolution, in the "mundane" society. However, once one endorses a view according to which it is possible to establish a mundane society of freedom based on human rights, one seems forced to admit that national independence is the sole condition of possibility of a personal, that is to say individual, independence. It is likely for this reason that, as soon as Japan fought the wars with China (1895), Russia (1905), and Korea (from the 1890s to 1910, when the latter was established as a Japanese colony), Fukuzawa had been stressing more and more that the independence of the individual has to be conceived as functional to better serve the nation, and not as leading to self-affirmation. Finally, Fukuzawa did apparently lose his trust in the emancipation of the people, and turned back to the *samurai* ideal of loyalty and obedience to the lord, now to be identified with the emperor (Walker 1979: 23–25).

In any case, that is to say both in the case where individualism is pursued for the sake of the nation – or, more in general, of a community – and in the case where individualism is pursued for the sake of the individual(s) as such, individualism cannot be realized insofar as there is not a certain, *specific* way of understanding the individual. It is not enough to say that the individual is guaranteed in its rights, as far as the rights concern something which is defined by means of its belonging to the individual, that is to say properties, abilities, capacities, thus leaving unclear what individuality as such properly is. One has to understand what the essence of the individual is in order to establish, among other things, a legal system which protects and, perhaps, even fosters it. In other words, the change from, say, collectivism and holism to individualism is not merely possible by means of "releasing" the above-mentioned "inner life" which was so far imprisoned – for instance in pleasure districts or in hermitages. It is, rather, necessary to shape a new kind of individual, with features which are absent in the pre-individualistic mind. Therefore, it is far from surprising that individualism has been one of the main issues in the Meiji era. The issue of individualism is, indeed, strictly connected to the socio-political as well as economic ideas of liberalism, which were vigorously and swiftly spreading in East Asia.

In this regard, there is one aspect of the issue of individualism which has efficaciously been pointed out by (Nakamura 1967). According to Nakamura, in the history of Japan up to the nineteenth-century encounter with the Western culture, there is a lack of strictly logical thought. This does not mean that the Japanese were unable to reason, but rather that in their thinking there was no clear distinction between universal, or generic, terms and individual terms. More precisely, in Japanese thought, and also in Japanese metaphysical thought, there has been lack of a conception of the individual *qua* individual (Nakamura 1967: 182). To what extent this lack can be traced back to the Chinese tradition is worth exploring further. As far as Japan is concerned, even one of the very terms to express the individual, namely *kobutsu* (個物), has been introduced into the Japanese language as a result of the encounter with the West.

Certainly, as we have already remarked, this does not properly mean that Japanese have been lacking the capacity to see individuals, or to differentiate between individuals and collections. Quite to the contrary, Japanese thought, as well as the Japanese scientific tradition, has mainly been empiricist. In Japanese traditional thought, following a trend present in Buddhism, only individuals can be properly perceived, and consequently, only individuals exist, while the *genus* 'in Buddhist logic is an object of inference' (Nakamura 1967: 193 – Nakamura refers here to the Buddhist logician Hōtan). One could therefore say that in the Japanese tradition there has always been a predominance of a kind of thought which has privileged the individual over the universal and the abstract. However, as Nakamura sharply points out, inasmuch as there is no clear elaboration both of the problem and of the respective logic of universals and of their relationships with the individuals, one cannot properly have a comprehension of the individual *as individual*. Indeed, one is lacking the capacity to see all individuals as belonging to the *genus* "individual" and, consequently, to accurately elaborate an idea of what makes the essence of each and every individual, that is to say what *individuality* means.

Nakamura's reflection permits to shed light on a possible relationship between logical thought and the socio-political ideal of individualism. Our discussion of this would be more fruitful if we were to consider a social science such as economics, which tends to put the focus on the individual agent (and oftentimes, considers only the individual agent). Indeed, the lack of an accurate logical consideration of the onto-logical and "epistemo-logical" relationships between universal and individual can be considered as hindering the capacity to conceive of all individuals as "really" equal and to precisely investigate what individuality means. This was, in my view, exactly the duty which Kitarō Nishida, a pure son of the Meiji Restoration, undertook.

The idea of individual to be found in Kitarō Nishida

A reader of Nishida's writings will easily find that he mainly focuses on the logico-ontological issue, while he seldom touches upon the socio-political and ethical issues of individualism. However, one must not neglect the fact that, probably from the very beginning of his philosophical endeavor, one of Nishida's main aims consisted in re-understanding Hegel's "concrete universal".[3] This implies that, for Nishida, the logic of individual and universal is to be restricted neither to a "purely logical", nor to a "purely epistemological" sphere. Nishida's inquiry into the relationships between the universal and the individual has, indeed, a highly practical significance. Such a significance (although this is not clearly expressed by Nishida himself) clearly concerns also the individual as an economic actor, that is to say as a point of reference within a net of mutual exchanges with a both the natural and human environment.

From a very general point of view, the general socio-political idea which emerges from almost all of Nishida's works corresponds to a liberal one, although quite vague. Nishida seems to take for granted, as undeniable evidence, that the individual must have the freedom to be the author of its own life as one finds in Nishida (1992: 109, 137–38), (NKZ 12/Nishida 2014) and (NKZ 8). Goto-Jones (2003) has particularly stressed this aspect of Nishida's thought. However, one could maintain that, in this regard, Nishida does not go any further than Fukuzawa. One could even underline that Nishida does not really tackle any of the main issues of both political liberalism and individualism. He almost does not deal at all with some cardinal questions of politics and of political philosophy, like rights and duties, immunities and benefits, sovereignty and subordination, among other major notions.

This is why, contrary to Goto-Jones, who has claimed that there is "a potentially valuable legacy for political and moral philosophy" (Goto-Jones 2003: 530) in Nishida's thought, I believe that Nishida's legacy does not consist in the ideas about ethics and politics that Nishida expressed, but rather in his logico-epistemological, ontological and phenomenological considerations about the relationship between universal and individual, as well as the self-consciousness of an individual as individual. Nishida's ideas in this regard can, and perhaps must, be relevant also for a philosophical reflection about politics and ethics, while Nishida's ideas about politics – right or wrong as they may be – seem to me not sufficiently justified and lacking the detailed analyses which a philosophical inquiry into politics and ethics would require.

That being said, there is one aspect of Nishida's thought which is of clear relevance for a philosophical investigation into the topic of "economic" and "political" individualism, and that, at the same time, finds in Nishida's own writings much more than a superficial and vague treatment, although it still requires us to step beyond Nishida's thought – and especially beyond his alleged political ideas and reflections. There is, indeed, a possible reading of Nishida's treatment of the essence of individuality which shows that the experience one has of oneself as individual is an experience of *given* indeterminacy exactly inasmuch as one is an individual, that is to say it is not reducible to any given, nor to come, community.

This (possible) result of Nishida's reflexive ideas and the respective conceptual horizons they disclose (but absolutely do not exhaust) can be better appreciated if one considers Nishida's path of thought as (at least partially) motivated exactly by the need to clarify what it means to be an individual. More precisely, Nishida's philosophy can be partially read as an attempt to explicate one's experience of oneself as an individual and what the *realization* of oneself as complete, socio-economic individual amounts to.

In his first published book, entitled *An Inquiry into the Good*, which is considered to mark the beginning of Japanese modern, that is to say conspicuously "Westernized" philosophy, Nishida wishes for an individualism which is different and independent from egoism (Nishida 1992: 131). Moreover, in the end, he conceives the maximum of self-realization as coincident with selflessness, that is to say the overcoming of one's small self and the unification with the universal self (NKZ 1/Nishida 1992: 79–81, 135, 161). Similar ideas can be found also in Nishida's last writing (NKZ 10/Nishida 1993). For an exhaustive and critical survey of the issue of unification in Nishida's thought, we refer the reader to the study by Dalissier (Dalissier 2009).

One can say that Nishida followed a path of thought according to which the question of the logico-epistemological understanding of the relationship between singularity and universality lies deeper and, so to say, at the core of the possibility to solve the questions concerning individualism and communitarianism. Indeed, in order to opt for one of these two views, the previous clarification of the phenomenological *and* ontological status of the individual is required. Nishida somehow endorses a view according to which the self-realization of the individual concerns both its happiness and its good. One is truly happy inasmuch as one realizes oneself. Following this, the realization of oneself corresponds to achieving the good. The good of oneself as individual is, however, not the good of oneself as the "empirical *ego*", that is to say a certain person which is *supposed* to have certain needs and goals. The self-realization of the individual must overcome the "limited" sphere of the ego one can believe one is, or is supposed to be. More generally, if one works for oneself as a self that one already is, then one somehow does not realize oneself, but rather a *simulacrum* of oneself. The "good" of oneself as a "genuine" individual, therefore, cannot be limited to the private interests of an ego. The latter cannot but lead to the failure of one's self-realization.

All these connections and disconnections of concepts and ideals could seem to produce a quite inconsistent and paradoxical, or at least confused, picture. However, the scenario which emerges from *An Inquiry into the Good* is rather a field of ideas which cannot be reduced to a collage of univocally pre-established concepts. I would suggest that there appears in *An Inquiry into the Good*, among other things, a genuine "exertion of the concept" that is exactly aimed at clarifying what is the individual whose good one is "individualistically" supposed to seek.

One could say that all of Nishida's philosophy aims at the understanding of what the good of that peculiar being which is conscious of itself as individual is and, overall, of the obscurity which characterizes the teleology of its life. In the Preface to the first edition of *An Inquiry into the Good*, Nishida famously writes that "it is not that experience exists because there is an individual, but that an individual exists because there is experience" (NKZ 1/Nishida 1992: Preface, xxx). This, however, does neither directly nor necessarily imply an ontological denial of the individual or of individuality as such. It rather means that the individual emerges in experience, thus being in principle something mutable and even vanishing, and that it is furthermore not something "fixed" beyond experience. In *An Inquiry into the Good*, Nishida seems to incline towards a "phenomenalistic" understanding of the individual, a kind of "Buddhist" view upon the self as being a deceptive phenomenon. Indeed, Nishida speaks of "pure experience" as something which precedes the subject–object distinction, the distinction between individual and the universe. Nishida declares that in pure experience we can find "reality as it is" (事実其儘). Since pure experience is said to precede individuality, one could easily draw the conclusion that in reality there are no individuals, and this is the reason why Nishida speaks of selflessness as being the true reality of the individual.

Yet, what Nishida really aimed at clarifying is exactly the ambiguous reality of an experience which is immediately given as *self*-awareness and, consequently, it contains a kind of internal fission. One could even argue that all of Nishida's philosophy is nothing but a meditation on this split unity; the most mature, but not necessarily conclusive, framing of which is, quite consistently, to be found in Nishida's theory of the so-called "absolute contradictory self-identity" (NKZ 8).

Nishida concentrates a great part of his theoretical efforts precisely in understanding and clarifying the essence of the individual, that is to say individuality. He is not content with only the epistemology or the ontology of individual substance. Nishida's main issue is the individual which emerges in experience as the individual one identifies oneself with while being aware of oneself. Experience is self-referential, and the self-appearance in experience is adequately understood only inasmuch as it is comprehended as a specification of the totality it appears in. At the same time, however, experience is a place of appearance of the individual which is somehow intuited as the unity which allows the determination of the individual itself (NKZ 3/Nishida 2015). In experience one intuits oneself, and also intuits that the "determined" self that one becomes conscious of is not properly one's own totality and cannot be properly identified with the unity which allows for the recognition of different aspects as belonging to one's same self.

On this perspective, the individual has to be considered as the inner specification of a universal, which is therefore something real and not an abstraction. Hence Nishida's perspective is not purely nominalist. Indeed, his philosophy does not embrace a view according to which individuals only are real. In a certain sense, as is most clear in the last phase of his thought, only individuals exist, but what exactly their existence as individuals is remains somehow linked to the reality of the universals and to their somehow internal (self-)negation.

The problems that Nishida deals with consist exactly of reconciling a "realist" view on the universals with the evidence that individuals are given as being non-reducible to any universal determination, as well as one of combining ontological holism with ontological pluralism.

As already mentioned, the late Nishida quite efficaciously framed this conflicting scenario in an ontology of "absolutely contradictory self-identity". Far from being a mere sophistic solution, and although it can sound like a mere speculative and abstract, not to say empty and verbal, meandering, Nishida's logical treatment tries on the contrary to be the most accurate and faithful expression of what self-awareness, self-consciousness and, in particular, what the (self-)experience of one's individuality actually *gives*. This is the reason why Nishida's philosophy can be, at least partially, considered as also a phenomeno-logical philosophy.

Before offering a general evaluation of this attempt by Nishida, we should briefly consider in some more detail his elaboration of the "given-ness" of individuality.

The "given-ness" of individuality according to Nishida

As previously mentioned, in order to properly understand what it means to be and to act, as well as to realize oneself as an individual, Nishida first of all tackled the issue of the individual from an experiential point of view. The key concept in Nishida's early philosophy, and somehow the grounding idea of his whole path of thought, is notably the idea of pure experience. This is not here the place to analyze this concept in all its nuances and difficulties. Suffice it to say that the individual has to manifest its meaning and its structure in experience. The individual must correspond to a specific kind of experience. More precisely, as we will now see, the individual which is at stake in individualism corresponds to a specific type of self-experience.

In order to achieve a clear insight into the essence of the individual, it is therefore necessary to understand the structure of the corresponding experience. This, in turn, requires a specific logical endeavor. To experience an individual *as* individual corresponds to a specific logical structure, in which the subject at stake is considered to be the bearer of a more or less numerous amount of predicates. The well-known problem is that predicates are somehow always universal. Therefore, at least in a traditional Aristotelian logic, the individual cannot be defined as such by these. One way out, which could permit to logically determine the individual, would be to admit *haecceitas*, that is to say a feature which is proper only of an individual, and cannot but characterize *one* individual. Nishida, however, does not seem to opt for this solution. Or, more accurately, he looks for a kind of both logical and phenomenological account of the experiential, though avoiding the recourse to any indexicality as well as to direct reference. This avoidance of such a solution is consistent with Nishida's endorsement of some "Hegelian" understanding both of logic and of indexicality.

Nishida, therefore, tries to re-articulate the relationship between the universal and the individual. Such a re-articulation is, though perhaps not sufficient, at least necessary in order to understand how the individual is defined (and self-defined) in relationship to what is common, that is to say what each individual shares with other individuals.

Nishida, in a certain sense, seems to be willing to logically tackle the idea that "one is nothing". Far from endorsing a superficial understanding of some Buddhist (but possibly also Christian and, in general, Western) understanding of the individual self as mere delusion, Nishida investigates the indeterminacy of the individual. Following Spinoza's *dictum*, according to which *omnis determinatio est negatio*, and, at the same time, espousing a view according to which individuals are maximally concrete, one is forced either to admit the concreteness of negativity, or that individuals cannot be determined. In a certain way, Nishida offers a theoretical framework, or at least a theoretical framework which allows one to develop a view in which the two previously mentioned options are combined: individuals are *positively* characterized as undetermined *and* negativity belongs to the status of individuals, both phenomenologically and ontologically. This aspect is explained with the uttermost gravity in (NKZ 10/Nishida 1993).

Deprived of any determination, the individual would remain something extremely vague. In other words, it would be hard to assume that individuals are actually grasped at all in this way. Moreover, if this were the case, the very same idea of individuals would be incomprehensible – or, better, *impossible*. This leads to the acknowledgement that the individual is undetermined *as* determined. Or, better, its inmost determination is indeterminacy.

In Nishida's thought we find this somehow paradoxical characterization of individuality as going hand in hand with the idea that individuality is maximally concrete inasmuch as an individual is self-referential. Indeed, only a being which is able to be aware of itself as undetermined is a true individual. In this way, Nishida somehow endorses a view in which selflessness is the innermost reality of an individual self. Thus, individuals do exist, but they are beings which are conscious of themselves as being void of determinacy.

The logical structure of individuals is, then, contradictory. Contradiction is, in turn, necessary to the existence of individuals, and individuals are the most concrete beings.

Consistent with this line of thought, Nishida proposes a view of the totality and its levels in which the most concrete reality is constituted by individuals, and concrete individuals are self-referential and self-aware entities. The self-referential structure of individuals is contradictory, because an individual acquires awareness of being itself only by means of its difference from other individuals as well as from universality. In this awareness, the individual is grasped as *undetermined*. It is grasped as something which cannot be grasped. However, this does not mean that the individual and reality are something irrational. It rather means that "reality as it is" is contradictory.

This is how Nishida tries to realize Hegel's idea of the "concrete universal". The individual is the negation of the universal, because any universality misses the individual. By saying this, one offers a universal definition of the individual, thus affirming the contradiction of what was just stated. In this contradiction, which should be comprehended as not merely verbal, but rather experienced in one's own self-consciousness, one realizes the reality of oneself. That which does not have this kind of self-awareness and this tension, cannot count as a real individual. Hence, only if an individual which *is* contradictory exists, the *feeling* of the tension between the two extremes, that is to say individuality and universality, as well as determination and indeterminacy, is possible. For this reason, one could say that the concrete individual is somehow coextensive with the two extremes. Consequently, the concrete individual corresponds to concreteness of the universal.

In the individual any *absolute* determination *is* concretely negated. No adherence to any supra-individual whole is possible, not to speak of a Pan-like fusion with the universe. Indeterminacy constitutes the inmost essential determination of the individual. As a consequence, in one's conscious and active self-determination one realizes one's determination as not-pre-determined and not-hetero-determined.

Nishida's attempt to elaborate a predicative logic which is not properly alternative, but rather complementary to the Aristotelian subjective logic (NKZ 4/Nishida 2000a), would finally lead to the acknowledgment that the universal essence of all individuals is their singular indeterminacy. Indeterminacy is what all individuals have in common. One could say that the more something is really determined, the more it is undetermined.

Back to the ethical, socio-political and economic individual agent

All these considerations seem to say nearly nothing about the socio-political, as well as ethical, determination of the individual. What does the contradictory determination of the individual as such mean for its social relationships, its socio-economic embedding, its rights, duties and immunities?

In this regard, Nishida does not say much, indeed. However, one first has to acknowledge that Nishida tries to better sharpen the kind of self-relationship which characterizes a true individual. In doing so, he happens to pinpoint some aspects of individuality which can be considered, at least potentially, more progressive than some views by Fukuzawa. As we stated, Nishida does not thoroughly discuss or investigate what, for example, individual rights are. However, he seems to endorse and somehow also to logically show the consistency of an ideal according to which the maximum good of an individual is the capacity to self-determination.

The dialectical relationship between determination and indeterminacy of the individual that we stressed above can also mean that the individual as such is essentially characterized by need and, thus, destined to an economic relationship with the others and with the environment. The autonomy of the individual, which is vindicated by both liberalism and individualism, is abstract if we do not realize that it has to go hand in hand with the dependence of each and every individual on a system of exchange with the others and with the environment, that is to say if we forget its economic embedding. We could even say that the overcoming of need and of economic dependency would correspond to the annihilation of the individual as such.

On the basis of what we saw in the previous pages, one should now be able to easily see why, according to Nishida, one must logically reject any kind of individualism in which the individual is considered *abstractly*, that is to say as if it were an atom, totally devoid of environment and spatio-temporal, biological and cultural embedding. It is, indeed, essential to the individual that its embedding be within a system of determinations. The latter, indeed, is necessary to the self-affirmation of the individual *as individual*, that is to say as irreducible to such determinations. The system of determinations necessary to the self-affirmation of the individual must also be understood in "environmental" terms.

If one recognizes the historical and, in general, the environmental embedding of an individual, which is particularly stressed and investigated by Nishida in the 1930s (Nishida 2012), then one has to acknowledge that the idea of "atomic individuality" pursued by an abstract individualism, which goes more or less necessarily hand in hand with egoism, does not lead to a genuine realization of the individual, that is to say of its individuality, but rather to its suppression. Such an abstract form of individualism is identified by Nishida with the one deriving from eighteenth-century Enlightenment ideas and ideals. According to Nishida, the latter sustains an idea of the individual which is highly abstract, because it does not acknowledge the socio-historical, and more generally environmental, embedding of each and every individual. Such an individualism, therefore, proposes an ideal of justice and equality which, being abstract, can even be harmful to the actual good of the individuals.

The critique of the individual of the Enlightenment is, among others, present in a highly problematic text, entitled *The Principle of the New World Order* (Nishida 1996 – reprint of the speech given during World War II). It is interesting to note that in this same text one can still glimpse a kind of libertarian idea, according to which the individuals, as well as the nations/peoples (国家民族 *Kokka Minzoku*), must be able of self-determination in order to reach the formation of a truly global world. That being said, by denying that the self-realization of a people can be achieved by means of what Nishida calls 'self-determinationism' (Nishida 1996: 18), which seems unavoidably linked to the principle of autonomy and independence, Nishida definitely distances himself from a genuine liberal perspective.

As a matter of fact, Nishida's insistence on the interdependence of all peoples and nations tends to overwhelm both the legal and political principle of independence and autonomy. Moreover, probably due to the situation and context in which Nishida had to deliver such a speech, the right to self-determination and the value of the individual(s) are totally neglected. However, this clear distance from a genuine liberal perspective taken in Nishida's later political statements does render even more dramatic his insistence on finding some super-individual, universal principle which requires the *self*-realization of the individuals, or the singular peoples/nations, in order to be genuinely *concrete*. One could, therefore, assert that until the end of his life Nishida had been struggling with the desperate need to harmonize the individual and the universal, and, more specifically, with the possibility to originally re-elaborate the individuality he had to experience as a son of the Meiji Restoration.

Nishida thinks that each individual tends, by means of its very own essence, to become absolute (Nishida 2000b). This can mean, simply, that each individual tends to overcome its own finitude, the latter involving need and desire. However, a true individual is the finite being which becomes aware of itself as individual inasmuch as it becomes aware of its environmental embedding. An individual, in other terms, includes its own environment, which is strictly connected to both its real and its imaginative desires and needs, in its own self-consciousness. Moreover, in the case of the human being, or, more generally, of a self-conscious being, the individual is also aware of itself as self-determining.

In this sense, the most accomplished form of individuality corresponds to the consciousness also of one's own responsibility. In turn, responsibility implies that at least a part of the life of the individual remains *undetermined*. The latter, however, is not to be properly understood as a lack of the individual, but it is rather a fundamental part of its essence. In a certain sense, we could repeat, even in a socio-political or economic context, that the individual is determined as undetermined.

The right, as well as the duty, to self-determination is thus granted to the individual inasmuch as this is not violating the rights of others. Autonomy and independence are the two main ontological features of individuality, which lead Nishida to partly endorse a monadic understanding of reality. However, Nishida explicitly distanced himself from Leibniz. Nishida, indeed, rejected Leibniz's ideas of the immortality of the monads and of pre-established harmony (Nishida 2000b). Quite interestingly, Nishida did this exactly in order to better respect the reality and concreteness of the individuals and their inner phenomenology. Individuals exist as such only insofar as they realize themselves independently from any pre-established harmony. In Nishida's view, the individual determines itself, and is real exactly in its contraposition to another individual. The difference between individuals is such that no wholly encompassing system of the individuals as monads is possible. As such, the society in which we find the "truest" realization of the absolute, which, from the aforesaid, cannot but be a society of plural individuals, is the society in which space for indeterminacy is granted and guaranteed. In other words, the "absolute" goal of a society should be to enable and foster human indeterminacy – also at a risk for social cohesion.

That being said, one cannot conceal that, in some aspects, Nishida did betray the self-experience of individuality and the logic it displays, that is to say the philosopher betrayed the logical consequences one should draw from it. Nishida, indeed, fell victim to a mistake quite similar to the one Marx attributed to Hegel – that is to say to *assume* an empirical reality as the incarnation of an idea, which, in turn, has a normative or teleological nature.[4] Nishida wishes, and somehow even foresees, a stage of humanity in which the only absolute community is humanity itself. In this regard, his kenotic view (Heisig 2001; 2012; 2015) of the relationship between the Absolute and the individual should urge him to acknowledge that there can *never* be any *given* totality one can be supposed to adhere to, and that *no single individual* can ever *be* either the absolute or its representative, just as there is no individual who can constitute either the unity or the continuity among a people and generations by his/her own self. Nevertheless, Nishida did actually declare *one* particular individual to be the symbol of the unity of a people and his species, as well as the symbol of the history of this very people, namely the Japanese Emperor and the Japanese Imperial family (see, in particular the reprints of very famous speeches by Nishida, in 2011 and Nishida 1996).

There have been, especially in the last twenty years, copious amounts of literature about Nishida's political engagements as well as about the political meaning of his thought. We may quote, among others, Lavelle (1994), Heisig and Maraldo (1995), Arisaka (1996), Goto-Jones (2008) and Goto-Jones (2010). Yet, it is not my aim to tackle this issue here, and I rather think that the literature produced so far already offers a quite comprehensive view on this subject. I would simply agree with, say, among others, Cestari (2008), in saying that Nishida's thoughts about politics are far from being something one can seriously take as a piece of political philosophy or a philosophy of politics. They are far from being ripe, accurate and scientifically discerning. Nishida's personal path from a traditional society to one which somehow puts the subject in front of its own individuality can be considered as similar to the paths of many East Asian intellectuals of his age. Therefore, Nishida's intellectual endeavor about the meaning of the individual can be considered as paradigmatic not solely for the Japanese, but for the East Asian history in general.

Therefore, I find that, whoever should want to evaluate Nishida's thought about politics, does it solely in order to save or condemn Nishida as a person. So, beyond the dubious interest in an *in absentia* trial to Nishida, one can simply state that Nishida does not offer much in terms of political philosophy and philosophy of politics – and looking at the few offerings he has done in this regard, one probably wishes he had been even more parsimonious. Moreover, one could probably observe, though, that the theory of the essence of the individual as consisting in indeterminacy seems to hint at a possible equality amongst all individuals, which is as good as ineffectual. It not only ignores the concreteness of the given social relationships, but also does not offer any clear insight into how these could or should be shaped in order to achieve the "universal" self-realization of humanity.

One could, nevertheless, remark that, by stressing the necessity of self-determination for the individual in order to realize itself as individual, and as self-determination is possible only inasmuch as an individual is aware of its own unavoidable indeterminacy, then Nishida's view did at least require a community to *grant such freedom*.

Indeed, in his pedagogical thoughts, Nishida stressed the necessity to foster the creativity of the individual.[5] This is consistent with the above-mentioned idea that individuals are such inasmuch as they do not follow any pre-fixed pattern of behavior. In this sense, Nishida's overall view of the individual could be considered as, at least partially, in accordance with John Stuart Mill's view that the space of individual freedom is necessary to the well-being of the individual, as well as to the development of society and, ultimately, the progress of humanity (Mill 1991: 73). Furthermore, this quite surprising conclusion would lead us back to considering what economics may consist of, when one agrees not to discard political economy in the name of a much less advanced understanding of the nature of exchange and trade between human beings.

One could say that Nishida has indeed anyhow *not* investigated the "material" conditions of possibility of a truly individual self-consciousness, viz. of a truly self-conscious individual. That being said, one should not ignore that Nishida has taken great pains to understand how an individual can understand itself and its own interest amidst its social and historical embedding. He has not simply proclaimed the right of the individuals to self-determination. He has rather tried to understand what kind of logic both governs and sustains individual self-determination. In this way, Nishida has offered a contribution to the understanding of what are the conditions of possibility for a true individual, and the implementation of a social system which "creates" and supports *individuals.*

The spirit of Nishida's thought, indeed the most original part of it, thus possibly extends beyond what he has been able to see, in his times and in his country. It extends first to some reflection on what emerged in modern East Asian philosophy when discussing this partially homegrown, partially imported notion of individual. It is then up to us, Easterners as well as Westerns, to materialize it by further developing it – or not.

Acknowledgements

The present chapter has been realized thanks to the support of the Japan Association for the Promotion of Science when the author was JSPS-Fellow at Hokkaido University. It is presented here within the official deliverable of the European Union program "Liberalization In Between Europe And China" (LIBEAC – a program of the European Union Seventh Framework *FP7/2007–2013*, registered under *grant agreement* n°PIRSES–GA–2012–317767).

Notes

1   There could be some objection to the idea that the consciousness of an "inner life" was already present in Japan, as well as in any non-Western and non-Christian culture, before the encounter with the Westerners. Janet Walker, indeed, has shown in her book (Walker 1979) that the literary style of the novel of the "inner life" was developed in Japan only in the Meiji era. However, I would suggest that the awareness of the "privacy" of ideas, feelings and thought is somehow independent of its elaboration and clear definition. In other words, the lacking of a clear theory of inner life does not imply a lacking of inner life. Maraldo (1994) has, in this regard, efficaciously shown that it is

a specific way of understanding and evaluating the inner life which characterizes the Western modern idea of the self and of its life. I believe that, indeed, to deny the awareness of the inner life would coincide with denying that a subject is able to distinguish, for example, between one's feelings and memories and outer objects. In other words, to negate any form of awareness of an inner life would coincide with the negation of self-awareness. The "cultural" issue concerns, in my view, the way of "understanding" this basic transcultural phenomenon. It is only by boldly assuming such a phenomenon that, indeed, the cultural differences can be better appreciated and evaluated. More generally, the difference between the individual life and the social or common life, be this a specific human society or the universe *tout-court*, is likely present, at least from a more "existential" and "religious" point of view, in any human culture. Before being a philosophical question, it can be somehow traced back to mythological narrations. The question concerning the autonomy and the independence of the individual subject, mainly conceived as a human being, and the society or, more generally, the totality of being, has seemingly been puzzling mankind since its "emergence", as not only the oldest writings, but also the "mythical" rituals testify. One could see these ancestral visions of the relationship between individual and totality (any kind of totality), as also containing *in nuce* the problem concerning the individual good and its desires, on the one hand, and the common or universal good and interests, on the other hand, which clearly constituted the center of almost all the oldest philosophical reflections worldwide.

2   The problem is, in other terms, a certain, specific kind of *self-consciousness*. The issue of the relationship between individual and community is, indeed, present in every society. The specific issue of individualism consists in the consciousness the individual has of oneself *as* an individual who cannot be reduced to its communal nature or embedding. That this kind of consciousness is grounded in a specific history, which is also embedded in theologico-political issues, has been convincingly argued by Dumont (1971) and Dumont (1983). Dumont derives some of his theses from Troeltsch (1911).

3   For a precise survey of Nishida's thoughts on the concept of the individual, see Tremblay (2000). Although Tremblay does not touch upon the political issue of the individual, she offers an overview on the individual from a logical-epistemological as well as a religious-existential point of view, which is fundamental for the present understanding of the socio-political implications of Nishida's thought. Another important contribution to the latter issue is offered by the same author in Tremblay (2007).

4   What Marx wrote in 1843–44 is quite explicit in this regard:

> Hegel conceives of society, family, etc., the artificial person in general, not as the realization of the actual, empirical person but as the *real* person which, however, has the moment of personality in it only abstractly [...] It is a consequence of Hegel's wanting to allow the essence of man to act for itself as an imaginary individual instead of acting in its actual, human existence, and it necessarily has as its result that an empirical existent is taken in an uncritical manner to be the real truth of the Idea, because it is not a question of bringing empirical existence to its truth but of bringing the truth to empirical existence, and thereupon the obvious is developed as a real moment of the idea.
>
> (Marx 1843–44: 39)

5   I credit this information to A. J. Zavala's presentation at the 13th Annual Meeting of the Nishida Philosophy Association, "The Educational Ideas and Practice of Nishida Kitarō: 1895–1935". For a discussion of Nishida's ideas about education, see Yusa and Lavelle (1994).

References

Arisaka, Y. (1996) 'The Nishida Enigma: "The Principle of the New World Order" (1943)', *Monumenta Nipponica*, 51/1: 81–105

Brindley, E. (2010) *Individualism in Early China: Human Agency and the Self in Thought and Politics*, Honolulu: University of Hawaii Press.

Campagnolo, G. (2013) 'Three influential Western thinkers during the "break-up" period in China. Eucken, Bergson and Dewey', in M. Ying and H.-M. Trautwein (eds), *Thoughts on Economic Development in China*. London and New York: Routledge: 101–35.

Cestari, M. (2008) 'The Individual and Individualism in Nishida and Tanabe', in C. S. Goto-Jones (ed.) (2008) *Re-Politicising the Kyoto School as Philosophy*, London and New York: Routledge: 49–74.

Craig, A. (2009) *Civilization and Enlightenment: The Early Thought of Fukuzawa Yukichi*, Chicago: Harvard University Press.

Dalissier, M. (2009) *Anfractuosité et Unification. La Philosophie de Nishida Kitarō*, Genève: Librairie Droz.

——(2010) 'Nishida Kitarō and Chinese Philosophy: Debt and Distance', *Japan Review*, 22: 137–70.

Dumont, L. (1971) *Homo hierarchicus: essai sur le système des castes*, Paris: Gallimard.

——(1983) *Essais sur l'individualisme. Une perspective anthropologique sur l'idéologie moderne*, Paris: Seuil.

Fukuzawa, Y. (1960) [1872–76], 学問のすすめ (An Encouragement of Learning) in 福沢諭吉全種 (Complete Works of Fukuzawa Yukichi), Vol. 3, Tokyo: Iwanami Shoten [English translation by D. A. Dilworth and U. Hirano, *An Encouragement of Learning*, Tokyo: Sophia University, 1969].

Goto-Jones, C. S. (2003) 'Ethics and Politics in the Early Nishida: Reconsidering Zen no Kenkyū', *Philosophy East and West*, 3/1: 514–36.

——(ed.) (2008) *Re-Politicising the Kyoto School as Philosophy*, London and New York: Routledge.

——(2010) *Political Philosophy in Japan: Nishida, the Kyoto School and Co-prosperity*, Leiden: Routledge.

Heisig, J. (2001) *Philosophers of Nothingness*, Honolulu: University of Hawaii Press.

——(2012) 'An Inquiry into the Good and Nishida's Missing Basho', *Comparative and Continental Philosophy*, 4/2: 237–51.

——(2015) 'Nishida's Philosophical Equivalents of Enlightenment and No-Self', *Bulletin of the Nanzan Institute for Religion and Culture*, 39: 36–60.

Heisig, J. and Maraldo, J. (eds) (1995) *Rude Awakenings: Zen, the Kyoto School, and the Question of Nationalism*, Honolulu: University of Hawaii Press.

Ikegami, E. (1995) *The Taming of the Samurai: Honorific Individualism and the Making of Modern Japan*, Cambridge, MA: Harvard University Press.

Lavelle, P. (1994) 'The Political Thought of Nishida Kitarô', *Monumenta Nipponica*, 49/2: 141–162.

Lee, M. (2013) 'Zhang Taiyan: Daoist individualism and Political Reality', *Frontiers of Literary Studies in China*, 7/3: 346–66.

Maraldo, J. (1994) Rousseau, Hakuseki, and Hakuin: Paradigms of Self in Three Autobiographers, in R. T. Ames, W. Dissanayake and T. Kasulis (eds), *Self as Person in Asian Theory and Practice*, New York: SUNY Press: 57–79.

Marx, K. (1843–44) *Zur Kritik der Hegelschen Rechtsphilosophie*, in K. Marx and F. Engels, *Werke*, Berlin/DDR: Dietz Verlag, Band 1, 1953. [English tr. by A. Jolin and J. O'Malley, *Critique of Hegel's Philosophy of Right*, Cambridge: Cambridge University Press, 1970.]

Matthew, J. (2015) 'A Comparative Analysis of the Civilizations of Fukuzawa Yukichi and Sun Yat-sen', *Global Tides*, 9, Article 2, <http://digitalcommons.pepperdine.edu/globaltides/vol9/iss1/2>.

Mill, J. S. (1991) [1859], *On Liberty*, ed. by J. Gray and G. W. Smith, London and New York: Routledge.

Munro, D. (ed) (1985) *Individualism and Holism: Studies in Confucian and Taoist Values*, Ann Arbor: University of Michigan.

Nakamura, H. (1967) Consciousness of the Individual and the Universal among the Japanese, in C. A. Moore (ed.), *The Japanese Mind*, Honolulu: University of Hawaii Press.

Nishida, K. (1992) *An Inquiry into the Good*, English tr. by M. Abe and C. Ives, New Haven: Yale University Press.

——(1993) *Last Writings: Nothingness and the Religious Worldview*, English tr. by D. A. Dilworth, Honolulu: University of Hawaii Press.

——(1996) 'The Principle of the "New World Order"', English tr. by Y. Arisaka, in Arisaka (1996).

——(2000a) *Logique prédicative*, French tr. by J. Tremblay, in Tremblay (2000: 58–97).

——(2000b) *La position de l'individuel dans le monde historique*, French tr. by J. Tremblay, in Tremblay (2000: 229–74).

——(2002–2009), 西田幾多郎全集 (*Nishida Kitarō Zenshu*) [*Complete Works of Kitarō Nishida*], Tokyo: Iwanami Shoten (quoted in the text as NKZ).

——(2011) 'Das Problem der Japanischen Kultur (1938)', German tr. by R. Elberfeld, in R. Elberfeld and Y. Arisaka (eds), *Kitarō Nishida in der Philosophie des 20. Jahrhunderts*, Freiburg-München: Alber.

——(2012) *Place and Dialectic*, English tr. by J. W. M. Krummel and S. Nagatomo, New York: Oxford University Press.

——(2014) *Problemi fondamentali della filosofia*, Italian tr. by E. Fongaro, Venezia: Marsilio.

——(2015) *De ce qui agit à ce qui voit*, French tr. by J. Tremblay, Montréal: Les Presses de l'Université de Montréal.

Nolte, S. H. (1984) 'Individualism in Taisho Japan', *Journal of Asian Studies*, 43/4.

Tremblay, J. (2000) *Le jeu de l'individuel et de l'universel*, Paris: CNRS Éditions.

——(2007) *L'être-soi et l'être-ensemble*, Paris: L'Harmattan.

Troeltsch, E. (1911) *Religiöser Individualismus und Kirche*, in Troeltsch, *Kritische Gesamtausgabe*, Bd 10, Berlin: De Gruyter.

Walker, J. (1979) *The Japanese Novel of the Meiji Period and the Ideal of Individualism*, Princeton: Princeton University Press.

Yusa, M. (2002) *Zen and Philosophy: An Intellectual Biography of Nishida Kitarō*, Honolulu: University of Hawaii Press.

Yusa, M. and Lavelle, P. (1994) 'Correspondence', *Monumenta Nipponica*, 49/4: 524–529.

7 The rejection of narcissism and social essentialism through the anthropology of Masao Maruyama

Masataka Muramatsu

Introduction: what is the meaning of autonomy, in particular in East Asia?

From the mid-nineteenth century, Japan and China have pursued modernization and Westernization in their own ways.[1] At times they tried to integrate Western civilization into their own, while at other times they insisted on the superiority of their culture over the forms of culture originated in the West and imported from there. As for the difference between these two modernizations, many subjects are left to discuss, which could help us understand some of the differences between Japan and China, as well as the difference between Asiatic cultures and Western civilizations.

On the level of abstract ideas, for example, the reception of the essential ideas which characterize Western philosophy, such as "Liberty", "Right", "Obligation", etc. in Asiatic countries could be a very interesting subject. The difference between the receptions of these ideas may reveal essential cultural differences among Asiatic countries. For example, what do Asian peoples understand under the term 'liberalism'? And do Chinese people understand the idea of liberalism in the same way that Japanese people do? It is very probable that our understanding of liberalism is very different from that of the Chinese. It is also probable that this difference may cause mutual misunderstanding. In the so-called "age of globalization", it may contribute to the mutual benefit between Japan and Asiatic countries, especially China and Korea, to clarify our intelligence of liberalism and that of other countries. This question leads us very naturally to the following question: *do we really understand Western liberalism? How do we understand Western liberalism?*

Some people say that Japan is a nation prone to liberalism, referring to its economic system. Others say, though, that Japanese liberalism is very limited and that it must be developed much further in the direction of individual liberty. Interestingly, some conservative politicians, though promoting economic liberalism, insist that traditional Japanese communitarianism must be revived, claiming that the individual liberties are so excessive that they will destroy traditional Japanese values.

I find that this kind of confusion suggests a possible misunderstanding about the terms "liberty" and "liberalism" among Japanese people. In Japan, it seems that the term "liberty" does *not* indicate self-examination or self-criticism, though these are ideally the necessary conditions of any autonomous decision based on individual liberty. In these circumstances, any self-decision could be justified under the name of "Liberty" unless it should violate laws. Then, the term "Liberty" or the term "Liberalism" would have a very abstract and empty meaning, because they would only signify the right to do whatever one wants to do. In other words, the term "Liberty" or the term "Liberalism" may permit many Japanese to behave as they wish without reflection and to justify their actions too easily. In a context of modernization, whether in Japan or in China, these people who side with liberal ideas should take a stand with respect to these terms.

In Japan, Fukuzawa Yukichi (1835–1901) had already noticed possible confusion, or misunderstanding of the concept of liberty at the very beginning of Meiji Era. "Liberty has the danger to be mistaken for selfishness. It is because of this that intellectuals must clarify the concept of liberty" (Fukuzawa 1866–70/2002: 231).

In order to avoid this possible confusion, we must look for the norms or the criteria of human actions which can be compatible with liberalism, or which even can promote liberalism. Confronted with this problem, we can ask ourselves whether traditional values in Asian countries could perform the role of normativity or prevent us from creating this norm. For example, what are the traditional and theoretical relationships between the concept of *Li* (「理」; Principle) in Confucianism and the reception of "Liberty" and "Liberalism"? This kind of research may contribute to the Chinese understanding of these concepts and, as well, we can ask the same question about the relationships between Japanese traditional values and the reception of "Liberty" and "Liberalism".

In order to shed light on this subject, we shall refer to the anthropology of Masao Maruyama (1914–96), one of the most representative intellectuals of postwar Japan. He became very famous just after the defeat of the Japanese nation in World War II with his work *Logic and Psychology of Ultra-nationalism* in 1946. In this historical document, he severely criticized the political leaders who had directed the war by analyzing their *conformist* psychology, and the Japanese political system, which permitted them to be very irresponsible with regard to the critical situation during the war. Then he actively fought against the revival of pre-war thought, which put respect of the traditional social hierarchy above all. His influence was at its height in particular at the time of the civil movement against the revision of the "Treaty of Mutual Cooperation and Security between the United States and Japan" around 1960. He also wrote many influential documents in which he tried to clarify the Japanese ideological elements which had hindered modernization in Japan, with a clear impact on the rest of East Asia, notably through war. It is certain that anyone who tries to understand postwar Japanese thought and the development of ideologies in East Asia can never neglect his philosophy and his influence on postwar Japan.

There is no doubt that one of Masao Maruyama's main goals was the creation of an autonomous individual in Japanese society. As Rikki Kersten states, for

Maruyama, who identified modernization with democratization, "the essential factor was autonomy. Without personal and social autonomy, there could be no democracy. It was autonomy that could guarantee the independence of the individual, and preserve individual identity within a democratic system" (Kersten 1995: 130).[2]

In order to create an autonomous individual, Maruyama continued to analyze the patterns in Japanese thought which had prevented the emergence of such autonomy. However, has Maruyama's attempt succeeded? In some ways, the Japanese people seem to be much more democratic and reflective than before. In others, however, we might argue the opposite because we can still see fanatical movements, for instance in some areas of downtown Tokyo, as well as odious comments against foreigners on websites. Does this prove the lingering power of the Japanese way of thinking that Maruyama targeted? We may answer yes to this question, but in order to avoid falling into pessimism, we must again take up his analysis and that will hopefully help to further his goal, as well as to understand better some aspects of the (lack of) reception of liberalism at the individual level in East Asia.

If Maruyama's endeavors failed to generate an autonomous individual, this failure seems to come partly from the lack of a clear conceptualization of such an individual. Who exactly, is an "autonomous individual"? For a start, some ideas come to mind: for example, could this be an individual who can decide for himself or herself without obeying any external authority? Is someone who lives alone and independently without asking for the help of others an autonomous individual?

In fact, an autonomous individual is someone who can decide his or her own criteria of behavior and thought through strict reflection and self-criticism. Adding to this, it is essential to avoid narcissism, that is to say, to escape from self-love ("*Jiai*" 自愛 in Japanese). This point has sometimes been mentioned in studies made on Maruyama's thought, but it has been neither clarified nor sufficiently analyzed. As such, this may be a key point to understand what has prevented the development of autonomous individuality in Japan. It is not easy to widen the lesson to other peoples, and we shall refrain from discussing the Chinese case more directly here – but no doubt our endeavor shall also open an analogous debate about China.

Now, if we fail to determine the features of any autonomous individual, we may fall into the danger of being satisfied with considering only ourselves as autonomous. In this chapter, I try to analyze the relationships of narcissism to some key concepts devised by Masao Maruyama and to insist on the importance of reservations when placing moral judgment on our own actions, intentions, and character. One of the motives of the argument in this chapter is the idea that we may have failed to create an autonomous individual because of the lack of a severe and powerful critic against Japanese narcissism, or Japanese self-love (*Jiai*). This could well serve as a lesson for a philosophical appreciation of the distinctive traits in cultural relationships between the West and Asia, and between Asiatic countries.

The rejection of Jiai: Japanese moral narcissism

A first reflection in the introduction above may remind us of one suggestive reference, to Karl Löwith's severe criticism of Japanese *Jiai* (self-love). Let us sketch the dangers of "self-love" with a reading of Löwith's text, the famous German phenomenologist and historian of philosophy who is referred to in Maruyama's very famous essay *"Japanese Thought"*.[3] Furthermore, considering the place Löwith takes in Maruyama's text, there can be no doubt that Maruyama should agree with him.

Löwith's essay, which tried to be a "justification of European self-criticism and a critique of Japanese self-love", was written in 1940 and would be put at the end of his book *Martin Heidegger and European Nihilism*. In this essay, he makes the following statement:

> In principle they [= Japanese] love themselves as they are; they have not yet eaten from the (Christian!) tree of knowledge and lost their innocence, a loss which places human beings beyond themselves and makes them critical of themselves. Along with this comes an extreme sensitivity, a delicate sensitiveness, as Chamberlain puts it, whose flip-side is a touchiness that avoids the truth and that knows nothing of reasonable considerations.
>
> (Löwith 1940/1998: 232)

Löwith adds that "The deeper ground for this naïve trust in one's own superiority is Japanese self-love, which believes the right and justice are embodied in Japan, the land of God" (Löwith 1998: 231).

Löwith was thus pointing a finger at the self-love and lack of self-criticism of the Japanese, attacking Japanese narcissism because it prevented the Japanese from facing the truth and making progress based on the knowledge of truth.

If the Japanese do not try to pursue their autonomy in this way, in avoiding being confronted with the reality, then they may be authorized not to take his comments so seriously, because it would lead only to the absence of progress. Nevertheless, Löwith later pointed to a far more serious danger to be found in Japanese *self-love* and this remark is even more important and addresses not only the Japanese but East Asian peoples as well: "The Orient does not endure the kind of inconsiderate critique, either of itself or of others, in which all European progress is grounded" (Löwith 1940/1998: 233).

Löwith thus points here to the sensibility that makes us all (Japanese or not, Asians or not) intolerant of criticism by others. But why is it that they (or we, as Japanese) cannot endure a so-called inconsiderate critique? Is it simply because they (or we) think, unconsciously or otherwise, that they (or we) are worthy in themselves (ourselves), and thus that others should not criticize them (or us)? This way of thinking goes so far in Japan as to think that others should *not* criticize our actions in any way. In other words, the Japanese (or we) tend to consider such criticism on their (our) actions as attacks upon their (our) very nature. We see thus here the crucial issue: the lack of distinction between *action* (to do) and *essence* (to be).

This lack of distinction between action (to do) and essence (to be) recalls the famous analysis of Dependence (*Amae* 甘え) by Doi Takeo.[4] "*Amae*" is a key concept in the analysis of Japanese psychology. Doi describes a kind of dependent character, which is especially seen in the attitude of Japanese children toward their parents. A person of the *Amae* tends, for example, to demand too much sympathy from friends or colleagues. He or she also has a tendency to think that his or her friends or colleagues should forgive his or her mistakes or faults as his or her parents would do. In short, a person who may be qualified with *Amae* cannot distinguish his or her private human relationships from his or her public ones.

In his essay, Doi points out the close relationship between this notion of dependence (*Amae*) and the consciousness of being wronged by others. Doi wrote:

> In this connection it is interesting to recall a recent comment by Masao Maruyama that almost all Japanese leaders in all walks of life are convinced that they are always surrounded by hostile critics, a consciousness which Maruyama calls "an ever-present sense of being wronged by others (higaisha ishiki 被害者意識)". This fact clearly indicates that all of these people harbor the desire to 'amaeru' that and feel frustrated in it. If the leading representatives of Japanese society are like this, how would the rest of the population feel, without even going so far as to speak of those patients who come to seek help from psychiatrists?

> (Doi 1966/1967: 334)

This sense of "being wronged by others" comes from the feeling that the critics are unfair and that the receiver of the criticism is merely misunderstood. Maruyama himself writes as follows (and the connection seems quite obvious):

> An idea is shared among many Japanese that a "good" political or social system essentially functions in good ways and a "bad" political or social system essentially functions in bad ways. Behind such an idea, they suppose an ideal society or an ideal political system. In addition, this ideal is considered as exemplary and unchangeable. According to this idea, real social or political evil must be a temporary deviation from this ideal, provoked by some malevolent persons who would like to violate this ideal state.

> (Maruyama: 1995–97, CMW, VIII–35)[5]

In this case, those who think of themselves as benevolent persons attached to this "ideal state" consider themselves as being the victims of the social or political evil provoked by "some malevolent persons who would like to violate this ideal state". One can easily see here a sense of "being wronged by others". There is no doubt that this sense of "being wronged by others" can easily transform into an assault against one's opponent. Even now, a great deal of slander against opponents, particularly seen on websites, can be explained by this kind of psychological reasoning. Now I will try to analyze what kind of logic/reasoning permits to see this kind of self-love rise.

Jiai and the essence of moral judgment

One of the risks of *Jiai* is, I suppose, the ignorance of the essence of moral judgment. To clarify this point, I will analyze some general features of moral judgment.

When it is required to place a moral judgment on someone's actions, who is then authorized to give moral evaluation to these actions? In some cases, a person with responsibility for those concerned with this action can finally decide upon the moral value. In other cases, it may be through public debates that the moral value of such actions is decided. In any case, though, the actor himself (herself) has no right to give a *final* moral judgment of his or her own actions. Moral evaluation is given by someone (or some institution, some external criterion) which transcends the actor (the law, customs, a court, public discussion, etc.).

This idea is closely related to that of Adam Smith, often seen as the forefather of economic liberalism, who insists on the importance for us to adjust our actions to the criteria of others. For example, Smith writes as follows:

> Whatever judgment we can form concerning them [= actions of others], accordingly, must always bear some secret reference, either to what are, or to what, upon a certain condition, would be, or to what, we imagine, ought to be the judgment of others. We endeavour to examine our own conduct as we imagine any other fair and impartial spectator would examine it.
>
> (Smith 1759/1976, part III, ch. 1: 110)

Jiai, however, allows one to neglect this important aspect of moral judgment and thus to judge one's behavior for oneself. Adding to this, we must take into consideration the fact that we are natively *narcissistic* and very tolerant towards ourselves. We must never forget that this narcissism has a strong tendency to invade moral judgments, especially moral judgments about our own actions or characters. Where it lacks any objective criterion which permits us to consider our actions from the point of view of the third person, there the essential feature of moral judgment is easily forgotten and narcissism prospers. In order to clarify this point, we shall take some imaginary examples, as is common in analytic moral philosophy.

Imagine that I claimed that the invitation I send to my colleague, Professor Smith, to an academic meeting would be very beneficial to him. I may be right or I may be wrong. Prof. Smith might, though, have taken my own benefit into consideration when he accepted my invitation. In this case, it is Prof. Smith, and never myself, who can decide whether or not what I have done for him is beneficial. I should not say, even in my own mind, that what I have done is beneficial to him, if I would like to respect the essence of moral judgment.

The former analysis also applies to the interpretation of our intentions. Let us imagine now the following situation: after a meeting, I notice that Prof. Smith has forgotten his wallet. Though I take the wallet with every intention to return it to him, I forget to do so. The next day, I forget my own wallet and I use some money from the wallet of Prof. Smith, but nevertheless I have every intention to repay it. At night, Prof. Smith remarks that I have his wallet and criticizes me. I apologize saying that I had the intention all along to return it to him. Though Prof. Smith accepts my apology, he criticizes me again, remarking that I have taken some of his money. He says that he cannot believe me ...

In this imaginary case, probably, I may repeat my apology saying that I had forgotten to give the money back. Anyway, it is not me, but Prof. Smith (or another third person) *only* who is authorized to judge on my intention. At least, Professor Smith is never morally compelled to accept my apology. If I insist, however, that he should accept my intention, saying that I know my intentions much better than others ever possibly can, it would betray again the nature of moral judgment, generally speaking.[6]

Even in such a case, the very structure of *Jiai* invites us to betray this moral essence. The self-love for oneself as one is pushes us to make the following statement: "I am right and must be respected as I am. I know myself much better than others. As for my intentions, those who wrongly misunderstand me must accept what I say regardless of my actions." We may perceive in such a statement the pathological form of self-love, or *Amae*.

Now, if our analysis is philosophically true and sound, we are then obliged to refrain from placing moral judgment upon our own actions. We must also take into consideration that our intentions are, and will be, examined by others and that, sometimes, the value of our intentions can only be evaluated by others (an example is a case of a trial where the motive of a crime is evaluated). If we respect the nature of moral judgment, and if we want to be moral beings, then we must refrain from placing moral judgments about our own actions for fear of the narcissism that easily invades and thus clouds that judgment. This kind of philosophical analysis goes much further than the Japanese case only, yet this danger got illustrated very sorely in the history of East Asia.

Social essentialism and moral narcissism

The danger of *Jiai*, which we can now translate as "Japanese moral narcissism", is even much more serious when it is closely connected with "essentialism". Here I use the term "essentialism" to designate the way of thinking which supposes an invariable essence in entities so as to explain the other elements concerned. For example, if we think that the Japanese are very kind to foreigners because of *their proper essence* and that this essence is invariable, we are "essentialists" in saying so. (In this case, when the Japanese are not kind to foreigners, they say that they are very sorry not to be kind, in spite of their essential kindness, because of some maliciousness which then *necessarily* happens to be on the side of the foreigners.)

It is very interesting that Maruyama attacks this attitude, which we may possibly call *"social essentialism"*[7] in his very famous essay "To be and to do" (「「である」ことと「する」こと」(*""de-aru"koto to "suru"koto"*, Maruyama 1995–97: CWM.VIII:24–44). After discussing the rigidity of social status in the Edo period of Japanese history (1603–1868), Maruyama states that manners, in behavior or communication, were considered to derive *a priori* from one's social status (who is who and who one is as such in society) in a given group and/or area. A *"samurai"* should thus behave as a typical Samurai should, and a merchant should also behave as a merchant (Maruyama 1995–97: CWM.VIII–27). We could say that this way of thinking, which Maruyama criticizes, represents a form of *social essentialism*.

This can be related to civilizational traits, and Maruyama himself pointed to a possible relationship between this way of thinking and Confucianism, by referring to the concept of *Li* (理; "Principle") in the latter, saying that in Confucianism:

> Principle had a transcendent character, unifying everything, but was at the same time immanent in each individual thing. This Principle, when endowed upon man, constitutes his Original Nature. Hence by investigating the Principle in each individual object, we should be able to understand our own Original Nature better.
>
> (Maruyama 1974b: 24–25)

Rikki Kersten properly comments as follows, after citing this same remark: "In other words, subjectivity was located outside the self, and moral status depended on external, material things. This link between nature and norms was the crux" (Kersten 1995: 54).

Here, the most important feature deciding what an individual's identity and essential nature is consists in one's social status, and all other aspects should be decided through this element. In this respect, the person situated in a higher position in the social hierarchy is considered to be naturally the better and more moral person, and whatever he/she (usually, he) does must be considered *a priori* to be essentially good. This thought was a burden that hindered the modernization of Japan. This thought, if indeed anchored in Confucianism, may be valid more widely in East Asia, from China to Korea and other parts of the world where Confucianism has been the cradle of civilization.

Adding to this, Maruyama severely criticized social essentialism in that it played a great role in the rise and prevalence of Japanese fascism, in which the authority of the decision-makers was decided only by their distance from the Emperor. Within this fascist system, one's distance from the Emperor, determined *a priori* by social hierarchy, decides the person's value and social status. This way of thinking is "essentialist" in that a "predetermined" status decides upon the degree of authority inherent in every human being *without* referring to *effective* individual action.

The dangerous connection between narcissism and essentialism

We shall now proceed to examine the relationship between this essentialism and *Jiai* which we have just analyzed. *Jiai* is much more dangerous when connected with essentialism. I have already pointed out the danger of *Jiai* in its relationships with the moral evaluation of human action and human intentions. Here I will refer to two characteristics of the resulting effect when connecting *Jiai* with 'essentialism' with respect to *human character*.

First, proponents of essentialism in *human character* claim that the nature of human actions must have a close relationship with one's character. In other words, the nature of one human action is evaluated by referring to the moral character of the actor. The actions of a kind person must be full of kindness. The actions of a mean person must be full of malice, etc. Those who believe in this kind of essentialism suspect that the actions of a malicious person must conceal some malicious intentions, even when and whether his or her action is in fact very beneficial to the party casting aspersion. This kind of reasoning is based on what we call "the moral essentialism applied to *human character*".

Second, because we, as human beings, are inherently narcissistic, we have the obstinate tendency to consider our own character or nature very positively. I may *very* easily say to myself something like the following: "Though I may sometimes be dishonest, I'm good at heart. Let others criticize me! I don't need them to know I'm a decent human being." If we adopt such a way of thinking, we are naturally led to approve of our own actions, misguidedly thinking that all of our actions, no matter how wrong they may be, derive from good intentions, and we thus abandon any spirit of self-criticism.

When this "moral essentialism" is connected with the idea that the human moral character is ultimately evaluated from a point of view of the first person, and when this connection permits us to justify ourselves without self-examination and by referring only to our own self-admitted "good" character, then we are referring to an attitude I would like to call "Moral Narcissism".

All of us may have seen individuals who indulge in statements of the type "I'm a good person", "I'm kind", and so on. Quite naturally, such sentiments are common in our daily life. I dare think, though, that these expressions bear a great difficulty from a theoretical point of view, because the terms that designate these moral features are significant with regard to our relationships with others. In fact, I think that these moral characteristics are terms that should be used by others and not by the one who is mentioned in this case. Suppose a person who considers his or her own self as being very tolerant, even though his or her companions say that he or she is on the contrary very intolerant. In this case, who will decide whether that person is tolerant or not?

One must not overlook the fact that moral character is something that can be proven *only* by action. In this sense, the description of one's character from the point of view of the first person is never effective. Conversely, a moral-narcissist thinks as follows: "I'm kind, because I think that I'm kind. Since the evaluation of my moral character relates to me, and since I know myself better than others, they are obligated to accept and follow my own judgment about myself." In this way, moral essentialists tend to systematically justify their behavior. I repeat that this psychological character by which one will evaluate him/herself in a very positive way and which lets such a person say that he or she is good *in essence*, should properly be called "Moral Narcissism".

Moreover, such "Moral Narcissism" based on essentialism is much more dangerous because, based on this notion, it carries with it the tendency to view a moral character as definite and static, that is to say, invariable, and thus character which is justified in this manner justifies actions of the same kind in turn. It is precisely for this reason that moral narcissists never forgive their critics.

The danger of vague loyalty

In this section, we shift the analysis from a philosophical examination of moral judgment to the anthropology put forth by Maruyama Masao, as we try to show the relationship between narcissism and social authority. As we come to social matters, the people considered as communities are at stake. Here we deal with the Japanese.

In some pathological cases, moral narcissists love themselves *simply because they are themselves*. We cannot, though, justify ourselves without any substantial evidence unless we are pathologically narcissistic. There are, however, some easy ways to substitute for this evidence.

For example, we have a tendency to satisfy our narcissistic desires by belonging to social groups that boast of a relatively high status in society. In some cases, we satisfy this desire by obeying an ambiguous authority based on a historical tradition. In this case, our moral character is justified and idealized. Here, the connection between moral narcissism and essentialism discussed above reveals its most dangerous form.

Here I provide a brief sketch of the danger in the connection indicated. In short, loyalty to an authority excuses those who are attached to it from examining their characters by thoroughly justifying them *only* through their attachment. From their point of view, they are good in essence because of their attachment to this authority. Adding to this, almost all their actions are good because they are derived from their good character (essence).

Furthermore, those attached to an authority are very aggressive towards those who deny their absolute goodness, all the more so because they consider themselves to be sincere and virtuous through their devotion to that authority. This lack of doubt in their own moral goodness and sincerity, along with the lack of self-criticism, allows them to consider themselves as victims whenever their actions are criticized.

Now, some people may obey an authoritative body because of their sincere attachment to it. Some people may insist on the practical utility of an authority by saying that it can integrate national subjects. Yet, some people may attach themselves to an authority because loyalty to this authority justifies their moral character without demanding any reflection. In other words, this kind of attachment to authority quite easily satisfies the common desire for self-love. The less this authority is conceptualized, the better it functions because its very ambiguity facilitates emotional identification. An ambiguous authority can expect a great deal of loyalty from those concerned, though it attacks suspected opponents very harshly. In this regard, Maruyama's arguments about the Japanese national polity, *Kokutai* (国体), which means "Japanese excellent and original national polity", are very suggestive.[8] Maruyama writes as follows: "Because the idea of national polity was a vague sort of ideological system, it conformed very well to the traditional Japanese intellectual approach of embracing all sorts of other ideas irrespective of principles" (Maruyama 1995–97: CWM, VII–215). Adding to this, any clear conceptualization of the "*Kokutai*" idea was carefully avoided, because such a conceptualization would lead to the relativizing of this fundamental concept of the state. We can say that the figure which *Kokutai* shows to each person is the very figure that he or she would like to see in *Kokutai*. Thus, *Kokutai* changes its ideological contents according to its interpreters because of its theoretical ambiguity. This is where some notions of political economy may be derived from this analysis of moral philosophy.

From the point of view of political economy, the wartime Japanese political economic system, which was closely associated with *Kokutai* ideology, could therefore also be evaluated differently. Let us explain: to some degree, it could be said that the wartime economical system, which was highly concentrated and administered, would *finally* make postwar economic development *possible*. Yamanouchi Yasushi points in that direction in mentioning Kazuo Ōkōchi, an economist who had much influence in wartime and postwar Japanese economic thought:

> Therefore, the trajectory on which postwar Japanese social science was established should not be sought in resistance to total war, but rather in the process of contribution to the rationalization of the wartime system, as represented in the case of Ōkōchi. In this regard, one should not overlook the fact that at the time of the postwar dismantling of the Zaibatsu (財閥, this word means industrial conglomerate or financial trust) Ōkōchi argued against disturbing the rationalization standards established for the Japanese industry during the war, and he was supported in this by an influential group of economists. The wartime economy possessed a certain degree of economic rationality in its own right, and Ōkōchi felt that the reforms achieved as a result of that rationality should not be reversed or allowed to lapse. Moreover, Ōkōchi contended that rather than the postwar reforms, it was the wartime mobilization system that was responsible for creating the configuration of labor power that was the main pillar of accelerated postwar growth.
>
> (Yamanouchi 1999: 24–25)

This remark is very suggestive because it reveals the potentiality of mobilization and centralization by means of the *Kokutai* ideology. If that is correct, it can then quite ironically be said that postwar economic prosperity in Japan, seemingly related to economic liberalism, is on the contrary a product of this *Kokutai* ideology, which is absolutely incompatible with liberalism in general.

We shall now return to the psychological analysis of *Kokutai* ideology, since the notion of *Kokutai* allows its believers to indulge a narcissistic attachment and justification without reflection. It can even play every ideological role for all Japanese, with the exception of demanding self-criticism, and thus, autonomy. In obeying *Kokutai*, one's behavior is already right and virtuous *in essence*.

Here we can see the traditional connection between historical authority and narcissism. Where this connection prevails, the seed of self-criticism vanishes. And any seed of liberalism vanishes with it. This is also where the danger of essentialism becomes much clearer, all the more so because *Kokutai* is regarded as an invariable and absolute good, and thus its believers consider themselves to be good in essence. Such a way of thinking is, needless to say, absurd when we take into consideration the analysis given above of the nature of moral judgment.

An issue in the "Old Layer" of Japanese historical thought and Japanese narcissism – and beyond Japan

The very famous concept of Maruyama, that of "Old Layer" could be interpreted in this context. Maruyama coined the term "Old Layer" to denote what, he thinks, constitutes the element in Japanese thinking which he characterizes as a "flowing energy that transforms and develops itself one after another" ("*tsugi tsugi ni nariyuku ikihohi* 「つぎつぎになりゆくいきほひ」) (Maruyama 1995–97: CWM–X, p.45).[9] Maruyama says that this "flowing energy" is closely related to the Japanese affirmation of "an eternal present". Such energy ties the Japanese to that present, exempting them from reflection on their past actions and on possible future actions. It is very possible that this energy has a strong capacity to make the Japanese very conformist by inviting them, either in ethical or aesthetic terms, to identify with it.

At any rate, one *basso ostinato* of Maruyama's philosophy is the urge to create an autonomous individual. The autonomous individual must avoid identifying himself (or herself) very easily with a given authority, all the more so because the authority allows him to forego any examination of his or her actions or reflect on them. In an age of relativism, absolute values cannot exist. Even when one chooses some authoritative body as providing him (or her) with values, one must always remember that all authorities are relative and examine his (or her) own actions and the authority. Therefore, narcissism is one of the most persistent enemies against such self-examination and the achievement of autonomy. Aware of this logic, Maruyama continues to severely criticize narcissism. In fact, without trying to escape from narcissism, one can never be autonomous, because he (or she) then forgets the essential element of autonomy.

After these remarks, let us add two different points related to how cultural analysis applies more universally than the Japanese case.

First, though Maruyama's analysis applies very well to Japanese thought and ethos, it can also apply to all the other cultures to some extent and degree.

Examining many cultures (especially in East Asia) we see that the lack of a transcendent element such as God permits such self-love, and we may say that the same type of narcissism or satisfaction through identification with authority can also be seen in China or in other countries – and more at large throughout the world in the age of secularization. Maruyama himself suggests this as a shared trait among the European cultures and the ethos at the end of "Old layer of Japanese Historical Thought".[10]

Second, I will briefly sketch the relationship between narcissism and liberalism by referring to another text by Maruyama. This will require more development in further works, but it is already possible to say that in his essay *Development and Features of the Japanese Consciousness of Liberty*, Maruyama distinguished between liberty that is sought to satisfy sensual desires and liberty that one needs in order to make decisions to act based upon reflection (Maruyama 1995–97: *CWM*, II–153ff.) Maruyama pointed out the difficulty in the Japanese language of going from this first concept of liberty to the second type. Is that in turn true only in the case of Japan?

It is not difficult to see, as a consequence, a relationship between so-called "liberalism" in the first sense and "moral narcissism", if one remembers well that moral narcissism is a *psychological* feature designed to love oneself as one already is. That being said, even liberty in the first sense must be protected from "our own" activities. However, we must never forget that moral narcissism should not come as *already* justified (or capable of justification) even if in the name of some relativism based on liberalism (taken in the first sense).

Conclusion

Though there has been much discussion about the idea of the autonomous individual in postwar Japan, the essential element required to become an autonomous individual that we find through the analysis and the rejection of "Moral Narcissism" as a plague seems to require in turn more discussion. As seen in the previous pages, if "we" identify with a "flowing energy that transforms and develops itself continuously", or with some substantial but ambiguous outside authority without cautious reflection, then we fall into moral narcissism through an excessively easy self-justification. Such identification prevents us from communicating deliberatively with those who stand on opposite sides, and the whole matter results in us becoming aggressive towards them. The history of Japan in East Asia may well have much to do with in this analysis.

Maruyama, like many philosophers, argues that human nature is neither good nor evil. We can only maintain the will to be "good and moral" (if we so choose) and to try to prove that will through substantive actions. In that case, it is absolutely necessary to be conscious that we will, and must, ultimately be evaluated by some objective criteria.

It seems impossible, though, to create from the ashes some new transcendent criterion that demands self-objectification and prohibits self-love in an age lacking any transcendent judging scheme (one example being the Christian God originated in the West). Maruyama himself always insisted on Japan's difficulty in finding such an objective criterion. How can we pinpoint, in this secular world, a criterion that might help us objectify ourselves?

In this respect, I will conclude by quoting the work of Karube Tadashi. The comment by this professor of Japanese political thought at the University of Tokyo seems very suggestive when, at the end of his introductory book on Maruyama, Karube cites a line from Japanese novelist Shoji Kaoru putting forth a coincidence of ideas with Maruyama. Karube quotes Shoji as follows:

> Amid the deluge of information that advances in step with the pluralization and relativization of values, we are already on the verge of confusion, even at the stage of selecting the information that is a prerequisite for personal development. Here it seems the only really effective thing to do is to choose a person we can trust, an intellect we can honestly believe in, and learn from their wisdom and their way of thinking.
>
> (Shoji 1973: 188 cited in Karube 2008: 171)

After this citation, Karube himself commented that:

> in a society in which we are caught in the cross fire of information and commentary on the great issues of the day, it may seem altogether too modest and naïve to be searching for someone we can trust. But perhaps that is all that is left to us.
>
> (Karube 2008: 171)

Shoji and Karube both insist on the importance of finding a *reliable* person to decide. My opinion is that in the age of secularization, it is the only reliable way to relieve ourselves from the morass of narcissism. I would only like to modify one element by changing the singular "person" into a plural ("persons") since too much trust in, or attachment to, only one person leads us very easily to self-satisfaction or identification with him or her. Because of this risk (of personalization which empowers a leader), it is better that we find a set of many reliable person*s*, whose advice might be conflicting at times. That could mean a defense of democracy, in Japan and beyond, in a liberalized world, since truly autonomous individuals must support these contradictions and make choices according to the better opinion they can form by themselves.

This analysis reminds us of the importance of associations that Maruyama emphasized. Maruyama seemed to think that it is very important to belong to associations (intermediate groups) in order to be autonomous. If we belong to several groups, our point of view on society shall be balanced without being one-sided. In other words, our loyalty should never get monopolized by one single system or ideology. The distribution of loyalty leads to the social pluralism and coexistence of different ways of thought.[11] This could apply to Japan and Japan's neighbors as well.

This reflection leads me to end by saying that the ethos of reservation of moral narcissism and the trial to search for reliable persons is essential, even nowadays, for the *creation* of the autonomous individual Maruyama was seeking. This path is very narrow. I hope, though, that my analysis is philosophically sound enough and that this ethos is strong enough to open a way towards achieving such a better society in Japan, East Asia, and beyond.

Acknowledgements

The first version of this article was presented on November 28, 2014 at the "Seventeenth Hokkaido University (HU) – Seoul National University (SNU) Joint Symposium" titled "How individual liberty/liberalism theory and community/communitarianism meet together in Europe and East Asia". I express my special thanks to all the participants.

Notes

1 The relationship between "modernization" and "Westernization" is of course very difficult and complex. For some intellectuals, "Westernization" meant "modernization" in itself. Other intellectuals thought that "Westernization" is only one (typical) form of modernization and that Japan or China had to seek their own form of modernization. Maruyama Masao, whose anthropology we study in this chapter, seems to belong to the latter group and to think that "Modernization" is in essence "Democratization".

2 Kersten's following remark is also very suggestive:

> Maruyama's demand for a modern consciousness is now revealed unmistakably as the demand for a popular autonomous ethos. There is no doubt about what was required in Maruyama's eyes in postwar Japan: an autonomous citizenry which was active, whose action was informed by values autonomously defined, and which was fully conscious of the responsibility to engage in this sort of active definition of political life.
>
> (Kersten 1995: 128)

3 Karl Löwith (1897–1973) stayed at Sendai (in northern Japan) in order to escape from the Nazis from 1936 to 1940. Löwith taught philosophy at Tohoku Imperial University. This stay gave him a chance to observe closely the Japanese way of thinking and the Japanese reception of European philosophy. As for the article by Maruyama Masao, we have adopted the abbreviated English translation, "Japanese Thought", in Maruyama (1974a).

4 Takeo Doi (1920–2009), the distinguished psychoanalyst, got his *Amae no Kōzō* (literally the "structure of *Amae*") first published in 1971. It is considered a representative analysis of Japanese psychology and the volume has been translated into several languages. The English translation is titled *The Anatomy of Dependence*.

5 The *Collected Works of Maruyama Masao* (*Maruyama Masao shū*), made of sixteen volumes, were completed by Iwanami-shoten in 1995–97. We indicate volume by roman numerals, followed by page number in arabic numerals.

6 This kind of assertion is a typical attitude of *Amae*, because in this case one insists that his (or her) claim should be far more respected than that of the others.

7 Maruyama himself never uses this term. We believe, though, that this term will make Maruyama's discussion easier to understand.

8 As for Maruyama's criticism against *Kokutai* ideology, see Sasaki (2012: 40–46).

9 This English translation comes from an essay by Morioka Masahiro (Morioka 2006).

10 Maruyama wrote: "When we turn our eyes to the European world, a century after Nietzsche said that God is dead, we cannot help remarking that the scenes seen there have become quite similar to those seen in Japan" (Maruyama 1995–97: *CWM*, X–64).
11 The present analysis originated from an endeavor to analyze the nature of the life of associations (intermediate groups) in Japan and in East Asia presented at the March 2013 meeting of the program "Liberalism in between Europe and China" chaired by Gilles Campagnolo and held in Aix-en-Provence.

References

Doi, Takeo (1971/1973) *Amae no Kōzō* （『甘えの構造』）, Tokyo: Kondansha. English translation: John Bester (1973), *The Anatomy of Dependence*, Tokyo Kondansha International.

Doi, Takeo (1967) 'Giri-Ninjō: An Interpretation', in R. P. Dore (ed.), (1967), *Aspects of Social Change in Modern Japan*, Princeton: Princeton University Press, 327–36.

Fukuzawa, Yukichi (1866–70/2002) *Seiyō-Jijō* （『西洋事情』, Things Western), in *Collected Works of Fukuzawa Yukichi*, vol. 1, Tokyo, Keiō-Gijuku University Press, 1–339.

Karube, Tadashi (2008), *Maruyama Masao and the Fate of Liberalism in Twentieth-Century Japan*, Tokyo, LTCB International Library Selection.

Kersten, Rikki (1995) *Democracy in Postwar Japan: Maruyama Masao and the Search for Autonomy*, London: Routledge.

Löwith, Karl (1940/1998) 'Afterword to the Japanese Reader', in *Martin Heidegger and European Nihilism*, New York: Columbia University Press, 228–34. This article was firstly published in Japanese in *Shisō* （『思想』）, No. 222, Tokyo, Iwanami Shoten.

Maruyama, Masao (1995–97) *Collected Works of Maruyama Masao*" (*Maruyama Masao shū* （『丸山眞男集』）, 16 vols. Tokyo: Iwanami Shoten.

Maruyama, Masao (1974a) "Japanese Thought", in Irwin Scheiner (ed.) *Modern Japan: An Interpretive Anthology*, London/New York: Macmillan: 208–215.

Maruyama, Masao (1974b), *Studies in the Intellectual history of Tokugawa Japan*, Tokyo: Tokyo University Press.

Morioka, Masahiro (2006) 'The Ethics of Human Cloning and the Sprout of Human Life', in Heiner Roetz (ed.), *Cross-Cultural Issues in Bioethics: The Example of Human Cloning*, Amsterdam, Rodopi: 1–16.

Sasaki, Fumiko (2012) *Nationalism, Political Realism and Democracy in Japan: The Thought of Masao Maruyama*, London: Routledge.

Shoji, Kaoru (1973) 'Kaisetsu – Toku ni wakai dokusya no tame ni' （「解説－特に若い読者のために」 *Notes: Especially for younger readers*), in Hayashi Tatsuo, *Kyōsan syugi teki ningen* （『共産主義的人間』, *The Communist Personality*), Tokyo, Chūkō Bunko.

Smith, Adam (1759/1976), *Theory of Moral Sentiments*, ed. D. D. Raphael and A. L. Macfie, Oxford: Oxford University Press.

Yamanouchi, Yasushi (1999), 'Total War and Social Integration: A methodological Introduction', in Yasushi Yamanouchi, J. Victor Koschmann and Ryuichi Narita (eds.) *Total War and 'Modernization'*, Ithaca NY, East Asia Program, Cornell University, 1–40.

8 Dual individualization in East Asia

Individualization in the society and in the family

Sang-Jin Han and Young-Hee Shim

Introduction

The primary purpose of this chapter is to conceptually sort out different types of individualization in East Asia and demonstrate their salient characteristics based on survey data collected from three cities of Seoul, Beijing, and Tokyo. We want to show that individualization in East Asia is a Janus-faced, dual individualization, involving a tendency of individualization of the West on the one hand and characteristics of "community-oriented individualization" (Shim and Han 2013) on the other. We also want to reveal that different types of individualization we develop are linked to different styles of liberalism in the context of East Asian development.

Let us begin by noting two aspects of individualization. One is individualization from the perspective of social change, or individualization in society in general. The other is individualization in the context of the family. The reason why we divide these two aspects of individualization is because in East Asia it is questionable to define individualization exclusively in terms of self-interests. In contrast, collective interests can be a strong motive of individualization. For instance, individualization in the context of the family might be different from individualization in society in general. This study attempts to reveal the individualization in society in general and individualization in the context of the family in three cities, utilizing a typology of individualization, focusing on "community-oriented type" of individualization.

It is well known that the family in East Asian countries has long been considered as one of the most important institutions, showing strong collective orientation and strong ties between family members and sharing some Confucian traditions. These days, however, the family in these three countries has been undergoing remarkable change. In this regard the most important change would be the family risk and individualization in urban transformation. While family risk manifests itself in high divorce rate, low fertility and low marriage rate, etc., the individualization could be considered as a deeper process of change in the relationship between individual and community, which forms the basis of the family risk. We will approach the issue of individualization within the urban context of transformation in East Asia. Since family risk has been already investigated (Shim *et al.*, 2014), we would like to show the extent, the variation in types, and explanations of individualization in society and in the context of the family as well.

There have been considerable debates on the characteristics of individualization in East Asia, particularly in Korea. Chang and Song (2010) claim that individualization in Korea is "aversive individualization" or "individualization without individualism". On the contrary, Hong (2012) claims that there actually developed individualism in Korea. In this context, we (Shim and Han 2010, 2013) have argued that the theory of social change grasped by individualization shows a delicate balance between transformation of individual and transformation of community. What comes out from the combination of these two concomitant changes is something like "family-oriented individualization," or "public-oriented individualization," embracing individual choices plus community orientation. This chapter will further support the claim that individualization in East Asia has such Janus-faced characteristics.

Another thing is that, there is a lack of empirical studies on individualization in East Asia as a whole. There have been some studies on individualization in East Asia, arguing that individualization in East Asia is different from that of the West (Suzuki et al. 2010; Ishida et al. 2010; Chang and Song 2010; Shim and Han 2010, 2013; Shim 2013; Shim, Kim and Kim 2014; Yamada 2010; Yan 2010, 2013). However, most of these studies used arguments based on historical unfolding of individualization or qualitative study in each country. And empirical studies on individualization in East Asia as a whole comparing East Asian countries are hard to find. This research is an attempt to fill this gap with a systematic survey of individualization in the three cities of Seoul, Beijing, and Tokyo.

In this context the research questions are as follows:

1   Is there a trend of individualization among the citizens of the three cities in East Asia? That is, to what extent are they individualized? Here we will see individualization in society in general, in the context of social change. In this regard I will discuss the typology of individualization in society in general.
2   If the citizens of East Asia are individualized in society in general, what are the characteristics of their individualization in the context of the family? Here we will discuss the typology of individualization in the context of the family, and see what is the most common type in East Asia. In this regard, we will discuss the issues of "*hikikomori*" in Japan, or "*balinghou*" in China.

We distinguish these two types, the individualization in general and the individualization in the context of the family, because individualization in the context of the family has special meaning in East Asia.

3   What is the meaning of the findings? What is the relationship between individual and community in the context of the family? Is there any characteristic of individualization unique to East Asia?

Analytical framework: theory and typology of individualization for East Asia

Individualization theory

The concept of individualization indicates a categorical shift in relations between an individual and the society (Beck 1992: 127). Here individualization means that individuals get unleashed from the previous frameworks of welfare financed by either the state or business firms or by the family and have to take care of their survival by their own means (Han and Shim 2010; Shim and Han 2010).

The individualization theorists give an account of the relationship between individuals and social determinants that is more complex than the "either/or" models of conventional social science. They see individualization as a form of emancipation from particular constraints. As Howard (Howard 2007: 9) aptly points out, these constraints revolve around several poles. The first is tradition, or the idea that people behave in certain ways and understand their experience on the basis of historically established forms of behavior and modes of interpretation. In this sense, individualization means the diminishing power of tradition to determine the specific content of behaviors and to justify actions. In place of tradition, human behavior becomes increasingly "reflexive", meaning that it is driven by deliberate human actions and choices and is shaped by self-awareness (Beck, Giddens and Lash 1994).

The second constraint that is lifted in the process of individualization is the close tie between individual identity and membership of specific social collectives, such as social classes, ethnic groupings, and local and national communities (Howard 2007: 9). The individualization thesis suggests that individuals decreasingly derive their identities from social groupings and no longer see their fates as being directly shared with other group members. According to individualization theorists, traditions and groups continue to play a role in individual experience; however, the meaning of tradition and group membership has shifted from an external imposition to a deliberate action or affiliation. Thus the act of conforming to a tradition or joining and submitting to a group is increasingly interpreted, queried, and challenged on the grounds that it is a reflexive choice, something done consciously and deliberately by individuals to inform self-identity and personal biography (Howard 2007: 8–9).

While the individualization thesis assumes growing scope for personal choice and individual decision-making, this does not mean that individuals are free to do whatever they like, unencumbered by social structures and norms (Beck and Beck-Gernsheim 2002). The individualization thesis suggests that social structure is not receding in its influence; rather, it is changing the demands it places on individuals. Individualization, according to Beck, is 'the social structure of the second modernity' and as such, it implies a transformation of social structures, not the liberation of individuals from social processes. Increasingly, social structures compel people to become individuals and take charge of their lives. Thus Bauman characterized the present era in terms of "compulsive and obligatory self-determination" (Bauman 2000: 32), and Beck suggests that today individuals are compelled, "for the sake of their own material survival – to make themselves the center of their own planning and conduct of life" (Beck 1992: 88).

Typology of individualization in general

Individualization consists of two distinct dimensions of emancipation, that is, emancipation from tradition and emancipation from community. One dimension is whether one's way of thinking is traditional or reflexive. The other dimension is whether one's goal is oriented towards collective interests or self-interests. One is about the mode of operation and the other is about the goal between collective interests and self-interests. Thus a typology made of these two dimensions will be useful in tracing not only the change of traditional versus reflexive ways of thinking/acting, but also the change of the orientation toward collective interests versus self-interests. By crossing these two dimensions of individualization as two main axes, we constructed the following four types of individualization (Table 8.1; Shim and Han 2013).

Type A is characterized by both strong collective interests and traditional way of thinking/acting, thus it can be called "conventional types of collectivism." This type can typically be found among those who consider collective interests to be more important than self-interest grounded primarily on traditional conventions. Type B is characterized by traditional ways of thinking/acting (for example, family-oriented), but tries to pursue self-interest for survival. The self-interests here can be interpreted as private interests. Thus it can be called "family-oriented striving individualization." This type tends to be frequently found among those who strive hard to get out of poverty for the welfare of the family rather than strictly for personal gain. The type labeled "family-oriented individualization" (Shim and Han 2010) can be classified as a category of this type. Type C is characterized by a reflexive way of thinking/acting closely associated with the mode of action pursuing and advocating public interests. A typical example is civil movements based on individual decisions to join through either on-line or off-line deliberations in pursuit of certain values of public

Table 8.1 Typology of individualization in general

| | | Goal of orientation | |
		Collective interests	Self-interests
Mode of thinking/ acting	Traditional	A Conventional types of collectivism	B Family-oriented striving individualization
	Reflexive	C Public-minded participatory individualization	D Self-centered libertarian individualization

Source: Shim and Han, 2013.

significance. Thus it can be called "public-minded participatory individualization." Han's study on the so-called "386 generation" reveals this type of individualization (Han 2007). Type D is characterized by both reflexive ways of thinking/acting and pursuit of self-centered individualizing tastes and preferences. This type can typically be found among the younger generations, namely teenagers or those in their twenties. Libertarian individualization may fully develop when such conditions such as cultural democracy, welfare state, and classical individualism are met (Baumann 2001; Beck 1992; Beck and Beck-Gernsheim 2002).

Typology of individualization in the context of the family

Since the above typology on individualization is about the very general situation in the urban transformation of a society as a whole and may not reflect the relationship of the individual and his/her family in the context of this family, we tried to make a typology of individualization in the context of the family which can better reveal the characteristics of East Asian family relationship such as strong ties between individual and community. In order to do so, we crossed two dimensions of individualization in the context of the family: the first is the mode of thinking/acting and the second is solidarity among the family, which are similar to the case of individualization in society in general. By crossing these two dimensions we elaborate the following four types of individualization in the context of the family (Table 8.2).

As shown in Table 8.2, type 1 is called "integrated community", traditional (or familial) in attitude and also having strong solidarity among the family. Type 2 can be called "fragmented community," traditional (or familial) in attitude but having weak solidarity among the family. Type 3 is called "community-oriented individual," reflexive (or individualistic) in attitude, but having strong solidarity among the family. Type 4 is called "self-centered individualization," reflexive (or individualistic) in attitude and also having weak solidarity among the family. In a Western theory of individualization it is assumed that the individualization process is moving from type 1 through type 2, type 3 to type 4.

Table 8.2 Types of individualization in the context of the family

| | | Solidarity among the family | |
		strong	weak
Mode of Thinking/ Acting	Traditional	1 Integrated community	2 Fragmented community
	Reflexive	3 Community-oriented individual	4 Self-centered individualization

Data and method

For this study, data were collected by a survey research. Questionnaire surveys were conducted to 1,609 people, 500 people respectively in three cities of Seoul, Beijing, and Tokyo in June 2012.[1] Socio-demographic characteristics of the respondents in three cities is shown in Table 8.3.

In terms of gender, there are more men in Beijing than in Seoul and Tokyo, while the proportion of gender is similar in Tokyo and Seoul. In terms of age, there is a bigger number of younger people (in their twenties) in Beijing, while there are more elderly people (over sixties) in Seoul. In terms of education, the proportion of college graduates is highest in Seoul, and lowest in Beijing. In terms of standard of living, the proportion of the middle class is highest in Tokyo and lowest in Beijing, while the proportion of the lower class is highest in Beijing and lowest in Tokyo.

The variables were measured as follows: as to individualization, two levels of individualization were measured: individualization in general and individualization in the context of the family. First, as to individualization in general, we asked questions on two levels, one on individualization in general and the other on individualization in the context of the family. As to individualization in general we tried to measure it by giving focus to the two aspects of individualization, that is, community-orientation versus individual-orientation, on the one hand, and tradition versus de-traditionalization on the other.[2]

Table 8.3 Socio-demographic characteristics of the respondents in three cities

(%)		Seoul	Beijing	Tokyo
Total frequency		(512)	(560)	(537)
Sex	Men	49.4	50.2	47.1
	Women	50.6	49.8	52.9
Age groups	Twenties	19.5	38.9	20.1
	Thirties	22.7	19.9	17.9
	Forties	21.1	20.2	17.4
	Fifties	18.4	13.9	11.8
	Over sixties	18.4	7.1	32.7
Education	High School and lower	26.2	47.3	37.6
	College and higher	73.8	52.7	62.4
Standard of living	Upper class	2.3	0.9	1.2
	Middle class	57.0	47.0	75.4
	Lower class	40.6	52.1	23.4
Marital status	Single	28.9	36.5	40.2
	Married	64.8	58.9	52.8
	Divorce/separation	6.3	4.6	7.0
Total percentage		100	100	100

They were measured with two items. Among the two items one item focused on the tradition-boundness versus de-traditionalization, and the other focused on the community-orientation versus individual-orientation. The questions focusing on the tradition-boundness versus de-traditionalization are: "Even if they are customs and authority, I don't have to respect them" versus "Customs and authority should be respected as much as possible." The other focusing on the community-orientation versus individual-orientation is: "It is more important to protect one's personal interests" versus "The development of the state and society should be considered first." They were measured on the five-point scale.

Second, regarding the individualization in the context of the family, as mentioned above, we tried to measure the relationship in a more concrete situation in the context of the family which can better reveal the characteristics of East Asian family relationships such as strong ties between individual and community, since the above questions on individualization are very general questions in the society as a whole and may not reflect the relationship of individual and family in the context of family. In order to do that, we first measured the mode of thinking/acting in terms of "attitude toward the family" through three items of statements on the attitude toward marriage and the family. The question is as follows: "If your child expresses an opinion like the following, how would you respond?" And the three items are as follows: (1) "If he/she says that he/she will live alone without getting married," (a) "I will persuade him/her to get married with various means such as matchmaking," versus (b) "Living alone can be a way of life if he/she wants it"; (2) "If he/she says that he/she will not have a child after getting married," (a) "I will persuade him/her to have a child by any means," versus (b) "Living without a child can be a way of life, if the couple wants it"; (3) "If he/she says that it is too difficult to live together and he/she will get divorced," (a) "I will tell him/her not to get divorced," versus "Getting divorced can be a way of life, if the couple wants it." It is OK even if the children do not get married." Each of these three involves emancipation from the tradition and from community. In order to see the distribution of the attitude toward the family, we gave point 1 to (a) and point 2 to (b) and added them up. And then we classified them into "traditional" (less 3 points) and "reflexive" (4 to 6 points) according to the summed up points.

And then, we tried to measure the solidarity of the family relationship in a more dramatic situation, like disasters or emergencies, to see the strength of the relationship between individual and community in East Asia better. The related question is: "If a disaster occurred, how much help do you think the following people or groups could give you?" And the answer is "a lot", "somewhat", "none." "A lot" was counted as "strong" and "somewhat" and "none" were counted as "weak". We crossed this with the attitude toward the family discussed above and made the following four types of family-oriented individualization (Table 8.2).

Individualization in society in general in three megacities

The two aspects of individualization in society in general: mode of thinking/ acting versus goal of orientation/interest

As mentioned above, in order to measure individualization in general, we tried to measure it by giving focus to the two aspects of individualization, that is, mode of thinking/acting, or tradition versus de-traditionalization, and goal of orientation, or community-orientation versus individual-orientation, on the other.[3]

The results are as shown in (Figure 8.1). The answers to mode of thinking/ acting or "Even if they are customs and authority, we don't have to respect them" turned out to be high in Seoul and Tokyo with more than 50 points, but low in Beijing with 42.3 points. And the answers to goal of orientation or "It is more important to protect one's personal interests" turned out to be relatively low in Beijing and Seoul with less than 50 points, and high in Tokyo with 54.0 points among the 100 scores. This means that among the citizens of three East Asian cities, Tokyo citizens are relatively more individualized, Beijing citizens are not much individualized, and Seoul citizens are in the middle.

One thing to note is that we can see some balance between the mode of thinking/acting and goal of orientation in three cities: 55.3 vs 54.0 in Tokyo, 42.3 vs. 40.2 in Beijing, and 50.8 vs. 46.7 in Seoul. The difference between the two dimensions of individualization in three cities does not seem to be big. Only those in Seoul seem slightly skewed, even if not much, showing they are individualized in terms of mode of thinking/acting, while they are not so much individualized in terms of goal of orientation or interests.

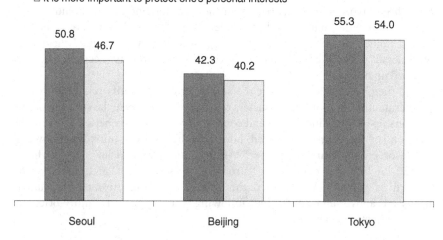

■ Even if they are customs and authority, we don't have to respect them

□ It is more important to protect one's personal interests

Figure 8.1 Mode of thinking/acting versus goal of orientation/interest in three cities

Distribution of individualization in society in general

As mentioned above, by crossing these two dimensions of individualization, that is emancipation from tradition and emancipation from community, as two main axes, we constructed the four types of individualization: they are type A, conventional types of collectivism; type B, family-oriented striving individualization; type C, public-minded participatory individualization; and type D, self-centered libertarian individualization.

When we classify the individualization in society in general into these four types (Table 8.4), those who belong to type A is 15.5%, type B 17.1%, type C 15.8%, and type D is 51.7%; thus the type with the highest proportion is type D (51.7%), that is, self-centered libertarian individualization, and three other types show similar distribution, with the lowest proportion is type A (15.5%), conventional types of collectivism, showing that more than half of the respondents are individualized into type D.

When we compare the distribution according the three cities (Figure 8.2), Type A, that is, conventional types of collectivism, is highest among Beijing citizens (28.0%), next highest among Seoul citizens (14.1%), and lowest among Tokyo citizens (3.7%), and type D, that is, self-centered libertarian individualization, which is closest to the Western type of individualization, is highest among Tokyo citizens (70.7%), next among Seoul citizens (52.1%), and lowest among Beijing citizens (33.0%), showing that Tokyo is the most individualized among the three cities. Type B, that is, family-oriented striving individualization, is similar among the three cities, and Type C, that is, public-minded participatory individualization, is similar between Seoul and Beijing citizens and lowest among Tokyo citizens.

When we break down the distribution of types of individualization by age groups for more detailed analysis of the distribution of individualization (Figures 8.3, 8.4, 8.5), it shows a different pattern by cities. In Seoul, where Type D is a dominant type, Type D is higher among the younger age groups, and lower among the elderly, while Type A is higher among the aged, and lower among the younger age groups, showing that Korea is in the middle of change. In Beijing, where Type A and D are almost equal, it shows a similar pattern as in Seoul, with Type A higher among the aged and type D higher among the younger, showing some change is occurring. In Tokyo, where Type D is a majority, interestingly

Table 8.4 Distribution of types of individualization in society in general in three cities

(%)	Conventional types of collectivism	Family-oriented striving individualization	Public-minded participatory individualization	Self-centered individual-ization	Total
Seoul	14.1	15.4	18.4	52.1	100.0(512)
Beijing	28.0	21.5	17.6	33.0	100.0(558)
Tokyo	3.7	14.2	11.4	70.7	100.0(829)
Total	15.5(248)	17.1(275)	15.8(253)	51.7(829)	100.0(1605)

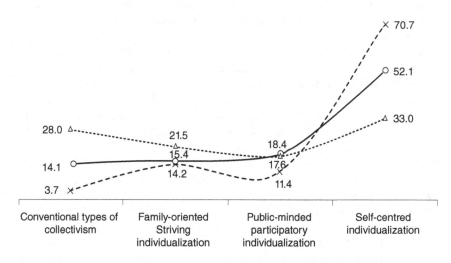

Figure 8.2 Distribution of types of individualization in general in three cities

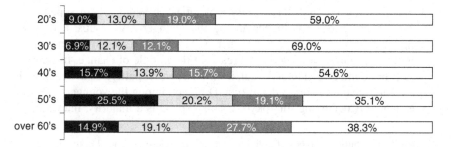

Figure 8.3 Distribution of types of individualization in general by age groups: Seoul

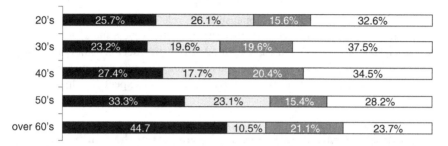

Figure 8.4 Distribution of types of individualization in general by age groups: Beijing

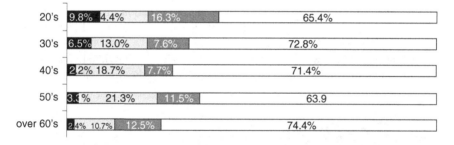

Figure 8.5 Distribution of types of individualization in general by age groups: Tokyo

Type D is higher among the elderly, and Type A is higher among the younger, against our expectation, showing no distinct pattern. This could be interpreted that much change has already occurred.

When we break down the distribution of types of individualization by gender, it also shows different pattern by cities. In Seoul, Type A is higher among men, and Type D is higher among women, showing that women are more individualized (or faster in individualization). In Tokyo, the situation is similar to that in Seoul: Type A is higher among men, and Type D is higher among women, showing that women are more individualized. In Beijing, it shows a completely different picture: Type A is higher among men, and Type D is also higher among men, showing that tradition and change are both led by men.

Individualization in the context of the family

The above results on individualization in general show that East Asia is not much different from the west, and also following the Western type of individualization. East Asia is well known for a strong family tie, but this is not so clear in the above results. Thus we have to ask a question again whether it is really so. In order to answer this question, we tried to measure the relationship in a more concrete situation in the context of the family which can better reveal the characteristics of East Asian family relationships such as strong ties between individual and community, as mentioned in the previous section. The two aspects we tried to measure are attitude toward the family and degree of expected help from the family when in disaster.

Two aspects of individualization in the context of the family: mode of thinking/acting and solidarity among the family

As mentioned above, in order to measure the mode of thinking/acting we used three items of statements on the attitude toward marriage and the family. The question is as follows: how would you respond (1) if your child says he/she will live alone without getting married, (2) if he/she says that he/she will not have a child after getting married, (3) if he/she says that it is too difficult to live together and he/she will get divorced? Each of these three has emancipation from the traditional way of thinking/acting. And in order to measure the solidarity of the family relationship, we used a more dramatic situation, like disasters or emergencies, to see how strong the relationship between individual and community is in East Asia better.

As shown in Figure 8.6, the distribution of reflexive (or individualist) attitudes toward the family in the three cities turned out to be quite high with more than

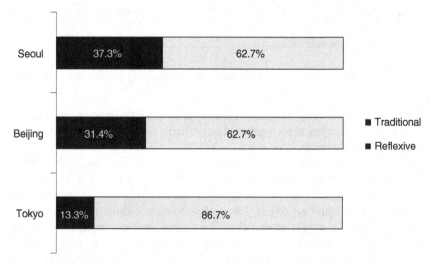

Figure 8.6 Mode of thinking/acting: traditional (familial) vs reflexive (individualistic)

60% in all the three cities; highest in Tokyo (86.7%), followed by Beijing (68.6%); and lowest in Seoul (62.7%). This shows that citizens are much reflexive (or individualized) at least in terms of mode of thinking/acting in the context of the family.

The answers to the question of "If a disaster occurred, how much help do you think the following people or groups could give you?" are as shown in Figure 8.7. Among the six institutions mentioned, the family turned out to be highest in the degree of expected help when in disaster, showing strong solidarity among the family (showing more than 60 points overall and more than 90 points in Beijing and Tokyo among 100 scores). Next was friends, neighbors, government, insurance company, and civic group (NGO), with Beijing being exceptionally high in expected help from the government (66.9).

These findings show that citizens probably have a contradictory attitude, because they show highly reflexive (or individualist) attitude in terms of mode of thinking/acting on the one hand, but show strong solidarity among the family, expecting a lot of help from the family when in disaster on the other. This might suggest that individualization is occurring in terms of mode of thinking or attitude on the one hand, but citizens still rely on the family in real situations such as in times of disasters or emergency, showing a Janus face in terms of individualization.

Individualization in the context of the family

As mentioned above we tried to make a typology of individualization in the context of the family by crossing two dimensions of individualization in this context of the family: that is, the mode of thinking/acting and solidarity among

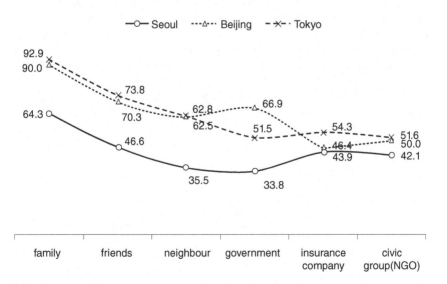

Figure 8.7 Degree of expected help when in disaster in three cities

the family. And the resulting four types are: type 1, "integrated community"; type 2, "fragmented community"; type 3, "community-oriented individual"; and type 4, "self-centered individual" (Table 8.2).

The distribution of the types of relationship between individual and community in the context of the family in the three cities is very interesting (Figure 8.8). As shown in Table 8.5, "community-oriented individual," or type 3, is highest among the four types, with 49.2%, almost a half of the respondents. Next is "self-centered individual," or type 4 with 23.6%; the third is "integrated community" type, or type 1, and the fourth is "fragmented community" type or type 2.

When we compare the distribution in the three cities (Figure 8.8), Beijing and Tokyo show a similar pattern, showing a surprisingly high proportion of type 3 or "community-oriented individual", with 70.6% in Tokyo and with 56.3% in Beijing, and Seoul is lowest with 19.1%. Seoul, on the other hand, shows a different distribution. In Seoul, the highest type is type 4 or "self-centered individual," with 43.6%, next is type 2 with 23.4%, and the third is type 3 with 19.1%, and type 1 is the last with 13.9%.

How can this be interpreted? The first thing is that the high proportion of type 3, that is, community-oriented individual, clearly shows the Janus-faced or dual characteristics of the relationship between individual and community in East Asia when compared with the individualization in society in general: that self-centered, Western-style individualization is going on in the society in general, but community-orientation is also going on in the context of the family.

Second, why the higher proportion of type 3 in both Beijing and Tokyo, the least individualized and the most individualized city in terms of individualization in society in general? As for Beijing it might be rather easy to interpret: that it could probably be because it is less individualized in society in general, and thus the relationship within the family is still strong, stronger than in Seoul. However, the high proportion of type 3 in Tokyo is not easy to interpret. Could it be possible that Tokyo citizens crave for stronger family relationship, because they are too much reflexive? Or perhaps it could be due to the effect of 3.11 Fukushima nuclear leakage incidents. There are some reports that after the accident, some changes occurred in Japanese people's attitude. For example, people began to care more about their families, and young people, who did not want to get married, now began to consider getting married (SBS News Report, May 10, 2011).

Third, as for Seoul, it can be interpreted that people's way of thinking is relatively traditional (or familial), taking value in traditional familial relationship,

Table 8.5 Distribution of types of individualization in the context of the family in three cities

(%)	Integrated community	Fragmented community	Community-oriented individual	self-centered individual
Seoul	13.9	23.4	19.1	43.6
Beijing	25.3	6.1	56.3	12.4
Tokyo	9.4	3.8	70.6	16.2
Total	16.4	10.9	49.2	23.6

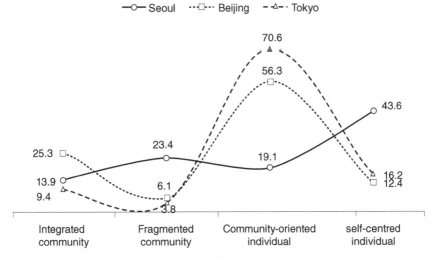

Figure 8.8 Distribution of types of individualization in the context of the family in three cities

but in reality solidarity of the family relationship seems very much weakened and fragmented, so that they do not think that they can get much help when needed.

An analysis of "community-oriented individual"

Since the type of "community-oriented individual" turned out to be highest among the four types we distinguished, it needs a more detailed analysis. In this section I will focus on socio-demographic factors influencing "community-oriented individual".

First, in order to see the effect of socio-demographic variables, we broke down the distribution by age groups (Figures 8.9, 8.10, 8.11). As a result we could see the different configurations of community-oriented individual in each city.

In Tokyo it is found that an overwhelming majority (70.6%) belong to type 3, that is, "community-oriented individual" (Figure 8.8), and they are evenly distributed among both young and elderly generations. In Beijing, where more than half (56.3%) belong to type 3 and it is evenly distributed among the younger and elderly generations. However, a close look at Tokyo shows that there are more elderly generation in type 3 and younger generation in type 4, that is, self-centered libertarian type, showing a move from type 3 to type 4 between the generations. A close look in Beijing also reveals that there are more younger generations in type 3 and more elderly generations in type 1, showing that they are moving from type 1 to type 3.

However, the situation is quite different in Seoul. In Seoul, nearly half (43.6%) belong to type 4, the next is type 2, "fragmented community type" (23.4%), and only 19.1% belongs to type 3. In Seoul as for type 4, the younger generations show higher proportion than the older generation, and as for type 1 and 2, older generations show higher proportion than the younger ones. And as for type 3, younger generations show higher proportion than elderly generation. From this we can clearly see the changes occurring in individualization among the age groups in Seoul, with more elderly generation in type 1 and type 2, and more younger generations in type 3 and type 4 (Figure 8.9).

Why are there so many type 3, or community-oriented, individuals in Tokyo and Beijing? More specifically why are there so many type 3, not only among the elderly but also among the younger generations in Tokyo and Beijing? This could be related to the economically difficult situations such as high housing price, difficulty in finding a job, etc., in both cities. In such a situation they have little they can do independently, and they have no choice but to rely on their families, even though they are reflexive (or individualistic) in mode of thinking. Thus they expect help from the family before they can stand on their own. For example,

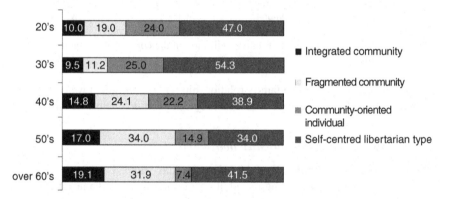

Figure 8.9 Distribution of types of relationship between individual and community in the context of the family in three cities (by age: Seoul)

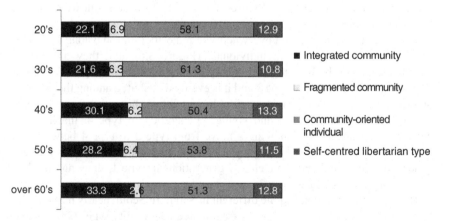

Figure 8.10 Distribution of types of relationship between individual and community in the context of the family in three cities (by age: Beijing)

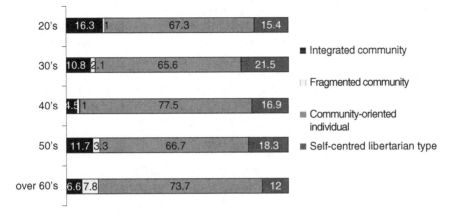

Figure 8.11 Distribution of types of relationship between individual and community in the context of the family in three cities (by age: Tokyo)

"parasitic singles" and "*hikikomori*" in Japan and "*kenlaos*" among the "*balinghous*" and "*jiulinghous*" in China could be examples (Li et al. 2013). A similar phenomenon can also be observed among the so-called "*baiksu*" in Seoul.

In Seoul, why is there a relatively high proportion of type 2, that is, "fragmented community," particularly among the elderly generations? This might be because their mode of thinking is still traditional (or familial), or taking value in a familial relationship, even though in reality the solidarity of the family relationship seems to have been weakened or fragmented.

In sum, in all the three cities, there seems to be a change going on in individualization, though on a different level. The individualization seems to be moving from type 3 to type 4 in Tokyo, from type 1 to type 3 in Beijing, and from type 2 through type 3 to type 4 in Seoul. This suggests that individualization is going on in all the three cities in East Asia, even though it is taking different paths, even though it is most advanced in Tokyo among the three cities.

Summary and conclusion

This chapter tried to reveal whether individualization is occurring and, if so, what kind of individualization is occurring in East Asia. More specifically, this study tried to argue that individualization in East Asia has a Janus face, showing a tendency of individualization of the West on the one hand and characteristics of community-oriented individualization on the other. For this we developed two typologies of individualization: the first, the typology of individualization in society in general, and the second, the typology of individualization in the context of the family.

Let us recall that the types in the first typology include "conventional types of collectivism" (type A), "family-oriented striving individualization" (type B), "public-minded participatory individualization" (type C), and "self-centered libertarian individualization" (type D). The types in the second typology included "integrated community" (type 1), "fragmented community" (type 2), "community-oriented individual" (type 3), and "self-centered individual" (type 4). For this we conducted a survey research in three cities of East Asia; that is, Seoul, Beijing, and Tokyo. The research findings are as follows.

First, as to individualization in society in general, self-centered libertarian individualization of the West (type D) turned out to be high in two East Asian cities, Tokyo (70.7%) and Seoul (52.1%), even though it turned out to be relatively low in Beijing (33.0%) (Figure 8.2). When we break down the distribution of types of individualization by age groups, it shows different pattern by cities. In Seoul, where "self-centered libertarian individualization" or Type D is a dominant type, Type D is higher among the younger, and lower among the elderly, while "conventional types of collectivism" or Type A are higher among the aged, and lower among the younger, showing that Korea is in the middle of change. In Beijing, where Type A and D are almost equal, it shows a similar pattern as in Seoul, with Type A higher among the aged and type D higher among the younger, showing some change is occurring. In Tokyo, where Type D is in a majority, interestingly Type D is higher among the elderly, and Type A is higher among the younger, against our expectation, showing no distinct pattern. This could be interpreted that much change has already occurred.

Second, as to the individualization in the context of the family, the "community-oriented individual" (type 3) turned out to be highest among the four types with 49% (Table 8.5). Beijing and Tokyo show a surprisingly high proportion of type 3 or "community-oriented individual", with 70.6% in Tokyo and with 56.3% in Beijing (Figure 8.8), showing the characteristics of the family relationship in East Asia. Seoul, on the other hand, shows a different distribution, showing the highest type in type 4 with 43.6%, with "fragmented community" type as the second (Figure 8.8). A closer analysis shows that there is a change going on in individualization moving from type 1 through type 2 and type 3 to type 4 (Figure 8.9).

Third, as to the more detailed analysis of the "community-oriented individuals," which seems to be the characteristics of individualization in the context of the family, it turned out that in Beijing and Tokyo, there are more "community-oriented individuals" not only among the elderly but also among the younger generations in their twenties and thirties. This seems because they are in difficult situation in real life even though they are individualistic in attitude. "Parasitic singles" and *"hikigomoris"* in Japan, *"kenlaos"* among the *"balinghous"* and *"jiulinghous"* in China could be examples.

These findings show that in East Asia people are very much individualized in society in general in urban transformation, but at the same time very much family-oriented in the context of the family. In this sense the path for individualization might be called "dual individualization." The implications of the findings for the future of the family are that even though the individualization is under way, it has special characteristics of family orientation unique to East Asia. It shows that the family has special meaning for East Asian citizens and thus the family, even though it faces many problems and crises, is still very important in East Asia. It also implies that there are more social and cultural conditions in East Asia, particularly in China, for liberalism to develop in the direction of socially sensitive or responsible liberalism than in the Western countries.

Notes

1 Surveys were conducted by Prof. Li Qiang of Tsinghua University in China, by Prof. Han Sang-Jin of Seoul National University in Korea, and by Prof. Li Tingjiang of Chuo University in Japan respectively.
2 These are to be related to "individualization typology" as mentioned above consisting of four types, that is, conventional types of collectivism, family-oriented striving individualization, public-minded participatory individualization, and self-centered libertarian individualization (see Table 8.1).
3 These are again to be related to the same "individualization typology" as mentioned above.

References

Baumann, Zygmunt (2000) *Liquid Modernity*, Cambridge: Polity.
——(2001) *The Individualized Society*, Cambridge: Polity.
Beck, U. (1992) *Risk Society: Towards a New Modernity*, trans. M. Ritter, London: Sage.
Beck, U., and Beck-Gernsheim, E. (2002) *Individualization: Institutionalized Individualism and its Social and Political Consequences*, London: Sage.
Beck, Ulrich, Giddens, Anthony and Lash, Scott (1994) *Reflexive Modernization: Politics, Tradition and Aesthetics in the Modern Social Order*, Cambridge: Polity.
Chang, K. and Song M. (2010). The Stranded Individualizer under Compressed Modernity: South Korean Women in Individualization without Individualism. *British Journal of Sociology*, 61(3): 539–64.
Han, S. (2007) 'The Formation and Differentiation of Post-Conventional Generations in Korea: A Search for the Agency of Social Change', *Theory and Society*, 11 (in Korean).
Han, S, and Shim, Y. (2010) 'Redefining Second Modernity for East Asia: A Critical Assessment', *British Journal of Sociology*, 61(3): 465–88.
Hong, C. (2012) 'Compressed Individualization and the Meaning of Democratic Implication of Gender Category in Korea', *Women and History*, 17: 1–25 (in Korean).
Howard, Cosmo. 2007. *Contested Individualization: Debates about Contemporary Personhood* in Howard, Cosmo ed. Palgrave Macmillan.
Ishida, M. et al. (2010) 'The Individualization of Relationship in Japan', *Soziale Welt*, 61(3/4): 217–35.
Li C., et al. (2013) *Experience, Attitudes and Social Transition*, Beijing: Social Science Academic Press (in Chinese).
Shim, Y. (2013) Two Types of Individualization: Family-centered Survival-oriented type and Twilight Divorce Type. *Society and Theory*, 23: 277–312 (in Korean).
Shim, Y. and Han, S. (2010). '"Family-Oriented Individualization" and Second Modernity: An Analysis of Transnational Marriages in Korea', *Soziale Welt*, 61(3/4): 237–55.
Shim, Y. and Han, S. (2013) 'Individualization and Community Networks in East Asia: How to deal with global difference in social science theories?', in M. Khun and S.

Yazawa (eds.), *Theories about and Strategies against Hegemonic Social Sciences*, Tokyo: Center for Glocal Studies, Seijo University, 197–214.

Shim, Y., Kim, M., and Kim, B. (2014) 'Two Dimensions of Family Risk in East Asia: Variations and Contextualization', *Development and Society*, 43(2): 239–67.

Suzuki, M. et al. (2010) 'Individualizing Japan: Searching for its Origin in First Modernity', *British Journal of Sociology*, 61(3): 513–38.

Yamada, M. (2010) *Kazoku No Restructuring, Shin-Yo-Sa*, trans. W. Jang, , Seoul: Greenbi (first published 1998).

Yan, Y. (2010) 'The Chinese Path to Individualization', *British Journal of Sociology*, 61(3): 489–512.

Yan, Y. (2013) 'Parent-Driven Divorce and Individualization among Chinese Youth', paper presented at an International Conference on "Life and Humanity in Late Modern Transformation: Beyond East and West", Seoul, Korea, 139–51.

9 Intensive secularization of engaged Buddhism to heal isolated people in East Asia

Active listening by monks in liberalized societies of Eastern Asia

Yoshihide Sakurai

Introduction

This chapter shows first the decline of subjective happiness and deterioration of wellbeing in Japan due to the more than twenty years of a stagnant economy and an aging society, as illustrated in a recent survey by the Cabinet Office. The signs of crisis in the face of postmodernity brought by the liberalization of society are there, blatantly present in East Asia. Using the example of Japan, this chapter displays traits that may concern South Korea and China in a not-too-distant future. This is a contribution to the study of how East Asian countries may respond to the increasing personalization and risk-society (the famous notion brought forth by Ulrich Beck), using their respective existing cultures, religions and social systems.

To overcome unhappiness and insufficient wellbeing among modern people, Buddhist monks have recently begun what they call "active listening". In this chapter, four cases will be studied, in which young and engaged Japanese monks threw off their conventional robes and jumped into the minds of the isolated: (1) Buddhist monks have continued to conduct exhortation in jails for more than 140 years; (2) even years after March 2011, engaged monks conducted their outreach support to the sufferers at the tsunami-hit areas by managing a community café; (3) young monks counseled citizens at street-corners by active listening to their grumbles; (4) the monk who took leadership of social education to prevent suicides of elderly people collaborated with municipal social welfare.

The change of demographic and industrial structures has caused upheaval in Japanese society. The National Institute for Research on Population and Social Security has issued a report on future demographic trends, which indicates that the Japanese population increased to 127,830,000 until 2004, yet declined thereafter continuously to the extent that it is expected to drop to 86,740,000 in 2060 and that people of 65 years old and more will occupy approximately 39 percent of the total population.[1]

Moreover, with the advance of so-called globalization, the manufacturing industry of Japan has shifted its production base overseas and the retail industry entered the fairly developed countries for market expansion. Population decline in local municipalities caused by natural decrease accelerated with the outflow of working generations to urban areas. In 2050 it is predicted that approximately 57 percent of Japanese nationals will live in the three major metropolitan areas, and that the population density of rural areas will be falling.[2]

Although Ulrich Beck is a sociologist widely known for his risk-society theory, personalization theory is another important idea in his studies. Beck warned about the personalization of risk management and excessive self-responsibility in modern society. In preindustrial society, family and community were the reproduction units of social life, and the family core functioned as a barrier to protect its members from dangers. Furthermore, the industrialization of society gave rise to labor unions and a class structure to represent the interests of individuals. In this way, individuals could avoid the risk they faced by affiliating to a community and/or associations.

However, with the rise of modern society, when individuals are increasingly released from traditional social institutions and constraints, it became a personal matter for people to determine which group they belong to. Moreover, what and when events are going to happen in the life course, such as entering school, work, marriage, and child-rearing, is all left to individual choice. On the one hand, to evaluate this positively, we may say human rights have been respected and society has become more liberal. On the other hand, however, personalization has led to the isolation of people. The more freely people can choose their lifestyle, the more stressful and uneasy it is when people actually have to decide by themselves (Beck, 1986; Beck and Beck-Gernsheim, 2011).

As the personalization of social life as well as social risk make progress, what kind of change will happen to people's consciousness? In other words, when we lost a sense of collectiveness, are we feeling more unhappy and anxious?

South Korean sociologist Han Sang Jin conducted a comparative study to see how East Asian countries may respond to the increasing personalization and risk-society, using their existing cultures and social systems. He argued that labor movement and family in South Korea still play a buffering role (Han 2011).[3] On the one hand, churches in Korea, whose members have exceeded about 30 percent of the Korean population, could also be seen as another buffer. On the other hand, in Japan, the number of single-person households has increased consistently, and is going to reach 37.2 percent in 2035. This ratio, about 33 percent in 2014, is 10 percent higher than in South Korea and Taiwan. The unionization rate, which is now 17.7 percent in Japan, is dropping. Christians in Japan form just 1 percent of the total population. Can religious culture and religious institutions help Japanese society respond to the risk of personalization? How did religions relate to the maintenance and creation of "bonds" that people are looking for? In this regard, China shows altogether different features, which are put in comparison in the last section of this chapter. Also explored are the cases in which Japanese monks tried to overcome excessive individualization and atomization of a liberalized society by active listening, not intended for their own sect members, but for citizens who wanted recognition by others. Before that, I discuss how people's relationships connect with subjective happiness, based on previous studies of "happiness" and "wellbeing" in the social sciences.

Researches on "happiness" and "wellbeing"

Here I will define "happiness" as a state of feeling subjectively sufficient, and "wellbeing" as a state where human rights and basic needs of people are secured. Psychology and psychiatry/brain sciences tend to see the former as more important, while jurisprudence, sociology, and social welfare studies focus on the latter. Research that deals with both sides is social psychology and behavioral economics. These constructivist and secular definitions may not be able to convince religious/moralistic or literal-minded/philosophical persons. Therefore, social sciences require operational and measurable definitions.

The Economic and Social Research Institute of the Cabinet Office started "the study group report: tentative index on the degree of happiness" in December 2011 and conducted its first social survey in 2012. Referring to this study, I will describe some interesting knowledge about subjective happiness.[4]

The decline of happiness in recent times

The degree of subjective happiness is measured using a scale from 0 to 10 with 10 being the happiest. When the present feeling of happiness is measured, the average result is 6.6 according to Internet research and 6.1 according to interview survey. This result also coincides with the life satisfaction in the "National Preference Index Survey" conducted by the Cabinet Office. As of 2005, it is 6.14. This index has hardly changed for ten years. But as of 1984, it was 7.2. GDP per person and life satisfaction were correlated during the economic boom until 1984. However, they began to correlate inversely after the oil shock and the liberalization of the labor market. This phenomenon was known as the "Easterlin paradox". But the Japanese case is more than that. Subjective happiness in Japan passed the saturation level and began to deteriorate, which has drawn the attention of economists and the government.

Relation between individual attributes and happiness

1   Age cohorts show a J shape in relation to happiness. That is, happiness is highest in the generation of teenelderly people, the "tens generation" (7.3), slightly drops for those in their twenties (6.7) and slightly increases again for those in their thirties (6.9), but reaches the lowest level for those in their forties and fifties (6.5), and slightly rises again for those in their sixties and seventies (6.6). Now, quite naturally, middle-aged people generally bear huge responsibilities to manage their family and their job. However, in Japan, many aged people are not freed from their burden and/or anxiety, because they may have to care for unmarried children and sustain long retirement years.

2   The level of happiness varies among those of different occupational status: housewife (6.8), financial insurance business people (6.3), government official (6.2), student (6.0), and unemployed (4.6). The high level of happiness shown by housewives is related to the stability of their lives in a country where this status is widespread and the norm.
3   The level of happiness also varies among married people, widowers/widows, single, and divorced persons, just indicated here in descending order. However, happiness for the married declines consistently from those in their thirties on.
4   Gender is related to happiness as men rate 6.3 and women 6.9.
5   Educational career does not seem to have any strong impact on happiness, but the level of income has.
6   A higher degree of trust in administration, justice and media, society in general, as well as in other people is also related to a higher degree of happiness. However, it can be argued that such people trust others just because they have a higher degree of happiness overall and/or vested interest, thus reversing the causality chain.
7   Income, health, and family relations are three significant factors for achieving higher subjective happiness. (See Table 9.1.)

How should we interpret these findings? Most of them appear to be common sense and widely accepted facts. The question for us is how to construct social structures that will lead to a higher level of happiness based on such knowledge. Owing to the increasing ratio of the unmarried young people and to their deteriorating working conditions (such as part-time employment and the widespread use of dispatched workers), Japan cannot immediately increase the number of married

Table 9.1 Feeling of happiness

Items	%
Household budget	62.2
Health condition	62.1
Family relations	61.3
Mental health	51.4
Employment status	35.5
Relationships with friends	35.4
Free time	34.3
Substantial leisure	24.2
Hobby, philanthropy, meaning of life	22.6
Fulfillment from work	21.5
Human relations in workplace	14.3
Relation with local community	10.2

Source: National Survey for nations' preference, Questionnaire 3 "What is important to be happy?", <http://www5.cao.go.jp/seikatsu/senkoudo/h23/23 senkou_03.pdf>.

people and full-time workers, who tend to have higher feelings of happiness. If we look at the National Preference Degree Survey of 2011 (Table 9.2), we see that matters that people expect from their government include a sufficient level of pension and of medical treatment, security in their employment and living environment, and food security as well as measures against disasters. On the one hand, much public expenditure is required to achieve these objectives. On the other hand, people are also looking for human relations with friends and their neighborhood, peace of mind, leisure time, and voluntary work, which lead to a sense of happiness.

Now let us formulate a hypothesis about the structure of happiness. Securing wellbeing is a necessary condition of the subjective feeling of happiness, but not a sufficient condition. For instance, human relationships are one of the sufficient conditions: through cultivating these, people are able to gain happiness by themselves. Another element that should also be added is 'value-consciousness'. Regrettably, most surveys in the past studied only how happiness is related to family, employment and the community, as well as to social relations, and any

Table 9.2 What do you want from the government in order to make you happy?

Item	%
Construction of pension system which is fair and secure	70.1
Realization of society that facilitates child rearing	69.3
Stable employment or living environment	42.6
High-quality medical service	32.3
Measures against calamities and a criminal measure	31.2
Safety and food security	31.2
Measures that assist small and medium-sized enterprises	26.5
Promoting a healthy public financial plan	25.4
Social environment without bullying, truancy, or shut-in	23.7
Opportunity for all people to receive high quality education	18.9
Reproduction of agriculture, forestry, and fisheries, and stable supply	15.5
Regional vitalization	15.1
Realization of society with few suicides	10.0
Contribution to economic development in Asia	8.1
Protection and promotion of consumer rights	7.7
Improvement in technology	6.2
Reduce greenhouse gas ratio to 25% in 1990, and lead in environmental technology	4.4
Reduction in traffic accident	4.1
Realization of society with high citizen participation in promoting public interest	3.8
Development of potential tourist spots, promote tourism	1.6
Others	3.6

Source: National Survey for the preference in 2011, Questionnaire 7 "What do you expect for the government to be happy? Choose five at most.",<http://www5.cao.go.jp/seikatsu/senkoudo/h23/23 senkou_03.pdf>.

questionnaire item related to value-consciousness was excluded. This is indeed lacking. However, since society is becoming more liberalized, pluralized and diversified in terms of value in recent times, it has also become more difficult to design such surveys that would question the connection between value-consciousness and happiness. Instead, it seems more efficient to explore some case studies in which people developed closer tie to isolated people, and their community as well, thereby enhancing wellbeing. We study such cases in Japan only in the next section.

Active listening by monks

Active listening volunteering

Hisayuki Murata is a professor at Kyoto Notre Dame Women's College who studied pastoral care and initiated the first active listening training school in Japan. Since then, the idea of "active listening" has spread among volunteers who provided care for aged people in nursing homes and hospitals. According to Murata, active listening consists just in listening to the voices of those who want to talk, and do so about their important life events. By doing so, the speakers reflect on themselves and find a new meaning in life, which makes them feel comforted and healed, without the use of religious discourse. Therefore, this concept of listening is somehow secularized, despite the fact that it was invented by Murata upon the basis of his practice of pastoral caring.

According to Japanese Buddhist traditions, especially the Jodo Shinshu sect (that is to say the "new True Teaching of Pure Land" denomination of Buddhism), "listening to Buddhist preaching" was long regarded as the most important training for all Buddhists. They believed in the idea that reflection on oneself could be achieved by listening to the teachings of Buddha and Shinran (1173–1262), the founder of this sect. Nowadays, modern active listening has gotten popularized and respect for the ordinary people has grown: people who can know the essence of life even if they are not religious saints. Clinical counselling also puts priority on listening to the voice of clients in medical care clinics during the initial and also recovery stage.

However, active listening is different from counseling in terms of practitioners, as well as in the process of treatment. For active listening, practitioners are non-professional and volunteers, therefore they do not make any contract for cure and do not intervene into the mind of those who talk. If the listeners and speakers could develop successful interactions, the latter would reflect on their lives and they would regain self-awareness. These positive side-effects of the process are unintended. Currently, the Buddhist community also appreciates the value of active listening, and several "active listening priests' group" have been established. Here let us have a look at the practice of listening carried out by some Buddhist communities.

Exhortation by monks

Ms. Keiko Horikawa published the book *Exhortation-Teacher* in 2014 when her interviewee, Fusho Watanabe, who was a priest of the Jodo-Shinshu Honganji denomination and an exhortation teacher for death-row inmates for more than fifty years, passed away. It was their promise that his life story would be disclosed after his death. This book carefully describes the way of exhortation-teaching and experience in the execution chamber, where repentance among death-row inmates and the experience of their last moments were so varied and emotion-inducing that an exhortation-teacher would himself be submitted to a huge degree of stress.

Otohiko Kaga is a psychiatrist and novelist who has worked at the Tokyo detention center. He studied the mental condition of death-row inmates in his two books, *The Sentence* and *Record of Death-row Inmates*, as follows. He found that death-row inmates have a unique sense of time: they do not know how long they are going to stay alive because the day of the execution announced during the trial is not known in the Japanese judicial system, and the sentence of execution by the Minister of Justice is made just before the last morning or on the previous day; therefore they suffer from several types of neurosis and often assert that they were falsely accused (Kaga 1979, 1980). The hero and narrator of *The Sentence* is a psychiatrist doctor in death row.

Fusho Watanabe, the preacher in the death row, suffered from alcoholism. As he recovered from his own mental problem, he acquired and applied his empathetic listening skills to death-row inmates, who experienced incredible ups and downs of their mental condition. His personal experiences and passions invoked compassion and found the acceptance of inmates, who so far had refused anything from his role as an exhortation-teacher. However, his exhortation would end with the execution of inmates, and he had no chance to see the recovery of inmates, which caused him huge regrets and mental stress. He could go on through these heavy challenges only by keeping a strong belief in "Pure Land" Buddhism.

In 2015, there were 1,865 exhortation-teachers in total, with 221 affiliated to Shintoism (namely to Jinja-Honcho and Konko-kyo), 258 to Christianity, 161 to so-called "new religions" (out of them 160 are members of the Tenri-kyo denomination), and 1225 to Buddhism (of many various denominations). They all belong to the National Exhortation Teacher Association, which was founded in 1956. Exhortation teaching consists of collective exhortation (preaching), individual exhortation (counseling), mourning day exhortation (mourning day for inmates' family and kin), funeral exhortation (funeral day for inmates' family), and so-called "casket exhortation" (at the death of the inmates).

Exhortation teachers have been recruited from, and trained in, religious sects, because their work has no payment and is so stressful that probably only religious persons could endure it. In the modern history of the Japanese jail-system, official prison guards and wardens governed all of the lives of the inmates and corrected their attitudes with the help of exhortation-teachers, which is in contrast with the role of the chaplain in the West, who responded to the religious demands of the inmates. Under the reform education system, Japanese exhortation-teachers have conducted active listening for serious criminals and death-row inmates.

In short, it turns out that there is a *tradition* of active listening in the religious tradition of Japan. What kind of features are there in *modern* active listening, in the different frame of a liberalized society? The next section presents such cases, where monks engaged in providing care for people suffering from disasters and where students engaged themselves for persons in need who just wanted someone to "listen" to them.

The "Café de Monk"

On March 11, 2011, the Great Eastern Japan Earthquake and the tsunami that followed killed 15,892 people and left 2,574 missing (revealed by National Police Agency on July 10, 2015). The total economic damage suffered from this earthquake and its direct consequences amounted approximately to USD 1,400 billion. The subsequent explosion of the nuclear power plant in Fukushima also led to the contamination of soil, large tracts of land and coastal areas, and to large-scale evacuation of residents. The overall damage done to the Japanese people, the economy and technical facilities is difficult to calculate.

The monks who lived in the affected areas conducted funeral ceremonies for the deceased almost every day for the first few months after the quake, and they provided counsel services to their fellow members as well as to others who had lost their families. Teiou Kaneda, a monk of the Soto Zen sect, wandered around the coastal areas, in search of those who suffered so as to listen to their laments. He served his clients with coffee and cake during their conservations, and called this coffee-shop-like activity "Café de Monk." Kaneda encouraged his followers to help more people using the skills of active listening and he has continued his efforts thereafter. He said:

> In order to realize Zen, reading Buddhist canons and practicing Zen meditation are not sufficient. Instead, stepping into this world is necessary. Indeed, there are teachings of Zen and the essence of Buddhism we can learn in everyday life. The things we learn cannot be articulated using words and concepts in books. However, we will finally realize those essences.[5]

Active listening and desire for recognition

The young priest of the Jodo-Shinshu Honganji denomination as well as the students of Ryukoku University have practiced active listening since 2012 at their university campus, Kyoto Tower,[6] and at bars run by monks. They have listened to more than 2,000 of what we could call "grumbles", which they classified into different categories and uploaded on their website (the so-called "reliance-upon-others" network). The data were then analyzed for studies on recent social trends and used to train "active listeners". They aimed at employing Jodo Shinshu views on life in an effective manner through the act of "active listening." It seems that most grumbles are usually related to school, work, love, and relationships with friends among the generations of people aged 10–19 and 20–29.

While I appreciate and agree with what the young students tried to achieve, I have two concerns about their activities. First, while I agree that listening to disaster victims, to people suffering from distress and sickness, is important, I am concerned about the effects of such "active listening" conducted by ordinary persons and young people (rather than by professionals trained in psychological sciences for instance), as well as about the potential *reverse* side-effects in isolating the speakers from their more natural mates. Of course, anyone may have troubles and, probably, members of the younger generation are also living with stress. However, given that both the young and middle-aged people still have the potential (time and energy) to expand their human relationships, isn't it more necessary to encourage them to be more self-reliant in the first place, instead of just complaining? Another concern relates to the division of voluntary active listening carried out by religious persons and by specialist counselors. As a matter of fact, most clinical psychologists who received education and training of counseling in Master's courses or at graduate schools have begun to work as temporary counselors in schools, hospitals and offices. A handful of veteran counselors can open their own clinics. It is probably more desirable that religious persons should acquire similar qualifications for counseling. While some actually did so, the number of such persons is still very limited. The negative consequence of this is that young professional counselors may not be able to make a living out of the university training, if "active listening" is regarded as something that can be freely provided by volunteers.

Let us summarize the background against which people of today may want active listening and why Buddhist monks can supply them with it. Many people have already realized that today is an era of "non-listening". Those who talk together in trains or coffee-shops seem to be relatively fewer, and many people, not only in Japan but in high-tech East Asian countries, live through looking at their smartphones and personal computers, moving their fingers restlessly upon all kinds of screens of various sizes and styles. They would like to be connected through these electronic media and have their existence recognized by others. However, the "others" that they want to connect with are not face-to-face neighbors, but friends through virtual networks. People of today are just so busy that they cannot *find* someone to talk to directly, even though they actually display a strong desire to have such opportunities. Now, active listening *can* generate face-to-face talking relations and, thereby, satisfy their needs for direct communications.

Engagement by monks and regional development

The case of Fujisato-town

Shunei Hakamada is a well-known monk who has engaged in promoting the wellbeing of local people living in Fujisato town in Akita prefecture, in the

Shirakami mountainous area, with a World National Heritage site known as "Beech Forest". On the one hand, this medium-size town is also famous for its high educational performance, as the place where the score of national achievement tests in elementary and secondary schools has ranked at the top for several years. On the other hand, the ratio of suicide is about 50 per 100,000 people, which is more than double that of the rest of Japan. When compared with neighboring Korea, in 2012, Korea's suicide rate was 28.2, which is higher than Japan's 21.4, yet less than in Fujisato. Furthermore, as for the ratio of "shut-in" persons (the phenomenon known as *hikikomori*), being in neither education nor employment, or staying at home under the protection of their own family, Fujisato also ranked at the top (8.74 percent), which is almost five times of the average of Japan (1.79 percent). How can we understand the imbalance between the outstanding performance in education and a high rate of suicide and "shut-in" persons?

According to national statistics, Japan had more than 30,000 people who committed suicide from 1998 to 2011, a period that started by following the so-called "Asian financial crisis" and whose sequel was long-term economic stagnation before a new major crisis stroke at international level. At that time, many Japanese manufacturing companies withdrew from the provinces and moved their factories to China and to Southeast Asian countries such as Vietnam, Laos and Myanmar, aiming at a cheaper labor force and huge markets overseas. As a result, high-school graduates could not find a secure job in their hometown and often had to work at temporary jobs, which were unstable as layoffs were frequent. As middle-aged persons went back to their original provincial towns from the metropolitan areas in order to take care of their aged parents, even those with graduate degrees could not find regular jobs that suited their specialties. Therefore, many young and middle-aged men suffered from a feeling of helplessness, and some even committed suicide or became "shut-in" at home.

In fact, not only the provinces but also major urban areas suffered from stagnation during this period and so-called "McDonaldization" of the economy. However, the suicide rate as assessed by prefectural offices in Japan still reflects a large discrepancy between the depopulated areas and the developing ones. The latter still have more opportunities for jobs. Moreover, the mechanization of agriculture and its relatively low competitiveness overall has gradually reduced the duties and workloads of aged people employed in farming, making them feel purposeless and not able to fulfill their roles in the rural conventional family. The rural and mountainous region of Akita in the north of Japan still retains much of a spirit of hardworking and industriousness, which shows in students studying hard and gaining high scores in national examinations. However, and also *because* of their emphasis on hard work, jobless people tend to feel small. If compared with Okinawa, the southern island nearest to Taiwan which has much higher unemployment rates, there are lower suicide rates in the southern parts: it seems as if people in Akita had a lower ability to cope with stress.

Active listening and local "cafés"[7]

Shunei Hakamada was born in a temple and a decree made him a monk whose fate was to inherit his father's temple of the Soto Zen sect. After graduating from Komazawa Buddhist University, he journeyed to Hokkaido and Noshiro town for his training. There, he met the so-called "hospice movement" at the age of 29. He learnt the concept and practice of terminal care, but he could not find any hospital to allow him to practice what he had learned, except during small preaching sessions once a week and for a very limited time. Feeling that what he was doing was far from enough as he realized the problem of high suicide-rates in Akita prefecture, and in Fujisato town in particular, was related to a depressive syndrome, Hakamada initiated a prevention movement against suicide with the help of twenty volunteers in the year 2000. He held lectures for citizens and aimed at overcoming the high ratio of suicide in Fujisato town, which was of 50 persons among 4,300 inhabitants from 1990 to 2004. He also held a community café once a week, in which elders in and outside the town could gather and chat with each other and with other people. In addition, he conducted an outreach "*izakaya* (Japanese pub) café" with villagers to enhance community integration. These activities are important for promoting the social life of elders in rural villages. One reason is that, after retiring from farming, most of them have very little chance for table-talk and easily tend to feel void and useless.

In addition to taking the post of public and voluntary organizations in Fujisato town, such as the head of special nursing home and head of educational board etc., Shunei Hakamada also works as a head missionary of the Soto Zen sect in Akita prefecture, where he gathers 150 household members in his temple.

Social welfare for working opportunities

Altogether, Fujisato was a very compact and conventional town, as its location in the Tohoku (Northeastern) district may explain since people there are seemingly strongly integrated by kinship and village-neighborhood network. In fact, people meet their friends easily everywhere in town. However, when the Fujisato municipality conducted research on "shut-in" people in order to find out how many people might need social support provided by the social welfare council, they found that 113 people had been staying at home for a long time without jobs. Even social workers were astonished by this number and the fact that local people were not able to realize the existence of these "shut-ins" earlier on. Their close kin and neighbors did not even ask about their sons and daughters in detail, because their families kept them secret and they did not readily think of seeking help from the municipal offices.

Now, the number of 113 shut-ins represents no less than 8.7 percent of Fujisato's population. Male shut-ins make up 66 percent of that figure, and their repartition among generations is as follows: 30 people are aged from 18 to 29; 31 are aged from 30 to 39; 41 are aged from 40 to 49, and 11 aged from 50 to 55. The span of the "shut-in time period" varies from half a year to over ten years. Some people simply cannot go out of their house, while some can still go out, at night or on holidays. Considering the background of the shut-ins, it was found that most of them were *not* the victims of school bullying or of mental illness. Conversely, many of them reported that they could not find a secure job near Fujisato town. And, after a relatively long time of unemployment, they had no choice but to stay at home and rely on the support received from their old parents. A long period of "shut-in" behavior finally made them suffer from "anthropo-phobia" and helplessness, which could be a potential cause of suicide.

To rescue these shut-ins from such critical situations, the social welfare council has set up an organization called "Commit", which runs a restaurant and encourages shut-in people to work there. They provide homegrown food (such as "*Soba*", or buckwheat noodles), for locals, and quiche made of local mushrooms, for tourists. Shut-ins that went there to work gradually readapted themselves to a working environment and began interacting with others, something they had not experienced for a long time. The "Commit" association also encourages local businessmen to provide short-term working opportunities for shut-ins so as to gain more experience and to bring former shut-ins to a job-placement office, as some shut-ins still felt uncomfortable sitting there in front of officials, and could not face the situation due to an excessive psychological strain.

Although "Commit" has offered job search assistance to shut-ins, secure jobs were very limited on the whole. In fact, the most secure and largest office is the municipality of Fujisato town itself, but it does not have enough capacity to hire shut-ins. The second largest job opportunity is at the nursing care house, but they only hire care-supporters who obtained the qualification "Home Helper level 2", or higher. Therefore, "Commit" provided training to shut-ins and helped them to achieve this level-2 course. It also applied for subsidies from the government and other funding organizations to run projects that hire shut-ins. The head of staff rightly and proudly stated the fact that "social welfare creates jobs in the region."

Social capital in the provinces

The case study done on Fujisato town focuses on the engagement of a Buddhist monk, Hakamada, and the activities of local social welfare offices in Fujisato town. Hakamada and the staff of these welfare services are indeed distinguished cases that have attracted observers from many locations: as a matter of fact, from more than 100 municipalities from all Japan. Indeed, religious institutions such as temples and shrines, and administrative institutions such as municipalities, play significant social functions in the provinces in the face of elements of social and individual crisis in modern society.

In order to strengthen the role of (here, Japanese) religious persons in developing such social capital in the communities, we ended up stressing the following three factors: (1) how, through innovation in cultural and environmental resources of traditional religion, they adapt to modern society; (2) how a better leadership and management by business people or talented people inside or outside of religion works out; (3) cooperation with various social actors that include not only denominational sects, but a larger community. These points overlap on the agenda with the re-vitalization of local communities and cities, where being innovative and open-minded is most important.

Debate on social capital, religious engagement, and wellbeing beyond Japan in contemporary East Asia

Social capital and religious engagement

Social capital is defined as the set of norms of reciprocal human relationships, trust in society and in the others, and social networks. Currently, the theory of social capital has attracted much attention in social sciences and public administration and the social function of religion in generating social capital is also studied.[8]

The relation between religion and wellbeing has been discussed in various religious traditions for a long time. Religious people preach that eternal peace, away from conflicts, and perfect salvation from sins can be achieved through religious practice and faith, rather than through secular pursuit of wealth and power. Even sociologists argued that those who are deprived from health, wealth, power, and meaning of life tend to join religious movements and/or engage in religious missions. People who feel happy would continue to stay in their religious groups, but those who still feel unhappy would leave and/or abandon their faiths. Therefore, if we ask the question, "are you happy now?" to those who belong to some religion, they might report a "yes" answer more frequently than non-religious persons who are not affiliated to any religious group.

Why do we feel happy believing in religion and joining religious groups? One possible, and the most influential, answer is that religion may provide strong relationships and ensure integrity among believers. Religious persons can meet good friends who provide comfort and necessary material support, and conversely they can also change roles to become providers, showing their compassion and charity. Religion also provides meanings of life and worldviews that help believers cope with different situations, even (especially) in times of hardship.

The frontier theoretician of social capital Robert Putnam also argued that friendship-networks that develop within religious networks and strong religious identity are linked to a higher level of life-satisfaction. First asking whether other forms of social relationship might enhance life-satisfaction of members, in turn the focus is on religious attendance. Studies confirmed that civic and social involvement did not have as much effect when compared to religious attendance, and demonstrated a strong correlation between the number of friends in a congregation and life-satisfaction mediated by a strong belief in Christianity (Lim and Putnam 2010).

This argument may well explain the wellbeing of more than half of the US population because of high attendance in churches (Smidt 2003) and engaged Buddhism movements in Theravada Buddhism countries (Sakurai 2013). However, East Asia displays huge contrasts, and in Japan the idea that religious attendance may generate happy feelings may perhaps apply to less than 10–20 percent of the Japanese only. Religious organizations with a clear-cut congregation-system are usually Christian churches and so-called "new religions" that hold regular weekly and monthly gatherings and activities.

Therefore, we have to consider what type of religious activities is related to wellbeing in the Japanese context (Yoshihide and Hamada 2012; Otani and Fujimoto 2012; Kasai and Itai 2013; Inaba and Kurosaki 2013), as well as in northeastern Asian countries since, in this chapter, I study the engagement of religious persons in these societies to help the general public face problems and suffering. While they suffer, the people do not *construct* a congregation or a community, as they have neither strong relationships nor any defined identity based on religious discourse. Conversely, monks just provided that, the opportunity through which people could feel recognized by others. In this sense, the "others" do not belong to any religious dimension yet, they rather exist in secular forms, in everyday life. The Japanese people who feel emptiness and helplessness because of a low self-esteem do desire recognition from others. So, by listening to people, monks offer just that and could become like substitutes of family, friends, neighbors and the general public, so as to offer a sense of recognition to people in need. Recognition by the divine nature of God is regarded as such as most important by most Christians; that is to say, they wish "to feel God's love." But for the Japanese in particular, and maybe Asian people more generally, recognition from others is the key factor.

Secularization of Buddhism and social action

In most East Asian countries, family and community have been the major providers of care to family members. For disadvantaged people, the "under-privileged" who suffer from illness, poverty, or other problems, Christian missionaries and Buddhist temples have long established day-care facilities and provided social support. However, since the social welfare system was established in the early 1950s and a national pension and medical scheme was also, in 1961 in Japan, engagement by religious groups in social actions has receded into the background. When religious organizations have set up social welfare corporations, it was in order to receive governmental subsidies and to hire the general public. In this sense, secularization has proceeded in religious institutions.

However, the increase of expenditure for social security, huge pension schemes coming to maturity, a heavier medical care and public assistance have all led the Japanese government to give up the idea of providing a complete state welfare and rather to adopt pluralism in welfare, which includes self-reliance, mutual assistance, private purchase of care services, and the mobilization of NPOs and NGOs to make up for lacks in public assistance. Since the beginning of the twenty-first century, Shinto shrines have provided spaces (shrine offices and precincts) for childcare. Buddhist temples, through offering funeral services, are trying to promote new social roles that transcend the traditional ones, based on neighborhood and denominational membership. Christian pastors offer spiritual care in terms of prayer and healing to terminally ill patients, many of whom are non-believers. So-called "new religions" also provide various social support to the general public. These examples show that there are some religious practitioners who do not feel restricted by regulations or religious customs. They are concerned about socially excluded people. Moreover, they try to develop a sense of trust in society even if connectedness among people is being weakened along with individualization in a liberalized environment.

Our case studies show that active listening offered by volunteers and monks displays a "second wave" of secularization of religion in Japan. It means that various religions improve self-recognition not merely through religious means, but by using secular counseling methods. The general public, concerned about the negative effects of religious solicitation, does favor this secular approach. Besides, ordinary people begin to recognize that Japanese Buddhism, which has been criticized as mostly "money-seeking funeral Buddhism" actually is an invaluable institution bringing comfort to bereaved families. However, at the same time, it would be challenging for religious institutions to conduct funeral services, praying and active listening on an exclusively voluntary basis. While most temples think such action should only be done at critical times, some bold monks want to promote active listening for a more secular use within the general public. This is how one may characterize the situation in Japan.

Economy, population, and social welfare regimes in East Asia

The concept of "welfare regime" refers to the institutional form of welfare (Esping-Andersen 1990). By focusing on whether receiving welfare service already requires employment and whether social welfare functions as a means of redistribution, Esping-Andersen provided a threefold typology by distinguishing northern European social democracies (where social-welfare services are financed by taxes levied on the public), "liberalism" in Anglo-Saxon countries (based on self-help, self-reliance), and a more conservative attitude to welfare in continental European countries (with welfare programs by the state and social insurance by companies).

Conversely, East Asian countries still rely a lot on families as the main care-giver and they have not yet developed uniformly institutionalized social welfare, because they have undergone their "modern nation" building process in various ways (capitalism in Japan, socialism in China, and development-oriented dictatorship in Korea and Taiwan after World War II: Nishimura, Kyogoku, and Kaneko 2014). Universal health insurance and pensions were established in the 1960s in Japan, but only in the 1990s in Korea, the 2000s in Taiwan, and in the 2010s as partial systems in mainland China, while there is still no government or state pension at all in Hong Kong.

At the beginning of the twenty-first century, Japan became the first country in Asia in terms of aging and a low birthrate (in East Asia) with a ratio of social welfare expenditures more than double that of these other countries. However, the speed of aging in Korea and Taiwan is higher than Japan, so the medical insurance and pension being enhanced would increase the fiscal burden in these countries from the 2010s on.

China also experienced an industrial and political process of urbanization that led to a low birthrate, but China had a one-child policy in cities and rural areas and only in the 2010s somehow relaxed that policy. Hong Kong controls public welfare expenditures strictly by promoting the role of individuals, and by putting stress on family and community. In fact all East Asian countries have already entered the stage of an aging society with falling birth rates so that they should modify the East Asian welfare regime based on families as care-givers (Tables 9.3 and 9.4).

Moreover, the fiscal burden relates not only to the change in population but also to the level of economic development attained by a country. While Japan has already experienced twenty years of stagnant economy and China has suffered a downturn since the years 2013–15, which in turn affects trading business with

Table 9.3 Population aging rate in East Asia

	1950	1970	1990	2010	2030	2050
Japan	4.9	7.1	12.1	23	31.3	38.8
Korea	–	3.1	5.1	11	24.3	37.4
China	4.4	4.9	5.6	8.9	16.23	23.07
Taiwan	–	–	6.2	10.74	23.9	–
Hong Kong	–	4.5	8.7	13.4	26.5	–

Sources:
Japan: Health, Labour and Welfare Ministry, Institute of Social Welfare and Population Problems, Annual Population Survey.
Korea: Population Census 2010, Future population estimation 2011 (Ministry of Statistics).
China: Chinese Statistics Press, Almanac of Chinese Statistics 2013.
Taiwan: Ministry of Interior, Bulletin of Interior Statistics, each year
Hong Kong: Hong Kong Census and Statistics Department.

Table 9.4 Total fertility rate in East Asia

	1950	1970	1990	2010
Japan	3.65	2.13	1.54	1.39
Korea	–	4.56	1.57	1.22
China	5.81	5.81	2.31	1.8
Taiwan	7.04	3.71	1.81	0.9
Hong Kong	–	1.97	1.28	1.2

Sources:
Japan: Health, Labour and Welfare Ministry, Institute of Social Welfare and Population Problems, Annual Population Survey.
Korea: Population Census 2010, Future population estimation 2011(Ministry of Statistics).
China: Chinese Statistics Press, Almanac of Chinese Statistics 2013.
Taiwan: Ministry of Interior, Bulletin of Interior Statistics, each year.
Hong Kong: Hong Kong Census and Statistics Department.

Table 9.5 Economic growth rate and social welfare fund rate of GDP

	Japan	*Korea*	*China*	*Taiwan*	*Hong-Kong*
Economic growth rate per GDP (2013)	1.54	2.78	7.67	2.11	2.94
Social welfare fund rate per GDP(2009)	22.2	9.6	4.6	3.5 (2005)	5.7 (2007)

Source: OECD Statistics, IMF World Economic Outlook Database.

Taiwan, Korea and Hong Kong, most East Asian countries face a deadlock in enhancing their social welfare systems due to the spread of economic stagnation, as it was the case in Japan earlier on for two decades or so (Table 9.5). As a result, the time in which familial care gets replaced by a public social welfare system may not last for long, and some other form of welfare model may emerge in the near future. Welfare pluralism, composed of several factors such as mutual assistance in family and neighborhood, social support from NGOs/NPOs, and religious charitable activities, may become increasingly important in the whole of East Asia, connecting to earlier practices and traditions.

In the USA, where the social welfare system is less developed than in continental Europe, say, many religious denominations provide services to needy people. FBOs (faith-based organizations) and/or FROs (faith-related organizations) were established outside churches and provide outsourcing of social services funded by the federal government. This outsourcing mechanism also became popular among northern European countries and the United Kingdom where Protestant and Anglican denominations were authorized and subsidized by governments. Of course, since the law is one of separation of politics and religion and also guarantees religious freedom, those countries maintain strict transparency in managing their subsidies in social services and they also monitor carefully whether religions deal equally with people in need who have a different religious faith (Inaba 2008).

Another factor is that the so-called policy of "neo-liberalism", which tends to reduce social security benefits and welfare expenditure, and promotes a growth strategy in general, has become prevalent even in East Asian countries, and welfare pluralism with outsourcing of social services to FBOs and FROs will spread, as they both put forward such a policy. In Japan, however, public concern over religion is so strong that the ideas of religious engagement in the public sphere and regarding religions as part of social capital are not yet widely accepted among social scientists or welfare specialists.

Concluding remarks: wellbeing and religion

In this chapter, I have discussed the potential of social capital that modern religion can generate, on the basis of the case studies in particular of monks who engaged in active listening and other social activities that enhance "wellbeing" in Japan.

The people who are listened to become more "happy", and at the same time persons who provide care also become happier, because they can share the happiness of others with others, and recognize their own ability in counseling as a "gift". Such an altruistic action sometimes makes people happy on both sides.

This is an active counter-policy regarding the de-population and the atomization of human relationships in the provinces in particular, which results in social evils such as suicide, the phenomenon of "shut-in" people and loneliness, all of which should be considered from the perspective of human wellbeing. People feel helplessness due to the lack of "significant others" who would be willing to listen to their voices. If they are listened to and recognized by others, they restore a sense of security and comfort, and then regain self-esteem through interacting and working with others.

The process of individualization in terms of population and social relations, which also relates to any specific social welfare system, will probably sooner or later become a common feature in East Asian countries. The growing fiscal burden that it entails may promote a backlash and neo-liberal policies concerning social welfare. East Asia may well develop a social space and a public sphere where multiple actors increasingly participate in social services to respond to the demand of the people, which is to promote social as well as individual wellbeing. In this chapter, the studies of several cases of the engagement of Buddhist monks in social services displayed that trend, naturally with its limitations. How individualization has proceeded in East Asian contexts and how religions should respond to such a trend with their own resources, this is what further studies are required to answer.[9]

Notes

1   The Press Releases of National Institute of Population and Social Security Research (January 30, 2012).
2   The National Land Development Council policy sectional meeting, long-term view committee "long-term view interim draft of a country" (February 21, 2011).
3   And in this same volume, chapter 8 by Han and Shim displays their results of major importance, first presented by Sang-Jin Han and Young-Hee Shim in 2013 as "patterns of Individualization and their Implications for Liberalism in East Asia,' in the conference co-hosted by Seoul University and Hokkaido University on "Individualization and Liberalism in Korea and Japan: Implications for Aging Society", December 13, 2013, at Seoul National University.
4   The Economic and Social Research Institute, Cabinet Office, 2011 "study group report-happy degree index tentative plan about the degree of happiness", <http://www.esri.go.jp/>.
5   Introduction of Café de Monk can be found on the website "Sotozen-Net", < http://www.sotozen-net.or.jp/teqw/j20130808.html> (accessed September 9, 2015). The "Café de Monk" active listening has been supported by the "Kokoro no Sodanshitu (Counseling room for Mind)" Group, which is composed of the chair of religious studies in Tohoku University, psychiatric and paramedical workers, and religious persons.
6   Located in Kyoto, this school of Buddhist teaching still active was founded in the seventeenth century. It is nowadays a university that has kept close link to the Honganji tradition in which it was founded.

7   With students, I conducted this case study in August 2014, visiting Fujisato town and conducting interviews with Shunei Hakamada, staff of the social welfare council, the former municipality staff, and the residents, both those who gathered at the café and those who did not go.
8   Besides the notion put forth by French sociologist Pierre Bourdieu, the concept of "social capital" is being promoted in the following areas: (1) citizens' political participation (ombudsman, jury system, policy advocating NPO), (2) economic promotion (vitalization of local area, solidarity of workers and the autonomy of working place, local production for local consumption, and local brands), (3) plans to deal with social problems (environmental measure, gender equality, education, welfare and reconstruction of medical system) (Yoshimura 2011: 126). Besides, I co-edited a book series called "Social Capital and Religion" (four volumes) with Inaba Keishin which is published by Akashi shoten. See Yoshihide Sakurai, and Yo Hamada, *Asia no shukyo to social capital (Asian Religion and Social Capital)*, 2012; Eiichi Otani, and Yorio,Fujimoto, *Chiikishakai wo tsukuru shukyo (Religion forms Community)*, 2012; Kenta Kasai, and Masanari, Itai, *Care toshiteno shukyo (Religious Caring)*, 2013; Keishin Inaba and Hiroyuki Kurosaki, *Shinsai to syukyo (Reconstruction of Earthquake Disaster and Religious Support)*, 2013.
9   I presented the first third of this chapter ("Researches on 'Happiness' and "'wellbeing'") and the section "Social capital and Religious Engagement" at the Yokohama Conference of the International Sociological Association in 2014.

References

Beck, Ulrich (1986) *Risikogesellschaft: Auf dem Weg in eine andere Moderne*, Frankfurt am Main: Suhrkamp.
Beck, Ulrich and Beck-Gernsheim, Elisabeth (2011) *Individualization: Institutionalized Individualism and its Social and Political Consequences*, London: Sage.
Esping-Andersen, G. (1990) *The Three Worlds of Welfare Capitalism*, Oxford: Polity Press.
Han, Sang-Jin (2011) 'Higashi asia niokeru daini no kindai no shakai henyo to risk yobo governance (Second Modernization in East Asia and Governance of Risk Hedge), in Ulrich Beck, Munenori Suzuki and Ito Midori (eds), *Risk ka suru nihon: Ulrich Beck tono taiwa (Risk Society of Japan: Talk with Ulrich Beck)*, Iwanami Shoten: 163–218.
Inaba, Keishin (2008) *Amerika niokeru shukyo no shakaikoukenn: jizenteki sentaku to shinko ni motozuita shakaihukusi sabis (Religious Engagement in the US: Charitable Selection And Faith Based Social Action)*, Tokyo: kokusai shukyou kenkyujyo newsletter 58: 11–16.
Kaga, Otohiko (1979) *Senkoku (The Sentence)* (in Japanese), Tokyo: Shinchosha.
——(1980) *Shikeishu no Kiroku (Records of Death-row Inmates)* (in Japanese), Tokyo: Chuô Koron Shinsha.
Lim, Chaeyoon and Putnam, Robert D. (2010) 'Religion, Social Networks, and Life Satisfaction', *American Sociological Review*, 75(6): 914–33.
Nishimura, Shuzo, Kyogoku, Takanobu, and Kaneko, Yoshihiro (2014) *Shakai hosho no kokusai hikaku kenkyu: seido saiko nimuketa gakusaiteki/seisakukagakuteki approach (Comparative Study of Social Security: Interdisciplinary and Political Scientific Approach to Reconsider Social Institution)*, Kyoto: Mineruba shobo.
Sakurai, Yoshihide (2013) *Tai jyoza bukkyo to shakaiteki hosetsu: social capital toshiteno shukyo (Theravada Buddhism and Social Inclusion: Religion as Social Capital)*, Tokyo: Akashi shoten.

Smidt, Corwin (2003) *Religion as Social Capital: Producing the Common Good*, Waco, TX: Baylor University Press.

Yoshimura Ririko (2011) 'Social capital to shukyo' (Social Capital and Religion), in Naoto Yamauchi, Toshifumi Tanaka and Okuyama Shoko (eds), *Social Capital no jisho bunseki* (*Empirical Research of Social Capital*), Tokyo: NPO Jyoho Center.

Part III

Liberalism, universalism and pluralism

10 Self-determination

What liberalism is it?

Lizhi Zhao

It seems that a considerable part of the international legal scholarship can hardly resist the temptation to regard so-called "liberalism" (in whichever sense this has to be defined) as the basis of contemporary international law after the Berlin Wall collapsed. As Martti Koskenniemi stated in 2006, in each realm at the heart of international law there emerges the need for justification of some assumptions of what the international community actually is, and how to shape it. One may label the whole of such assumptions a "*liberal* theory of politics". (Koskenniemi 2006: 5)

Nonetheless, it pertained to Gerry Simpson to put forward an intriguing argument that there exists more than one form of "liberalism" in the current social world, and Simpson did so five years earlier than the reprint of Koskenniemi's *From Apology to Utopia*. In his article, Simpson characterized one type of liberalism as "Charter liberalism" and another as "liberal anti-pluralism". Simpson further explained that the former was summarized starting from the United Nations" reluctance to assess the democratic or humanitarian credentials of its members, while the latter embraces the idea of such credentials like a state will, and should, be treated as a determinant criterion of assessing its status in the international community (Simpson 2001: 537).[1]

This finding should inspire those interested in studying the development of self-determination in international law, in order to discuss the relationship between liberalism and self-determination both from a historical and from an empirical perspective. This is precisely what I shall do here. In addition, how this topic relates to views on China, in China and by Chinese authors/lawyers can be an intriguing subject. Indeed, one result of Chinese authorities" being generally antagonistic to Western ideologies is that China's scholarship usually chooses to dilute the liberal color of the painting of the contemporary international law. Besides, in fact, China's own theories and practice of modern international law never run away from the shadow of these two kinds of liberalisms, whether positively or negatively.

To give here only one example of this: China's attitude toward the two kinds of liberalism, as well as international law as a whole, can actually be well illustrated by Su Changhe's analysis of the Five Principles of Peaceful Coexistence. They are the following: mutual respect for each other's territorial integrity and sovereignty, mutual non-aggression, mutual non-interference in each other's internal affairs, equality and cooperation for mutual benefit, and peaceful coexistence.[2] As an early stage researcher from China, I do not aim so much at evaluating the value of either one of the two kinds of liberalisms, but rather to probe into a new angle of his field of study. That approach is of interest to the legal framework and institutionalist approach that law and economics are about, so that one may hope that dealing with international forms of liberalism may provide something new for law and economics and for Chinese international legal studies as well.

A reminder of Simpson's two liberalisms

Straight from the shoulder, Simpson points out that those two kinds of liberalism, which are found in international legal arguments, originated in nothing but the split between two modes of interpretation. These are either viewing liberalism as a comprehensive doctrine that helps promote social good from some almost utopian version of it, or "reasonably" calming it down within the bounds of so-called "proceduralism", while emphasizing diversity.[3]

However, there is actually no one-to-one correspondence between such a split in political outlook and the opposition of Simpson's two liberalisms. In the context of international law, it is the only truth that either "Charter liberalism" or "liberal anti-pluralism" embodies both interpretations of liberalism, namely, they aim at promoting the international community's wellbeing through the advocacy and practice of plural diversity and procedural justice. The genuine divergence of the two doctrines lies in the focus put on who the legal subjects are.

Charter liberalism transplants classical liberalism onto the international community, basically formed by nation-states, and treats sovereign equality and territorial integrity of these states as the "international edition" of some individual rights in municipal laws, which overall constitutes a mechanism for maintaining world peace and order (or, speaking in a more high-sounding way, promoting human well-being).

Liberal anti-pluralism, in contrast, contends that states are only entitled to participate in international affairs based on the premise that they safeguard *bona fide* the fundamental rights of their own nationals, that is, they perfectly practice classical liberalism all the way from the municipal level first. Both arguments present a set of procedural requirements while their emphasis differs due to their substantial opposition.

Now, in fact, from a Chinese point of view, a number of Chinese international lawyers have admitted the logical connection between these liberal political doctrines and international law. However, most of them (with some major exceptions like Su Changhe already mentioned) seem less interested in exploring the differences inside the system of liberalism in the international order *per se*, and that remains true despite the fact that they do notice some of the main elements of either kind of liberalism put forward by Simpson, as their works exemplify.[4]

The distinction between the two kinds of liberalisms may prominently feature the development of human rights in international law and serve as a frame for many more aspects of human behavior and exchange (including exchange of material goods and services). Simpson, amongst most international lawyers today, pointed out that the introduction of an international human rights mechanism has modified, to a large extent at least, the view on absolute sovereignty that sees all affairs within its territory not subject to international supervision (Simpson 2001: 556). For Simpson, the UN's criticism of *apartheid* in South Africa and white rule in Rhodesia/Zimbabwe, in particular, is supposed to be considered the milestone that first linked internal state affairs with status in the international community (Simpson 2001: 557). From then on, especially during the late 1980s, there has been remarkable development of the normalization of human rights (or "democratic") standards within and outside the UN system. Theories of a new "judgmental" and "substantive" liberalism naturally followed the practice of the globalization of human rights, be there economic sanctions or not, which challenges the pluralistic and procedural attitude of Charter liberalism in almost all directions:

> The core norms of the old liberalism, it is argued, no longer capture the reality of the new transnational order (Slaughter), are morally bankrupt (Tesón) or are in the process of radical modification (Franck).
>
> (Simpson 2001: 559)

It is worth noting that Simpson only slightly mentions the right to self-determination, one of the most important parts of the so-called third generation human rights, in reference to both liberalisms. While he notices that most advocates of liberal anti-pluralism are supporters of the right to self-determination (Simpson 2001: 561, 563), he also stresses that "Statism is a liberal theory of international law. Liberalism is as much about non-intervention and self-determination as it is about justice" (Simpson 2001: 563, note 134). One may regard it, nonetheless, as a bit unfortunate that Simpson did *not* expand on the topic in the essay, considering that the issues of South Africa, South-West Africa/Namibia (under the rule of South Africa then) and Rhodesia signally raised the questions of self-determination.[5] Hence, the following issue arises in this chapter: *which* liberalism does self-determination embody? One may also ask just as well whether there is *only* "one kind" of self-determination today.

"Two self-determinations" after World War II

Undoubtedly, national self-determination in international legal discourse is one of the youngest offspring of modern international law. Although Lenin and Woodrow Wilson formed their respective ideas about self-determination during and after World War I, their ideals could never find successful acceptance within the international community that was haunted by doubts over the Treaty of

Versailles. The treaty's mechanism had determined that the rearrangement of sensitive territories would almost completely depend on a range of secret agreements between the Allies and the other powers rather than on plebiscites or referenda (Hannum 1996: 13-14).[6]

Most scholars therefore tend to view Article 1(2) and 55 of the Charter of the United Nations as the very beginning of the incorporation of self-determination into an international legal system. However, as some lawyers also admitted, such progress was remarkable not because of the global acknowledgement of the importance of self-determination, but rather because of the significance of the Charter itself (Cassese 1965: 43; Nawaz 1995: 91).

The crucial engine that pushed the right to self-determination into the orbit of customary international law is the movement of decolonization under the flag of the Declaration on the Granting of Independence to Colonial Countries and Peoples, opening the age of newly independent states across Africa and Asia. The overwhelming movement, which followed the incorporation of the right to self-determination into basic human rights by the two leading international human rights instruments, the International Covenant on Civil and Political Rights (ICCPR) and the International Covenant on Economic, Social and Cultural Rights (ICESCR), touched China as well. This reality is now one with which Chinese thinkers and lawyers have to cope.

Nevertheless, to keep to the general setting, the battle over the interpretation of self-determination had already begun: it dates back to the moment this point was included in the Charter, since the UN's framework document never made a clear definition of self-determination. Antonio Cassese summarizes, in a tone full of regrets, that in fact the wording of self-determination in the Charter, inferred from the debate between the drafters, does *not* include any "mainstream" interpretation of the term. One may think of what could be the right of the peoples under colonial rule to independence, the right of minorities to secede or even the right to domestic democracy (Cassese 1995: 42).[7] In other words, such a paradox has left considerable room for the dynamic development of self-determination alongside changes in the international political environment. The theories and practice of self-determination were practically dominated by the enthusiasm during decolonization and before the adoption of the Helsinki Final Act in 1975 (generally seen as putting forward an ongoing legal right to internal self-determination).[8] The new context unsurprisingly led to the reinterpretation of the term as well as to the documents "inexplicitly" involving the issue. A typical instance of this is how Michael Reisman offers an innovative comment on Article 21(3) of the Universal Declaration of Human Rights, that is:

> The will of the people shall be the basis of the authority of the government; this will shall be expressed in periodic and genuine elections that shall be by universal and equal suffrage and shall be held by secret vote or by equivalent free voting procedures.

> (Reisman 1990: 867)

Although there is no content evidently related to self-determination in the Declaration adopted twelve years before the UN Resolution 1514 on decolonization, Reisman holds that it was the wording of Article 21(3) that dispelled for the first time the traditional idea excluding self-determination from a state's internal affairs.

The hidden logic behind the development of the term is that the right to self-determination, now as a basic human right, should be an ongoing right rather than a one-off deal in the name of "independence" (Salmon 1993: 269).[9]

In 1991, Thomas Franck furthermore attached unusual importance to self-determination in the postwar era by *re-evaluating* the meaning of Article 1 of the ICCPR, which says that the determinacy of self-determination is supposed to be much greater to promote the right to democratic governance inside states other than decolonization(Franck 1992: 60). Still, his statement is rather modest if compared with that of Reisman, who had already presented a more radical attitude eight years before. He stated in a flinty tone that the implementation of "ongoing" self-determination should not reject legitimate interventions that can serve as an effective path to enhance the free choice of peoples under democracy and liberty (Reisman 1984: 644).

Though Reisman and Franck stepped forwards, other lawyers were and might still be reluctant to stand with them in the same camp. For instance, Cassese never discarded the idea that the word "freely" in Article 1 of the ICCPR makes clear that any possibility and form of foreign intervention gets merely eliminated (Cassese 1995: 55). In sum, "orthodox" scholarship on self-determination encapsulates the belief that: "[t]he rules designed to permit peoples under foreign colonial rule to achieve independence were considered to constitute the legal core of this concept while all other possible interpretations were largely retained to be merely political demands" (Hilpold 2006: 36). The challenge to that assertion, however, increasingly sharpened as new situations surfaced one by one.

Choosing to stick to or to break out of the context of decolonization brings about two apparently different versions of self-determination, but the arguments and debates over both may have started much earlier than we thought. Essentially, it would be difficult for us to recognize the substance of the confrontation if we cannot grasp its real drive, namely, the much more complicated (and perhaps paradoxical) game between liberalism and the theories and practice of self-determination in the past, present and future. The economic factor is of full momentum in that regard and, even if international law texts do not always give it prominence, one cannot but include it as the background of any reflection that includes matters of war and peace in the international context.

Struggle and collaboration between self-determination and liberalism in history and the present

"Two self-determinations" patterns may be related to liberalism in its early history. It is hard to determine whether (or not) modern scholars have reached the consensus on the real origin of the conception of self-determination in history.

Apparently, most agree that Thomas Hobbes was one of the first philosophers to emphasize the importance of the self-determination of peoples and nations. He said: "There are very few so foolish that they had not rather govern themselves than be governed by others" (Przetacznik 1990: 56). In addition, it is also non-negligible that one believes that John Locke's theory of the Social Contract, commonly regarded as the first elucidation of early liberalism and individualism, may be another significant source of the idea of self-determination especially from its internal aspects.

Noticeably, there is a seemingly "sought-after" opinion according to which Hobbes and Locke's ideological sprouts of self-determination are all rooted in liberalism *and* individualism (Hilpold 2006: 13), which remains doubtful though when examining in full detail their philosophical stand. For Hobbes, how much residual room was there for individual autonomy in face of the bloodcurdling Leviathan that hates any power sharing?

Therefore, there may be a more persuasive restoration of truth, which might be that the war between external and internal self-determination can trace its chronicle to the beginning of the Enlightenment. Another early contributor to the idea of self-determination is Immanuel Kant, another important character in Western liberalism, whose thought has been introduced into China with a long history.[10] Apart from the faith in liberty and individual freedom, Kant strongly opposed to destroying a country as a *moral* person by incorporating it "as a graft in another State" as well.[11]

The most crucial aspect of the early practice of self-determination might have been North America. To some extent, it is convincing to say that the prominent revolution led to a double achievement – overthrowing what the colonial peoples saw as tyrannical rule as well as exercising the right to external self-determination by establishing an independent state by means of just war. Though it is debatable whether (or not) the American Revolution was the first case of self-determination in its proper sense (Umozurike 1972: 152-153), the founding of the United States of America is beyond question an encouraging victory of liberalism in history. Similar events occurred following the French Revolution, which for the first time legislated for referenda and plebiscites as the unique legitimate path to decide the status of a sensitive territory – this holds although the principle was not always implemented impartially (Cassese 1995: 12).

Besides, early thoughts of self-determination were not all the patents of liberal thinkers. For instance, famous Polish canonist Stanislaw of Skarbimierz was believed to have defended "the right to self-determination and independence of non-Christian peoples" (Przetacznik 1990: 56) at a time much less progressive than his proposition. It may be remarkably noteworthy for its incredibly resembling the modern rights of minorities and cultural diversity. Yet, in general, the relatively more mature practice of early thoughts of self-determination, either in its external or internal aspects, could hardly have parried the words and deeds of liberalism. The superficial honeymoon period, however, was destined to last not for long, when no proof was given that liberalism would be the unconditional contrary of colonialism.

Major conflict and "minor compromise" between liberalism and self-determination in the colonial centuries

Classical liberals kept on criticizing colonialism, and yet they have hardly touched the essence of the human-right-based decolonization in the modern sense. Instead, most of them opposed colonial activities mainly from the perspective of utility.[12]

Moreover, an ironically conspicuous historical fact is that the most prominent colonial powers from late seventeenth century to the early twentieth century were liberal states[13] and states more or less influenced by liberalism. While sometimes the government of the metropolitan state appeared willing to grant the inhabitants of the colonies citizenship and civil rights to some degree,[14] it would have never recognized the entitlement of the colonial peoples to self-determination by claiming their own statehood. In particular, Oji Umozurike's conclusion that the independence of the Thirteen Colonies was the very first case of self-determination is under suspicion since the successor United States actively participated in dividing old empires" colonies in the late nineteenth century as well.

Behind colonialism, we can possibly have a glimpse at liberalism's gloomy side magnified in by modern international law before 1945: the paradoxical reconciliation between individual freedom and social order. Completely treating sovereigns as individuals in the international community, "international communitarian liberalism" must have ensured that sovereign freedom could be preserved only by a normatively international order. In return, such a normative order was ultimately legitimate only if sovereigns recognized the capacity and reputation of the order to preserve their own vested interests, including colonies and mandated territories definitely. An almost "naked" reconciliation was adorned with the Rule of Law to display a legitimate social order "which is objective, one that consists of formally neutral and objectively ascertainable rules" (Koskenniemi 2006: 71). Or, just as how Sir Hersch Lauterpacht commented on the British Guiana Arbitration 1897, the matters of "high political importance" would always have "eventually resolved itself into a lengthy legal contest" (Lauterpacht 2011: 157). At last, the most discouraging fact was that people under colonial rule were excluded from the realm of the "individuals" of the "liberal" *civitas maxima* composed by "civilized countries".

The long-term restraining context determined that liberalism and self-determination conflicted in most situations. Indeed, the two ideas might have compromised with each other, particularly in the dissolution of the Ottoman Empire and the conclusion of the House of Habsburg. But these are also precisely the two cases that prove Hurst Hannum's argument according to which the enthusiasm of nationalism helped the Allies in justifying the arrangement for a new Europe after World War I. And this, while the advocates and founders of the League of Nations (including President Wilson himself) never had the faith in the universality of the right to self-determination (Hannum 1996: 13), let alone in the case of the potentially turbulent Africa and Asia.

A dialectical unity of the two forms of liberalism and self-determination in the postwar era

As mentioned in the previous section of this chapter, it seems inappropriate to evaluate provisions of the UN Charter on self-determination in a utopian vision. Yet quite a few international lawyers are reluctant to recognize the international legal effect of the term mentioned by Article 1(2) and 55 of the Charter for its semantic ambiguity in drafting (Pomerance 1982: 9; Sinha 1974: 336-337; Hannum 2011: 33). Anyhow, obviously, the genuinely authentic provisions that first provided the General Assembly Resolution 1514 with legal ground is Article 76(b), which makes it clear that the new trusteeship system shall aim to promote the "progressive development towards self-government or independence" of each trust territory and its peoples. Certainly, Article 76(b) of the Charter marked the recognition of the identity of colonies, which were being granted their independence as "individuals" of the "liberal" international community for the first time.

Furthermore, as Cassese pointed out, the international practice following the founding of the UN put the issue of self-determination onto a more liberal track. For instance, either conventional or customary international law is believed to have granted the entitlement of peoples under colonial rule or foreign military domination to resorting to armed liberation movement in extreme cases to implement their rights. More significantly, as Article 1(2) of both the ICCPR and the ICESCR demonstrably states that peoples of a territory shall not be deprived of the right to freely dispose of their natural wealth and resources, Third World states successfully complete the final piece of the puzzle of decolonization through the guarantee of their national sovereignty (Cassese 1995: 99-100). In other words, this provision made the personality of newly recognized individuals of the *civitas maxima* adequate at least in a formal way.

Needless to say, all issues of self-determination against the backdrop of decolonization were "chiefly raised as a question affecting sovereign states rather than peoples as such", especially referring to Cassese's comment on about "economic self-determination" (Cassese 1995: 99). The "state-centric" element was particularly reflected in the fact that the debate before the UN forum revolved around the possibility of reconciling the respect for national sovereignty of developing natural resources and interests of foreign investors. That eventually gave birth to the Declaration on Permanent Sovereignty over Natural Resources (1962) as well as Article 1(2) of the two Covenants (Cassese 1995: 100).

In this context, the liberal political doctrine applied to international relations was still merely a municipal analogy, which simply equated sovereign states to citizens and an imaginary "world federation" to a civil society – only to enlarge the scope of "citizenship" (the statehood). In such discourse, it would never have been surprising that the theories, proposals and activities of non-liberal states – such as the Soviet Union and other pre-communist countries (including China, perhaps) – once constituted the main impetus to enhance the movement of decolonization. Such discourse of the "international liberalism" set up a harmony between different ideologies in a seemingly paradoxical manner.

Nevertheless, the transformation of the right to self-determination towards acknowledged collective human rights at worldwide level also signaled the end of that paradoxical harmony. Quite a few delegates of the Human Rights Committee viewed the Working Party of the drafting of the ICCPR initially reducing the draft of Article 1(3) to an obligation that targeted the colonial powers as discriminatory. As a result, the final text of Article 1(3) has inserted the phrase "including those" before "[the states] having responsibility for the administration of Non-Self-Governing and Trust Territories", which makes it clear that the provision applies to all peoples rather than only those under colonial rule or alien subjugation (Nowak 2005: 13).[15]

This shift, which went beyond mere decolonization, brought about, however, the debates over the legal nature of self-determination. On the one hand, although it had been widely accepted in numerous international legal documents that the implementation of the right to self-determination should not harm state territorial integrity, some scholars and members of the international community never abandoned the view that such a right could indeed be violated by a denial of the right of secession from a multinational state (Nowak 2005: 23). On the other hand, renowned lawyers and diplomats (particularly from Western liberal countries) hold that the internal aspects of self-determination are as important as its external ones. Their standpoint can be perfectly illustrated by Manfred Nowak's comment that internal political self-determination has to be exercised together with Arts 19, 21, 22 and 25, which provide civil rights and freedoms within a sovereign state (Nowak 2005: 24). That is convincingly demonstrated by the fact that Article 1 contains the "permanent character" of the right to self-determination and such permanence is remarkably featured by its internal aspects (Nowak 2005: 15-16, 24).

Apparently, the historical facts following the introduction of the ICCPR echoed such a pro-liberal interpretation of self-determination. The collapse of communist regimes in Eastern Europe – most of which were solid advocates of decolonization – especially the dissolution of the Soviet Union and Yugoslavia, was regarded as a triumph of the implementation of the right of peoples to both external and internal self-determination. Such an "end of the history" naturally inspired the proposal of the right to democratic governance, which seemingly brought the opposition between Simpson's two liberalisms into the public arena before the international community.

However, such opposition has never been absolute, or has hardly been the whole truth. Supposing that there indeed exists a diametrical conflict between the two forms of liberalism, the presumed practice of post-decolonization external self-determination, such as in the cases of the Soviet Union, Yugoslavia, Czechoslovakia and East Germany, did not challenge one of the most theoretical foundations of Charter liberalism. The latter *de facto* equates sovereign states to citizens of the *civitas maxima*, and the sole alteration is the increase (or reduction) in the number of such citizens, whose subtext is hardly different from that of decolonization. Liberal anti-pluralism, in that sense, only applies to internal political self-determination that put much more emphasis on municipal law than its external counterpart, since the latter will never necessarily result in the practice of so-called democratic governance. It is not rare for modern international lawyers to criticize the possible irrelevance of self-determination to the promotion of democracy and the protection of human rights – with a Chinese background, Hua Fan did so (Fan 2008: 176-95).

Furthermore, most liberal anti-pluralists are also reluctant to challenge the Charter-based international order, at least the Charter itself, in terms of the argumentation over self-determination. For example, Reisman defends his "legitimate-intervention-supported self-determination" with a perspective of proclaiming and safeguarding the true meaning of Article 2(4) of the Charter. (Reisman 1984: 644) Franck, likewise, recalls that the normative content of the right to self-determination began with the Charter (Franck 1992: 60).

From this point of view, the internal logic of liberal anti-pluralism can still find room within the structure of Charter liberalism: so-called "outlaw states" are simply partly disfranchised individuals in the *civitas maxima*, which is not unacceptable even in a liberal state either. Another typical instance is Gregory Fox, who deems internal political self-determination an effective way to prevent the split of a state, made complete and compatible with the principle of territorial integrity (Fox 1995: 734).[16] From this angle, liberal anti-pluralists, who tend to concentrate on the internal aspects of self-determination, reach some quite loose consensus with Charter liberalists. Quite a few lawyers disagree about whether to discuss external and internal self-determination in a strictly separate way (Nowak 2005: 24, note 96), which might slightly rest upon such an idea.

Besides, it is noteworthy that one can hardly ignore the gap between academia and the reality of global politics. On the one hand, in a theoretical sense, a number of lawyers tend to transform self-determination into a basket to contain other human rights that may raise great concerns in the international community, from the rights of indigenous communities to those of women.[17] On the other hand, in practice, especially at the podium of the UN, it is still not easy to persuade states to agree to push self-determination beyond its traditional interpretation in international law. The latest report on the rights of peoples to self-determination from the Third Committee of the General Assembly can be a fair example.[18] In other words, even if it seems likely that more and more lawyers take delight in conceiving the establishment of a totally individual-centric global village, the order-based international community as a whole is far from prepared to do so.

Epilogue

The final issue is whether there is a Line of "Liberal Self-Determination" Emerging in International Law with consequences for the legal and material life of "world-citizens". Is that the case?

One should relate insights into the relationship between self-determination and liberalism to issues that rose about Simpson's reasoning at first. Simpson stressed that the core distinction between Charter liberalism and liberal pluralism is their opposite attitude toward sovereign equality. While Simpson is right in that the liberal logic of international law is experiencing some kind of transformation, this simple dichotomy remains dubious.

First, as sovereign equality is the leading principle of the Charter, most liberal anti-pluralists at least appear more conservative than Simpson believes. Fernando Tesón's statement, for example, is especially worth pondering. Although he insists that the international community is supposed to permanently reject recognition of the statehood of non-liberal states, Tesón keeps his argument within the bounds that international organizations like the UN should only admit the membership of liberal states (Marks 2000: 44). This seemingly radical standpoint precisely reveals his bottom line. In other words, it might be more reasonable that anti-pluralists prefer to delimit the boundary of Charter liberalism rather than to deny sovereign equality.

More significantly, history has proved that sovereign-equality-based international law only exists in ideology. Slaughter, no matter what surprising views she expressed to challenge traditional international law, advisably pointed out that the system of either the League of Nations or the UN, preponderantly influenced by the major powers, provides the equality between states only before the law, which is well illustrated by Article 27 of the Charter (Slaughter 1992: 1925).

Moreover, one cannot but remain skeptical of Simpson's dichotomy even if we admit the existence of two types of liberalisms according to their difference on sovereign equality. Writings of opposing lawyers reveal that the latter are essentially divided on the issue of the international legal subjects. For Charter liberalists, the most or "mainstream" qualified subjects can only be sovereign states. Their anti-pluralist counterparts, though not interested in totally negating the crucial role of states, concern themselves with or even tend to magnify the significance of non-state participants like individuals, enterprises, NGOs, etc., and thus have proposed several scenarios for international order reformation beyond the current state-centric structure.[19]

Besides, as is well known, there are two separate and sort of opposite strands of liberal theory of politics. The ascending strand refers to individual consent to legitimize political normative order, while the descending one stresses that one may preserve individual rights and freedoms only by a normatively compelling political order, which excludes any deviating individual preferences (Koskenniemi 2006: 72, 75). Connected with the above analysis, it is clear that Charter liberalism is more concerned with constructing and consolidating an ideal global order based on the "steerable" sovereign equality. Liberal anti-pluralism, on the other hand, theoretically focuses more on the consent of *all individuals*, except that of the individual *states*.

Thus, one may discover first that one can hardly strictly categorize internal self-determination as either of the two liberalisms in the current international legal discourse, where other human rights including claims of minorities and indigenous peoples are considerably involved. For instance, Franck has stated that the right to self-determination (especially internal self-determination) has evolved into a principle of political inclusion, but how can it disregard any suspicion vis-à-vis the new situation where not all claims for internal self-determination are necessarily about the right to participate?[20] Likewise, how can Charter liberalists and statists respond to the Draft Nordic Saami Convention aiming to build a trans-territorial indigenous organization? The development of internal self-determination might indicate the decay of Charter liberalism to some extent, but it does not naturally mean the victory of its rival.

Of course – at least on a formal level – a practice of external self-determination seems much closer to Charter liberalism all along after World War II. During the period of decolonization, such "liberalism" concentrated on the retroactive recognition of the "international citizenship" of the peoples under foreign subjugation and their consent to the brand-new international legal order. It might execute a similar mission through the acquiescence in "remedial secession" – implied by advisory opinions of the Supreme Court of Canada and the International Court of Justice (ICJ) regarding Quebec and Kosovo respectively. However, for most of the time, the international community, especially the major powers, will not hesitate to warn about the legitimacy of post-decolonization secession so long as it appears threatening to the stability of global or regional order. A good case in point can be the international lawyers' effort to draw the line between the unilateral independence of Kosovo and Russia's annexation of Crimea from both substantive and procedural perspectives.[21]

Besides, it seems to us that undoubtedly all indications are that the international community has agreed gradually to give a more free interpretation of self-determination from the traditional context of decolonization. This course officially commenced with the adoption of the UN Declaration on the Rights of Indigenous Peoples by the General Assembly in 2007, which is the first international legal instrument that confirms the right to self-determination of a people living in a sovereign state other than peoples under colonial domination and foreign occupation. Moreover, one will consolidate further such a confirmation by dialogue, drafting and adoption of an optional protocol to the Declaration in future.[22] Though it is unknown whether the approval of the indigenous peoples" right to self-determination will usher in the movement of internal self-determination by other sub-state groups,[23] progress is to some extent a tribute to classical liberalists who *opposed* colonialism at the very beginning (as mentioned earlier in the chapter).

All in all, from the angles of politics and philosophy, economics and social life, self-determination was, is and will always be bound up with liberalism – just like modern international law as a whole. But generally speaking, the existence of a genuine "liberal self-determination" in international law, let alone what kind of liberalism it belongs to, will continue to be under suspicion so long as there is a tension either between international law and international politics, or between a newly emerged utopia of global governance and the obstinate state-centric reality.

Nevertheless, that contemporary dilemma does *not* make meaningless the need to revisit the relationship between liberalism (whatever it should be) and self-determination, and this holds especially for China's international law research. For a long time, Chinese authorities and scholars regard both liberalism and self-determination as paradoxical: they were somehow useful in terms of academic research but rather sensitive in terms of political and ideological opposition.[24]

Perhaps it is then time, in 2015 and in the future, for the Chinese to further envisage both concepts described in the previous pages from a more pragmatic perspective and without political bias, insofar as to re-examine the inherent link between liberalism and international law as a whole. It is impossible for China to reverse its steps towards reform and opening up, and the way forward is to become more responsible for international affairs, which lies in any foreseeable future. This is encouraging since changes have been happening, and probably one more change is needed in that regard.

Acknowledgements

The author would like to extend his sincere thanks to the LIBEAC project sponsored by the European Commission. He is very grateful to Professor Tomáš Karásek from Charles University in Prague, who took the time and trouble to arrange his academic visit to Prague. His heartfelt thanks also go to Mr Aleš Karmazin from Charles University in Prague for his considerate help during the visit, to Mr Liu Lun, Ms Shen Jie, Mr Duan Wen, Mr Yang Ken, Mr Li Zhemin and Ms Shao Yangyang for their constructive assistance during the work. Last but not least, the author wants to thank Professor Gilles Campagnolo from Aix-Marseilles University for his inspiring and enlightening suggestions during the writing. The author is particularly grateful to his doctoral dissertation supervisor, Professor Bai Guimei, for her kind and patient guidance of his study of self-determination all along. The author himself is responsible for any potential errors or mistakes in the chapter.

Notes

1 Although Simpson puts scholars like Anne-Marie Slaughter, Fernando Tesón, Michael Reisman, Thomas Franck and John Rawls under the same signboard of "liberal anti-pluralism", he does not deny that beyond the consensus there are considerable dissimilarities among them. Inasmuch as this is a fact, this chapter will concentrate on their commonly negative attitude towards the discourse of sovereign-equality-based international law while disregarding their differences.

2 In his article commemorating the sixtieth anniversary of the establishment of the Five Principles by China and India, Professor Su pointed out that the core of the jurisprudence of the Five Principles embodies "公道" (impartiality), "共生" (mutualism), "平等" (equality) and "团结" (inclusiveness), most of which embrace the tenor of Charter liberalism at least literally. In contrast, he sharply criticized the doctrines of liberal anti-pluralism as the continuity of the arbitrary antithesis of civilization to barbarism in the era of colonialism (Su 2014: 4-22).

3 As Simpson himself correctly discovered, the conception of liberalism from the perspective of international relations in the postwar era is considerably fragmented (Simpson 2001: 540), and such further distinction is excluded from the theme of this chapter.

4 See, for instance (Wang and Jiang 2004); Liu Zhiyun, "世界秩序理论视野下的国际法" ("The International Law from the Perspective of the Theories of World Order"), *Journal of Gansu Political Science and Law Institute*, General No. 109 (Liu 2010: 87-93) and others. Compared to these other scholars, Su Changhe did make some beneficial in-depth studies on various modern liberal thoughts in terms of international relations (Su 2004: 15-20).

5 The issue of South-West Africa/Namibia directly related to self-determination, confirmed by the International Court Justice's advisory opinion in 1971. See the ICJ, *Legal Consequences for States of the Continued Presence of South Africa in Namibia (South West Africa) notwithstanding Security Council Resolution 276 (1970)* (1971), <http://www.icj-cij.org/docket/files/53/5595.pdf>. In addition, the fight against *apartheid* in South Africa and white rule in Rhodesia, according to Cassese, typically pushed the formation of the customary rules of internal self-determination in international law (Cassese 1995: 131).

6 Such an opinion is still disputable since a number of lawyers insist that the original intention of such international instruments after World War I was exactly the reverse of the unintentional end-result but not the aim, at least in words. But Hannum's opinion is widely supported by Third World countries including China.

7 One may also exemplify this issue with Michla Pomerance's argument that the Declaration on the Granting of Independence to Colonial Countries and Peoples did not genuinely conform to the UN Charter, since the latter had never clearly regarded colonial rule, so long as there was not abuse, as the violation of the Charter as well as human rights (Pomerance 1982: 11). Similar opinions have been relatively rare after the Cold War, however.

8 Quite a few scholars have made positive comments on the right to self-determination from an internal aspect according to Chapter VIII of the Helsinki Final Act (Cassese 1995: 287). One must mention Thomas Duncan Musgrave (Musgrave 1997: 99) and Jean Salmon also coped with some aspects of the right to self-Determination (Salmon 1993: 269).

9 Furthermore, quite a few scholars agreed that *continuity* constitutes the basic characteristic of internal self-determination. For instance, James Anaya directly called internal self-determination "ongoing self-determination" and external self-determination "constitutive self-determination" (Anaya 1993: 151) and Bai Guimei has extensively written on self-determination in international law (Bai 1999: 72).

10 See Chapter 2 in the present volume.

11 See Immanuel Kant, "Toward Perpetual Peace", quoted in the collection of essays on liberalism by David Sidorsky (*The Liberal Tradition in European Thought*: Sikorsky 1970). Although this quote seemingly focuses on the territorial sovereignty, most advocates of internal self-determination, including liberal anti-pluralists of course, are also greatly influenced by Kant's political doctrines. However, this is not the place to discuss this point deeper in this chapter.

12 For instance, Adam Smith specifically argued that allowing the independence of all colonies would be economically beneficial for British people in the average. In this regard, the book *An Inquiry into the Nature and Causes of the Wealth of Nations* should be treated as a source both for economists and for lawyers, both for general theoretical economics and for international concerns (Smith 1811: 343–484).

13 The terms "liberal/non-liberal states" used in this chapter only refer to the states whose political and social systems are based (in general) upon the doctrines of liberalism (or not) without any value judgment involved though.

14 For instance, the French revolutionary authorities once announced that each and every person living in the French colonies, no matter what the color of the skin may be, was entitled to enjoy constitutional rights (Umozurike 1972: 10).

15 Interestingly the former Socialist Federal Republic of Yugoslavia, a communist country at variance with the Soviet Union though, proposed such an insertion.

16 Even though it is not easy to decide whether Fox is a liberal anti-pluralist, one may think that his opinion finds common ground with Franck's view of self-determination as a principle of "inclusion", namely the right to participate in domestic political life (Franck 1992: 59; Bai 1999: 62).

17 Fergus MacKay, the former representative of Canadian indigenous peoples, used to point out that indigenous communities in fact wield the right to self-determination as a framework of ensuring their fundamental human rights and the integrity of their culture (Bai 1999: 145, note 2). In addition, the correlation between self-determination and women's rights has become another non-negligible issue amongst human rights topics. See, for instance among essays gathered by Karen Knop: "Women and self-determination in Europe after World War I" (Knop 2002: 277-326).

18 During the 68th session of the General Assembly, the UN Secretary-General submitted a report on rights of peoples to self-determination, which quoted the comments and conclusions of the Human Rights Committee and the Human Rights Council about the violations of indigenous rights. Nonetheless, the final report of the Third Committee still concentrated on the rights of peoples under colonial domination and foreign occupation, leaving other questions unmentioned. See "Rights of peoples to self-determination – Report of the Third Committee", *UN Doc. A/68/455*, <http://daccess-dds-ny.un.org/doc/UNDOC/GEN/N13/592/85/PDF/N1359285.pdf> (accessed December 3, 2013).

19 Representative proposals include Slaughter's trans-governmentalism (Slaughter 1997: 183-97) and Franck's suggestion to transform the UN General Assembly into a bicameral parliament, to which one should add a second chamber of representation apportioning seats based on population (Franck 1995: 171).

20 One can well exemplify this point by the American indigenous peoples' claims that are believed to relate to their peculiar isolationism (Barsh 1993: 279-85).

21 See, for instance, Anne Peters, "Crimea: Does 'The West' Now Pay the Price for Kosovo?", published April 22, 2014, <http://www.ejiltalk.org/crimea-does-the-west-now-pay-the-price-for-kosovo/>.

22 Remarkably, it would be the first optional protocol to a mere declaration rather than a well-formed treaty or convention in the history of international law. About some of the initial discussion on the dialogue and drafting of the protocol, see the UN Economic and Social Council, "Expert Group Meeting on the theme 'Dialogue on an optional protocol to the United Nations Declaration on the Rights of Indigenous Peoples': Note by the Secretariat", *UN Doc. E/C.19/2015/8* (February 17, 2015), <http://daccess-dds-ny.un.org/doc/UNDOC/GEN/N15/043/24/PDF/N1504324.pdf?OpenElement>.

23 Lawyers do have the concern that general principles laid in the Declaration on the Rights of Indigenous Peoples may inspire other ethno-cultural sub-state groups, especially certain national minorities, to propose similar claims just as indigenous peoples did (Kymlicka 2011: 192).

24 There is always a clear dichotomy within China's attitude toward self-determination. On the one hand, as one of the main advocates of decolonization after World War II, China usually shows its distinct favor upon the claims for self-determination of peoples under colonial domination and foreign occupation. An example is Palestine's struggle for statehood and the right to self-determination of indigenous peoples living in the United States, Canada, Australia and New Zealand (considered as the earliest victims of colonialism). On the other hand, China is generally very negative towards internal self-determination – either the controversial right of sub-state groups to secede from a sovereign state or linking self-determination with "democratization" of a state involving foreign interference – particularly when such issues are directly relevant to its own interests (such as that of Tibet, Xinjiang, Hong Kong and Taiwan).

References

Anaya, J. (1993) 'A Contemporary Definition of the International Norm of Self-Determination', *Transnational Law & Contemporary Problems*, 3: 131-64.

Bai, G. (1999) *Self-Determination in International Law*, Beijing: The Chinese Overseas Publishing House.

Barsh, R. L. (1993) 'The Challenge of Indigenous Self-Determination', *The University of Michigan Journal of Law Reform*, 26: 277-312.

Cassese, A. (1995) *Self-Determination of Peoples: A Legal Reappraisal*, Cambridge: Cambridge University Press.

Fan, H. (2008) 'The Missing Link between Self-Determination and Democracy: The Case of East Timor', *Northwestern Journal of International Human Rights*, 6 (1): 176-95.

Fox, G. H. (1995) 'Self-Determination in the Post-Cold War Era: A New Internal Focus', *Michigan Journal of International Law*, 16: 733-781.

Franck, T. M. (1992) 'The Emergence Right to Democratic Governance', *The American Journal of International Law*, 86: 46-91.

——(1995) 'Fairness in Fairness Discourse', *Proceedings of the Annual Meeting (American Society of International Law)*: 167-72.

Hannum, H (1996) 'Self-Determination in the Post-Colonial Era', in D. Clark and R. Williamson (eds.), *Self-Determination: International Perspectives*, London: Palgrave Macmillan, 12-44.

——(2011) *Autonomy, Sovereignty, and Self-Determination: The Accommodation of Conflicting Rights*, Philadelphia: University of Pennsylvania Press.

Hilpold, P. (2006) 'The Right to Self-Determination: Approaching an Elusive Concept through a Historic Iconography', *Austrian Review of International and European Law*, 11: 23-48.

Knop, K. (2002) *Diversity and Self-Determination in International Law*, Cambridge: Cambridge University Press.

Koskenniemi, M. (2006) *From Apology to Utopia: The Structure of International Legal Argument*, Cambridge: Cambridge University Press.

Kymlicka, W. (2011) 'Beyond the Indigenous/Minority Dichotomy', in: S. Allen and A. Xanthaki (eds.), *Reflections on the UN Declaration on the Rights of Indigenous Peoples*, Oxford: Hart Publishing, 183-208.

Lauterpacht, H. (2011) *The Function of Law in the International Community*, Oxford: Oxford University Press.

Liu, Z. (2010) 'The International Law from the Perspective of the Theories of World Order', *Journal of Gansu Political Science and Law Institute*, 109: 87-93.

Marks, S. (2000) *The Riddle of all Constitutions: International Law, Democracy, and the Critique of Ideology*, New York: Oxford University Press.

Musgrave, T. D. (1997) *Self-Determination and National Minorities*, Oxford: Clarendon Press.

Nawaz, M. K. (1965) 'The meaning and range of the principle of self-determination', *Duke Law Journal*, 14(1): 82-101.

Nowak, M. (2005) *U.N. Covenant on Civil and Political Rights: CCPR Commentary* (2nd Edition), Kehl: Norbert Paul Engel Verlag, e.K.

Pomerance, M. (1982) *Self-Determination in Law and Practice: The New Doctrine in the United Nations*, The Hague: Martinus Nijhoff Publishers.

Przetacznik, F. (1990) 'The Basic Collective Human Right to Self-Determination of Peoples and Nations as a Prerequisite for Peace', *New York Law School Journal of Human Rights*, 8: 49-109.

Reisman, M. (1984) 'Coercion and Self-Determination. Construing Article 2(4)', *The American Journal of International Law*, 78: 642-45.

——(1990) 'Sovereignty and Human Rights in Contemporary International Law', *The American Journal of International Law*, 84: 866-76.

Salmon, J. (1993) 'Internal Aspects of the Right to Self-Determination: Towards a Democratic Legitimacy Principle', in C. Tomuschat (ed.), *Modern Law of Self-Determination*, The Hague: Martinus Nijhoff Publishers.

Sidorsky, D. (ed.) (1970) *The Liberal Tradition in European Thought*, New York: G. P. Putnam's Sons.

Simpson, G. (2001) 'Two Liberalisms', *The European Journal of International Law*, 12: 537-71.

Sinha, S. P. (1974) 'Has Self-Determination Become A Principle Of International Law Today?', *Indian Journal of International Law*, 14: 332-61.

Slaughter, A. (1992) 'Law among Liberal States: Liberal Internationalism and the Act of State Doctrine', *Colombia Law Review*, 92(8): 1907-96.

——(1997) 'The Real New World Order', *Foreign Affairs*, 76: 183-97.

Smith, A. (1811) *An Inquiry into the Nature and Causes of the Wealth of Nations*, Hartford: Peter B. Gleason and Co.

Su, C. (2004) 'Liberalism and World Politics: The Enlightenment of Liberal International Relations Theory', *World Politics and Economics*, 7: 15-20.

——(2014) 'Reflection on the Five Principles of Peaceful Coexistence and Chinese Theoretical System of International Law', *World Economics and Politics*, 6: 4-22.

Umozurike, O. (1972) *Self-Determination in International Law*, Hamden: Archon Books.

Wang, J. and Jiang, S. (2004) 'Philosophical Foundation of Liberalism in the International Law', *Journal of Guangxi Administrative Cadre Institute of Politics and Law*, 19(3): 23-25.

11 Slaughter's liberal theory of international law

Comments from a Chinese perspective

Guimei Bai

This chapter first explores the concept of liberal theory in international law, initiated and developed by Professor Anne-Marie Slaughter and her followers. But emphasis will be on human rights law, which is actually the heart of her theory. Second, this chapter will focus on the role of the States in international human rights law. I try to apply Slaughter's theory to see if it will help in compliance with international human rights conventions. Here, I make an in-depth study on United Nations (UN) human rights treaty bodies. I choose international human rights law as the entry point of this study for I consider Slaughter's liberal theory easier to be applied to this area than any others in international law, and international human rights law is perhaps the only branch of the subject in which individuals and groups are in the center and which has blurred the distinction between international law and domestic law. Third, the limits of the liberal theory will be discussed after comparing the European experiences and that of UN treaties.

In all cases, and in all three sections, one must keep in mind that the legal institutions are what frames the course of exchange, spiritual and material, between people. In other words, that without a legal frame there is no economy. Therefore, economics is highly concerned with the evolution of the legal system and the bodies that bear some authority. This is not only an institutionalist point of view, it is also about how the economy effectively works, and why I, as a lawyer, feel deeply concerned with the applied aspect of law and economics, while trying to provide some of the necessary keys to understanding with a perspective from China.

A brief introduction to Slaughter's liberal theory of international law

As is the case in general law, there are different liberalisms or liberal theories in international law, as well as different understandings or interpretations of these approaches or schools.[1] Liberal theories in international law are commonly divided into two types: classical liberalism and new liberalism. The former emphasizes "the virtues of tolerance, diversity and openness together with an agnosticism about moral truth" (Simpson 2001: 539). The latter is manifested mainly by Anne-Marie Slaughter in her works published at the turn of the twentieth to the twenty-first century.

Gerry Simpson characterizes her theory as "liberal anti-pluralism" (Simpson 2001: 537) and there are many critiques of Slaughter's theory by international scholars (Alvarez 2001: 183; Marks 1997: 449; Kennedy 1999: 9 for instance). Yet, her transposition of positive liberal theory of international relations into international law has stimulated some Chinese international lawyers.[2] As Slaughter has repeatedly indicated, her theory of international relations theory has the following four characteristics:

(1) It is a bottom-up view rather than a top-down one. In contrast to the top-down view, Slaughter's theory "assumes that international order is created from bottom up" (Slaughter and Alvarez 2000: 242). According to this bottom-up view, the making of international law is, suggested by Slaughter, composed of three levels.[3]

First, individuals and groups operating in domestic and transnational society make rules governing themselves. Second, governments make rules regulating individuals and groups operating in domestic and transnational society; parts of governments may also cooperate with one another to make rules binding themselves on matters of common concern. Third, states make rules governing their mutual relations. It seems that Slaughter is dealing with the sources of international law:

> [T]he first level of law is the voluntary law of individuals and groups in transnational society. The liberal focus on state–society relations leads first to an examination of rules arising out of the interactions of individuals, private groups and organizations across borders.
>
> [...] The second level of law is transnational and trans-governmental law. [...] The result is a growing body of transnational and "trans governmental" law. Transnational law has many definitions. I mean to include here simply national law that is designed to reach actors beyond national borders: the assertion of extra territorial jurisdiction.
>
> [...] At the third level, a liberal approach to international law would also incorporate the traditional sources of public international law – treaties and customary law.
>
> (Slaughter and Alvarez 2000: 242–45)

In Slaughter's liberal theory, the focus is on the rules arising from individuals and groups in their interactions both within and across borders, which are, in the eyes of positive or realist international lawyers, soft laws that are not legally binding on states. However, this change of the focus from state-made treaties and customs to those standards or codes of conduct distinguishes Slaughter's theory obviously from the traditional state-centric approach.

(2) It is an integrated view rather than a view of separation between the international and domestic spheres. The blurring of the distinction between international and domestic law is the second characteristic of Slaughter's liberal theory, which is an inevitable result of the bottom-up view. The reason for the integration of the two spheres is that:

Global problems have domestic roots. Law that directly regulates individuals and groups thus is more likely to get at the root of the problem. Law that has a direct impact on individuals and groups will thus have the greatest impact on international order.

(Slaughter and Alvarez 2000: 245–46)

It is commonly discussed in international law textbooks that these two laws are closely related. But that does not mean, at least in theory, that they can be obscured. Slaughter's theory blurs the two in order to pave the way for individuals and groups to break the border of states and reach international law directly. This blurring not only makes unnecessary the distinction between public and private international law but also puts all kinds of international law, such as international trade law, international investment law, and international human rights law, etc., into one basket. As Slaughter explains, "the Liberal theory of international law advanced here sweeps all those bodies of international law into a specific account of how law contributes to international order" (Slaughter and Alvarez 2000: 241). But this chapter only focuses on international human rights law, which is actually Slaughter's main concern as well.

(3) It assumes state–society relations, in which national states play a different role from what the traditional theory of international law preserves for them. In Slaughter's theory, states are no longer billiard balls. They are transparent in the sense that the atoms of varying composition of the state are playing roles in international law. Slaughter's assumption of state–society relations is also a challenge to international lawyers since most of them, even those who regard individuals as subjects of international law, do not deny that international law is the one mainly regulating interstate relations. What is the concept of state–society relations? It is "the plethora of ways in which domestic institutions interact with individuals and groups in domestic and transnational society" (Slaughter and Alvarez 2000: 246). It refers to relations not only within the billiard balls of states but also across their borders.

(4) Slaughter's theory fragmentizes a state into different government institutions, which could be generally called governments. It concentrates on the specific interactions between individuals and these institutions. These government institutions are primarily legislative, executive, administrative and judicial. They are playing an important role in protecting rights of individuals both inside and outside the jurisdiction. As Slaughter indicates:

By departing from the traditional conception of States as unitary actors on the international stage, it is possible to understand these relations in the context of a trans-judicial and trans-legislative dialogue, in which courts and legislatures acknowledge and evaluate foreign law. It also facilitates the conceptualization of a transnational legal process encompassing disaggregated judicial, legislative and executive interaction.

(Slaughter 1995: 517)

This disaggregation of states into government institutions attempts to further reduce the role of states in international law in order to bring about the bottom-up theory of international law.

To sum up, Slaughter's liberal theory of international law is an approach to transform the law from a top-down system into a bottom-up one. The heart of this approach is the changing of the role of states in international law or the transformation of international law from a state-centric system to an individual-centric one. Therefore, international human rights law is precisely the area that is the most fit for her theory.

The role of states and civil society/NGOs in international human rights law: an attempt to apply Slaughter's theory

As Antonio Cassese aptly summarized (Cassese 2005: 59–60), the realization of full respect of human rights can never depend on states. One should turn to the civil society or non-governmental organizations (NGOs) at both the domestic and international level. In short, we should depend on ourselves. This is a reflection out of the disappointment from an experienced human rights scholar for the reality of the enforcement of international human rights law, especially for the role or the behavior of states. In reality, individuals, the holders of human rights in international human rights law, are merely beneficiaries (Henkin 1990: 21, 37). In other words, they are not the subjects of the law. It is states, the parties to the international human rights conventions then that are the subjects.

But in contrast to other international treaties, the balance of rights and obligations of the state parties is almost absent. By ratifying human rights treaties states promise to undertake obligations provided in the treaties to respect, protect and fulfill human rights within their jurisdiction. They are the duty bearers with very few, if any, rights to enjoy directly from the conventions.[4] Then why do states ratify international human rights treaties, besides economic treaties and more traditional diplomatic treaties about war and peace? This very complicated issue is not within the range of this chapter. But it is by no means irrelevant to the topic – the role of states in trading goods according to shared common goals with regard to persons who trade, and the role of states in international human rights law. In this section, I first explore the role of states, both liberal and non-liberal ones, in implementing human rights obligations; second, the role of civil society or NGOs in international human rights law will be briefed; third, I attempt a deeper study on the so-called "FRA" in Europe and try to apply Slaughter's theories to the practice of this institution.

States are obligation carriers and also implementation barriers.

Differently from other branches of international law, states are the treaty obligation carriers but they have very few rights in the sense of the law of treaties, which is regulating reciprocal relations between states. Usually a treaty should create obligations and rights for states that ratify it on an equal footing. Reciprocally, a right granted by treaty to one state party bears the obligation of the other state party to respect that right and vice versa. This is so both for bilateral and for multilateral treaties or conventions. But the balance between rights and obligations as a result of reciprocity between states does not exist in international human rights treaties because the subject matter of those treaties are human rights and the right holders are not other states but rather individuals. As is provided in most human rights treaties, each "state party [...] undertakes to respect and to ensure to all individuals within its territory and subject to its jurisdiction."[5]

It is obviously clear that the right–obligation relationship in human rights treaties is not between the state parties but between individuals as the right holders and the relevant state parties as the obligation carriers. Yet human rights are not treaty rights, namely they are not created but "recognized" by the human rights treaties. [6] And the relationship between the state parties and the individuals within its territory and subject to its jurisdiction is not regulated by the law of the treaty. In other words, there is no reciprocal rights–obligations treaty relationship under the human rights treaties since the substantial rights are rights of the individuals who are not parties to the treaty. The state parties do not have human rights.[7]

To sum up, it is obvious that the role of states under international human rights law is to undertake obligations to respect, protect and fulfill human rights within their territories or their jurisdiction. They are obligation carriers, both in theory and in reality.

However, the problem is that not all the state parties take human rights conventions seriously, or not all states at all times take human rights treaty obligations seriously. Even states like the United States sometimes change their policies on human rights when state interests are at stake. Violations of human rights are likely to be ignored or excused.[8] There have always been debates on sovereignty and human rights.[9] Which prevails when the two collide? The answer might either be simple or complicated, or the issue itself might be regarded as a pseudo-proposition. States and individuals may have different attitudes towards this issue – assuming it is an issue. And their attitudes might change in different circumstances from different perspectives.

When there is a humanitarian crisis or serious human rights violations in State A, State B might claim humanitarian intervention and argue that the sovereignty of State A cannot be used as a shield, while State A will protest against State B for its intervention in its internal affairs by alleging a concealed interest of petroleum or other economic or military considerations. Then the third states would be divided into at least three groups: the one on A's side, the one on B's side and the one in the middle, the big silent group. What is happening? Who is seriously concerned about the human rights of individuals? What is the focus then? These are questions that do not need an answer.

Such a scenario has been repeated again and again since international human rights law came into the domain of international law, whether during or after the cold war. Sometimes the United Nations and its institutions are utilized by both sides, such as the General Assembly and the Security Council, particularly the former Commission on Human Rights and the present Human Rights Council.[10] This is a political struggle among sovereign states with human rights as a disguise. Human rights have been politicized by states both at international and at domestic level. From a macroscopic view, human rights law has been developed in the cracks of political and diplomatic struggles within and among the states.

In international human rights law, the role of states has a dual character. On the one hand, like international human rights treaty parties, they could be the most vigorous promoters of human rights if they faithfully do what they pledged in the treaties – to respect, protect and fulfill the human rights of individuals within their territories and under their jurisdiction. On the other hand, if they do not take human rights treaties seriously or take it as a window-dressing (Hathaway 2001–2: 1940),[11] or, even worse, utilize them as political and diplomatic tools to fight against each other for their self-interests, they could be the most powerful barriers against the promotion and protection of human rights. In fact, international human rights law emerged after World War II when people in the world found that it would be hopelessly impossible for states with fascist regimes to protect human rights. Those states actually are not simply barriers of human rights protection but rather the violators themselves.

By the term "barriers", I mean the role states are playing in human rights protection by means of taking some measures that do not break the rules of international law. States could be barriers in many ways, which include: refusing to ratify human rights treaties or ratifying them as window-dressing;[12] making too many reservations to human rights treaties;[13] refusing to accept individual communication and inquiry mechanisms of treaty bodies;[14] rejecting UN human rights special rapporteurs' visits;[15] not submitting or delaying state reports to treaty bodies, etc.

Those are only at the international level, where states are on the defensive with state sovereignty as a powerful weapon; while at the domestic level, the barring strategies are various and with different degrees for different states on different occasions. States may insist on a political system that is not easy for human rights promotion.[16] States may make and carry out policies that are restrictive or preventive of human rights, and the one-child policy and the policy of Hukou have brought many problems for human rights in China, for instance.[17] States may promulgate laws or take emergent measures to derogate human rights treaty obligations in emergencies, such as anti-terrorism laws.[18]

So what? Is it in the hands of any to remove states from the international society for the sake of human rights protection? This kind of dream never comes true. Anyhow, states are the main actors and play a very important role, either positive or negative, in international human rights law. What can be done is, as Slaughter proposed, to transform the focus. This could imply not relying as much on states as on NGOs or the civil society, born from the active exchange of goods and information between people.

Civil society/NGOs are the most active in international human rights law

Slaughter's bottom-up approach seems most fit for international human rights law because the heart of her approach is an individual-centric character and individuals are in the center of international human rights law. Compared to other international law fields, individuals, civil society or NGOs are the most active in the making and implementation of international human rights law.[19] There are some famous human rights NGOs, such as Amnesty International, Global Rights, International Committee of the Red Cross, Human Rights Watch, International Federation of Human Rights, UN Watch, Human Rights Foundation, etc.[20] However, the human rights NGOs that I am talking about in this chapter are ordinary ones, but they play the same kind of role and do similar things in human rights protection and human rights education. Generally speaking, it appears to be just as Wolfgang S. Heinz commented:

> NGOs collect critical information, advise victims how to complain, complain themselves publicly about weaknesses of state agencies, and even support legal cases before national, regional, and international expert committees and courts.
>
> (Heinz 2010: 493)

But that is only one single part of the whole picture, drawn by NGOs which are bigger and have a greater reputation in the world and whose activities are more often reflected in the mass media. There are hundreds of thousands of human rights NGOs, which have played and are playing important roles in the promotion and protection of human rights both internationally and domestically. Their activities include short-term campaigns for a specific goal and long-term programs of human rights research and education.

When the Charter of the United Nations was drafted, it was human rights NGOs that played a critical role in inserting a stronger version of human rights provisions into the Charter than what appeared in the earlier Dumbarton Oaks proposals (van Boven 1990: 210). According to the former US Secretary of State Edward Stettinius' report to President Truman, the NGO input brought to the 1945 San Francisco Conference by "the group of American consultants representing forty-two leading American organizations and groups concerned with the enjoyment of human rights and basic freedoms to all peoples":

> A direct outgrowth of discussions between the United States delegation and the Consultants was the proposal of the United States delegation in which it was joined by other sponsoring powers that the Charter [Article 68] be amended to provide for a Commission on Human Rights.
>
> (van Boven 1990: 210–11)

This proposal was accepted.[21] Some NGOs together with a group of smaller countries fought for the inclusion of an international bill of rights in the UN

Charter but failed because of the objection principally from the major powers (Buergenthal 2006: 786).

Ever since then, domestic and international NGOs (or in Slaughter's term, the civil society) never stop pushing for the development of international human rights law, particularly by participating in the process of the making and the implementing of international human rights treaties, as well as by promoting human rights education.

NGOs are active in international human rights lawmaking, including that of treaties promoting economic rights and documents protecting the right to development

Though states are the only actors in the actual making of international human rights treaties, NGOs can play an important role in that process, as they did in the San Francisco Conference. NGOs influence the drafting of human rights treaties by directly participating in the debates or even submitting proposals to the UN institutions. As was recorded in the *travaux préparatoires* of the *International Bill of Human Rights*, NGOs participated in the debates on the drafting of the texts though only at the level of the Commission on Human Rights and its drafting group. At that time they could not submit proposals in their own name (van Boven 1990: 211).

Yet, their concerns could be brought to the negotiation table by sympathetic governmental representatives. Now things have changed tremendously and NGOs are entitled to submit drafting proposals in their own name. NGOs are very active in the process of drafting many human rights conventions, including the Convention on Elimination of All Forms of Discrimination against Women (CEDAW, 1981) and the Optional Protocol to CEDAW (OP CEDAW, 1999), the Convention against Torture and Other Cruel, Inhuman or Degrading Treatment or Punishment (CAT, 1984), the Convention of the Rights of the Child (CRC, 1989), and the most recent ones, such as the Convention on the Rights of Persons with Disabilities (CRPD, 2006), as well as the one in its drafting process at the moment when this chapter was being written, that is, the Convention on the Rights of Older Persons. This is not the place to detail NGOs' contributions to all of the above-mentioned conventions, so let me provide only two examples: the CEDAW and the one that can be drafted on the rights of older persons.[22]

When CEDAW was being drafted the UN Commission on the Status of Women called on NGOs to make comments, on the same footing with member States of the United Nations on the draft articles which were contained in the report of the Working Group (Burrows 1985: 420) in time for its 26th session (1976). The All African Women's Conference submitted its draft texts though it was not discussed in the 26th session of the Commission. A Group of NGOs made an amendment proposal on the draft text. The group proposed that in the Convention NGOs should be given the right to submit information and recommendations relating to the observance of the provisions of the Convention. But unfortunately the proposal was rejected (Burrows 1985: 456). About twenty years later, when the OP CEDAW was being drafted, "a draft Optional Protocol for the Women's Convention was prepared by a non-governmental group of experts, sponsored by the Women in Law Project of the International Human Rights Law Group and the Maastricht Centre for Human Rights" (Evatt 2002–3: 551, note 187).

The Convention for the Rights of Older Persons is now being drafted. The process began in 2011, when the first session of the Open-Ended Working Group (OEWG) was set up by the General Assembly in its resolution 65/182 of December 21, 2010. By July 2015, six sessions had been held by the OEWG. NGOs from all over the world participated in all the sessions and played important roles.[23] As The Hon. Susan Ryan AO, the Australian Age and Disability Discrimination Commissioner, the Honorable Susan Ryan, summarized as follows:

> More progress has been made among international civil society groups, some of which have started to write up their own draft conventions! The international NGO community has formed an alliance called the Global Alliance for the Rights for Older People (GAROP). This consists of a network of international age-related NGOs who are in support of a new convention. An Australian branch of GAROP, led by COTA has been formed and is active.
>
> (Ryan 2014)

NGO participation in the process of drafting human rights conventions has taken similar forms: making presentations in the session panels; submitting documents (such as reports, recommendations or research papers) to UN working groups; making statements at the sessions; organizing meetings among different NGOs; writing their own draft articles or even a whole convention;[24] organizing NGO alliances to work together; etc.[25] Of course, when the major actors in international human rights lawmaking are still sovereign states, NGOs' efforts do not always end in success; sometimes the results are disappointing.[26] As mentioned above, some NGO proposals were rejected or even not discussed at all.

NGOs are active in the implementation of international human rights conventions

Lawmaking is only the first step; the critical step is actually the implementation. The implementing mechanisms of the treaty bodies depend heavily on NGOs' support. As Elizabeth Evatt, the former Chair of the CEDAW Committee, recognized, "NGO support was an essential element in making the work of the Committee effective" (Evatt 2002: 535). Compared to lawmaking, the more important task for NGOs is to push the governments of the state parties to carry out their treaty obligations after ratification.

Taking the reporting mechanism of the treaty bodies as an example, NGOs are playing different roles at almost every stage of the reporting process. First, they try to influence the drafting process of the state report by attending hearings or consulting meetings organized by the government of the reporting state. Second, if they are not satisfied with the finished state report they will write their shadow or parallel reports and submit them directly to the treaty bodies. NGOs in Mainland China began to write shadow reports three years ago when the Chinese report on the Convention of Rights of Persons with Disabilities was prepared.

Besides, the committees of the other conventions (except that of the *International Covenant of Civil and Political Rights*) have also received a range of shadow reports from Chinese NGOs (including that of Hong Kong and Macao) since 2009. The number of the reports submitted by NGOs in Mainland China, however, is very limited.[27] Human rights treaty bodies depend heavily on accurate information and those reports may provide what they need. With that detailed and on-the-ground information from NGOs, members of treaty bodies can ask government delegations questions in order to shed light on issues the government would otherwise like to keep concealed.

Third, when the list of questions raised by the treaty bodies is ready for the state parties on their reports, NGOs will participate in the discussions, if any, organized by the government. Or they can organize workshops with governmental officials invited for the same purpose. Their efforts at this stage are to influence the government's answers to questions.

Fourth, when the state report is being reviewed by the human rights treaty bodies, NGOs are provided opportunities to brief their opinions on the human rights situation in the countries in question. They may lobby the members of the treaty bodies during the break, particularly the country rapporteur for the review.[28] They may disseminate their shadow reports and other relevant materials in the conference halls where the reports are being reviewed. In fact, this is a good chance for NGOs to have face-to-face contacts with the governmental officials in order to exchange ideas on the report and on the specific human rights problems in the country.[29]

Last but not least, the follow-up stage after the review is the most important of all in this circulating reporting flow path because if the implementation of the concluding recommendations given by the treaty bodies to the state party cannot be carried back into the domestic level the reporting mechanism of the treaty bodies would perform practically no function at all. NGOs can do a lot in various ways to contribute to the accomplishment of this longer-term task, which will last till the next report to be reviewed, usually seven or eight years.[30]

NGOs promote human rights education

Human rights education is another field in which NGOs are the most active. Since the first UN decade of human rights education started in 1995,[31] there have emerged many full-time or part-time programs on human rights education. Some are jointly organized for students with different disciplinary backgrounds. Human rights NGOs' efforts in this field are crucial to helping in establishing and maintaining human rights education programs in developing countries.

Let us take the Raoul Wallenberg Institute for Human Rights and Humanitarian Law (RWI) as an example. RWI has human rights education programs in Sub-Saharan Africa, Asia, Europe, Middle East and North Africa. In China, RWI began their activities in human rights education early in 1998, when the first round of donation of books on human rights law was delivered to thirteen Chinese universities. Why is that of tremendous relevance to China? In 1998, thirteen universities, academic institutions and libraries were selected throughout China to receive a collection of literature consisting of some 400 titles with emphasis on human rights law. There followed four other donation rounds (in 2002, 2003, 2006 and 2007), and in each round there were about eighty brand-new books in English published by famous publishers on international law and human rights law. Peking University was there but also twelve other universities and academic institutions. For each round, the list of the thirteen universities or academic institutions would be adjusted somewhat in order to cover more institutions, especially the ones in western China.[32]

For the period 2001–7, RWI, together with the other two Nordic Institutions, the Norwegian Centre for Human Rights and the Danish Institute of Human Rights, held annual training courses and altogether trained more than 200 Chinese university teachers in how to teach international human rights law, and many of them have now become leading human rights teachers in China. Since the training lasted for a long time period, some of the first trainees became trainers for later courses. According to a follow-up study on the previous course participants carried out in 2010, undergraduate and graduate level human rights courses have now been established at around 100 universities in China.

Besides, RWI has relatively long-term projects of human rights education. Since 2004, RWI has been collaborating with the National Prosecutors College in Beijing and its provincial branch colleges throughout China to strengthen the human rights component as part of the professional training for prosecutors, including training the trainers and textbook compiling, etc. The most important project on human rights education that RWI has been doing in China since 2004 is the Human Rights Master Program at Peking University. The program was initially launched and has been maintained with substantial support from RWI. To date, more than 200 students have graduated from the program. Many are working in human rights related careers or doing further studies on human rights.[33]

Human rights education is so important that many NGOs like RWI are insistently making efforts to promote its development, particularly in developing countries or countries in transition, like China. It is a fact now recognized as true: individualism is something enhanced through education, and if human rights education is absent or poor and if individuals do not know what rights they have or they should have, it is quite understandably difficult for international human rights conventions to be implemented within the territory of the state parties. How could a bottom-up approach *à la Slaughter* be applied when there is no "ground" to do so?

The European Union Agency for Fundamental Rights: model for Slaughter's liberal approach?

From the above-mentioned interferences of NGOs in UN human rights lawmaking and in the circulating process of state reporting, at least two points of Slaughter's theory might be applied here: first, the bottom-up view; second, the inextricably linked relationship between international and domestic spheres. The other two characteristics of Slaughter's liberal approach, state–society relations and the fragmentation of states, are missing. Let's leave this for the moment and come back to it after one example of practice, by the so-called "FRA", is examined.

"FRA" stands for the European Union Agency for Fundamental Rights, one of the European Union's decentralized agencies, established on 1 March 2007 under Council Regulation 168/2007/EC of 15 February 2007. The EU set up this agency to provide independent, evidence-based assistance and expertise on fundamental rights to EU institutions and member states. It is an independent EU body. If the EU were considered a state, then the FRA could be regarded as a National Human Rights Institution.[34] It has a director[35] to guide and manage the Agency, a Management Board for defining the Agency's work program, and a Scientific Committee of experts for ensuring the quality of the Agency's work. The Founding Regulation identifies eight tasks. But Gabriel Toggenburg subsumed them under three major functions, namely data collection, the production of expert opinions, and the establishment of a communication strategy (Toggenburg 2008: 392).

There were heated debates on the nature and position of the FRA as the newest and the only EU agency on human rights, particularly in the early years after its establishment.[36] Anyway, this chapter's interest is neither the theoretical debate on the FRA's legal nature nor its political position in the EU but rather what it is practicing for human rights protection, especially the approach with which it is operated. I would like to analyze the FRA's practice in order to find out to what extent Slaughter's liberal theory is actually tested in the field of human rights by the Agency. However, the FRA's practice may not turn the whole theory into reality, but the ways in which it is operating might have some influences upon the EU society. But this is by no means to say that the FRA is intentionally practicing any theory.[37] From a perspective of international human rights law, this is, however, precisely a primary attempt to construe the FRA's practice with Slaughter's theory.

The so-called "bottom-up view"

Slaughter points out that the traditional view of international law is top-down, which means sovereign states are the major actors in international lawmaking and enforcement of the law. Civil society could only be represented by their home state at the international level. The "bottom-up view" approach is to make a dramatic change of the situation and bring the people from the grass roots to interact with the international platform.

Observation shows the FRA is exactly practicing with the "bottom-up view" approach. We can see this from its strategies and substantial activities. From Slaughter's "bottom-up view", the highlight is the FRA's annual meeting of the Fundamental Rights Platform (FRP). As Morten Kjaerum and Gabriel N. Toggenburg indicated:

> This is a unique and interesting feature of the EU fundamental rights landscape. Whereas a variety of consultation mechanisms exist, especially with the European Commission, the Platform is innovative in that it provides for the structured and long-term engagement of an EU body with hundreds of NGO participants who regularly meet both electronically as well as physically.
>
> (Kjaerum and Toggenburg 2012: 6)

The critical element of the FRP is the regular participation of hundreds of NGOs in the FRA's engagement with human rights protection. Though there is quite a long list of criteria[38] for being selected for the participation of the FRP, which is on the basis of application, almost all applicants have been approved because, according to statistics of 2012, FRA has accepted 90% of the total number of applicants as Platform participants. The reasons for rejecting the rest are either formal or the willingness of the applicants.[39] It is this FRP strategy that brings NGOs from different parts of the EU with different thematic focuses. Up to the year 2015, 395 civil society organizations participated in the Platform. The mere existence of the FRP makes Slaughter's "bottom-up view" possible for the FRA because the FRP opens a permanent communication channel that enables the civil society members to bring their inputs to the FRA both through the annual meetings, conferences and thematic seminars and electronically through email as well as the 'e-FRP'. The civil society's inputs include mainly:

> First, planning input required to draft the Annual Work Programme; second, evaluation input required to gain feedback and thereby enable the director and the Management Board to ensure that the Agency performs the tasks entrusted to it; and third, information input which allows the Agency to track developments on the ground, such as developments in Court rooms, the field of employment, the social sector, academia, etc.
>
> (Kjaerum and Toggenburg 2012: 10)

However, practice shows that most of the NGOs are at the national and EU level. At the time of writing, only 71 local civil society organizations of the total 395 participate in the Platform.[40] The figure reduces a little bit of the applicability of Slaughter's "bottom-up view" approach.

An integrated view is that the integration of international and domestic spheres is also possible and is another attempt at transformation in Slaughter's liberal theory. Actually the strict separation of the two spheres is a natural result of the state-centric character of international relations and international law. With sovereign states as the major subjects of international law and non-intervention as one the fundamental principles of the law, there is an invisible wall that prevents individuals from entering into the international sphere. Individuals and groups or civil society are kept inside the billiard balls (the states). In order to promote the "bottom-up view" individuals and groups must break through the wall. Before that can be done the blurring of the two spheres is a better alternative maneuver.

The platform provided by the FRA to the civil society is just a good experiment if not to break the wall but certainly to create the interaction between the two spheres. First, the participants of the annual Fundamental Rights Platform meeting are from different levels. The FRP was established exclusively as a forum to establish a European civil society platform on human rights issues. After a number of successful meetings officials from the European Commission and members of the Parliament found it very useful to be present in order to listen to the concerns and issues raised by civil society. Even international organizations join the Platform meetings as well.[41]

They all attend the meeting on the same footing. Individuals are not represented by the member states (but by NGO representatives). Second, the thematic issues that they discuss are mixtures of international (between member states) and domestic (internal affairs of member states) ones. Since the issues can be common to many member states, the EU as a whole may be considerably interested in them. On the other hand, the issues are also relevant at the national level as people still live domestically. This is to ensure a joined-up approach.[42] Third, the procedure or precisely the strategy of the FRP meeting is propitious for breaking the wall: messages that pour out from the meeting are not stored there or are stored just for publication in the report.

Those messages were formulated by all participants throughout the whole FRP meeting, and more specifically during both the Working groups and "The Floor is yours" sessions. They aimed at outlining strategic guidelines for the areas of freedom, security and justice, and were then transmitted to the Council of the European Union (and other policymakers), in order to feed into the final discussions on the new strategic guidelines.[43] The messages from NGOs could also be transferred to the European Parliament or the European Council. The FRA is three to four times a year requested by the Parliament or the Council for its opinion on draft legislation, or is requested to do studies or surveys about certain human rights issues. The messages from the meeting of the Platform are obviously significant to attract attention to certain issues.

Apart from the FRP the FRA host every year a Fundamental Rights Conference (FRC). At these highly interactive conferences the officials, politicians from the EU institutions and Member States participated in an engaged manner discussing specific issues: the legal protection of irregular migrants, access to justice in times of crisis, juvenile justice, migration, etc. By hearing substantial voices from both civil society and governments, the FRA apparently succeeds in acting as a chief coordinator of almost all human rights issues within the EU.[44]

Transparent state–society relations

This is one point on which to debate as well: is it possible at all, to be wished and/ or laudable? Slaughter's most serious critique of the state-centric international law is her "billiard ball" analogy. States in international law are like billiard balls on the pool table. They collide against each other or roll at the same or different directions on the table. Nobody knows what's going on inside the ball, let alone allowing the compositions of the ball to play some role. These are the traditional interstate relations. In Slaughter's liberal theory, the transparent state-society is in contrast to the billiard ball. Instead of the states interacting like billiard balls in interstate relations, the compositions of the states, that is, individuals, private groups and organizations across borders, interact at the international level. This is the concept of Slaughter's state–society relations.

For the FRA, through the FRP annual meetings and the e-FRP, interactions are manifold. As Kjaerum and Toggenburg summarized, there are three different modes of interaction (2012: 17).

- Platform–FRA: FRP participants provide frontline knowledge of Civil Society to the FRA, thereby allowing the latter to address the right issues and to display relevant advice, corresponding to the expectations of the agency's stakeholders;
- FRA–Platform: the FRA opens channels allowing Platform participants to provide input on Agency activities and, indirectly, on policy developments at EU level in a wider sense;
- Platform–Platform: annual meetings, conferences and thematic seminars allow Platform participants to network amongst the relevant Civil Society organizations, to hold discussions and exchange promising practices.

From its annual reports, we can see that the FRA's work involves all kinds of actors, especially those related to fundamental rights, such as EU institutions, EU member states, and other national actors, including national equality bodies, human rights institutions and civil society organizations. Take anti-discrimination as an example, as is emphasized in the report, "countering discrimination requires strong cooperation between all relevant actors," and these actors "took specific steps in that direction in 2014."[45] For the application of Slaughter's theory, the most important thing here is that the FRA provides the platform where all actors are able to interact, exchange views, information and experiences, and cooperate. It is a good model of transparent state–society relations.

The transformation of states into governments

This means somehow the "disintegration" of states into governments, and is the last characteristic of Slaughter's liberal theory. In the context of the FRA, it means the actors on the platform should not only be the member states but also the governmental components, such as the parliaments, courts, the administrative bodies, etc. The interaction among those components of states should replace the interaction between states as billiard balls. My understanding of this approach is that state sovereignty will in the end be crippled by dispersing state power at the international level. But this does not apply in the FRA's context because it is not an international society.

In summary, the practices of the FRA, especially the FRP strategies, match most of the characteristics of Slaughter's liberal theory. The FRP provides a regular and permanent platform for civil society to dialogue face-to-face with the FRA, other EU institutions, agencies and organizations, and member states. This matches the "bottom-up view".[46] The thematic issues chosen for each FRP meeting do not distinguish between international and domestic spheres. This strategy breaks the confines of those dichotomies of international and domestic, public and private, etc. All issues relevant to human rights could be covered. This matches the "integrated view". The FRA brings all actors at all levels to the same platform and they interact on the same footing. This makes a transparent "state–society" relation. The only missing matching point is the transformation of states into governments. But this is the limit of my attempt to apply Slaughter's theory. Perhaps the EU and the FRA are the most promising targets – but that is beyond the purpose of this chapter on China.

An attempt to apply Slaughter's liberal approach to international human rights law

Now, to come back to a larger world – international human rights law, as was analyzed previously, *individuals* are in several aspects playing important roles and influencing the development of international human rights law. Besides what I have discussed above, NGOs are also functioning in monitoring, information collection and litigation among other themes: a bottom-up view can be roughly applied. The second characteristic, the integrated view, is the easiest to be found in international human rights law. Or more precisely, there is no other branch of international law, where the relationship between the international and domestic sphere is more closely linked than that of human rights law.

In international law, individuals may play many different roles, such as heads of states, foreign ministers, diplomats, consuls, governmental representatives, aliens, refugees, asylum seekers, etc. Actually those roles can be summarized by two kinds of status in the law: those who have immunities from jurisdiction of another state and those who do not. The treatment of aliens (including refugees and asylum seekers, who in a general sense are also aliens but have different types of treatment under international law) is an important part of traditional international law. Maltreatment of aliens that might commit delinquencies gives rise to state responsibilities to the home-state of injured aliens. Before international human rights law emerged, individuals did not have independent status in international law. Issues arising from the above-mentioned status are dealt with under either immunities of state jurisdiction or the treatment of aliens (by diplomatic protection).[47] It is self-evident that they are all issues of horizontal state–state relations. Domestic political system or state structures, etc., are all within the opaque billiard balls. In that "world" they are not visible. International and domestic spheres are sharply separated.

But international human rights law has apparently turned that "world" upside down, at least formally. The horizontal state–state relation has been replaced by a superficially vertical relation.[48] The integration of international and domestic spheres has been realized in international human rights law. In fact everything provided in the human rights treaties would be illusion if the two spheres were still separated. All human rights – economic, political, social, civil and cultural, cannot be well respected, promoted and fulfilled without domestic implementation because the rights holders are mostly citizens of the state parties. Economic, social and cultural rights need states to take short-term and long-term positive measures to ensure that their commitments are accomplished, including measures to eliminate discrimination; political and civil rights need states to restrain themselves from abuses of those rights, including positive measures to prevent the rights from being violated.[49]

In order to perform their human rights treaty obligations states may have to make new laws or amend exiting laws that are not consistent with the provisions of the treaties or may even have to make political reforms. In short, all these must be done domestically. The integration of international human rights law with domestic laws and policies is necessary for human rights protection – this is not always the case for every state party to human rights treaties, for instance in the case of window-dressing mentioned previously in this chapter. But this is only what is required by international human rights law. The reality and the degree of the integration depend on the attitudes of states. This will be discussed in the next section. And the other two characteristics of Slaughter's liberal approach, state–society relations and the fragmentation of states, are so far simply missing.

The limits of Slaughter's liberal theory of international law

The core of Slaughter's liberal theory of international law is her attempt to change the structure from top-down to bottom-up or from state-centric to individual-centric. "Liberal IR theory thus literally turns the world upside down for international lawyers" (Slaughter and Alvarez 2000: 241);[50] at least regarding public international law, the fact is that we are still living in a world where states are the primary actors. Individuals have superficially been moved to the center only in international human rights law and environmental law. Even in these fields, there are limits to Slaughter's theory.

Human rights and environmental law are exceptional in public international law

There are many branches of international law, such as law of state territory, law of the sea, law of aviation, law of outer space, law of diplomatic and consular relations, law of treaties, law of international institutions, etc. It is hard to deny that voices of individuals, groups and civil society/NGOs are rarely heard in these fields. It is correct to say: "From the perspective of Liberal theory, human rights law is the core of international law" (Slaughter and Alvarez 2000: 246). It is also not wrong to say that from an empirical perspective of a public international lawyer, human rights law is one of the two exceptional fields, where states are not in the center, as far as their rights and interests are concerned. Those are certainly not the subject matter of these two laws. But I should indicate that humanitarian law, international refugees law and, in some sense, international criminal law may be considered as part of international human rights law.

However, even in the field of international human rights law and environmental law, individuals are merely the beneficiaries of the law because the lawmakers (precisely the contracting parties of international treaties and conventions) are states. But in fact, compared to other branches of public international law, the status of individuals has been elevated in at least two aspects. First, human rights conventions have been made so that individuals (as holders of human rights) are protected directly by international treaties. Second, the mechanism of individual complaints has been set up so that individuals as victims of human rights violations (mostly by their own states) can make claims (usually called individual communications) in the relevant human rights bodies established by human rights conventions. Up to August 2015, almost all of the nine UN core human rights conventions have set up this mechanism.

After all, all that cannot happen without states. First, it is states that make the human rights treaties or conventions and make the mechanism of individual complaint possible. Second, the coming into force of neither the human rights convention nor the mechanism of individual complaint automatically binds the states if they do not ratify the instrument in question. All human rights treaties need to be ratified by states according to their own domestic procedures. Otherwise they are not binding upon states, which means individuals as their citizens or under their jurisdiction cannot become practical beneficiaries of human rights treaties. Third, the mechanism of individual complaint is optional for states in all human rights treaties, either in the treaty itself as one clause or in the form of a protocol to the treaty. This so called "contacting in" strategy gives states more leeway to exercise sovereign power.[51]

In short, when states have the final say whether individuals can be beneficiaries or whether they can use the international remedy mechanisms, the status of individuals in international human rights law is self-evident. This is just like a little monkey in the big hand of the Buddha.[52] It is impossible to utterly turn this world upside down because individuals cannot escape from the powerful hand of the states.

State sovereignty is the last but difficult obstacle

It goes without saying that individuals as holders of human rights should be in the center of international human rights law. But since the final say is on the part of states it is not easy to turn the world upside down. The obstacle is state sovereignty – a difficult one.

State sovereignty has been the most important fundamental principle of international law. Others are concomitant, such as non-intervention, and state equality. But state sovereignty is a principle to regulate state-to-state horizontal relations. It shouldn't conflict with human rights. However, in international law state sovereignty means independence and that follows the principle of non-intervention (to be left alone). Nevertheless, international human rights law is an exception to this "leave-me-alone" principle because international concern is at the heart of all mechanisms of human rights protection provided in international human rights treaties. The stronger the mechanisms are, the better human rights are protected. That is the assumption on which all human rights treaties are based. "Never let it alone" is what "we the peoples" (as it is addressed in the UN Charter) learned from the brutal historical lessons before and during World War II. Sovereign states have made international human rights law, as we discussed previously. But how can or in what circumstances does the state sovereignty become an obstacle? In the first place it happens at the international level between states. Circumstances may be summarized as follows.

First, states may refuse to ratify human rights treaties including related protocols. Second, states may make reservations when they do the ratification on whatever provisions if not prohibited by the treaties. Third, states may criticize other states for their bad human rights record in order to win diplomatic battles; in return the targeted states may use the principle of state sovereignty as a weapon to fight back. Last but the worst, when there is humanitarian crisis taking place in a sovereign state unilateral humanitarian intervention by other states may be refused under the disguise of state sovereignty. The situation may be more complicated when intervention is disguised.

The international community has tried and is still trying to solve this problem. Particularly after the Rwanda genocide in mid 1994, which the international community failed to prevent and stop, and the humanitarian intervention in Kosovo by NATO, which was criticized for its real purpose and for violations of international law on the use of force,[53] Kofi Annan called on the UN members in 2000 to find a solution.[54] After five years of continuous joint efforts the three pillars of so-called "Responsibility to protection" (R2P or RtoP) was finally stipulated in the Outcome Document of the 2005 United Nations World Summit.[55] However, when R2P was considered to be first tested in Libya in 2011 the result was not optimistic because the two non-Western permanent members Russia and China were dismayed at NATO's misuse of the UN Security Council resolution,[56] which did not include regime change in Libya. That caused the two countries' veto after veto on the similar draft resolutions of the Security Council on Syria.[57]

Though R2P is still being promoted by the UN and NGOs, there does not seem to have been substantial progress. In fact, non-intervention is still one of the fundamental principles of international law. Even in the field of human rights, China insists on this principle in theory and practice. China is not a party to any of the optional protocols on individual communications. Here I would like to add something to the paradox that Slaughter threw out at the end of her lecture: both the extremely democratic countries and the extremely non-democratic countries "are likely most strenuously to resist strong enforcement mechanisms" (Slaughter and Alvarez 2000: 249). Have a look at the status of the optional protocols on individual complaints and you will find the bars all blank of both signature and ratification under the United States, Democratic People's Republic of Korea and People's Republic of China.[58] It seems that it is not very easy to get rid of this difficult obstacle – state sovereignty.

Politicization of human rights

The politicization of human rights has been witnessed both in bilateral and in multilateral international relations. The Sino American annual confrontation on the matter of most favored nation (MFN) in their trade relations lasted for several years in the early 1990s because of the economic sanctions against China for the cracking down of the June Fourth Movement in 1989. It ended in 1994 at Clinton's administration.[59] But the fighting did not stop there. The US Department of State publishes an annual report on human rights practice of the world, often including criticisms of China.[60] As a response, China issues its own report on US human rights violations right after the US publication. China started to fight back officially in 2000 (in 1999, the fighting was in the form of an article published by Xinhua News Agency under Ren Yanshi, a pen name) when the *Human Rights Record of the United States in 1999* was published by the Information Office of the State Council. Then year after year this fight continues.[61] In multilateral international relations, the former UN Human Rights Commission was notorious in politicizing human rights. The *Report of the High-level Panel on Threats, Challenges and Change* said in 2004:

> We are concerned in recent years States have sought membership of the Commission not to strengthen human rights but to protect themselves against criticism or to criticize others. The Commission cannot be credible if it is seen to be maintaining double standards in addressing human rights concerns.
>
> (Annan 2004: 74, §283)

The most notorious struggle might be the hopelessly endless rounds of the fight in the former UN Human Rights Commission between China and the West since the early 1990s. As the targeted state, China tried all her efforts to make the no-action motion approved, before the Western proposal could be passed in order to use the 1235 procedure against China for her human rights practice. China had continuously foiled resolutions proposed by Western states on her human rights practice with no-action motion approved.[62] This fight lasted until the last day of the Human Rights Commission.

The UN Human Rights Commission was over politicized, which was one, if not the only one, of the main reasons for the Commission's being replaced by the UN Human Rights Council in 2006.[63] It seems that states are playing a game – the international human rights game. This game is still continuing unfortunately in the new Human Rights Council. Taking the membership of the Council for an example, it was criticized because UN member states have political considerations rather than human rights when they decide which country should be elected to the Council or have its membership renewed. Principle has given way to expediency.[64]

The Universal Periodic Report (UPR) mechanism also witnesses politicization or selectivity. The UN members' intervention[65] during the reviewing sessions, for instance, has exposed some problems. The UPR encourages UN member states to intervene when other states are being reviewed under the UPR mechanism. On the one hand, from different considerations, however, "[o]n many occasions, interventions congratulated States for their success on human rights, converting the UPR into a 'pat-on-the-back' exercise" (Redondo 2008: 731). Similar comments were made by UPR-info:

> Very often the speaking time is taken over by the so called "friendly" States to the SuR [*Nota:* SuR stands for "states under review"]. As we have seen in the section on statistics, the regional group of the SuR tend to be very active during the interactive dialogue. Sometimes these friendly States take a lot of time to praise the SuR's accomplishments rather than make constructive critiques.
>
> (UPR-info[66])

On the other hand, for diplomatic or political reasons, some interventions are really critical, sometimes aggressive. To avoid substantial criticisms from UN member states, some states being reviewed try to attract as many interventions as possible so as to shorten the time of each intervention, sometimes to only about 40 to 50 seconds. The most obvious consequences of human rights politicization are the phenomena of double standards. As Juan Mendes said recently to the media: "So 'double standards' is very much the name of the international human rights game, I'm afraid."[67] This double-standard approach is common practice not only in state-to-state relations but also in international institutions. In the UN Security Council, for instance, if the permanent members are involved in any serious human rights violations, one cannot expect any action from the Security Council.[68]

In summary, if Slaughter's liberal theory could be applied to the real world, there are real difficulties. International human rights and environmental law are the two exceptions, but still with some limits. The most arduous task is to override state sovereignty. Otherwise the ghost of politicization or selectivity will always dance with human rights law whether you like it or not. Though things are much better in Europe, particularly for the FRA model, such a mechanism is hard for other continents to follow. What is presented in this chapter is perhaps not the limits of Slaughter's liberal theory, but the confines of current international human rights law instead. The next question is what to do from there, realistically.

Epilogue

Slaughter's liberal theory of international law has brought us new perspectives. It reminds international lawyers that the ultimate goal of international law should be the maximum respect of human dignity; that individuals and groups should be the main actors; that sovereign states are instruments to be used in the long journey to the ideally glorious world, where individuals are in the center.

Before any world gets turned upside down, what one should and can do is, first, to strengthen the role of individuals in the making and implementation of international law in order to centralize them; second, to weaken the roles of states by restricting state sovereignty. These two efforts are logically linked to each other: the stronger the roles of individuals are, the weaker the states' roles will become.

Recalling the historical development of international law, though full of frustrations, the trend is by and large progressive, from the abolishing of the right to war to the emergence of international human rights and environmental law and to the prevailing mechanism of individual complaints. As presented in this chapter, individuals are moving or getting closer to the center by participating in the process of lawmaking and monitoring the implementation of the law. Though these two branches are still exceptional compared to the rest of the whole international law, the international society may slowly get used to ways that are prevailing in the field of international human rights law, such as the rights-based approach, gender-main-streaming, NGOs' participation and interaction with states – and so on towards the future.[69]

Acknowledgements

The author would like to extend her sincere thanks to the LIBEAC project sponsored by the European Commission. She is grateful to Professor Gilles Campagnolo at Aix-Marseilles University and Professor Tomáš Karásek at Charles University. Both of them took the time and trouble for arranging her academic visit. Her heartfelt thanks also go to Mr. Jean-Sébastien Gharbi and Mr. Aleš Karmazin from the two host universities for their considerate help, and to Mr. Liu Lun, Ms. Zhang Qi and Mr. Chao Yi, who did some of the desk research. Last, but not least, the author wants to thank Mr. Zhao Lizhi from the bottom of her heart for his hard work in collecting materials, adjusting endnotes and the English language. She is especially grateful to Professor Morten Kjaerum for reading part of the manuscript on the FRA and for his comments. The author herself is responsible for any potential errors or mistakes in the chapter.

Notes

1 For different types of liberalism in international law, see in particular Simpson (2001).
2 For example, Professor Xu Chongli at Xiamen University, in his article entitled "The Construction of 'Jurisprudence' of International Law: the Disciplinary Intersection of International Law and International Relations", says that it is theoretically feasible to form a "liberal school of international law within the 'jurisprudence' of the subject by analyzing the principles of international law with the new liberal theory of international relations". As a result, the first issue of the *Journal of International Relations and International Law* (in Chinese), edited by Professor Xu Chongli and Liu Zhiyun, was published in 2011, with one volume published annually.
3 Here Slaughter did not bother applying her theory to the enforcement of international law but considers that at least the lawmaking should be like that.
4 For the unbalanced state obligations under human rights treaties, Liu Huawen makes a point in *Lun Guojia Zai Jingji Shehui He Wenhua Guoji Gongyue Xia Yiwu De*

Buduichenxing ("The Unbalancedness of State Obligations under the International Covenant on Economic, Social, and Cultural Rights") (Huawen 2005).

5 Article 2 of the International Covenant of Civil and Political Rights (1966), <http://www.ohchr.org/EN/ProfessionalInterest/Pages/CCPR.aspx> [accessed August 20, 2015].

6 "To recognize" is here the word used by most of the human rights treaty in order to emphasize that human rights provided in treaty are not created by the treaty. For the texts of human rights treaties, see the website of the Office of the UN High Commissioner for Human Rights, <http://www.ohchr.org/EN/ProfessionalInterest/Pages/CoreInstruments.aspx> [accessed August 20, 2015].

7 State parties of human rights treaties may have some procedural rights, for instance, one state party may submit a communication complaint to the treaty body to claim against another state party if both of them accepted the state to state communication system provided by the treaty. See, for example, Article 41 of the International Covenant of Civil and Political Rights (1966), <http://www.ohchr.org/EN/ProfessionalInterest/Pages/CCPR.aspx> [accessed August 20, 2015].

8 It can be typically exemplified by the US Army's widespread use of torture on terrorist suspects and prisoners of war in the Guantanamo Bay detention camp of Cuba, as well as in prisons of Afghanistan and Iraq. The US government and its lawyers keep on defending the action by excluding the application of international humanitarian and human rights law treaties for several excuses (Renren 2012: 131–52).

9 There has been a huge literature on this topic – just to mention a few examples here: W. Michael Reisman, "Sovereignty and Human Rights in Contemporary International Law", *The American Journal of International Law (AJIL)* 84, No. 4 (1990): 866–876; Xu Yirang, "批判人权高于主权的谬论" ("The Absurdity of the Idea that Human Rights Weighs over Sovereignty"), *Philosophical Researches*, No. 10 (2000): 35–36; Wade M. Cole, "Sovereignty Relinquished? Explaining Commitment to the International Human Rights Covenants, 1966–1999", *American Sociological Review* 70, No. 3 (2005): 472–495; David Chandler, *From Kosovo to Kabul and Beyond: Human Rights and International Intervention* (London: Pluto Press, 2006).

10 There have been several instances of humanitarian crisis since the end of the Cold War: the Rwanda Genocide (1994), the Srebrenica Massacre in Bosnia (1995), the massive human rights violations during the Kosovo War (1998–1999), the Syrian Civil War (2011–), etc. Relevant international debates about them can easily turn to apparently endless political games between major powers.

11 In this article Hathaway made a quantitative study of the relationship between the ratification of human rights treaties and state practice. Hathaway's study has encountered some critical reflections. For a critique of Hathaway's study, see Ryan Goodman and Derek Jinks, "Measuring the Effects of Human Rights Treaties", and Hathaway's reply to this critique, see Oona A. Hathaway, "Testing Conventional Wisdom", both articles are published in *EJIL 14* (2003): 171–200.

12 Up to August 2015 there were fifteen states which have only ratified fewer than five international human rights treaties amid the total eighteen (including nine optional protocols): Bhutan (4), Brunei Darussalam (3), Fiji (3), Kiribati (3), Marshall Islands (3), Federated States of Micronesia (3), Myanmar (4), Niue (1), Palau (3), Saint Kitts And Nevis (4), Samoa (4), Sao Tome And Principe (2), Singapore (4), Tonga (2), and Tuvalu (3). See the Office of the High Commissioner for Human Rights (OHCHR), "Ratification of 18 International Human Rights Treaties", <http://indicators.ohchr.org> [accessed August 20, 2015].

13 The International Convention on the Elimination of All Forms of Discrimination against Women is the one that has been made the most reservations. Up to May 2015, there are in total sixty-two states which have made declarations or entered reservations against some provisions of the Convention. The most reserved article is Article 29, concerning dispute resolution and interpretation of the Convention, with thirty-nine reservations. Article 16, concerning the equality of women in marriage and family life,

is subject to twenty-three reservations. It is also worth noting that Article 2, concerning general non-discrimination, has seventeen reservations, although the Committee on the Elimination of Discrimination Against Women (CEDAW) has specifically stated that such a reservation is impermissible in General Recommendation No. 28. There are also some reservations that are not specific to an article within the Convention but rather a general reservation to all aspects of the Convention that would violate a stated principle, such as Islamic Sharia. For relevant literatures on reservations to human rights treaties, see Gong Renren, "论人权条约的保留：兼论中国对《公民权利和政治权利国际公约》的保留问题" ("Reservations to Human Rights Treaties: on China's Reservations to the International Covenant on Civil and Political Rights"), *Peking University Law Journal* 23, No. 6 (2011): 1106–1120; Ineta Ziemile (ed.), *Reservations to Human Rights Treaties and the Vienna Convention Regime: Conflict, Harmony or Reconciliation* (Martinus Nijhoff, 2004); etc.

14 For instance, up to August 2015, Singapore, Democratic People's Republic of Korea, Iran and some small states either had only signed and ratified one of the nine optional protocols to international human rights treaties, or even had not joined any of them. The two great powers, the United States and China, had taken no action on seven protocols either. In addition, most Arab states keep on being very conservative about such instruments and mechanisms as well. See the OHCHR, above, note 12.

15 For instance, in June 2014, Belarus objected to the mandate of the special rapporteur by the Human Rights Council, since it "did not consider the mandate as a tool for cooperation in the area of human rights because of the obvious political motivations behind its creation". See the OHCHR, "Human Rights Council discusses human rights in Belarus and in the Democratic People's Republic of Korea", <http://www.ohchr.org/EN/NewsEvents/Pages/DisplayNews.aspx?NewsID=14743&LangID=E> [last modified June 18, 2014]. Special rapporteurs may be involved in other troubles in the concerned state during the performance of his duties as well, typically exemplified by the International Court of Justice's advisory opinion on the immunity from legal process of Dato' Param Cumaraswamy, Special Rapporteur on the Independence of Judges and Lawyers of the UN Commission on Human Rights, in connection with certain civil lawsuits instituted against him before Malaysian courts for his comments on certain cases. See the ICJ, *Advisory Opinion of Difference Relating to Immunity From Legal Process of a Special Rapporteur of the Commission on Human Rights* (1999), <http://www.icj-cij.org/docket/files/100/7619.pdf> [accessed August 20, 2015].

16 Arbitrary or tyrannical regimes are naturally regarded as the most difficult barriers for human rights protection, such as extreme communist reigns like the Khmer Rouge of Cambodia and the Kim family of the Democratic People's Republic of Korea, as well as military dictatorships like Chile under the rule of General Augusto Pinochet and Iraq dominated by Saddam Hussein, and so on, in history.

17 For a general overview of the former, see Kenneth Pletcher, "One-child policy", <http://www.britannica.com/topic/one-child-policy> [accessed August 20, 2015]; about the *hukou*, see "China's Hukou System", <http://geography.about.com/od/chinamaps/fl/Chinas-Hukou-System.htm> [accessed August 20, 2015].

18 Anti-terrorism legislation can easily encounter criticisms for potential threats to human rights protection even for liberal states, which can be typically exemplified by the Patriot Act of the United States, the Prevention of Terrorism Act 2005 of the United Kingdom, and the Anti-Terrorism Act 2005 of Australia, etc. The United Nations have noticed and shown considerable concern for the tension between counter-terrorism and human rights. See the OHCHR, *Human Rights, Terrorism and Counter-terrorism: Fact Sheet No. 32* (2008), <http://www.ohchr.org/Documents/Publications/Factsheet32EN.pdf> [accessed August 20, 2015].

19 For the role of NGOs in human rights protection, see for instance, Philip Alston and Colin Gillespie, "Global Human Rights Monitoring, New technologies, and the Politics of Information", *EJIL* 23, No. 4 (2012): 1089–1123; Peter R. Baehr, *Non-Governmental*

Human Rights Organizations in International Relations (Houndsmill: Palgrave Macmillan, 2009); Makau Mutua (ed.), *Human Rights NGOs in East Africa: Political and Normative Tensions* (University of Pennsylvania Press, 2009); Scott Calnan, *The effectiveness of Domestic Human Rights NGOs: A Comparative Study* (Martinus Nijhoff, 2008); etc.

20 For brief introductions to some of the most famous human rights NGOs, see Robin Toal, "The World's Top Ten Human Rights Organisations", <http://www.fundsforngos.org/featured-articles/worlds-top-ten-human-rights-organisations/> [last modified February 11, 2014].

21 Article 68 of the Charter of the United Nations reads: "The Economic and Social Council shall set up commissions in economic and social fields and for the promotion of human rights, and such other commissions as may be required for the performance of its functions."

22 About NGO activities for other conventions, see Brett (1995) but also Cynthia Price Cohen, "The Role of Nongovernmental Organizations in the Drafting of the Convention on the Rights of the Child", *Human Rights Quarterly* 12, No. 1 (1990): 137–147; Janet E. Lord, "NGO Participation in Human Rights Law and Process: Latest Developments in the Effort to Develop an International Treaty on the Rights of People with Disabilities", *Journal of International and Comparative Law* 10 (2003–04): 311–318; etc.

23 In the second session of the OEWG, 20 NGOs were accredited to the Working Group. See the UNDESA, "List of NGOs accredited to the OEWG", <http://social.un.org/ageing-working-group/newngosecondsession.shtml> [accessed August 31, 2015].

24 See the HelpAge International, "A New Convention on the Rights of Older People: A Concrete Proposal" (March 2015), <http://social.un.org/ageing-working-group/documents/sixth/HelpAgeInternational.pdf> [accessed August 31, 2015].

25 For instance, the Child Rights Connect was initially set up in 1983 as the Ad Hoc NGO Group for the drafting of the Convention on the Rights of the Child (CRC). Similar cases include the Disabled People's International (DPI) and the International Disability Alliance (IDA) for the Convention on the Rights of Persons with Disabilities (CRPD). In 2011, the Global Alliance for the Rights of Older People (GAROP) was born out of the need to strengthen the rights and voice of older people globally and is active in pushing the drafting of an international convention on the rights of senior citizens.

26 For instance, even for the Convention on the Rights of the Child (CRC), which has been regarded by some scholars as one of the greatest achievements of NGOs' participation, they failed in their effort to raise the minimum age for recruitment into armed forces and participation in hostilities to eighteen years (Brett 1995: 101).

27 For some relevant information, see the OHCHR "Reporting status for China", <http://tbinternet.ohchr.org/_layouts/TreatyBodyExternal/Countries.aspx?CountryCode=CHN> [accessed August 31 2015].

28 In order to improve their work efficiency, treaty bodies appoint one rapporteur for each country to be reviewed. For example, Ms. Heisoo Shin from Republic of Korea was the rapporteur for China in 2006 for the combined 5th and 6th state report on the Convention of Elimination of All Forms of Discrimination against Women (CEDAW). And the one for the combination 7th and 8th state report was Ms. Yoko Hayashi from Japan in 2014.

29 But it also depends on the attitudes of (particularly the head of) the governmental delegation.

30 The content of their activities depends on that of the concluding recommendations. It may include promotion of the making and amendment of laws, and monitoring compliance with the concluding recommendations by state institutions in order to push them to take specific administrative measures to correct their wrongs or to provide remedies for the victims of human rights violations, etc. However, there are still various challenges to such activities within the special procedures of the Human Rights Council (Gutter 2007).

31 See the resolution of the United Nations General Assembly, *UN Doc. A/RES/49/184* (December 23, 1994), <http://www.un.org/documents/ga/res/49/a49r184.htm> [accessed August 31, 2015]. It proclaimed a ten-year period beginning on January 1, 1995 the United Nations Decade for Human Rights Education.

32 The twelve institutions mentioned here are the Chinese Academy of Social Sciences, Fudan University, Jilin University, Nanjing University, Tsinghua University, Sun Yat-sen University, Wuhan University, Xiamen University, China University of Political Science and Law, Sichuan University, Yunnan University, and National Prosecutors College.

33 For more about the program, see Rhona Smith and Guimei Bai, "Higher Education in Human Rights within China – A Ten-year Review of the Peking University Model", *Asian Journal of Legal Education*, 2(2) (2015): 81–99.

34 But since the EU is certainly not a nation but, as described by international lawyers, an entity *sui generis*, then the FRA is also an agency *sui generis* in the eyes of international lawyers. By the standards of the Paris Principles, it might be identified as a mixture of the model of the institute and the commission (Toggenburg 2008: 387).

35 The first director of the FRA is Morten Kjaerum, who used to be the founding director of the Danish Institute for Human Rights and now is the Director of the Raoul Wallenberg Institute for Human Rights and Humanitarian Law.

36 For critiques and other debates on the FRA, see Bal Sokhi-Bulley, "The Fundamental Rights Agency of the European Union: A New Panopticism", *Human Rights Law Review* 11, No. 4 (2011): 683–706; Emanuela Lombardo and Mieke Verloo, "Institutionalizing Intersectionality in the European Union? Policy Developments and Contestations", *International Feminist Journal of Politics* 11, No. 4 (2009): 478–95; etc.

37 This is only an analysis of an "outsider", so speak, as can be construed in two senses: in a geographic sense from outside of Europe; in an academic sense a non-professional in European law.

38 According to the Code of Conduct of the FRA, there are nine requirements for selection. See ibid., 13–14.

39 Of the 10 percent of applicants that did not become Platform participants, half failed because they did not reply to the Agency's written request for clarification concerning their applications. The FRA rejected most of the remaining 5 percent of applications for formal reasons, such as the nature of the organization or its geographic scope (Kjaerum and Toggenburg 2012: 14).

40 See the FRA, "Partner Organisations", <http://fra.europa.eu/en/cooperation/civil-society/participant-organisations> [accessed September 8, 2015].

41 According to the records of the previous seven FRP meetings, the most active participants other than civil society representatives include officials and working group members from the European Council, European Commission (in particular the Directorate-General for Justice and Consumers) and European Parliament. Members of the committees of international human rights treaties (such as the Committee on the Elimination of Racial Discrimination (CERD) and CRPD) have been welcomed to the Platform as well. The participation of official representatives of EU member states, nonetheless, has been relatively limited so far.

42 For example, at the 7th meeting, the issues of Roma integration, anti-Gypsyism and Children at EU borders are international (among member states) ones; the issues of age, women (violence and security), and children are domestic ones. See the report "Future fundamental rights priorities in the area of freedom, security and justice – The contribution of civil society", *7th Fundamental Rights Platform meeting Conference Report (long version): 10–11 April 2014, Vienna (2014)*: 15–18, <http://fra.europa.eu/sites/default/files/frp-2014-meeting-report-full_en.pdf> [accessed September 8, 2015].

43 See the *7th Fundamental Rights Platform meeting Conference Report (long version)*: 12.

44 I think the European civil society might take this for granted. But to an outsider, this is really very interesting. Especially taking it as an application of Slaughter's theory and assuming the EU community were the international society and there were a platform for civil society to discuss human rights issues together with sovereign states on the same footing and their messages were transmitted to a world lawmaking or policymaking institution, how wonderful it would be!

45 See the FRA's annual report, "Fundamental Rights: Challenges and Achievements in 2014" (2014): 27, <http://fra.europa.eu/sites/default/files/fra-annual-report-2014_en.pdf> [accessed September 8, 2015].

46 A blemish in an otherwise perfect thing is that the proportion of real local NGOs is rather small. That's why the FRA encouraged more local NGOs to apply for the FRP in its 2014 report. See the *7th Fundamental Rights Platform meeting Conference Report (long version)*: 13.

47 For state immunity, see Jürgen Bröhmer, *State Immunity and the Violation of Human Rights* (London: Martinus Nijhoff, 1997). For the treatment of aliens and diplomatic protection, see Vasileios Pergantis, "Towards a 'Humanization' of Diplomatic Protection?", *ZaöRV* 66 (2006): 351–97; as well as part of the International Law Commission's report to the General Assembly covering the work of the Commission's 58th session (A/61/10), *Draft Articles on Diplomatic Protection with Commentaries* (2006), <http://legal.un.org/ilc/texts/instruments/english/commentaries/9_8_2006.pdf> [accessed September 8, 2015].

48 "Superficially" here means it is not vertical in a real sense as it is in the European Union. International human rights law cannot be applied directly to individuals in the state parties.

49 About the implementation of international human rights obligations of states, see Asbjørn Eide, "Economic and Social Rights", in *Human Rights: Concepts and Standards*, ed. Janusz Symonides, (Paris: UNESCO, 2000), 109–74. Though that chapter focuses on the economic and social rights, the debate over how a state respects, protects and fulfils those rights can be linked to civil and political rights protection to a large extent, which the author has mentioned in the chapter as well.

50 When I first got access to this theory I was really very excited. As one of the international lawyers specializing in human rights, I was encouraged, for what international human rights law needs is just an upside-down world as Slaughter's theory is trying to build.

51 The procedures of considering individual complaints or communications from individuals have been provided in four international human rights conventions (Article 22 of the CAT, Article 14 of the ICERD, Article 31 of the ICCPED, and Article 77 of the International Convention on the Protection of the Rights of All Migrant Workers and Members of Their Families) as well as five optional protocols to such conventions [the respective optional protocols to the ICCPRT (1st), CEDAW, CRPD, ICESCR, and CRC (on a communications procedure)]. See the OHCHR, "Human Rights Treaty Bodies – Individual Communications", <http://www.ohchr.org/EN/HRBodies/TBPetitions/Pages/IndividualCommunications.aspx> [accessed September 10, 2015]. China, the United States and the Democratic People's Republic of Korea are non-parties to any of these optional clauses or protocols though they are parties to the conventions. See OHCHR, above, note 12.

52 The metaphor derives from the Chinese classical novel *Journey to the West*. Sun Wukong, the mighty Monkey King, rebels against the Heaven and destroys the Jade Emperor's forces. The Buddha comes to admonish Wukong, and makes a bet with the Monkey King that he cannot escape from the Buddha's palm. With great confidence, Wukong takes a great leap and then apparently flies to the end of the world in seconds, just seeing five pillars. To prove that he has won the bet, Wukong marks the pillars with a phrase declaring himself "the great hero equal to heaven". Afterwards, he leaps back and lands in the Buddha's palm, only to find out, astonishingly, that the five "pillars" are in fact the five fingers of the Buddha's hand. As Wukong tries to escape, the Buddha

turns his hand into a giant mountain and seals the Monkey King inside it for five centuries as punishment and redemption.

53 Since it was not self-defense and not authorized by the Security Council. These are the two exceptions to the non-use of force principle provided in the UN Charter.

54 See Kofi Annan, "We the peoples: the role of the United Nations in the twenty-first century – Report of the Secretary-General", *UN Doc. A/54/2000* (March 27, 2000): 189–253, <http://unpan1.un.org/intradoc/groups/public/documents/un/unpan000923. pdf> [accessed September 8, 2015].

55 More than 150 countries voted for the document, allowing armed intervention through the Security Council "should peaceful means be inadequate and national authorities are manifestly failing to protect their populations from genocide, war crimes, ethnic cleansing and crimes against humanity." See *A/RES/60/1* (October 24, 2005): § 138–40, <http://www.un.org/en/preventgenocide/adviser/pdf/World%20Summit%20 Outcome%20Document.pdf> [accessed September 8, 2015].

56 The Resolution 1973 of the UN Security Council on Libya was passed because Russia and China withheld their vetoes. See the Security Council, "Security Council Approves 'No-Fly Zone' over Libya, Authorizing 'All Necessary Measures' to Protect Civilians, by Vote of 10 in Favour with 5 Abstentions", <http://www.un.org/press/en/2011/ sc10200.doc.htm> [last modified March 17, 2011].

57 From 2011 to 2014, China, with Russia, has vetoed four draft resolutions of the Security Council on issues of Syria. See "Security Council – Veto List", <http://research.un.org/ en/docs/sc/quick> [accessed September 10, 2015].

58 See above, note 12.

59 See Ann Devroy, "Clinton Grants China MFN, Reversing Campaign Pledge", *The Washington Post*, 114(27) (May 27, 1994): 2, <http://tech.mit.edu/V114/PDF/V114-N27.pdf> [accessed September 10, 2015].

60 The report, started from 1977 and issued by the US Department of State, covers over 100 countries on human rights practice. About the publication history, see "Country Reports on Human Rights Practices", <http://onlinebooks.library.upenn.edu/webbin/ serial?id=crhrp> [accessed September 12, 2015].

61 The latest one is *Human Rights Record of the United States in 2014*, <http://www. chinahumanrights.org/html/2015/HRRUS_0629/2808.html> [last modified June 29, 2015].

62 It was the case at the 46th, 48th, 49th, 50th, 51st, 52nd, 53rd, 55th, 56th, 57th, and 60th Sessions of the former UN Human Rights Commission from 1990 to 2004. See Xinhua News Agency, "Chronology of Defeats of Anti-China Human Rights Attempts", <http://www.china.org.cn/english/international/93203.htm> [last modified April 16, 2004].

63 See the resolution adopted by the General Assembly, *UN Doc. A/RES/60/251* (April 3, 2006), <http://www2.ohchr.org/english/bodies/hrcouncil/docs/A.RES.60.251_En.pdf> [accessed September 12, 2015].

64 See Amy Knop-Narbutis, "The U.N. Human Rights Council: Politicized or Political?", *The Baines Report Policy Perspective*, <http://www.bainesreport.org/2010/11/ un-human-rights-council-politicized-or/> [last modified November 10, 2010].

65 UN member states intervene in the review when the review session is being held in Geneva. Each review starts with the presentation by the State under Review of its National Report and of its responses to the advance questions. Following this presentation, an interactive dialogue takes place during which UN member states take the floor to ask questions and make recommendations on the human rights situation in the concerned state under review. See UPR-info, "What is the UPR", <http://www. upr-info.org/en/upr-process/what-is-it> [accessed September 13, 2015].

66 UPR-info, *Analytical Assessment of the Universal Periodic Review: 2008–2010* (2010): 13, <https://www.fes.de/GPol/pdf/UPR-Info_Analytical_assessment.pdf> [accessed September 13, 2015].

234 *Guimei Bai*

67 Said by Juan E. Mendes (UN Special Rapporteur on Torture) when he was interviewed by Reuters on the arrivals of refugees in Australia, see "Double standards – name of the international human rights game", <http://www.rt.com/op-edge/239725-australia-abbott-refugees-report-un/> [last modified March 11, 2015].
68 See David P. Forsythe, "The UN Security Council and Human Rights: State Sovereignty and Human Dignity", *UN Security Council in Focus* (May 2012): 12, <http://library.fes.de/pdf-files/iez/09069.pdf> [accessed September 13, 2015].
69 Like many, maybe most, international lawyers, including the Chinese, I am sometimes very much entangled in the conflict between the ideal goals of our discipline – peace and human dignity – and the reality. Probably the best thing to do is not to give up the ideals and face the reality with confidence and wisdom.

References

Alvarez, José (2001) 'Do Liberal States Behave Better: A Critique of Slaughter's Liberal Theory', *European Journal of International Law* 12, No. 2: 183–246.

Annan, Kofi (2004) 'A More Secure World: Our Shared Responsibility – Report of the High-level Panel on Threats, Challenges and Change', *UN Doc. A/59/565* (December 2, 2004): 74, para. 283, <https://www1.umn.edu/humanrts/instree/report.pdf>.

Brett, Rachel (1995) 'The Role and Limits of Human Rights NGOs at the United Nations', *Political Studies* 43: 96–110.

Buergenthal, Thomas (2006) 'The Evolving International Human Rights System', *AJIL* 100(4): 783–807.

Burrows, Noreen (1985) 'The 1979 Convention on the Elimination of All Forms of Discrimination against Women', *Netherlands International Law Review* 32: 419–60.

Cassese, Antonio (2005) *International Law*, 2nd edn, New York: Oxford University Press.

Evatt, Elizabeth (2002–3) 'Finding a Voice for Women's Rights: The Early Days of CEDAW', *The George Washington International Law Review* 34: 515–53.

Huawen, Liu (2005) *Lun Guojia Zai Jingji Shehui He Wenhua Guoji Gongyue Xia Yiwu De Buduichenxing* [*The Unbalancedness of State Obligations under the International Covenant on Economic, Social, and Cultural Rights*], Beijing: Peking University Press (in Chinese).

Gutter, Jeroen (2007) 'Special Procedures and the Human Rights Council: Achievements and Challenges Ahead', *Human Rights Law Review* 7: 93–107.

Hathaway, Oona A. (2001–2), 'Do Human Rights Treaties Make a Difference?', *Yale Law Journal* 111: 1935–2042.

Heinz, Wolfgang S. (2010) 'The Effectiveness of Domestic Human Rights NGOs: A Comparative Study' (book review), *European Journal of International Law*, 21(2): 493–94.

Henkin, Louis (1990) *The Age of Rights*, New York: Columbia University Press.

Kennedy, David (1999) 'The Disciplines of International Law and Policy', *Leiden Journal of International Law*, 12: 9–33.

Kjaerum, Morten and Toggenburg, Gabriel N. (2012) 'The Fundamental Rights Agency and Civil Society: Reminding the Gardeners of Their Plants' Roots', 2 *European Diversity and Autonomy Papers (EDAP)*: 6, <http://aei.pitt.edu/38199/1/2012_edap02_pdf> [accessed August 15, 2015].

Marks, Susan (1997) 'The End of History? Reflections on Some International Legal Theses', *European Journal of International Law*, 8: 449–77.

Redondo, Elvira Dominguez (2008) 'The Universal Periodic Review of the UN Human Rights Council: An Assessment of the First Session', *Chinese Journal of International Law*, 7(3): 721–34.

Renren, Gong (2012), 'US Government Policy on Torture after September 11th and Its Impact', *Social Sciences in China*, 8: 131–52.

Ryan, Susan (2014) 'UN Convention for the Rights of Older Persons', *Australian Human Rights Commission News*, <https://www.humanrights.gov.au/news/speeches/un-convention-rights-older-persons> [accessed August 20, 2014].

Simpson, Gerry (2001) 'Two Liberalisms', *European Journal of International Law*, 12(3): 537–71.

Slaughter, Anne-Marie (1995) 'International Law in a World of Liberal States', *European Journal of International Law*, 6: 503–38.

Slaughter, Anne-Marie and José E. Alvarez (2000) 'A Liberal Theory of International Law', *Proceedings of the Annual Meeting [American Society of International Law]* 94 (April 5–8): 240–48.

Toggenburg, Gabriel N. (2008) 'Analysis and Reflections: The role of the new EU Fundamental Rights Agency: Debating the 'sex of angels' or improving Europe's human rights performance?', *European Law Review*, 33(3): 385–98.

van Boven, Theo (1990) 'The Role of Non-Governmental Organizations in International Human Rights Standard-Setting: A Prerequisite of Democracy', *California Western International Law Journal*, 20: 207–25.

Xu Chongli (2015) 'The Construction of 'Jurisprudence' of International Law: the Disciplinary Intersection of International Law and International Relations', <http://www.360doc.com/content/15/0701/09/2369606_481866592.shtml> [accessed August 15, 2015].

12 Liberalization of Russian foreign economic relations in North-Eastern Asia

A viewpoint on Chinese and Japanese business

Igor Botoev and Olga Tugulova

Introduction

At the beginning of the twenty-first century, under the existing conditions of the world economic globalization and a growing shortage of traditional energy resources, major economic powers have paid close attention to the Siberian and Far Eastern regions of Russia. It is worth noting that the mere geographic position of countries such as China and Japan, located in close proximity to these underdeveloped Russian territories, naturally leads them to consider doing business there. Leading Chinese and Japanese companies have fully realized the prospects of large-scale investment generally in the development of production and rich natural resources, not only in the border territories, but also in the central regions of the Asian part of Russia.

Moreover, the Russian side, while completely experiencing the weight of economic sanctions in 2014 and 2015, has been making many efforts to reallocate major economic interests in favor of the Asian region. This "Eastern vector" of Russian development is to a great extent aimed at further deepening economic cooperation with the countries of this region: China, Japan – and also, naturally, Korea and Mongolia. We will consider the case of Chinese economic development with regard to Russia, with a major addendum about Japanese investors and their state of mind when dealing with an ever and ever stronger Chinese presence in the Eastern regions of Russia.

As a matter of fact, many problems happening in the middle of the second decade of the twenty-first century in Russia, such as a sudden drop of the Russian ruble currency and the fall of hydrocarbon prices, were caused partly by the Ukrainian crisis as well as by many other noteworthy political and economic reasons. But such new geopolitical conditions take another major turn, which is the change of the Russian government's approach towards the Siberian and Far Eastern regions in order to foster their development, which appears more and more urgently required. This is especially true for regions that have common land borders with Mongolia and China, as well as regions facing the sea to Japan and Korea. These are such regions as Buryatia on the Eastern shore of Lake Baikal, the environs of Irkutsk, the regions of Zabaikalskii, Amur, Khabarovsk, Primorye and the island of Sakhalin off the coast and neighbor to the northernmost large island of Japan, namely Hokkaido. The new conditions of the global economic game have forced within a decade the Russian leadership to reconsider its position with regard to "Western" paths of development and so-called economic "liberalism", to change deep-seated features inherited from former Soviet times, and to rotate the vector of development to the "East".

This "Eastern vector" of the present geopolitical developments in contemporary Russia has determined a shift in emphasis towards countries lying at the North-East Asian border of Russian Siberia, and the two main countries by size and international economic power are obviously China and Japan. Did senior officials in the Russian central government in Moscow discover all of a sudden that to pay maximum attention to the development of the weakly developed regions of Siberia and Far-Eastern Russia bore promises which may be very rewarding? In any case, there was and there is plenty of room for major investments and, as a consequence, foreign direct investment (FDI, henceforth) has indeed been brought to Siberian lands in huge amounts from these two major neighboring economic powers in particular – one may add that this has been especially and all the more effectively true after economic sanctions have been taken by Western countries, thereby adding a constraint to the already limited exchange between them and Siberian promising lands and markets. And there is nothing surprising in the fact that many experts in the field of investment policy focus on the study of issues related to the investment climate that is improving in Russia in general, and in the Siberian and Far East regions in particular (Novoselova 2008; Drahokoupil 2009; Bayulgen 2010; Holm 2013; Turlai 2014; Iwasaki and Suganuma 2014). We will make use of these sources and others (from official press services, available on the World Wide Web) to discuss, first, the case of Chinese business that has become well established in this region, and second, the relationships with Japanese businessmen in what has thus become (at least) a threefold economic game.

The case of Chinese business

Pushing the initiative: from 2010 on, a new course for joint projects

During the 2010s Sino-Russian relations have reached, perhaps, the highest level in the history of their mutual trade and economic development. China is henceforth one of the most important economic partners of Russia, if not the first one. Matters of sheer size on both sides (in terms of space, resources and demography, with large figures and blatant disequilibrium in terms of population density) could easily explain this fact, yet one must also put forth in the 2010s a common higher understanding of the multifarious issues at stake.

The partnership with China is particularly relevant in terms of the development of Russian Siberia and the Far East. Accelerated socio-economic development of these regions has been officially declared "one of the main national priorities of Russia in the twenty-first century".[1] The Russian government has developed a number of programs designed to ensure governmental decisions, such as the program labeled "Development of the Far East and Trans-Baikal up to 2013" and its sub-program on the "Development of Vladivostok as a center for international cooperation in the Asia-Pacific region", which was furthered in the so-called "Strategy of socio-economic development of the Far East and Baikal region up to 2025". Russia thus considers the potentialities of Siberia and Far Eastern Russia as a major opportunity to take a prominent role and major economic stand in the Asia-Pacific region.

In November 2011, on the initiative of the President and the Prime Minister, a "Foundation for the Development of the Far East and the Baikal region" was formed as a basis to support infrastructure projects, development of investment activities in this macro-region. In May 2012, the Ministry for the Development of the Russian Far East (*Min-vostok-razvitiya*) was established to coordinate the implementation of government programs and to enhance targeted federal programs.

In 2014 was passed the act "On Territories of advancing priority for social and economic development in the Russian Federation".[2] It was adopted with the intent to create optimal conditions to attract business, investments and to accelerate socio-economic development. The first grounds for its implementation were defined in the Primorye and Khabarovsk Krai (a *krai* is an administrative region). It planned to provide a five-year tax-holiday on profits, mineral extraction, land and property, together with preferential rates for insurance premiums on these "territories of advancing social and economic development".

Now, at least three out of the nine designated areas already have several Chinese resident companies (including Baoli Bitumina, Melco International Development Ltd among others). From the viewpoint of China, this is therefore also a major developmental factor deserving attention.

Besides, an experience in attracting foreign investment in Russian special economic zones should be noted. Special economic zones (SEZ henceforth)[3] are large federal projects aimed at regional development by direct foreign and Russian investments, targeting the hi-tech economy industries, import-substituting production, shipbuilding and tourism. The first such zones were created in 2005. All the SEZ have a special legal status that provides a set of tax and custom preferences to residents and also guarantees the access to ready-to-use engineering, logistic and business infrastructures. The costs of projects that get realized within a SEZ amount in average to 30-40 percent less than usual (in comparison with Russian general practice in other zones). Currently, about 370 investors from more than 20 countries have thus invested in the Russian SEZs. And there are many Chinese resident companies among them: Lifan Motors is based in the SEZ of Lipetsk, ABC Steel and Solar Systems, for instance, in the SEZ of Alabuga as well as many more of them in other zones.

One landmark event happened in 2009 when was adopted the Program of cooperation between the Russian Federation Far East and Eastern Siberia regions and the North-Eastern regions of the People's Republic of China. That agreement, approved by the leaders of both countries, included more than 200 specific projects related to all areas of bilateral cooperation at the regional level.

Since then, Sino-Russian relations have rapidly strengthened. In September 2012, the Asia-Pacific Economic Cooperation (APEC) summit was held in Vladivostok and widely commented on in the Chinese media. Russia's role in Asia and its strategic objectives and priorities were featured very well during the summit and appeared prominently. For Russia, the APEC summit was a good opportunity to demonstrate the geopolitical and geo-economic ambitions, as well as to display the economic landscape of the country. Russian President Vladimir Putin announced the turn of the Russian economy towards Far Eastern regions. All related forum events were part of the promotion of development in Siberia and the Far East. In assessing the results of the summit for Russia, it was written that:

> For the first time became the host of the forum, Russia, has appeared as a link between the Asia-Pacific region, the main strategic area of the twenty-first century, and the Euro-Atlantic region, which occupied a central position in the global agenda of the last century.
>
> (Samokhin 2012)[4]

In practical terms, the results of the summit were to open up new prospects for the development of Russo-Chinese relations. It is noteworthy that the value of the first transaction at the APEC summit 2012 that Russia and China concluded amounted to no less than USD 200 million. In addition, it should be noted that, within the framework of the Russian–Chinese investment-funds, talks were held on about ten major investment projects in agriculture and logistics.

From 2012 to 2014, and according to statistics given by the Head of the Office of the Central Committee of the Communist Party of China, Li Zhanshu, the heads of both states, Vladimir Putin and Xi Jinping, have met eight times, telephoned each other four times, and exchanged official letters more than thirty times. It was pointed out that a record number of economic agreements were signed that relate to the following issues:

- supply of gas through the so-called "Eastern route" (that route goes from the Yakutsk gas production center, in the north of Eastern Siberia, and the Irkutsk gas production center, near Lake Baikal, through the main gas pipeline, significantly nicknamed "Power of Siberia"),
- supply of gas through the so-called "western route" (through the pipeline named "Altai" that links the gas fields in Western Siberia and the Xinjiang Uygur Autonomous area in the western part of China),
- mining,
- infrastructure development on the border between the two countries,
- logistics,
- tourism,

- agriculture,
- other agreements that help to build trade, which in 2014 reached a record USD 90 billion a year.

During that period the level of accumulated Chinese direct investments grew 2.5 times. Not only is this impressive quantitative rise noteworthy, but the terms and conditions for the inflow of Chinese capital in Russia have greatly improved.

In particular, at the meeting of the presidents of both countries on May 8, 2015 an agreement was signed between the Russian Direct Investment Fund (RDIF), the Russia–China Investment Fund (RCIF) and the China Construction Bank (CCB) on the establishment of credit facilities which will facilitate lending to large Russian companies on the part of Chinese banks. The bank Vnesheconombank has signed a general framework agreement for an amount of 8 billion USD from the China Development Bank (China Development Bank, CDB). The funding will be spent on development of the Far East and Siberia, namely, the implementation of infrastructure projects, projects in the field of communication technology and agribusiness.

It should also be noted that Chinese investors are interested in a variety of sectors within the economy. As the *People's Daily* observed,[5] nowadays there is almost no sector left where there would not be Chinese investment in Russia. The volume of Chinese investment in the Russian economy therefore continues to grow – and, in the first quarter of 2015, the amount of Chinese FDI rose by more than 14 percent compared to the same period in the previous year.

Russia's decision to increase participation of foreign capital in commodity projects in the Russian Far East is likely to attract even more foreign investors to the region. The goal for the Russian side is therefore clear, but what may one expect from Chinese investors? The development of closer cooperation between China and Russia is mutually beneficial for both parties. Moscow's "Eastern vector" coincides with Beijing's strategy to revive the older industrial base in the North-Eastern regions of China. Both countries have positioned themselves as the largest neighbors and partners for strategic cooperation. China is actively involved in diversifying its energy imports, and Russia hopes to achieve export-diversification of energy resources.

Chinese investors seem to hope that the new policy on the part of the Russian authorities will be conducive to economic development by exploiting so much more of the natural resources in the Far East that it will boost investment and stimulate the creation of a high-grade industrial chain in the trade relations between China and Russia.

There are clear examples: the Government of the Zabaikalskiy Krai and the Chinese Zoje Resources Investment Corporation have signed an agreement to lease to the Chinese fallow lands and pastures. This farmland area consists of 115,000 hectares (or 280,000 acres) and the term of lease is forty-nine years.[6] For this area, bordering on the Russian side, with China to the south and Mongolia to the south-east, runs to 1,500 km as a whole. The total cost of the lease term amounts to 176 million yuan. According to the news agency Chita.

Ru, China plans to invest some 24 billion rubles in developing agriculture in this region. It is expected that the production of the agricultural enterprises of both countries will focus on the regional, but also international markets, naturally including China as both the investor and the first consumer-market. The project will be implemented in two stages: the first stage goes from 2015 to 2018. If it is successful, China will get another plot of land and the total area of the lease will be extended up to 200 thousand ha (or 486,000 – close to half a million – acres).

Another striking example appears to foster imagination on how Chinese economic development affects Russia, and how Russia has definitely turned to realize how many benefits could (and should) be made of the "Eastern vector". It is the following: the Dongfang Electric Corporation of China is ready to invest 78 billion rubles in the energy sector of the Russian Far East. These funds will be spent on reconstruction of the existing power-generating facilities and grid complex, on the modernization of the thermal power station-2 in the Far Eastern "capital" city of Vladivostok, as well as the development of solar energy and power in the Sakha (Yakutia) Republic (the main northern region, a federal "subject-area" of Russia consisting mainly of ethnic Yakuts and Russians).

These specific examples of cooperation between the two countries reflect the mutual interest and the prospects for further cooperation. However, it should be noted that despite such huge amounts the level of development of Russian–Chinese investment cooperation still in 2015 does not fully meet the level reached in the previous good political and trade relations between the two countries.

Towards 2020, ambitious investments and goals

As set by the leaders of Russia and China, the task of increasing Chinese direct investment in the Russian economy in 2020 up to an amount of 12 billion USD looks very ambitious indeed. However, according to the Ministry of Commerce of China, there has been a truly significant increase in the inflow of Chinese direct investment in Russia. At the end of 2013, such FDIs amounted to 4 billion and 80 million USD against 660 million USD in 2012 (+ 518, 2 percent). The total volume of accumulated direct investment reached 7 billion 661 million USD (+ 113, 9 percent).

Moreover, in 2014, the Central banks of Russia and China signed an agreement on currency swap (150 billion yuan or 815 billion rubles), and also extended the list of areas in which Russia and China can carry out their calculations in their respective national currencies, which will contribute to the development of bilateral economic relations by extending potential trade and direct financial investments.

The main directions Chinese investment activities take in Russia are still in mining, forestry, energy, trade, household electrical appliances, communications, construction and services. The largest investments of Chinese companies in Russian assets proper are

- The purchase by China National Petroleum Corporation of a 20 percent stake in the project "Yamal LNG" of the Novatek company (estimated at USD 810 million);
- The purchase by China Investment Corporation of a 12.5 percent stake in the so-called "Uralkalii" company (estimated at USD 2 billion);
- The embedding of China International Engineering and Construction Company ferrous metallurgy (NFC) in a joint project with the corporation Metals of Eastern Siberia in the Republic of Buryatia (estimated USD 750 million);
- Investments of the State Grid Corporation of China in joint projects with the Russian state company Synthesis (estimated USD 1.1 billion);
- purchase by China Construction Bank of a 2 percent stake in *Vneshtorgbank* (valued at USD 100 million);
- And a purchase by Russian-Chinese investment fund (RCIF) of a 42 percent stake in the timber holding "Russian forest products group" (RFP Group) (the value of the transaction amounted to USD 110 million).[7]

Despite all these impressive figures, and despite the measures taken by the Russian government to improve the investment climate in the macro-region of Siberia and the Russian Far East, Asian investors still seem to remain quite skeptical about its investment attractiveness. In particular, Chinese businessmen in Russia often talk about the model of a "fattening pig" where, at first, they are invited to actively invest, yet, thereafter, when the project goes to a good level of profitability, they end up losing their business one way or another.[8] Such a negative experience has had a strong influence on the next generation of investors in Russian business, as well as on Russia's image altogether.

The improvement of administrative procedures and the development of a clear algorithm of interaction between investors and authorities seem to be prerequisites for success in attracting more investments in Siberia and Russia's Far East. The experience that China herself built at home in attracting foreign investment also clearly shows that the higher the level of public services that investors receive, the greater the likelihood that they will invest more. In addition to high-quality consulting services, it is important to increase the level of efficiency of services provided to investors. A mechanism of a "one window" counter allowing all discussions on emerging issues to be held in one place and to help efficiently remove barriers to mutual understanding would be effective.

The key to success on both sides (that is, for the Russian side to see FDIs grow in this region, and for the Chinese side, to take full advantage of investment opportunities) also lies in the right choice of priority sectors, based on an analysis of the real needs of Asian markets. According to Chinese entrepreneurs, cooperation has great potential indeed in the agricultural sector, especially in the production of soya beans and livestock. Russia has a major output productive capacity while China is a large market for agricultural products, as China imports for her 1.5 billion population grain, meat, and vegetables in large quantities. Some very successfully implemented projects can provide an example to China's importers, just as Japan has done in searching for clean wheat from the Siberian plains or for mineral bottled water from Lake Baikal. The Japanese case, which will be discussed further below in this chapter, is pointing to what can be achieved on a larger scale regarding China: investment in innovative businesses, automotive industry, processing industries, production of organic food, and so on.

Now, for the effective implementation of such projects, it is thus necessary to develop transport infrastructure, and build new railways, roads, bridges and ports. Transport communications in Russia should become attractive for the provision of international transport transit services that will make them more affordable for Russian producers in different regions of the country as well. The position of Siberia and the Far East is unique geopolitically as a "bridge" between Europe and Asia: this assumes a particular type of involvement and renewed importance in the process.

For example, the Northern Sea Route though the ices of the Arctic Ocean bordering Siberia to the north is much shorter than the path from the Asia-Pacific Region to Europe going all around Asia via the South Seas, which makes the Northern Sea Route cost-effective and attractive to international maritime carriers. Many of the shortest routes – cross-polar air for aerial transportation – indeed lie over the territory of Siberia and the Far East. Airports in such cities as Novosibirsk, Krasnoyarsk and Khabarovsk can become the basis for a system of multimodal transport and logistics centers in Eastern Russia, while several modes of transport may interact as their paths cross there.

Cooperation in the field of transport infrastructure has indeed significant prospects. Following the meeting of Vladimir Putin and Xi Jinping, China is ready to finance the construction of the railway as far as the port that lies in the northern Far East (Vanino), as well as railway lines within Siberia proper (for instance, with the railroad link Kyzyl–Kuragino).

Siberia's geopolitical position thus makes Russia a key country for the implementation of yet another project related to Chinese economic development, that is China's project named "the economic belt of the Great Silk Road", which will become a new basis for the development of the strategic partnership between Russia and China, as it will allow both countries to strengthen relations in the format of a so-called "Eurasian Economic Union". This project is indeed planned with the intent to build a trans-Eurasian highway, a public work that has begun with the construction of the high-speed Moscow–Kazan highway, with the participation of Chinese capital. The idea underlying the "Silk Road project" also involves the development of the Trans-Siberian and Baikal–Amur Railways, which will potentially almost double the volume of traffic on this route.

According to Chinese entrepreneurs,[9] energy resources and mineral reserves in Siberia and the Far East (140 major oil and gas fields are already being developed in the macroregion, and another 220 fields are planned for development)[10] are the key to sustained interest in China and maintainance of its steady economic growth. That entails the development of more transport infrastructure, as well as counting as another important aspect of cooperation in the Sino-Russian border areas.

At the same time, the collapse of the Chinese stock market in the summer of 2015 revealed the pre-crisis state of the economy of China. Structural problems of the Chinese economy, the so-called "bubbles" (bubble in the real estate market, credit market bubble, industry bubble), will negatively affect the development of the world economy, including the Russian economy. As the largest economy in the world is dependent on the import of raw materials, its fall will lead to a reduction in energy demand and falling prices for oil and gas, which will immediately affect the revenues of Russia. Also, many Russian projects with Chinese investment are at risk. The development of the situation will depend on the measures the Chinese authorities will take, but it is obvious that the further development of Russian–Chinese relations should be based not only on export–import contracts, but also on joint scientific-technical projects.

Borders between countries and limits to economic development: business and power-play

When one talks about borders, though, diplomatic issues come to mind, and while Russia and China have repeatedly imposed mutual territorial claims throughout decades of more or less difficult political relationships, the final demarcation took place in 2005. On the Russian side, major territorial concessions are regarded as having been made in favor of the Chinese side regarding a section of the so-called "Big Island", and two parts of the Big Ussuri Island and the Tarabarov Island (a total area of 380 km^2). Bearing that in mind, and in contrast with one unresolved issue regarding Japan (four islands off the coast of Hokkaido, known as North-Eastern Territories in Japan), territorial and border issues were fully resolved between Russia and China.

All this indicates that Russia has pushed a quite loyal and amicable policy in fostering relationships with China. If the country's leadership, by conducting a good-neighborliness policy, made concessions to China and resolved territorial disputes, there may be common understanding in relying on the support of China's position towards Russia in international affairs. As far as Chinese economic development is concerned, it may clearly impact FDIs and economic development of the macro-region under scrutiny here.

While the attitude of China with her great interest in the natural resources of the Far East may be called potent but cautious, one must also take into account Japan, which demonstrated a steady growth revival during the same 2013-15 so-called *'Abe-nomics'* period, both in capital turnover and in terms of investment activity in Russia. Japan is naturally the strongest potential competitor to China in the region. In addition to that economic competition, and since the territorial issue between Russia and Japan is not closed, the Chinese side has proffered an opinion on the topic – since the above-mentioned disputed islands (Big Island, Big Ussuri and Tarabarov) did belong to China in the period of the Qing Dynasty ...

Looking towards the future, among the most important problems in the border regions of Russia and China are the issues of how to organize migration and cross-border trade. The intense movement of people and goods across the state border requires a powerful cross-border infrastructure (including issues concerning customs, transport, financial transfers). Another important issue is the interaction of the two countries in the field of environmental protection in the border regions. On both issues, to conclude relevant agreements between the Russian and Chinese sides requires growing confidence and the development of a monitoring system toward the implementation of decisions that are being made by the authorities of both nations. It is necessary to solve such problems and keep the main key orientations of policy in mind.

The main direction of the foreign policy of Russia towards China is to strengthen Russia's position in the Chinese market, as a supplier of products of fuel and energy complex by expanding sales of petroleum products to the Chinese market. The main need of the Chinese economic powerhouse can thus be accommodated, under the condition that the implementation of projects related to the export of energy to China is furthered. Electricity surely brings in the issue of expanding cooperation in the field of nuclear power and, therefore, of nuclear power plant construction. Cooperation in the investment sphere would also aim to attract Chinese investment in the construction of such infrastructure facilities by the establishment of joint ventures in various industries.

However, it should be noted that China's participation in the development of the resources of the Eastern regions of Russia in the years 2015-20 will most significantly still come to buying and importing various raw materials, and processing them on Chinese territory. There are no (not yet) large refining joint ventures that would generate high added value in Siberia and the Far East. At the same time, Chinese businesses that own huge free-working capital can buy successful Russian companies.

Yet, there are some factors hindering the development of successful trade and economic cooperation between the two countries, in particular a corruption mechanism embedded in mutual trade, which results for instance in officially traded volumes of goods being understated and revenues to the Russian budget from customs duties being unduly reduced. There are arguments over an unfavorable investment climate in Russia as Chinese businessmen tend to point to the intricacies of the legislation, and to the bureaucratic barriers on the part of both federal and local authorities. Other unfavorable elements are: some degree of general instability in Russia's domestic policy towards foreigners, which does not give them the opportunity to build long-term plans of business development; the mere fact that Russian businessmen themselves have but little knowledge of Chinese business culture; a relatively underdeveloped infrastructure in Russia, especially in its Asian part; the undeveloped market of tourist services and the high cost of services. The level of understanding of the partner country in society (in its business circles in particular) also has a significant impact on building relationships and successful cooperation, as shows with China and, above all, with Japan, as we shall see in the second part of this chapter.

Now and again, the 2010s have seen much being done for the rapprochement of the Russia and China on both sides – high level visits were conducted, the scope of foreign interests was expanded, reciprocal China–Russia national, language and tourism theme years were held, large-scale projects were carried out. All of this contributed to a better understanding between the Russian and the Chinese. According to the Levada Center and All-Russian Public Opinion Research Center reports of January 2015, 80 percent of Russians had a positive attitude toward China, and about 50 percent believe that China is a strategic partner for Russia. Conversely, according to surveys of the American Pew Research Center (2014), more than 66 percent of Chinese respondents also have positive feelings toward Russia.

There are some mixed feelings though, since, on the one hand, Russia seems to enjoy warm feelings from the older generation of Chinese partners, based on past Soviet–Chinese friendship and common historical development in both countries. But, on the other hand, the younger generation of Chinese citizens has grown up partly tuned to the Western culture and, above all, American culture; the young have learnt English and there is poor knowledge of Russia among them, so it might be feared they will have a tendency to treat Russia as a country that compensates for economic weakness through political aggression and which, being in dispute with the West, may in the future depend more and more on its relationships with China.

Under these circumstances, it is all the more necessary to prevent the image of Russia from changing to that of an aggressive empire. Russia's image, an image of care for the welfare of the population and of respect to neighboring countries, would thus be more attractive to the younger generation of Chinese citizens. Moreover, the United States often has a negative image among the Chinese population. One can read:

> The personal popularity of Russian President Vladimir Putin is a significant factor in the positive image of Russia in China. Only Russian President Vladimir Putin and USA President Barack Obama are enjoying in China the status of a recognizable foreign Head of State character (and Putin is probably even at a better level than Obama on the scale of personal popularity). Most leaders of other countries are virtually unknown to the Chinese man in the street.
>
> (Smirnova 2014: 24)

On the other hand, the image of Russia as a superpower also continues to cause concern among the Chinese. Russia is suspected of maintaining a desire for territorial expansion. So, although the efficiency of Russia's actions on the referendum in Crimea aroused the admiration of the multitude of ordinary Chinese Internet users, at the same time the actions of Russia in Crimea caused Chinese people to recall comparisons within history about the role of Russia and the Soviet Union on the issue of, say, Mongolia's independence from China.

Forming a positive image of Russia in China will therefore require, on the one hand, a clear statement of the position of Russia, and, on the other hand, long-term communication endeavors through all available information sources: joint activities, translated into Chinese versions of the Russian mass media, films, literature, art, etc. One should also explain the humanitarian and legal component of Russia's position on major international crises, past and present during the 2010s (Kosovo, Afghanistan, Iraq and Syria), some of which there is a convergence of views with China. It is necessary to explain the changes in the tax, customs, immigration legislation to the representatives of business organizations as well as the advantages they can enjoy in the case of residence in free economic zones and areas of priority development (like the SEZ), and organize for them, also in China, seminars about investment, which may for instance cover success stories about Chinese entrepreneurs' activity in Russia.

This is probably how things may turn to be in the next decades to overcome the remaining limits to economic development between both nations. Such treatment of issues upon the basis of what geo-strategists have called "soft-power" is a key to future relationships of Russia in the region, towards China but towards other powers as well, among whom Japan quite naturally, for historical, political and obvious economic reasons, comes first. This is the second part of the present study.

The case of Japanese business

In contrast with the push on relationships between China and Russia since at least 2010, it is only in April 2012 that Japanese Prime Minister Shinzo Abe made the first official visit to the Russian Federation in ten years. In addition to the agreements to reconvene the talks on the signing of the Treaty of Peace between Japan and the Russian Federation, both parties reached an agreement on the further improvement of economic cooperation. In this perspective, the leaders of Russia and Japan reached an agreement on the joint development of Siberia and Far Eastern regions of Russia, on the cooperation in the field of infrastructure developments and on natural environment protection. Additional special agreements were made as well on the cooperation in the field of energy resources, including the construction of liquid gas production objects in Siberia and the Russian Far East. Both parties agreed to bring up a so-called "Platform for Russian-Japanese Investments" in order to help Japanese companies in realizing business projects in Russia. This summit meeting opened the door for Japanese interests to economically backward Siberian and Far Eastern areas of Russia.

According to information gathered from the Japanese *Teikoku* Data Bank, 239 representative offices of Japanese companies were registered in Russia as of July 2013.[11] The major part of these companies carries on business activities in Siberia and the Russian Far East. Stakeholders are the Japanese top product- and trade-companies. Of their representative offices 20.8 percent are located in Siberian and Far Eastern regions such as Primorsky Krai, Khabarovsk Krai and Sakhalin Oblast (an *oblast* is a type of administrative region). The results of the official visit of the Japanese prime minister suggested the possibility of a quick growth of the Japanese business-structures, in particular in the weakly developed regions we consider here.

Therefore, in January 2012, a round-table conference was held in Moscow with top Russian representative offices of Japanese companies. The geopolitical aspects of the issue as well as the perspectives of economic developments in Siberia and the Far East regions became the main staple of conversation. Representatives of such leading Japanese companies and economic authorities as Sumitomo Shoji, Marubeni, JBIC, Sojitsu, Mitsubishi Shoji, Toyota Tsusho, Komatsu, Itochu Shoji and Mitsui Bussan participated in this round-table conference.[12]

Positive trends of Russian economic development as a whole, such as Russia's solid GDP growth since 2000, declining inflation and the upswing in demand, were spoken of with a single voice by panelists. Participants in the talk made a pointed reference to the significant improvements of macroeconomic indicators especially at times of stagnation in the World economy. According to the 2014 IMF forecast, the Russian Federation will come in fourth in GDP volume after China, USA and Japan by 2020.[13] Yet, unfortunately, in the opinion of the majority of participants, this forecast was deemed to be over-optimistic. The high level of geopolitical and economic risks may hamper this prediction and not allow Russia to keep permanent growth in economic indicators at the same level. Moreover, political and/or strategic turmoil (like terrorist threats, ethnic and inter-religious conflicts), along with a high level of government bureaucracy and imperfections in the fiscal system, are causing special concerns among Japanese business persons. When these elements are brought in, the issues between the three major regional powers (China, Russia and Japan) are at stake.

On the one hand, the great mass of the Russians seems to be displeased with the high level of corruption at the various levels of power. This disaffection can lead to the increase in social and political activity followed by negative effects on Japanese investors. But, on the other hand, anti-corruption elements within the opposition movement, according to Japanese experts, can encourage the further development of economic reforms, otherwise stagnant, and enhance the modernization of the Russian economy. The Russian authorities' appropriate assessment of this process will potentially become a most important signal for foreign investors.

The main reason for fears being regularly raised is the high dependency of the Russian economy on hydrocarbon world prices. Russia has achieved some economic and social stability by reason of strong hydrocarbon prices in the early years of the twenty-first century, but there is no guarantee of stability in these prices, as one can see from the fact that in the summer of 2015, they reached their lowest point since 2009. Shale gas production in North America and the unstable political situation in the Arab regions of the world can reduce the export of natural gas from Russia to European countries, and the financial losses suffered as a consequence may be fatal to the Russian economy (Bayulgen 2010).

However, could not these losses be recovered by natural gas and oil export to such countries as China, Japan and Korea? In the case of Japan, a primary focus will be in liquid gas production and transportation throughout the Sakhalin-2 and Sakhalin-3 projects.

The unpleasantness of the climate for investment from the legislative perspectives in Siberia and the Far Eastern regions may bring difficulties for Japanese business structures, as it did for Chinese business. The Russian authorities have to create a special system of differential taxation and free economic zones that can improve Russia's image as a country welcoming foreign investments. Those free economic zones, which are already in place and successfully used by Chinese companies, fall short of meeting Japanese business standards. Measures dealing with the simplification of business company registration procedures, the securing of visas and quotas for highly skilled foreign specialists are thought of as urgently needed.[14] Will they be put in place as soon as possible?

One reason this issue is at stake is related to the rise of activity of Chinese business in Eastern Russia from year to year, as shown above, and the competition that follows, since it has also caused some concern among representatives of the Japanese capital investors. The particular interest of the Chinese in the natural resources of Siberia and the Far East, which has deep historical roots, may in the near future become a serious problem for Japanese investment. Indeed, as noted above, the successful course of Russian–Chinese talks on territorial issues (in contrast to Russian–Japanese talks) gives an even more powerful impetus for the expansion of the Chinese presence in the Siberian and Far Eastern market. Chinese companies have already taken strongholds in strategic sectors of the Russian economy related to wood processing, mineral extraction and exploitation of energy resources, and Japanese companies have to face very serious competition in these areas of investment activity.

Despite the recognition by the Russian authorities of the importance of the Siberian and Far Eastern regions, according to some representatives of the Japanese business community, the central government still pays insufficient attention to the infrastructure problems of these outermost regions. The state administrative apparatus, the main bodies which are concentrated in the capital city, cannot fully implement control over all the political and economic processes on the giant expanse to the East of the Urals. An imbalance in favor of the Western part of the national productive capacity makes the placement position of Siberia and the Far East even more unfavorable for foreign investment (Turlai 2014).

For instance, the only transport artery is in the form of the Trans-Siberian Railway, which should provide economic links to the central and peripheral regions of Russia, and cannot cope with all of its functions to the full. Works for the construction of an alternative means of communication are not promoted as fast as would suit the interests of Russia and of its foreign economic partners, which are potential investors.

This underdeveloped logistics system in the border regions of Siberia and the Far East does not allow for the necessary extension of transportation infrastructure for goods from Russia, and the backflow equipment and materials required for the construction of various production facilities within the country. Seaport terminal facilities are particularly important for Japanese businessmen, since the geography is such that they cannot use direct land transportation only, as it is the case for Chinese businessmen. At the same time, Japanese companies producing automotive and construction equipment have already felt that urgent need for the development of infrastructure, and not only for the release of the final product, but also for its subsequent service. Japanese experts noted the fact that the raw material orientation of Russian industry was particularly noticeable in the Siberian and Far Eastern regions of the country.[15] The increasing volumes of natural resources extracted should be accompanied by further processing within the country, which again would create new opportunities for economic cooperation between Russia and Japan. In that sense, some divergences in business practices in these Russian regions from China and from Japan seem to emerge, whether primary resources are extracted merely for export to the closer neighbor, or to develop a chain of processing centers to further export more value-added products. The needs of both partners to Russia are clearly not identical, and it is therefore only logical that the structure of their FDIs will be different.

The demographic aspect of the economic development in these lesser developed areas of Russia as well can trigger a few questions from the Japanese businessmen. Negative demographic indicators, in the long term, can be a serious problem for the continuation of Japanese investments in the Russian economy. In addition, the available production capacities in the Eastern part of the country cannot always find necessary personnel to employ within the small population of these regions. This, in turn, can lead to the problem of acute shortages of highly qualified personnel who are necessary for the introduction of advanced foreign technology.

Russia's desire to build up around itself "a common Eurasian economic space" is clearly seen since the beginning of the twenty first century. In order to become an attractive center, Russia must make considerable efforts to change its negative image in Japan and other partner countries. Along with measures expected from the Russian side, the round-table participants also discussed a range of issues related to the possible affirmative action of Japanese companies in efforts to improve Russia's image and business climate as a whole.

The image of Russia which has formed in Japan as a result of a long confrontation in the first half of the twentieth century keeps on disturbing potential Japanese investors. The average Japanese person still regards Russia as an enemy country, which has opposed the "Land of the Rising Sun" during a series of wars and conflicts in the Far East, from the war of 1905 to the end of World War II in 1945, not to speak of the Korean peninsula as a bone of contention. This is especially true for the regions of Siberia and the Far East with their harsh climate and a history of internment of Japanese prisoners of war after World War II. Moreover, in the second half of the twentieth century, the Cold War found Japan and Russia on different sides of the barricades again. At that time, Japan was on the side of the former geopolitical rivals of Russia, led by the United States and opposed by many competitors among the former socialist countries of Eastern Europe (at first Eastern Europe was on the side of Western Europe allied to the United States, but then reversed its position).

Even after the collapse of the Soviet Union, Russia's image has not changed significantly, despite a huge breakthrough for the countries of Eastern Europe. According to representatives of the Japanese business community, the change of the negative image of Russia can play a big role, and Japanese businessmen can help in changing that image by themselves with necessary support brought at the official level.

Samples of successful work achieved by the flagships of the Japanese economy in Siberia and the Russian Far East, such as the Sakhalin gas project in Sakhalin Region and the Sollers-Bussan project (Sollers is a Russian automotive company) in Vladivostok,[16] can be actively publicized in the Japanese media, and that may also attract new entrants to joint development projects in the Eastern regions of Russia. Such examples would serve as models and help change the overly cautious and biased attitude of the Japanese companies to the economic opportunities of the Russian market. The most striking point is that such an attitude is not so typical for commercial structures from the United States, from EU member countries (leaving aside politically motivated sanctions), or from China and Korea whose willingness to cooperate at the economic level and lack of reluctance to deal with Russia allowed them to take a leading position in investment activity in Russia, and partly in the Siberian and Eastern regions. This factor plays a particularly important role in the case of small and medium-sized companies from the Japan Sea coast prefectures, which face the Russian coastline and have had strong links with many Siberian and Far Eastern regions for a long time. Though cultural, scientific and educational contacts may be rapidly developing at different levels, trade and, moreover, FDIs are clearly insufficient for full economic development.

In addition, many stereotypes concerning Russian economic reality remain firmly rooted in the minds of the Japanese people and the business community as well, whereas they do not, in fact, fully reflect the true picture. Can problems such as the bureaucratization of the management system, far from perfect legislation, the lack of qualified personnel and obvious endemic bribery be overcome by adapting the features of Japanese business to Russian conditions? The question is open for the future.

As a result, the round-table participants of January 2012 displayed mitigated approval on the prospects of the Russian economic space for big foreign investments. Significant progress in the modernization of the economy at the beginning of the twenty-first century gave new impetus to the process of integration of Russian business into the world economy. Yet, to further strengthen Russia's position, the study of Japanese public opinion on the Russian situation leads one to think that Russia would need to make maximal efforts to maintain the previous rate of economic growth, and that Japan could do much more in that regard than is done presently for that purpose, in particular when considered in comparison with Chinese active business and investment. In any case, the existence of such business forums as the one held in 2012 indicates a rising level of interest from Japanese businessmen in the development of Russian–Japanese economic relations. Coordination of Russian and Japanese business efforts with the full support of the governments of both countries may help solve many issues in the economically lesser developed areas of Russia.

Conclusion

In the middle of the second decade of the twenty-first century, the Russian Federation is keen on negotiating its access to the Organization for Economic Cooperation and Development (OECD), which mainly consists of the European and Asian leading industrialized countries. The process of the affiliation assumes a set of economic reforms and legal business measures addressing the internal economy. These reforms will modernize domestic legal and economic systems in line with international rules. From the perspective of European and Asian countries, the deals made between Russia and China already play a major role at the international level and observers are convinced that they will do so even more in the future.

For the purpose of an open economic policy, the Russian government is forced to pay particular attention to the adaptation of the internal economic and legal realities to the demands of the global market in order to create favorable conditions for prospective investors from the countries of North-Eastern Asia, China and Japan above all. The growth of FDI indicators suggests that some work in this direction is already under way. However, as the experiences of the Chinese and Japanese companies show, there are still many problems that prevent this macro-region from being as attractive to new investors as it could be proportionally to its potentialities.

Volatility in the main indicators of economic growth and a high level of geopolitical risk are the principal concerns to stress on the part of Chinese and Japanese businessmen. One of the main reasons for such fears is a significant dependence of the Russian economy on world prices for hydrocarbons. A factor of no little significance is the solution of the territorial problems that exist in the Russian Federation with Japan and China. We have shown that it is being solved in different ways and with varying levels of success with both partners.

Articles in the official press, in the business press, proceedings of business meetings, round tables and analysis of real work experience show that Chinese and Japanese businessmen share one view about the excessive prevalence of the state sector in the Russian economy, which leads to high levels of bureaucracy and corruption in management and supervisory bodies of the state. The imperfection of the tax system and shortcomings in legal support lead to numerous examples of conflicts between the Russian state administration and representatives from foreign business. Underdeveloped logistical systems both in central and in the border regions of Russia also create difficulties for Chinese and Japanese companies to operate efficiently.

Finally, many issues are raised simply by the low level of service at excessively high prices. The demographic factor has to be taken into account, since negative demographic indicators in the long term can also become a serious problem for the expansion of foreign investment. Coordination of Russian and foreign business activities with full-scale support from the side of the Russian governmental structures may hopefully help to solve many problems with the aim to improve the investment climate both from China and from Japan. The overall image and well-being of the less-developed regions of Siberia and the Russian Far East and their people are at stake.

Notes

1 *Presidential Address to the Federal Assembly, December 12, 2013*, <http://kremlin.ru/events/president/news/19825> [last accessed June 12, 2015].
2 "O territoriyakh operezhayushchego sotsial'no-ekonomicheskogo razvitiya v Rossiyskoy Federatsii" (December 29, 2014).
3 The reader may find more information available at a technical level at <www.russez.ru> [last accessed August 10, 2015].
4 Available < http://ru.apircenter.org/archives/1889> [last accessed August 1, 2015].
5 Article by Y. Zagrebnov, "Russian Economy Receives Chinese Investment", was published in *Renmin ribao* online, June 15, 2015. It is available at <http://russian.people.com.cn/n/2015/0615/c31518-8906971.html> [last accessed June 24, 2015].
6 The reader may find more information available at a technical level at <http:// www.chita.ru> [last accessed June 24, 2015].
7 *Main results of investment cooperation between Russia and China (2006-2013)*, Press service of the Ministry of Economic Development, <http://ruchina.org/china-russia-article/china/612.html> [last accessed June 20, 2015].
8 A. Gabuyev, 'Far Eastern Investors', <http:// http://www.kommersant.ru/doc/2674988> [last accessed June 24, 2015].
9 'Paradox in the Future Development Trend of Siberia and the Far East and Its Impact on Sino-Russian Relations' [*Eluosi Xiboliya he Yuandong diqu weilai fazhan qushi zhong de beilun ji qi dui Zhong-E guanxi de yingxiang*],<http://bbs.tianya.cn/post-worldlook-247527-1.shtml> [last accessed June 14, 2015].
10 The latest Russian energy resources data, policy developments, energy demand and supply projections, energy prospects and their implications for global markets may be found in the following sources, and more of the like: *World International Outlook*, Paris: International Energy Agency, 2011; *Scenarios of development of Eastern Siberia and the Russian Far East in the context of the political and economic dynamics of the Asia-Pacific up to 2030* [*Stsenarii razvitiya Vostochnoy Sibiri i rossiyskogo Dal'nego Vostoka v kontekste politicheskoy i ekonomicheskoy dinamiki Aziatsko-Tikhookeanskogo regiona do 2030 goda*], Moscow: Editorial, 2011; 'Mineral Resources of Russia. Economics and Management' [Mineral'nyye resursy Rossii. Ekonomika i upravleniye], *Scientific and Technical Journal*, Moscow: Geoinformmark, 2012-15.
11 Information available at <http://www.tdb.co.jp/report/watching/press/p130703.html> [last accessed August 20, 2015].
12 Information available at <http://www.jftc.or.jp/shoshaeye/pdf/201203/201203_11.pdf> [last accessed 20 August 2015].
13 See <https://www.imf.org/external/russian/pubs/ft/ar/2014/pdf/ar14_rus.pdf> [last accessed 20 August 2015].
14 The reader may find more information available at a technical level at <http://www.jetro.go.jp/world/russia_cis/ru/reports/07001623> [last accessed 20 August 2015].
15 Available at <http://www.jftc.or.jp/shoshaeye/pdf/201203/201203_11.pdf> [last accessed August 20, 2015].
16 More information <http://sollers-auto.com/ru/about/structure_sollers/Sollers_Bussan/> [last accessed 20 August 2015].

References

Bayulgen, O. (2010) *Foreign Investments and Political Regimes: The Oil Sector in Azerbaijan, Russia, and Norway*, New York: Cambridge University Press.

Drahokoupil, J. (2009) *Globalization and the State in Central and Eastern Europe: The Politics of Foreign Direct Investment*, London: Routledge.

Gabuyev, A. (2015) 'Far Eastern investors', <http:// http://www.kommersant.ru/doc/2674988> [last accessed June 24, 2015].

Holm, N. (ed.) (2013) *Russia: Select Trade and Investment Analyses*, New York: Nova Science Publishers.

Iwasaki, I. and Suganuma, K. (2014) *Economics of emerging Markets and Foreign Direct Investment Empirical Evidence from Russia and Hungary*, Tokyo: Nihon-hyoronsha.

Novoselova, L. (ed.) (2008) *China: Investment Strategy and Perspectives for Russia*, Moscow: IFES RAS.

Samokhin, A. (2012) 'APEC summit 2012. Results for Russia', <http://ru.apircenter.org/archives/1889> [last accessed August 1, 2015].

Smirnova, L. (2014) 'Russia – China: 20 proposals for economic, scientific and humanitarian partnership', <http://russiancouncil.ru/common/upload/Russia20China.pdf> [last accessed June 20, 2015].

Turlai, S. (2014) *The Impact of Regional Economic Integration On Foreign direct Investment: Theoretical, Methodological, Empirical Aspects*, Moscow: Infra-M.

Zagrebnov, Y. (2015). 'Russian economy receives Chinese investment', <http://russian.people.com.cn/n/2015/0615/c31518-8906971.html> [last accessed June 24, 2015].

13 Talking politics in China

Media and "social management" in a China facing fast-pace modernization

Santiago Pinault

Introduction: what is the present Chinese system?

Since 1978 and the shift to Deng Xiaoping's leadership, with an enormous economic change in favor of what one may call, at first, some kind of "framed capitalism", it is not only difficult to accurately label the economic system existing in China – this chapter may be seen as an attempt to find a more precise and appropriate term – but also to adequately name the current Chinese socio-political regime as a whole.

Moreover, may not this endeavor be pointless if one accepts the following argument: "it was, and it remains made of a strange combination of despotic tradition and modernization program (the question of which "ism" the Chinese Communist Party (henceforth: CCP) would choose to carry this modernization out was a secondary question)" (Au 2012: loc. 551).[1]? Nevertheless, it is only natural to seek adequacy in names, since it is a basic task in building knowledge to distinguish units that make sense in a dense and moving reality. This might be "nominalism" but we assume having to name realities, as Jean-Pierre Cabestan recalls:

> Studied by numerous comparatists, among them Juan Linz and Guillermo O'Donnell, the process of transition from totalitarianism to authoritarianism is not debated any longer among specialists on China. The issues moved towards finding a definition and the main traits of Chinese authoritarianism: "fragmented" for some (Lieberthal), "responsive" for others (Weller), completely "competitive" for Levitsky and Way or "electoral" (Schedler), like, for example, the Russia of Putin. Steve Tsang suggested the notion of "consultative Leninism" and it also obtained success. Actually, the family of authoritarian regimes is particularly vast, and this designation does not tell us much, either about competing present strengths, or about strong tendencies on the move.
>
> (Cabestan 2014: loc. 202)

Likewise, after he lived and investigated for a long time in China, Australian journalist Richard McGregor confessed that he still did not know exactly what to think:

Is it a benevolent, Singapore-style autocracy? A capitalist development state, as many described Japan? Neo-Confucianism mixed with market economics? A slow-motion version of post-Soviet Russia, in which the elite grabbed productive public assets for private gain? Robber-baron socialism? Or is it something different altogether, an entirely new model, a "Beijing Consensus", according to the fashionable phrase, built around practical, problem-solving policies and technological innovation?

(McGregor 2010: loc. 129-30)

One may also think, with McGregor, that Western political analysts have difficulty in defining the Chinese current political model since "that it is prided over by a Communist Party makes it even more jarring for a Western world which, only a few years previously, was feasting on notions of the end of history and triumph of liberal democracy" (McGregor 2010: loc. 221).

Since it seems next to impossible even for specialists to guess if the Chinese regime is a transitional regime heading towards some uncertain future or an already well-known regime or even something else totally new for the rest of the twenty-first century, it may appear reasonable to refrain from naming it for now: perhaps, one will be able to label the current political situation only retrospectively. However, as the whole economic and political system seems to display some stable traits, it is conceivable to agree with Cabestan when the latter offers the following minimal characterization:

> Our hypothesis is that the Chinese political system can easily be included within the category defined by Samuel Huntington of "established one-party state". It is also that the CCP, seeing itself as a "government party" (*zhizhengdang*), achieved the organization of what we called a "new authoritarian equilibrium" and that this equilibrium could last even if economic growth were to slow down and if protests or other opposing movements multiply. In short, [...] as it could adapt and modernize itself, the current regime is consolidated and this will probably follow.
>
> (Cabestan 2014: loc. 230)

One thing is sure: beyond the model that the Chinese regime ideologically or pragmatically created and still invents in its daily adaptation to changing times, the CCP wants to remain the one and only pilot of China. The CCP opened the country to capitalism and accepted that decisions be decentralized, letting different economic agents enjoy some (relative) autonomy, but the CCP keeps control, wants to manage and to control society.

Concrete observation proves the shift from totalitarianism towards mere authoritarianism, even if the Party retains many tools to spy on the population (and foreigners present on Chinese territory). In one word, the regime may have adopted a form of "new macro-management" of society – a term that Anne-Marie Brady coined (Brady 2012: 194), among other "new terms" that she lists and explains as follows:

Party theorists coined a new phrase to acknowledge the consequences of all these shifts [in social and political control] of Chinese society: "the 'work-unit member' became a 'member of society'" (*danwei ren biancheng shehuiren*). This means Chinese people no longer have their lives ruled by the *danwei* or the collective. Like citizens in other modern industrialized nations, they have become atomized units within society.

(Brady 2012: 188)

As the first section in this chapter shows, the CCP, in so doing, may have made one step towards Westernization, while quite paradoxically Western countries that face threats of terrorism think of reorientating some of their own values and, while not changing basic liberal economic features, modify their socio-political environment. Would differences between these opposite regimes be of such a nature that, in some foreseeable future, they vary but only in degree? Following this perspective, a second section discusses how liberal democracies as well as the Chinese regime manage "pluralism" and "monism" within their own respective territories, and finally, a third section debates issues of transparency *vs.* opacity in the public debate, thus leading to discuss how "talking politics" evolves in more (or less, much less) liberal socio-political environments.

Different ways to manage (or set free) the psychology of masses and one whole people

We can assess a difference of nature between, say, three types of regimes, according to the manner in which they think of managing the thoughts of citizens:

1   Some regimes shape public opinion by asking everyone to actively adopt some behavior deemed as "'correct", to think according to some guide-rules and to play a large role in the "organization of enthusiasm".[2] This can be called "totalitarianism".
2   Some regimes set limits to what can be thinkable and encourage their population to do and think in a "*good*" way.
3   Some regimes assume no control on opinions or behaviors, only settling to repress violence between people who do not share any same view in common, except the idea that they can still live near people with whom they do not share anything. This may be called a purely "libertarian" model.

Being extreme cases on a wide spectrum, models 1 and 3 are quite easy to name because of their form. But they are, if not totally utopian, just asymptotic ideals (or counter-ideals, for that matter, depending on the point of view that is adopted by the observer) since no society has ever fully attained either one or the other. Actually, no organization ever found a way to control *all* of its population, be it with modern technology, which, far from giving absolute control in a scenario "à la *1984*" by George Orwell only stretches the cat-and-dog game between controllers and those who try to escape coercion – with all digital traces left by everybody while using it, the game becomes more high-tech than ever, but its principle remains "old hat".

The second type, as a middle way, finds illustrations in most cases of actual regimes and we would like to suggest that *both* China and most liberal Western democracies are indeed representatives of this model, albeit with quite important differences. The present thesis is that, analogous to the economic background, their divergences in other matters may well appear, in the end, as differences in degree, and not in nature, at least not fully and when one compares some other aspects of socio-political life. Where the autonomy of individuals, and the tolerance for ideas or behaviors by minorities or the extent to which thought control is practiced by public bodies, are at stake, divergences may at first seem obvious – but we would like to call these into question too. Actually, each and every political power (from the second type model) actively tries to control the way of thinking and of living, as well as the memory of its citizens. To what degree they try and succeed (or not), this may be indeed only where they differ.

In this perspective, one must seek reliable indicators that enable us to distinguish authoritarian regimes and open regimes, for instance, with the following:

- The existence of the "rule of law" and a "state of right", and the legal ability and effective possibility to truly use legal power and truly defend oneself against the State;[3]
- Limits in punishment that a given political power can impose upon the people: the very fact of the existence of the death penalty is a good example of the level to which any political regime thinks it can crack down on citizens, and to which degree a judicial body is assured that it has the ability to judge in such an irreversible way. The same may be said perhaps with regard to the use (or not) of torture;
- Effective equality of practice and rights between individuals and groups, notably according to their gender, skin color or sexual habits, is another indicator;
- Prohibitive laws (which prevent or prohibit some ideas or some behaviors) are also clear indicators, more than "positive" laws (those prescribing some ideas or behaviors) so as to decide where the limits are set in any given socio-political environment.

Now, if one considers these criteria, then the following traits may appear to be only secondary: the traditional classification of regimes with their boundaries – as defined by the number and/or the identity of the leaders (in an aristocracy, a democracy or a plutocracy), the way regimes come in place (by hereditary succession, cooptation or elections), the duration of mandates held by governors (life-long, with a scheduled expiry-date, or without any for that matter). One may as well think of other traditional classification schemes. All these boil down to secondary traits. One may, for instance, be convinced think that democracy is the best way to fulfil the promise of a fairer state, because it would represent more capably the needs of its people, but this is not so obvious. On the one hand, the numbers of the non-voting population in many democracies, where there exists the right to vote but voting is not compulsory, shows, for example, that in some societies the people are more concerned to live in peace than to actively take part in political life.

On the other hand, for some years, in China, the CCP has tried to recruit entrepreneurs in order to be more representative of all the country and among social strata where the most active forces are present. That was the main motive of Jiang Zemin's "Three representatives" policy, adopted at the Sixteenth Congress of the CCP in 2002, to make sure that the CCP would be the most adequate reflection of Chinese society, through this special opening to the private sector of the economy.

Furthermore, as French philosopher Henri Bergson once wrote,[4] if one takes two opposite points over a whole spectrum (that is to say, a line of differences *in degree*), one can always find a difference of nature between these points even if, to reach each of them, there exists a continuity. So, to put things in perspective, is neither underestimating the authoritarian aspect of the Chinese regime nor pushing to the extreme some "impure" features of liberal democracies: it is recalling that one has to refrain from adopting a *non*-critical view about democracy, as one may judge that is too often the case in Western texts (Chinese critics do not hesitate to point at this lack of self-criticism). The tendency to see in Western regimes an "end to History" (with a capital letter), a political equilibrium point towards which the rest of humanity would necessarily tend, in a kind of progressive schema that reminds the French scientist and revolutionary Condorcet's *Esquisse d'un tableau des progrès de l'esprit humain* (*A Draft on the Progress of the Human Mind*), in the hope for the best future of mankind – this is quite insufficient indeed. And conversely, this lack is particularly felt among peoples living under a dictatorship: some may even regard such Western complacency as a benevolent yet underlying form of neo-colonialism.

In this perspective, there are Chinese political thinkers and analysts who easily conclude that Western thinkers would have to "make [their] perceptions much more sophisticated than the black-white dichotomy of liberty against tyranny or democracy against authoritarianism" (Pan 2010: 2). To put some emphasis on the limitation of power, a criterion like the factual existence of the death penalty puts on the same side some of the states within the United States of America, Japan and China. One of these countries is a Western democracy, another is a non-Western democracy, and the third is an authoritarian country: even if there are distinct names for distinct regimes, on this precise issue, they share the same ability to legally kill a human being. Beyond regimes, their names and their history,[5] one has to consider the extension of the effective power and functioning of the legal system and its (in)dependence on/from political aspects. As French philosopher Bertrand de Jouvenel showed in his volume published in 1945 on power (Jouvenel 1945), democracies are neither necessarily pacific nor do they guarantee citizens against any excess of unlimited power. In the case of the death penalty, for people executed within a legal system, the fact that power may come from an aristocratic elite, the whole population, some one-party state or else, may be of less importance than the mere fact that one gets killed. In other words, if Socrates is a human being, not all human beings are Socrates.

It is also possible to differentiate the nature of political regimes with regard to the degree of liberty that they give to their citizens: one may try to appreciate whether some autonomy is given to individuals because there is no other choice available for the economic and socio-political good governance of the city in terms of efficiency and whether statesmen do this out of conviction – re-enacting the well-known difference between "ethics of responsibility" and "ethics of conviction" put forth by Max Weber. Such a distinction may be reversed, though, to consider that "responsible" statesmen may actually be more dangerous for the exercise of freedom. In other words, if it is by facts that one should distinguish the nature of regimes, then one should pay special attention to cases where some political men in power could have to deal with the effective possibility to enforce a set of particular ideas and behaviors upon the people, or to control and lead *and yet* conscientiously choose not to do so, considering it would be *useless* for the proper functioning of a decentralized society.

In the China of the beginning of the twenty-first century, it seems that there is no longer any real attempt being made to shape wholly the thinking and behavior of the people, as it once existed – China was somehow close to model 1 above when Mao Zedong tried to build China according to the "Red book" and "Mao thought" during his reign. After that period, the aim has become merely to frame and, strictly speaking, to put limits on and safeguards to what is "thinkable" within the country. It is in that sense that one may conceive of the Chinese regime as being "authoritarian", yet no longer "totalitarian", to recognize with Brady that "political stability has been strengthened in recent years, because the Chinese Party-state has increasingly preferred softer means of political and social control over coercive tactics" (Brady 2012: loc. 5380).

In the era of the Internet, and both markets and capital are openly accessible, when (part of) the population becomes wealthier, it seems practically impossible to control and prevent *a priori* all types of behavior that could be judged non-compliant by the Party, even the CCP. One may fancy that, if that were effectively possible, the Chinese regime would still be totalitarian, but this is a piece of political fiction, whereas one has to deal with facts. Therefore, in order to understand "authoritarian", when naming the Chinese regime at the beginning of the twenty-first century, one must think of it as synonymous with "totalitarianism technically constrained/forced" or "soft totalitarianism" or even, say, a "humble" attitude.

One proof that the Chinese regime remains somehow totalitarian, however, lies in its will to control national thinking in the sense that, if the CCP actually tolerates the existence of Non-Government Organizations (NGOs) in the country, the CCP still actively limits their activities and refuses the very idea that "civil society" may act independently from political control. Since this limitation applies to the economy, the most significant issue is to what extent Chinese capitalism is "liberal", and in which form this claim would make sense. The CCP *a fortiori* rejects the idea that civil society could come into conflict with political power. Practically speaking, no Chinese may legally sue the state or the CCP, and the very idea makes no sense.

In the twenty-first century, the CCP may still have lost more of its power over society, yet the wish to manage social change in itself remains effective, and efficient. Brady suggests that "the CCP is working on building up a managed civil society in China" (Brady 2012: 199/loc. 5795) and that

> China currently has a freer media environment than at any other time since 1949. This more tolerant attitude to a greater diversity of views in the public sphere has done much to create acceptance of the continuation of CCP rule.
>
> (Brady 2012: loc. 5688)

In turn, Cabestan gives this quite non-laudatory version of the situation in China:

> The current Chinese political system knows various vulnerabilities. The great majority of the 85 billion-members in the Party have their card more for career than out of ideal. The CCP ideology is incoherent and contradictory. The organization itself is disorderly and infected by corruption. The communist power has difficulty in reducing inequalities and managing demonstrations and social conflicts. It tries without success to put a corset on the Internet. If it succeeds in controlling most of the ethnic minorities, its policy in Tibet and Xinjiang failed. NGOs and non-official religious organizations multiply, favoring the emergence of a true civil society. And, even if they stay in the minority and are disrupted, partisans of a progressive democratization, inspired by the Taiwanese experience, are listened to more.[6]
>
> (Cabestan 2014: loc. 6029)

In spite of all, the CCP means to remain the official and unique pilot of Chinese history. The idea of the checks and balances between the legislative, executive and judiciary remains non-applicable in Chinese reality and these are thought of only as Western political notions. In an authoritarian regime, nobody can confront political power without getting punished for it: at the same time as the CCP tries to form the most representative body reflecting the country, its power remains quite limitless, however disinterested, representative or able to convey information both ways (to and from the people) it may be. The regime's acting in the most adequate manner possible in terms of good governance obviously does not guarantee good will and may also be regarded as tricking the Chinese people into an order that is fundamentally divergent from all others – if the difference is with other regimes. In order to reach this goal, the CCP has set up its domination through necessarily developing tools to control information, censorship and all new departments:

Rather than strengthening the Department's relatively powerless Literature and Art Bureau, the leadership of the propaganda sector decided to set up a new Cultural Reform Office (*Wenhua tizhi gaige bangongshi*). Under the Cultural Reform Office, three sub offices were created, in charge of "industry development" (*shiye fazhan chu*), "research" (*diaoyan chu*), and "liaison" (*lianluo chu*). This structure reveals that the new Cultural Reform Office is perceived as a think tank that develops strategies in close coordination with industry representatives across the country.

(Brady 2012: loc. 3173)

For the CCP, the issue is to keep control of the Chinese society without any delegation either of potentially neutral state institutions or of a civil society that it would let them emerge. Now, is it because CCP chairmen do not believe in the capacity of the people to live and organize by themselves? Although there are some elements of what is otherwise called a liberal democracy in the West, although there are some tangible elements beyond the merely formal right to vote for candidates designated directly by the CCP upper levels,[7] these few tokens remain a kind of special case in the control of the population. With an equal number of candidates to vacant positions, the system ensures that candidates are elected, but something else is happening. Before, owing to the anonymity of votes, the results indicated to the top level, through the rate of abstention, whether the choice of high ranking CCP officials was good. Now that the CCP officials nominate more candidates than there are vacant positions (with an average of 10 percent) they have more information on what the down level wants. Has China thus instituted a "limited democracy", like "controlled/framed capitalism"? If one thinks that even Western democracies are in some ways limited, albeit by other means, then the question of whether the difference between regimes is in degree or in nature resurfaces. Let us now consider how different regimes intend to be (or to remain) the narrators of the history of their nations, shaping media and minds as much as economic facts and social life.

Monism, pluralism and national "narratives"

A simple distinction can be made between monist and pluralist societies: in a totalitarian society, by definition, pluralism cannot exist. This does not mean, however, that any society without pluralism is totalitarian. But where it is the case, then everybody has to conform to, on the one hand, a model of thinking and behaviors, and, on the other hand, an economic plan, both given by a central authority. The elaboration, implementation and adaptation of these models generate series of social and economic problems. A moral issue is also raised, of course, since no power can homogenize a whole population without repression, even with the best propaganda tools. But there is also a practical issue, namely: who defines initially the model, according to what scale of values or theoretical model? Who may change this model, and how, in order to adapt it to the new necessities of the moment?

In the categorization mentioned in the previous section, at the other extreme of the spectrum (case 3: the libertarian model), the people *only* have to conform to one idea: accept the fact they do not *have* to agree with each other. Individuals or social groups formed by people sharing the same values can live side by side with others, and remain almost like total *strangers*. This kind of tacit social contract (respect and non-aggression) is not as evident as it could seem at first sight. This is why the regulatory powers, economic, political and judiciary, have to define and apply a few rules that clarify how divergence of many kinds between ways of life (religious, sexual, cultural, even philosophical, for leisure, or in visions of the world or what art consists in) may coexist upon one single piece of land, how people can express themselves or to what extent they can try to convert others to their own thinking. The permanent risk consists in regulating inflation in temporary fads, as much as in prices.

In the middle category of regimes, say, a republican model, for instance, the necessity is therefore to find some equilibrium between common basic values that ensure some unity within a given population living on the same territory and their divergences, which cause *de facto* pluralism. In order to achieve the first goal of governments, to protect order, the latter have tools not only to forbid some behaviors or some thoughts, enforced within the legal system, but also to create or to manage this basic common understanding aiming at unity. Public education allows the diffusion of "good" (here, republican) behavior and "good" (here, republican) thinking. The teaching of history forms a united narrative of the history of the country, with taboos (like the Algerian war of independence in France, or the June Fourth Tiananmen "events" in China) and choices that have been adopted in the syllabi elaborated by official bodies in charge of programs for schools. There can never exist any absolutely universal, exhaustive or neutral view, given the limited amount time for teaching.

As a consequence, political discourse, as broadcast and debated in the public media and by *cooperative* private ones as well, is endowed with a capacity to *name* things, or events, and give them what modern public opinion has led to call the greatest "fourth power". Putting a label on things, and deciding who is a "rebel" or a "terrorist", confers the power to qualify what is good or bad and right or wrong:[8] with whom to talk to in public, which topics are important to discuss and which one can ignore, what is beneficial or detrimental in past or present events, if this particular event is called a "riot", a "strike" or a "revolt", legally a "war" or an "aggression", and so on. There is not even the name of a country that is safe from this oriented nominalism (is it Myanmar or Burma? the Malvinas or the Falkland Islands?). Words shape mentalities. Furthermore, some countries' Ministries of Cultural Affairs promote accepted forms of art, while they repress others; preserve some historical heritage in preference to another, giving content to national identity. The economy, which benefits from tourism, for instance, is closely connected to this policy, but it also promotes some self-understanding of national life.

Now, China is a *monist* country where the CCP is the one and only party – well, actually there are eight authorized parties, essentially for small minority groups and obeying the CCP, and they are more like alibis for the regime (Cabestan 2014: ch. 10). Thus, the structure of the Chinese political system has two faces. One, formally, consists of political and legal institutions that imitate some institutions of "liberal democracies", just as a front. A second face is more informal in terms of true power, yet it is official since it consists of CCP institutions. This deeply arcane aspect may have no legal existence and yet it enables decisions to be made in profound opacity: who would know its funding, through channels that combine private and public finances? If known, this system, organized as a pyramid, operates top-down, while what *is said* behind closed doors and after official speeches is not made public. Meetings and internal discussions have different audiences, and public opinion is to be controlled. What is organized is a form of "internal pluralism", tolerated within the organization and almost equivalent to a political caste. Is there not a political class of statesmen in democracies as well? Even where differences of standpoints prevail, they are largely controlled by the central direction with noticeable examples of punishment for reluctant members.[9] Such pluralism is without doubt more complex than a binary struggle between so-called "crypto-Maoist" conservatives and "pro-Western" intellectuals (Piquet 2014: 402; Lam 2012: 11).

A more subtle analysis is the typology of models divided into six groups that Sébastien Veg applies to Chinese leaders in the CCP. The system or ideology that these groups support are called "Chinese model", "nostalgia for Mao", "New Democracy", "social democracy", "liberal constitutionalism" and "neo-confucianism" (Veg is quoted by Cabestan 2014: loc. 218 n. 29). The CCP has no problem with such (accepted leeway for) pluralism in itself, the main point being that it never moves outside particular circles and that debates shall be not be public (Frenkiel 2014).

In mainland China such tolerated pluralism is organized within the Party and bounded by the Party.[10] Party members know, from experience, the numerous tacit prohibitions that rule behavior, in particular which ideas one can express. In the Maoist period, contradictions were expressed publicly and used for internal factions struggle during the Cultural Revolution. In the post-Deng Xiaoping CCP, apparent contradiction is avoided and everything is expressed within the Party. In the same way, in contrast to any idea of a national "permanent revolution", the CCP emphasizes stability. Political and social experiments are authorized and sometimes encouraged as long as the change they may cause to the Party line in future times is considered beneficial to the overall unitary project of China. In economics, this attitude is responsible for quite major successes – and some upheavals as well. But they are, on the one hand, always led first at provincial or lower level, and, on the other hand, always with top-level approval.

The population – all individuals who do not belong to the CCP – can only participate in politics at the cantonal, district or lower levels, where all citizens of the People's Republic of China (PRC) "who have reached the age of 18" (except those deprived of political rights according to law)[11] can vote for local People's Congresses. Candidacy, if officially open to everyone, is managed by CCP leaders, each direct top-level designating candidates for the election in "unequal number". In other words, the number of candidates has to exceed by 33 percent to 100 percent the number of vacancies (Cabestan 2014: loc. 4369). This introduces some leeway and uncertainty in choice. At the same time, this space of choice for pluralism is moderated, as for each level, state institutions are paralleled by equivalent institutions that belong to the Party. True power remains in the hands of the CCP as unique organizer.

Concerning "thought management" and strong information control, the frustration that citizens may feel, especially in the face of rising economic inequalities, will naturally be felt more strongly in times when economic growth is slowing down. Massive discontent could be fatal for CCP officials and open the door to populist leaders, later bringing a new era of instability, perilous to the present elites. Once China turned to modern economics, economic growth became the ground upon which the CCP has based its legitimacy. Elite groups, within and outside the CCP, also access more "unframed" information sources, but this does not come as a problem for the CCP, since these elites are often educated abroad (notably in the USA, a country that remains undeniably attractive for Chinese leaders), know other political systems, bring back with them a noticeable and necessary measure of insight, but would easily regard themselves as "special" and having less in common with the common people than with educated foreigners. Small groups do not form a practical danger to power as long as they invest their strength in economic wealth. So, if no protest comes against the CCP in the mass media, Chinese leaders may let them comment freely, while within the elites, political criticism can be expressed as long as it is not expressed or published at popular level. If and when it is, then (self)censorship is omnipresent and the feeling is shared anyhow that the country has to show a united front in competing with the West.

It is also known that there are two current directives, ordained by the CCP, which limit topics one can speak about in China. The first directive, unpublished, is only known through leaks by Chinese scholars in the *South China Morning Post*: the *Qi bu jiang*, or "seven subjects you cannot speak about" appeared as a refocusing line directly related to the debate on constitutionalism that has agitated Chinese scholars and CCP leaders for years. The second directive, known as "number 9", was published in August 2013 "with a very similar content" to the first one, more visible since it was "published in September 2013 in a Chinese journal in the USA, the *Mingjing Magazine*" (Piquet 2014: 403). The seven forbidden subjects are listed as: universal values, civil society, citizen rights, judiciary independence, freedom of the press, past errors of the CCP, and privileges of capitalist elites (Piquet 2014: 403-4).

A common denominator to both directives is the fact that the CCP shall retain a monopoly on control in the country without any counterbalancing power. Chinese leaders strongly protect a system that allows them to rule arbitrarily (not "irrationally") and cannot accept civil society in the sense developed since the eighteenth century in Europe, notably with checks and balances along the line of French political philosopher Montesquieu. The very concept of civil society, as the idea that some non-governmental organizations may oppose the State, is problematic, and while separating powers creates equilibrium between institutions that people can objectively or subjectively distrust but use one against the other. This would create disharmony. And Confucius' character of the "benevolent emperor" may become an official inspiration for Chinese leaders in the first decade of the twenty-first century showing "a way to build a new Confucian *contrat social* to replace the breakdown of Maoist egalitarianism" (Niquet 2012: loc. 2362). Or one may evoke a Machiavellian ideal of a wise Prince rather than looking for some efficient "socialist state of law": all concepts that lead to liberal democracies are seen as threats for the current system insomuch as they would endanger its stability.

In a typically liberal democracy, say, Western countries, limitations of freedom in the name of harmony are present, but differently set. Political power limits what can be expressed, or even personally thought, on sensitive subjects such as historical events (Shoah, colonial wars, slavery, for instance) or gender, racist and discrimination issues. It is forbidden to broadcast commercials encouraging the sale of drugs, smoking or prostitution, both for potential sellers and for the buyers of such activities. Some "opinions" are by legal constraint made "crimes". Freedom of the press ensures that through public debate no (formal) distinction is made between the right to criticize authorities within circles of the elite and public opinion in the mass media. One can see differences between media, though: literature, which is more confidential, enjoys more freedom than some performances or live shows, cinema or TV. A few books only become "social facts" and have great impact on society; and more tolerance exists for ideas expressed therein, especially when authors use fiction. Other media, especially audiovisual and the Internet, generate quasi-permanent debate in a system of free speech, where repeatedly proposals come back to prosecute non-conformist ideas. What can be said, *who* can say it, what humor is, and where the limits are in offensive or dangerous speech: these are some of the great issues for statesmen and judges.

Beyond legal and moral questions, many debates bear on tacit interdictions on what can be expressed in the media, for example when extremist political parties are invited onto TV shows. Whether quasi-racist opinions, conspiracy theories, and anti-religious thinking should be authorized with equal rights to others – this is debated and defended in the public sphere. Tacit rules direct what honest people may express with common sense, recognition and respect. As with cigarettes, sexism and humor, one may think differently about how to dress, with whom to speak, whether to use a polluting car, go hunting or attend corrida: tacit normality evolves with time and a phenomenon of spontaneous homogenization of thinking and behavior leads to forms of (self)censorship, "reasonably" acceptable if inexorable.

As soon as limits are set that do not aim only to avoid physical aggression, then such a model is also in danger of inflationary intervention by governments in managing thoughts and behaviors. In democracies, formal rights to deeply criticize the regime itself are recognized and anti-democratic programs are supported in elections. One may face concrete difficulties to be present in the media and official condemnations from political leaders, or some unofficial hostile talk from experts or "second-hand dealers in ideas" of all sorts, as liberal thinker Friedrich Hayek called them in *Intellectuals and Socialism* in 1949. This is, in a way, absolutely normal since minority views spread with difficulty, a normal part of the struggle for ideas. Things change if political parties or non-democratic ideas do threaten the existing order with a chance to win elections or become more popular than traditional views: will free speech and tolerance for radical critics of democracy be criticized in turn? Voices will rise asking for their interdiction. Is it that free speech can be maintained only as long it remains riskless? Some Third World states have faced such trouble (*coup d'état* in Algeria in 1992 or in Egypt in 2011 after a completely legal and electoral victory by Islamists). Is China at risk?

Democracy also faces issues of efficiency since electoral processes and discussions take time, and of representativeness since in most cases, when a parliament is representative, it is hard for a majority to emerge. Some democracies choose a so-called "Presidential Democracy" with more power in the President's hands and electoral rules favoring the emergence of a few parties only to facilitate building a majority, while some have enjoyed a traditional two-party system for long, favoring tradition and stability. In all cases, electoral rules are designed in a more or less artificial way to ensure political representativeness for the population, the members thereof being free to practice their economic activities besides. Trouble comes when such equilibrium meets changes and discontinuities at one or the other level. If a new government wishes to apply a *totally* different policy, for instance an economic policy, in the country, or if power and such policies change with each new election, then progress cannot be constant, and any consistent action is denied. Conversely, if governmental parties decide only adjustments to what was decided in previous mandates, or if the political stratum agrees globally on some consensus view only with a difference in emphasis on priorities, then extreme parties remain in the margins – which in turn puts them in the position to say they are the only real alternative to the "establishment". Economic goals are at stake since what the alternative may be has to be clarified.

Now, where extremes parties may cause instability, democratic politics obviously faces political contradictions that a regime like the one guaranteed by the CCP does not have to face. Only succession rules were a problem in communist China, but, after Deng's leadership, they were fixed and are now clear and accepted. But what continuity is there to find when a monist political class within a single party has gotten rid of its ideology (revolutionary, for instance)? If the stability of the system is the goal, what to base it on? In both cases, one can observe that at the beginning of the twenty-first century, more policies are merely pragmatic, and gradual changes are preferred. Anti-liberal revolutionary stands as well as liberal "shock doctrines" (such as that advocated by Milton Friedman) for economies in transition both tend to find fewer supporters.

In the end, whatever the regime, the state cannot avoid seeking to acquire power over people, as French philosopher Michel Foucault saw. Liberal policies allow some leeway for the latter and for individuals *caring for themselves*. In

China, even with a more decentralized decisional process compared to that of the past, everything is organized or permitted by or with the CCP, which is a unique pilot standing beyond legal and state institutions. Where democracies shape limits within a common agreement on leaving expression to private initiative, some effects may be reckoned as not entirely different when China implements capitalism – yet, if one compares both systems on transparency and free speech, great differences in principle imply huge variants in practice in the media.

Opacity and silence or transparency and noise in a globalized world?

To discuss the Chinese case, let us borrow a distinction made by a "liberal" economist and Nobel-prize winner, Amartya Sen, in *The Argumentative Indian*, between both conceptions of secularism in France and in India:

> There are two principal approaches to secularism, focusing respectively on (1) *neutrality* between different religious, and (2) *prohibition* of religious associations in state activities. Indian secularism has tended to emphasize neutrality in particular, rather than prohibition in general.
>
> It is the "prohibitory" aspect that has been the central issue in the recent French decision to ban the wearing of headscarves by Muslim women students, on the ground that it violates secularism. It can, however, be argued that such a prohibition could not be justified specifically on grounds of secularism, if we accept the "neutrality" interpretation of secularism that has powerfully emerged in India. The secular demand that the state be "equidistant" from different religions (including agnosticism and atheism) need not disallow any person individually [...] from deciding what to wear, so long as members of different faiths are treated symmetrically.
>
> (Sen 2005: 19-20)

The former model (say, France) is distinguished by Sen as consisting in creating a neutral state that does not hesitate to confront religions[12] and empty the public space – as far as possible – of religious presence, containing the expression of religiosity to the private sphere. In the latter model (India), conversely, neutrality is insured by allowing people to practice the seven religions present in the country in all equality. One model neutralizes pluralism (judged dangerous) by *silence*, while the second makes them equal through the right to make *noise*. If this distinction is now applied by analogy to the information world, then the liberty to freely inform oneself in China follows the French model of secularism (*silence*), when liberal democracies follow the Indian model (*noise*).

The analogy just drawn has limits, like all analogies. Yet, concerning history or political debates, the CCP has clearly chosen *silence*. Debate (*noise*) remains within the Party and within universities (including the Cadets schools), but people have to respect the official version of facts in the media and the public sphere; also, evidently, when dealing with foreigners. Also, regarding geographical mobility, the *hukou* (household registration) system makes a rigorous and totally unequal distinction between rural and urban Chinese:

> One important procedural injustice is that the household registration (*hukou*) system confers substantial benefits on those registered in urban areas and discriminates greatly against citizens with rural registration – it is extremely difficult to have one's rural registration converted to urban status, even if migrants have worked in a city for years.
>
> (Lampton 2014: loc. 866)

This is mitigated by the distinction between the information that the common people and the elites can access, since for example "Opinion polls on political subjects are strictly controlled and their results published abroad or within the Party (*neibu*), as Chinese people say, so for a restricted audience (CCP executive, scholars and official intellectuals) if they are about sensitive subjects. (Cabestan 2014: loc. 142)

Chinese authorities also strongly *redesign* history, as authoritarian and/or totalitarian regimes have always done, accessing one official unique narrative. In more open regimes, some competition on narration about the past is allowed and public education aims at teaching some spirit of criticism along authorized narratives. Books can also be published that give another version of past events, with some restrictions for some topics. Yet not all democracies choose transparency in official discourse concerning history.[13] Choice for noise or silence (which would mean oblivion in some cases),[14] the choice of unique narratives or competition between narratives is thus partly independent from the regime. Now, China chose silence and, for past events like Tiananmen Square, on 4 June 1989, to erase collective memory. At the same time, the history of Modern China is taught conform to Deng Xiaoping's wish to pretend that China during the Mao period and China after Mao are the same country. That great inspiration of Deng let all communist symbols in place (the name of the CCP, the face of Mao on *renminbi* coins, the red national flag, the portrait and Mausoleum of Mao in Tiananmen Square), insisting on continuity while the system wholly shifted with the introduction of capitalist measures.

History is used to unite the people against common enemies. Cases of nationalist effusions against America or anti-Japanese protests in 2005 (McGregor 2010: Afterword, loc. 5276-95) or in 2012 (about the nationality of the so-called Diayou or Senkaku islands) are symptomatic: at times, authorities will let people demonstrate (or even secretly organize their demonstrations, asking them to stop when they do not need them anymore) to send a message to foreign countries. They may also ask them to stop if they fear that social protest will endanger business relationships or could become independent, leading to some civil society movement: "Activist effusions sometimes fall under conscious manipulation; the Chinese government uses it to turn on the tap of protests in order to support its international claims. It uses those emotions as gesticulation oriented towards China's partners" (Godement 2012: 186).

More generally, in order to keep control of what common Chinese can read or listen in the media, the CCP tries to preserve monopolistic control of the means of diffusion of information, in particular television and radio, and a strong control on publishing, cinema and works on literature or cultural in general (Cabestan 2014: loc. 696).

Because of the central place it has taken in everyday life, and although it is normally an open network, the Internet has locks in China. Chinese authorities develop, thanks to controlled firms, their own tools such as the Baidu search engine allowing propaganda services to better control results given by the search. When independent firms are active, like Alphabet for example (and its famous search engine: Google), if they do not cooperate in some degree of censorship, then they are forbidden to act and one cannot use their tools when connected on a Chinese network. Using tools such as virtual private networks allows firms to easily bypass prohibitions and censorship, but only few people use them and they come mainly from elite circles, so this is less of a problem for the authorities. The choice for silence is not the only one possible, though. If some websites or pages are embarrassing, one can *a priori* ban sites and close them if they are created on national soil and when they are detected (complete silence), or one may ask search engines to erase results and let the site exist (incomplete silence), or, finally, one may create or promote many popular websites that occupy all the first pages of results in order to bury the embarrassing results in a mass of pre-designed information (designed noise). The latter is a technique used in "open societies" by private firms when they want to control what can be read on them, as well as by public institutions.

Beyond the *passive* control of what Chinese people can see and know within Chinese territory, "China has also adopted many of the means of persuasion more commonly seen in Western democratic societies such as spin doctors, political PR, and careful monitoring of public opinion" (Brady 2012: loc. 5443). Propaganda services also use TV as "the main organ for Party thought work directed at the masses, which means it is the most heavily censored tool of mass communication in China (Brady 2012: loc. 5661). One may consider that television takes part in a global communication control:

> Most Chinese people have access to a TV; as part of a national project even nomads have been given TVs (with portable satellite dishes and solar power generators) and migrants have special facilities available to them in many cities. China's primetime TV dramas and documentaries always feature an underlying educational message, intertwined with the usual mix of sexual titillation, violence, and unfulfilled romance which is the stuff of popular TV drama series around the world. CCP propaganda specialists have long understood that political messages are best presented to the masses through entertainment.
>
> (Brady 2012: loc. 5662)

This method is not, of course, used only in China or authoritarian/totalitarian countries, but globally, and in the USA since the early 1940s. What differentiates

China, as an authoritarian regime, is the fact that the press is under control and some scandals get covered up with remarkable efficiency, very much more than in Western countries, where the press and politicians always find informal accomplices to divulge stories. One can remember, regarding China, the SARS scandal in 2003 (Lampton 2014: 156-57) or Sanlu's contaminated milk powder in 2008 (McGregor 2010: ch. 6), which was efficiently hidden during the Olympic Games.

The problem for Chinese authorities is that their country is also embedded in an international environment. And Chinese market socialism is characterized by a generalized decentralization (McGregor 2010: loc. 3970) after China's "shift from a centrally planned economy to a mercantilist one" (Brady 2012: 193). Not only do local governments play a "pivotal role in promoting their own economies" and "each locality operates in a way like a stand-alone company" (McGregor 2010: loc. 3473), but China also needed to enter international organizations to benefit from international trade. That led to changes in national rules and practices. For example, despite numerous arrangements tailored for China in order for it to enter the WTO in 2001, some demands of the Organization have nevertheless led the CCP to:

- "publish all the legislation and rules applicable on state level and give specifications on task allocation between the different political levels" (Cabestan 2014: loc. 3705);
- create a "socialist state of rights" (Cabestan 2014: loc. 5953), a first step toward a true state of rights;
- fight against corruption, this being "more and more seen as a supplementary cost to add at the price of numerous economic transactions"

(Cabestan 2014: loc. 7185).

While European institutions allowed (or forced) national legislations in Europe to evolve,[15] the fact that international institutions are external to China led towards more transparency. The CCP remains an opaque organization, and one can hardly know how decisions are really taken, or how unofficial meetings take place, yet the CCP cannot govern through arbitrary decisions and recruiting members to represent the population helps channeling information needed for central decisions (bottom-up) whether this fits (or not) the Leninist ideal of "democratic centralism". This system could be more efficient to guide a population that is not given the choice since to trust CCP or to accept its leadership means also trusting its ability to remain adapted in an open environment where foreign investors need economic, political and social visibility and where there are few clear and transparent rules.[16]

As capitalism has been introduced for more than three decades in China, the CCP has not relaxed its efforts, on the contrary. Is it sustainable to do so for long? The CCP tried to slow down the speed of some of the changes, actually, since the turn took one generation instead of a few months as was claimed for the revolutionary process under Mao. The Chinese people could adjust their mentality gradually and the regime did not force on the same people so many changes as before: they could avoid becoming schizophrenic while passing from contempt for (liberal) entrepreneurship to the glorification of the market as a new model.[17] Notice that this "capitalistic" dynamic was easier to create in China since it already existed in Western countries and Chinese authorities just had to join … and catch up. Notice also that Japan had paved the way in East Asia. But China is now the "workshop of the world", thanks to already existing globalization, elaborated initially without China. The gamble of the CCP was that it was easier that way, and also easier to manage society in an authoritarian way to achieve such success. The media were in charge of "talking politics" for the people.

Conclusion

As economic development leads to technological development, fast urbanization and new, complex problems to solve for authorities, will it lead always to more decentralization and autonomy of economic agents? The necessity to find new resources and new clients for manufactured products drives China to more openness towards other countries. Chinese leaders have more and more to attend international meetings and protect the national interest. The media also play the role of advertising this aspect of economic and political life. As crises come from time to time, a non-interventionist policy is difficult to maintain, and internal and external pressures may threaten the opacity of the CCP system, which governs like the Nocturnal Council in Plato's *Laws*.

Is the Chinese regime undergoing a slow transition, then, one that began forty years before the moments when crisis shook the economic structure? The answer to this question will determine whether China will become: (a) a democracy, liberal or of a new kind; (b) a form of imperial regime, as it existed before the 1920s, yet with a modernized state and more decentralized economy; (c) a strong power under some charismatic leader, a king elected by peers (without hereditary succession) or a military leader,[18] once totally emptied of its Marxist remainders, to protect the population enough for it to gain support, so that it will be satisfied and prefer the status quo to any new revolution that would make the country enter a new era of uncertainty; (d) some patient (re)foundation of a truly socialist regime, the first ever, since the former Soviet Union was only able to become state capitalism according to some commentators.[19]

Nevertheless, whatever its future, it is hard to conceive that the CCP will be able to control the whole society since current technologies make management of information by silence quite futile, like retaining water in the hand, and moreover with an increasingly well-educated population. It will be more difficult to keep silence on decisions and the CCP may probably have to justify them more to the population and foreign investors. Management through *noise* also deludes the people, by deluging the population with controlled information and propaganda. In all cases, the Chinese regime wishes to avoid contestation and has to follow its transition. Opacity and double institutions reach their limits as people come to realize that they cannot work for justice.

Will China go closer, then, to Western liberal democracies? Without a strict enforcement of their views and narratives of the past, these also limit tolerable ideas and marginalize opinions that are non-compliant with society (when not forbidding them). Western democracies do so because they face threats (terrorism or attacks from various organizations, even more than classic wars between nations). They are more and more tempted to control their population on the Internet or through daily tools such as IFRD cards and mobile devices. Beyond the categorization of regimes, some traits relative to the formal organization of states produce effective behavior that is not always so different in nature, if naturally in degree. Would then, conversely, Western models evolve towards some Chinese system based on media control and more opacity, as long as the authorities offer security?

Notes

1 Original text (we reproduce the French for the reader to judge the negative judgment made in the quote in its original form):

> Il était, et il est toujours, fait d'une étrange combinaison de traditions despotiques et d'un programme de modernisation (la question du 'isme' sous lequel le PCC allait choisir d'accomplir cette modernisation était à l'évidence une question secondaire).

2 See Elie Halévy's famous *L'Ère des Tyrannies* (*Era of Tyrannies*), published in 1938.

3 That is the meaning of the second American amendment, which may be interpreted as leaving to the state the "monopoly on violence" (as Max Weber famously put it), yet leaves the people the possibility to defend themselves (even using guns in practice) against legal authorities and official bodies of government power once all peaceful means have been used and as a solution of last resort.

4 On the influence of Bergson in Chinese thought, see Campagnolo (2013: 116-21).

5 Realistic pragmatism rules international relationships: the question of the nature of the regime or of its (possibly formerly) alleged (political, ideological or religious) ideology may actually be of very secondary importance. What a regime *was*, that is just to be taken into account in order to anticipate what it could become, or who its *clients* are. The real question is: what is the regime currently doing? For example, if a regime is/ was communist (in the Chinese case, we let the reader choose the tense) or if some leader was once a member of a "terrorist" organization (as in the cases of many leaders, from very different sides, or even Nobel Prize winners like South-African President Nelson Mandela, Palestinian authority leader Yasser Arafat or many Israeli statesmen who had been Hagana hitmen before 1947), that matters less. Someone who was a "terrorist" may change strategy in order to attain political goals.

6 Original text:

> Le système politique chinois actuel connaît de multiples vulnérabilités. La grande majorité des 85 millions de membres du Parti l'est plus par arrivisme que par idéal. L'idéologie du PCC est incohérente et contradictoire ; l'organisation elle-même est indisciplinée et gangrenée par la corruption ; le pouvoir communiste peine à réduire les inégalités et à gérer les protestations et les conflits sociaux ; il s'efforce sans succès de corseter Internet ; s'il parvient à contrôler la plupart des minorités ethniques, sa politique au Tibet et au Xinjiang a échoué ; les ONG et organisations religieuses non officielles se multiplient, favorisant l'émergence d'une véritable société civile ; et, quoique minoritaires et désorganisés, les partisans d'une démocratisation progressive du régime, inspirée de l'expérience taïwanaise, gagnent en audience.

7 Duchâtel and Zylberman remind us that all candidates in Chinese elections belong to
CCP:

In countryside and urban areas, positions for directors are naturally reserved for
Party members. Exceptionally, an independent can conquer the power on
countryside: he will be immediately integrated within the Party. Above all, more
than private firms, internal promotions often depend on CCP membership.

(Duchâtel and Zylberman 2012: 10)

The original French reads:

Dans les campagnes et dans les quartiers urbains, les postes de direction sont
naturellement réservés à des membres du parti. Exceptionnellement, un indépendant
peut conquérir le pouvoir à la campagne : il est alors immédiatement intégré dans
le giron du parti. Surtout, bien davantage que dans les entreprises privées, les
promotions internes dépendent souvent de l'appartenance au PCC.

8 "Good *vs.* bad" may be substituted with the dichotomy "normal *vs.* abnormal" here. It
suffices to consider how relatively these explicit (even legal) or tacit judgments concern
behaviors. In France, in the early twenty-first century, youths may be surprised to see
how people smoked earlier on screens and posters: it was "normal" to smoke and take
photos of smoking celebrities, but it has become forbidden to show cigarettes or pipes
in the public space. The question is then what to do with these clichés of famous
individuals who are always associated with cigarettes or cigars, such as French actor
and director Jacques Tati, poet Jacques Prévert, or the revolutionary icon Che Guevara
smoking a Cuban cigar. The issue of censorship and/or small instances of "à la *1984*"
rewriting of history may lead to the erasure of cigarettes on photos, for example. Many
historical commemorations were once not considered as "sexist" or "racist", and for
longer than they have become prohibited (people painted themselves in black for
Sinterklaas in the Netherlands, for instance). More serious economic matters may be at
stake: in China, individuals with an attitude displaying any kind of entrepreneurial
mentality were labeled "rightists" and jailed under Mao. The same became the models
of a "new Chinese man" after the turn operated under Deng's leadership, yet they had
never changed their behavior. In the words of French philosopher George Canguilhem
(*Le Normal et le pathologique*), the same person is one day seen as a "pathological"
member of society (and power tries to disqualify such opponents as mentally or
psychologically sick) and the other day not only as a "normal" member but a model,
and an example for the people.

9 Cabestan comments in that way a famous case that happened in the 2010s, when Bo
Xilai was expelled from the Standing Committee in 2012, since by

openly campaigning for his promotion to the Politburo Standing Committee of the
Communist Party of China, he [Bo Xilai] had tried to modify at the same time the
style of official leaders' political life and rules for promotion within the Party. In
other words, he had directly challenged Hu Jintao and his successor, Xi Jinping, as
well as the whole communist aristocracy's *modus operandi*.

(Cabestan 2014: loc. 7233)

10 There was more tolerance for Hong Kong, but the electoral reform imposed by Beijing
in 2014, in spite of many protests in a traditionally former British liberal context may
lead one to think that the slogan "One China, Two systems" could gradually disappear.

11 According to the PRC Constitution chapter 2, article 34.

12 As to France, this means except Alsace and Moselle where, according to the Concordat
of 1801, public organs remunerate priests of Christian and Jewish cults, and religious
symbols are not forbidden in public administrations, where religious teaching is
maintained. In the whole of France, despite a long and strong anti-clerical tradition,
there also exists some tolerance for Christianity, based upon a *cultural* legacy from
history, noticeable in the presence of crosses or chapels scattered in the countryside,
and audible since Christians may listen to bells ringing before mass, an audible presence
which is forbidden to other religions.

13 For example in Chile, where democrats obtained the end of the Pinochet's regime (1973-90) in exchange for an amnesty concerning abuses on human rights during the first years of the regime and collective amnesia in the media or education.

14 In Rwanda, after the genocide, it is free speech, the verbalization of memories in Gacaca courts, which permitted a step toward national reconciliation between culprits and victims.

15 Sometimes European demands give national leaders excuses to adopt unpopular measures in their country that they blame on Europe, although they may agree with them (possibly voting them in Brussels or Strasbourg). Parallel cases of political schizophrenia allow some Chinese commentators to compare the "State and Party" system with the national-European system with its double level of legislatures, see Zhao (2014).

16 Nevertheless, rationality and transparency are two different things: a system can be rational but opaque in the short-run (to take a quick decision), without either consultation or justification, while in the long run this could weaken it since players cannot anticipate decisions.

17 Richard McGregor gives the example of Nian Guanjiu, who was jailed several times in Mao's China because he did some private trade and then, always commerce-minded, became a successful entrepreneur in Deng's China: "Nian had morphed from subversive capitalist into a state-sponsored business celebrity" (McGregor 2010: loc. 3814). Nian had an entrepreneur mentality before the economic shift in China, but one cannot apply the reasoning to a whole population and ask them to change their mentality when educated in another system a few years before.

18 One has to keep in mind that "a future social or political crisis would give rise to questions concerning the Army's position, and the role it could play in this crisis, therefore in the current regime's survival" (Cabestan 2014: l. 5608).

19 Here is a warning in this direction:

> The CCP is not ready to build communism in China because this can only be constructed in an affluent society [...]; any time before one can share wealth, one has to create it. Before one can build communism, one has to go far in a phase of capitalist development. In this way, Deng transformed Marxism into an "ideology for national development". As a consequence, the Party's Charter, in its Preamble, states that ideal communism as followed by Chinese communists will be potentially constructed only when a socialist society will be completely developed and advanced. [...] China will still be in the primary stage of socialism for a long time to come.
>
> (Duchâtel and Zylberman 2012: 90-91)

References

Au, L. Y. (2012) *La Chine: un capitalisme bureaucratique: Forces et faiblesses (Arguments et mouvements)* [China's Rise: Strength and Fragility], Paris: Syllepses.

Brady, A.-M. (ed.) (2012) *China's Thought Management*, London: Routledge (Kindle version).

Cabestan, J.-P. (2014) *Le système politique chinois: un nouvel équilibre autoritaire.* [The Chinese political system: a new authoritarian equilibrium], Paris: Presses de Sciences Po (Kindle version).

Campagnolo, Gilles (2013) 'Three Influential Western Thinkers during the "Break-Up" Period in China: Eucken, Bergson and Dewey', in M. Ying and H.-M. Trautwein (eds.), *Thoughts on Economic Development in China*, London and New-York: Routledge, 116-21.

Duchâtel, M. and Zylberman J. (2012) *Les nouveaux communistes chinois* [The New Chinese Communists], Paris: Armand Colin.

Frenkiel, E. (2014) *Parler politique en Chine: Les intellectuels chinois pour ou contre la démocratie* [Talking about Politics in China: Chinese Intellectuals for or against Democracy], Paris: Presses Universitaires de France.

Godement, F. (2012) *Que veut la Chine?* [What does China want?], Paris: Odile Jacob.

Halévy, Elie (1938/1967) *L'Ère des tyrannies*, Paris: Gallimard. *The Era of Tyrannies: Essays on Socialism and War*, translated by R. K. Webb (with a note by F. Stern), London: the Penguin Press.

Jouvenel, Bertrand de (1945) *Du pouvoir*, Geneva: C. Bourquin.

Lam, W. W.-L. (2012) 'Le renouveau maoïste et le virage conservateur dans la politique chinoise' [The Maoist Revival and the Conservative Turn in Chinese Policy], *Perspectives chinoises*, 2: 31–43.

Lampton, D. M. (2014) *Following the Leader: Ruling China, from Deng Xiaoping to Xi Jinping*, University of California Press, Kindle version, March 7, 2014.

McGregor, Richard (2010) *The Party: The Secret World of China's Communist Rulers*, New York: Harper and Collins (Kindle version).

Niquet, V. (2012) '"Confu-talk": The Use of Confucian Concepts in Contemporary Chinese Foreign Policy', in A.-M. Brady (ed.) *China's Thought Management*, London: Routledge (Kindle version), 76-89.

Pan, W. (2010) 'Western System Versus Chinese System', The University of Nottingham, July 2010, <https://www.nottingham.ac.uk/cpi/documents/briefings/briefing-61-chinese-western-system.pdf> [last accessed September 30, 2015].

Piquet, H. (2014) 'Le "rêve chinois" en question: le débat sur le constitutionnalisme en Chine' (Interrogating the "Chinese Dream": the Debate On Constitutionalism in China), *Revue française de droit constitutionnel*, 2(98): 389-411.

Sen, A. (2005) *The Argumentative Indian: Writings on Indian History, Culture and Identity*, London and New York: Penguin Books.

Zhao, S. (2014) *Debating Political Reform in China: Rule of Law vs. Democratization*, London: Routledge.

Index

Printed in the United States
By Bookmasters